ORACLE® *Oracle Press*™

Oracle8 Tuning

Michael J. Corey
Michael Abbey
Daniel J. Dechichio, Jr.
Ian Abramson

Osborne **McGraw-Hill**

Berkeley New York St. Louis San Francisco
Auckland Bogotá Hamburg London Madrid
Mexico City Milan Montreal New Delhi Panama City
Paris São Paulo Singapore Sydney Tokyo Toronto

Osborne/**McGraw-Hill**
2600 Tenth Street
Berkeley, California 94710
U.S.A.

For information on translations or book distributors outside the U.S.A., or to arrange bulk purchase discounts for sales promotions, premiums, or fund-raisers, please contact Osborne/**McGraw-Hill** at the above address.

Oracle8 Tuning

234567890 AGM AGM 998

ISBN 0-07-882390-0

Publisher Brandon A. Nordin	**Copy Editor** Sally Engelfried
Editor-in-Chief Scott Rogers	**Proofreader** Pat Mannion
Acquisitions Editor Scott Rogers	**Indexer** Rebecca Plunkett
Technical Editor Ian Abramson	**Computer Designer** Sylvia Brown
Project Editor Mark Karmendy	**Illustrator** Roberta Steele
Editorial Assistant Ann Sellers	**Series Design** Jani Beckwith

This book is dedicated to my four wonderful children—
Jordan Noah, Naomi Liba, Nathan Mordecai, and Ben James.
I fantasize about how wonderful it is going to be to meet
my children's children.

Michael Abbey

To my wife Diana and son Paul

Dan Dechichio

To my late mother, Lily, I only wish you could have been here to
see me author a book. I know you would have been so proud.
To you, I dedicate my first book.

Ian Abramson

About the Authors...

Mike Corey, Chief Operating Officer of Database Technologies, Inc. in Wellesley, Massachusetts, has collected quite a following in the Oracle community. He has dedicated numerous hours, months, and years to helping ensure the user community has the active ear of Oracle Corporate. Mike has worked with Oracle products since early version 4. He has worked with Oracle on a variety of platforms from PCs all the way up to IBM mainframes. Mike's specialties include database administration, performance tuning, Data Warehouses, and very large databases. Mike is a frequent speaker on these topics all over the world. Mike can be reached via email at mcorey@dbtinc.com.

Michael Abbey is a successful author, and has co-written five works in the Oracle Press series. Michael's thirst for knowledge about Oracle the company and the software has been fueled by 11 years of exposure. He is a frequent presenter at conferences throughout the user community, and has become a point of contact for users around the world. His forte is performance tuning, disaster recovery, and instance management. His passion for Pink Floyd and Boston almost, but not quite, exceeds that for Oracle, with which he is comfortably numb. Michael can be reached via email at masint@istar.ca most any time of the day or night.

Daniel J. Dechichio, Jr., Lead Oracle Database Administrator with the First National Bank of Boston, has been working in the computer field since 1979, Oracle specifically since 1985. He has a Bachelor of Science in Mathematics from Northeastern University and an MBA, with a concentration in Database Management Systems, from the University of Massachusetts. He is also active in the Northeast Oracle User Group, where he is the representative to the IOUG-A.

Ian Abramson lives in Toronto, Ontario, Canada. He has over 11 years of experience with Oracle products. Ian has extensive experience in Oracle Data Warehousing, system development, and database administration. Ian has served as the technical editor on a number of Oracle Press publications including *Oracle8: A Beginner's Guide* and *Oracle Data Warehousing*. He is a regular presenter at Oracle User Conferences and is a member of the International Oracle User Group—Americas Conference Committee. In his spare time he dreams of playing goalie in the National Hockey League (NHL).

Contents At A Glance

Contents

Foreword

The transistor was invented fifty years ago and with it the Information Age was born...or was it? Thirty-five years ago, IBM made corporate computing routine by providing a standard platform for developing business applications. Maybe this was the start of the Information Age. Fifteen years ago, Apple and Microsoft scaled the usage of computing by several orders of magnitude through the introduction of the personal computer. Surely this was the dawn of the Information Age. Surely, with today's influence of computers in day-to-day life, it's not hard to accept that we have progressed deep into the Information Age.

Actually, we're just getting started and for most of the world's population, the Information Age is just beginning. Less than 5 percent of the world's population uses PCs and not many more have access to online information. In the richest country in the world, the United States, 70 percent of the population is disenfranchised and doesn't use computers. In Europe, the number is far less. In California, the home of the computer industry, our goal is to place four computers in each classroom by the year 2000. I think if we were really in the midst of an information age, we would demand more. The simple fact is, we will not have an information age until we substantially reduce the cost and complexity of computing.

The Internet has changed everything. None of the other developments of the last 50 years—the transistor, the mainframe computer, or the PC—will establish the Information Age with near the potential of the Internet. They are the equivalent of steam power in the Industrial Age. Now, computing and communications have come together to create an environment that includes us all. The cost of entry and ease of use will improve by orders of magnitude. The potential exists for the first time since the invention of the telephone and television to revolutionize the way we conduct business and the way we communicate.

This cannot happen through the proliferation of personal computers that cost over $8,000 every year. This will never happen with the complexity of mainframe computers sitting on the desktop. It will only happen through a standard, low-cost appliance that provides universal access. Imagine computers integrated with our telephones, faxes, and televisions for a few hundred dollars. With complexity moved to the network and low cost and simplicity moved to the end user, the delivery model and distribution economics of telephony and broadcast television will be replicated in computing. It's more than innovation...it's inevitable. The Information Age will be delivered by the advent of a new approach called network computing and a new device called the Network Computer.

The implications are profound. Information is being captured at the source and digitized, eliminating all limits to its movement, access, management, and communication. Real-time access to knowledge, in order to make immediate decisions and react to customer situations, is transforming the way companies create and deploy their strategies. Whole industries are disintermediating by removing the physical structures used to provide products, services, or information to their customers and users. And the work force can now access information in any media, any time, anywhere.

Network Computing will have a tornado effect on the business and civic communities. It will have a profound effect on the way we work and live. It will enable opportunities for new wealth creation by allowing flexible access to best-of-breed practices anywhere in the supply chain, anywhere in the world. It will shake every industry.

The economic principles behind the structure of the enterprise will have to consider the instantaneous availability of information and knowledge anywhere across the value chain. The focus of economic activity will transcend the individual firm and address instead the industry value chain. The new world of Network Computing will minimize transaction costs, maximize production quality, and reduce transaction cycle time. It has more potential to change industry ROEs than any business process that has been "re-engineered" in the last ten years.

Accessing knowledge will become more important than accessing energy. The gap between leaders and laggards will be based on knowledge availability, and will widen even further based on such availability. In this context, it is unacceptable that only 5 percent of the world's population has access to computing.

This fundamental change will occur in the most basic industries, like the automotive industry. The integrated supply chain in the automotive industry starting with the consumer, through the dealership network, the car assemblers, and extending toward the Tier 1, Tier 2, and Tier 3 suppliers, will be fundamentally restructured. Massive consolidations are happening downstream in the distribution side, and upstream with the suppliers. These changes require information availability across the totality of the automotive supply chain. Such drastic restructuring of this traditional industry cannot happen without the convergence of computing and communications into Network Computing.

Imagine the possibilities in education. We have the opportunity to end the intellectual decline of our nations. "Virtual Universities" are being built and great teachers with superior content will become as famous as rock stars, with commensurate compensation because their constituencies will grow thousandfold. Why shouldn't the greatest teachers with equivalent followings make as much money as Michael Jackson or Madonna?

These and other profound changes to our work place, our community, and our classrooms are enabled with Networked Computing. Network Computing, with a goal of creating a network society where everyone can participate, targets new markets, return on invested capital, "communications" rather than "computation," "exploring" rather than "tutorial-based" education, and much more. Network Computing will succeed in creating unimaginable wealth in our businesses and personal lives...we are finally on the road to creating the Information Age.

The importance of technicians, business people, and even executives having a fundamental understanding of how to manage and move information is as essential in the next millennium as engineering and manufacturing knowledge was in the century we are now bringing to a close. Oracle8 stands alone in the information industry as the most powerful tool for managing information that exists today. To ignore the concepts and principles of how to use it in business, government, and education would be equivalent to ignoring engineering or chemistry principles in the Industrial Age. Four precepts we've held constant in business for over 50 years are going to change dramatically over the next 10 to 20 years. These are the business structures, business processes, economic models, and attitudes/cultures. Without understanding and dealing with the bedrock changes that are coming as a result of knowledge management, market positions that have been held for years can be lost.

The authors of this book have provided the first steps to gaining the technical knowledge to Oracle8 that will equip businesses and institutions with the tools of the second millennium. As developers or users, we will see our lives forever changed. Access to information will be the difference in market-based economies, and this text is an important part of the arsenal needed to make that difference.

Raymond J. Lane
President and Chief Operating Officer
Oracle Corporation

Acknowledgments

I want to thank my wife, Juliann, and my children, John, Annmarie, and Michael. Without their understanding and infinite patience this book would not have been possible. I would also like to thank my partner, David Teplow. While working with David in building our consulting business, Database Technologies, Inc., I have grown both technically and professionally.

I would also like to extend a special thanks to Mike Abbey. Michael is a great technical resource and a very good friend. The longer I work with Mike, the more respect I have for him. I would also like to welcome a new author on board, Ian. It's a pleasure to work with you.

It is very clear to me that at many critical points in my life the people I have had the privilege to interact with have given me the skills needed to accomplish this book. To these many people, I would like to give thanks.

To the teacher who allowed me to continue to work with the school's computer system after all I had done to it: Denver Deeter, my High School Teacher.

To the many fine people at Honeywell Inc., who introduced me to Oracle: Terry Carlin (Hoser), Fred Powers, Rob Strickland, and Tom Kenney.

To the Numerous people at Oracle who have helped me both professionally and technically, a small but incomplete list: Andy Laursen, Mark Porter (alias, Video Lad), Scott Martin (Inventor of SQL*Trax), Kevin Walsh, Rama Velpuri, David Anderson, Gary Damiano, Ray Lane, and Judy Boyle.

Over the years, being very active within the Oracle usergroup has helped me tremendously. To those many people who have helped me: Geoffe Girvin, Merrilee Nohr, Buff Emsile, Bert Spencer, Warren Capps, Emily Bersin, Tony Ziemba, the late Chris Wooldridge, and so many more.

To the people at Osborne/McGraw-Hill who have worked so hard to put this book on the shelves: Scott Rogers, Ann Sellers, and staff.

To the many others I have worked with: Jim Hussey, Pat McDonald, Dan Lebel, George Noll, Mike Calisi, Darryl Smith, Ed Barry, and the late Skip Rochfort.

As you can see it takes a lot of people to make this possible. I hope you enjoy reading the book.

Michael J. Corey

Oracle8 Tuning is the second work Mike and I have updated for Oracle8, this time with the equal participation of Dan Dechichio and Ian Abramson. I wish to thank a number of people who have given me support, have helped me work with Oracle, and have been able to take the time to learn what I have. Dane Harris of Exocom Systems in Ottawa had an opportunity on some Oracle contracts when I worked for him in 1988. That's where it all started. Thanks Dane! Thanks to Ira Greenblatt and Eric Anttila at the Office of the Auditor General in Ottawa, Canada, where I worked for five years. Ira and Eric supported me and eagerly gave the office and me the opportunity to stay current with Oracle's emerging technology. Their trust in my abilities and skills has allowed me to get to the level of expertise I have mastered. Many thanks to my coauthors, Mike Corey, Dan Dechichio, and Ian Abramson, with whom I have produced *Oracle8 Tuning* over the past number of months. Thanks to Glen McLeod, who has lived up to his image as Mr. Unix. Thanks to my folks Rhoda and Sydney Abbey, as well as many professional colleagues including David Teplow, Ken Jacobs, Nancy Taslitz, Mark Farnham, Pete Sprukulis, Karen Besseling, Scott Rogers, Ann Sellers, Mark Karmendy, Susan Phipps, Mark Kerzner (the UTL_FILE guy),and Jack Jung. *Oracle8 Tuning* has always been "more than a feeling." Lloyd Sheen, Jim Rawlings, Karen Pallister, and Mike McPhee at SFI were very kind to line me up with software and provide a helping hand with SQL-Programmer. Many thanks to Mike Mallia, Bob Blair, and can't forget Dragan Stevanovic for putting up with my shenanigans at work that keep me realizing it is fun to work in IT.

Michael Abbey

There are a number of people that I would like to thank who have given me help and support throughout my career. I would like first and foremost to thank my family, my wife Diana and my son Paul, who have given me support and understanding during my long hours and the everyday demands put on a front-line Database Administrator. They have been there when I needed them and have helped me to achieve the success that I have, both personally and professionally. I would also like to thank the Database Administration Group at the First National Bank of Boston, especially Marguerite Hatch, Emily Bersin, Yi Wang, and Jim Hussey, for their welcoming of a new member to their group and making work both challenging and fun. I have been quite fortunate to have met and worked with a number of very talented people throughout my career. There are too many to mention individually, so I would like to thank all the people with whom I have worked, and who have helped me to grow both professionally and personally. A special thanks to my three co-authors: Mike Corey, for introducing me to the International Oracle User Group Community; Michael Abbey, for his untiring wit and persistence with leading the charge for this revision of the book; and Ian Abramson for his invaluable contribution to this revision of the book.

Daniel J. Dechichio, Jr.

There are people we meet at times in our lives who make a profound impact on us. These people inspire, challenge, and improve us. I would like to thank all these people.

My greatest inspiration in life is my family. You were there when I needed you. You inspired me to reach for my goals and helped me achieve my dreams. To Susan, my wife, thanks for putting up with me and for making this ride so much fun. To my children, Baila and Jillian, remember to reach for the stars. There are no limits to what you can do.

The people we meet everyday are another inspiration to me. To my friends, I want to thank you. Michael Abbey, you are the king. You inspire me to great heights and give me the chance to work with the best. To Michael Corey a big thanks. HEY THANKS! To my friend Jack Chadirdjian, you've been a friend since the beginning of time, and will be until the end. Thanks. To Mark Kerzner and all the Wackers, thanks for everything (especially for my first god-daughter). Thanks to the Abramsons, Astroffs, Orleans, Rzepas, and the Weiskopfs. To everyone else I forgot to mention, I give you all a big thanks!

Finally I would like to thank my parents. To my dad, Joe Abramson, you were always there in those cold arenas watching me play hockey. It's something I still cherish and it epitomizes how you have always been there for me. To my late mother, Lily, I only wish you could have been here to see me author a book. I know you would have been so proud. To you, I dedicate my first book.

Ian Abramson

Introduction

ou are in possession of (or looking at acquiring) a very complex piece of software. Perhaps you are looking for the quickest way to get the biggest bang for your tuning dollar. *Oracle8 Tuning* is the source of one-stop shopping as you dive head first into performance tuning. We offer you a set of guidelines to follow that will allow you to enjoy optimal performance of the Oracle8 Server, with a stress on Microsoft Windows NT 4.0. Oracle8 is a highly configurable product. Part of the dilemma many database administrators face is where to start.

Oracle8 Tuning is designed to allow you to spend 95 percent of your time attending to issues that will get you 95 percent of the attainable performance gain. Even though Oracle8 is a very complex product, it is highly tunable once you look at issues related to memory, CPU, I/O, application tuning, and the overall configuration of the software and hardware infrastructure.

Readers using Oracle7 will find more than enough information on their versions to keep their databases purring like an infant Siamese kitten. We highlight Oracle7.x specifics at the end of each chapter, pointing out what will work and what will not. The heart of the discussion is Oracle8, but most of the material applies to version 7 as well.

Suggestions pertaining to very large databases (VLDB) stand out in some chapters with an icon. So many database management techniques need that extra effort when dealing with information repositories in excess of many terabytes of information. The first production release of Oracle8 can support a repository up to 512 petabytes, where a petabytes equals 1,024 terabytes. Databases of this size were unthinkable not too long ago. With the emergence of a suite of 64-bit microprocessors to choose from, of which DEC Alpha led the pack, Windows NT databases in that 512 petabyte range are looming over the horizon.

Oracle8 Tuning complements the books you may already have. We present a set of rules in each chapter that could literally be cut and pasted into their own document and be a stand-alone guide to tuning. Keep a copy of this book close at hand; when asked to lend it to your colleagues, suggest they get their own. *Oracle8 Tuning* falls into the category of those books you run across in other people's libraries and say to yourself, "I used to have this, but someone borrowed it and I haven't seen it since." You then open the front cover and see the following text on page 1, "From the library of ..."; guess whose name follows!

CHAPTER

1

Installation

ou are now in possession of a very complex piece of software and are wondering what to do next. Relax—it's not as bad as you may think. In fact, it's probably better than you could imagine. Whether you have just acquired it or you have used it for some time, you will find that Oracle is a very tunable product once you master the nuances and idiosyncrasies of how to reach tuning nirvana. It's overwhelming before you get started, but, with this book, tuning is an attainable goal. There is light at the end of the tunnel. Like that little engine that turned "I think I can" into "I know I can," you can scale that tuning dilemma before it conquers you.

The central purpose of *Oracle8 Tuning* is to provide database administrators, application developers, and other interested parties with some basic solutions to issues that involve getting the most out of Oracle. Two things we constantly hear are, "You know, one of the things I *like* so much about Oracle is that it is so tunable," and, "You know, one of the things I *hate* so much about Oracle is that it is so tunable."

We believe both statements reflect where you are in your knowledge of how Oracle works. When first getting started with Oracle (or any other complex software product), you are barraged with a set of concepts. You then try to weed through those concepts, looking for a theme. When the theme is determined, you can begin to study how the concepts are applied. You find guidance through the following means:

- Reading (or ploughing through) copious amounts of technical documentation received with the product

- Requesting support through contracted support services that the vendor provides

- Rubbing shoulders with coexplorers and learning from your mistakes and successes, as well as those of others

- Devouring the gamut of technical material you find in user group publications and other forms of technical writing

- Trying this, trying that, retrying that another way, back to this, no that...

After a while, you are familiar with how to go about getting what is most important with any software—you want solutions and you want them quickly. Once you know the basic tuning issues, you then embark on the long, winding road to make the most of the knowledge gained on your journey. It's a vicious circle: the more you know, the more you find that you can tune.

Follow the suggestions outlined in *Oracle8 Tuning.* Take advantage of our collective 41 years of Oracle experience to succeed in real-life problems today. We have focused on areas we know and have had experience in, and our expertise will provide the biggest bang for your tuning investment buck.

Oracle8 Tuning will provide you with a survival guide to enable quick and competent database and environment tuning. We will present rules to be used as guidelines when tuning Oracle. These rules outline a fundamental tuning methodology, and they are designed to assist you when making tuning decisions. We then provide you with the skills that will get you through the tough times when our rules may not apply; all you need are the tools that Oracle provides out of the box. You do not need extra hardware or software to take advantage of the information in this book. Just remember: Rome was not built in a day. *Oracle8 Tuning* will point you in the right direction.

NOTE
Many issues covered in this chapter help you make decisions during the installation that affect availability and usability of the database down the road. These are best made early in the game rather than waiting until after your applications have been running for a while and interrupting them to attend to the types of issues we cover.

This chapter will deal with the common issues that arise during the installation process. Our goal is to help you avoid some common pitfalls. Many of our suggestions may seem like common sense, but trust us, we see these same mistakes, over and over again. In fact, rumor has it that we have been known to make some of these same mistakes. Just when we think we have a process memorized, Oracle changes it. For example, you may know that with version 6, the default behavior of import was IGNORE=Y (this flag determines how object creation errors are handled; N means report the object creation error before continuing). With Oracle7 and 8, however, the default behavior of import has been changed to IGNORE =N. This leads us into our first topic, the README file.

README File

Every Oracle product out of the box contains a README file, which contains a summary of changes and "gotchas" (things that happen to you when you install Oracle and neglect to read this file beforehand). One of the first things you should do during installation is locate all the pertinent README files and review them. Oracle has not yet reached the level of, say, McDonald's, the fast-food restaurant that is standardized around the world (but this may have something to do with the fact that cooking a hamburger is not as complicated as keeping your Oracle database operating). Until Oracle reaches that level of standardization, you must locate README files the old-fashioned way—by looking in every directory. As you can see from search results in Figure 1-1 against Windows NT and Figure 1-2 against HP-UX, Oracle places these README files anywhere and calls them most anything.

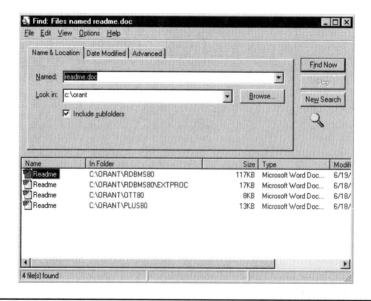

FIGURE 1-1. *README file location in Windows NT*

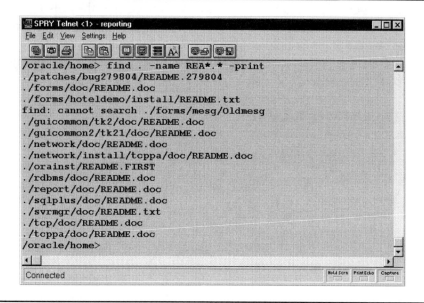

FIGURE 1-2. *README file location on HP-UX*

When installing Oracle8, the Oracle for Windows NT folder created during the installation contains a shortcut called Oracle8 Server Readme. Information in this file is crucial to successful management of the Oracle Server and related products. The next listing highlights the nature of information in the README files.

The size of a ROWID, stored in either external binary format (datatype 11) or a CHAR buffer, has not changed in Oracle8, therefore, the size and datatypes of host variables used to hold Oracle8 ROWIDs has not changed. Applications that employ ROWIDs to fetch rows from the database will be compatible with Oracle8 as long as the ROWIDs are obtained from the server and are otherwise unmodified.

However, in order to address a larger number of rows commensurate with larger databases, the encoding scheme for ROWIDs has changed. When fetching Oracle7 ROWIDs into CHAR datatype buffers it was possible to interpret the string of digits as 'BBBBBBBB.SSSS.FFFF' (Block.Slot.File). This interpretation no longer works under Oracle8. Oracle8 ROWIDs must be treated as opaque data items whose constituent elements cannot be accessed directly. Any applications that attempt to interpret or construct ROWID contents will fail.

What's especially nice about the README files is that they also contain hardware and operating system-specific notes. A list of known bugs is also addressed with the new release of the software. By looking through these README files, you can also learn about new utilities that may make the installation go smoother.

INSTALLATION RULE #1
Read the README files, where Oracle places the most up-to-date information on the product you are about to install. The README files are also where you might learn about useful new utilities or operating system specifics.

Information contained in these README files will assist you with a successful install or upgrade and with issues such as:

- **Compatibility issues** Some of the syntax supported under versions 2.x of PL/SQL does not work with PL/SQL 8. The README points you at an initialization parameter file entry PLSQL_V2_COMPATIBILITY to allow version 8 to support all the version 2 syntax.

- **Upgrading from earlier releases** A file called README.802 contains upgrade information specific to installations moving from release 8.0.2 (the last beta release) to 8.0.3 (this, the first production release).

- **V6 compatibility** The flag that allowed nonversion 6 software to imitate the behavior of Oracle V6 has been desupported; this may have an impact on installations upgrading from version 6 or with the V6 compatibility flag turned on in their Oracle7 applications.

- **Patches supplied with Oracle8 Server** When using Developer 2000 or SQL*Forms, there could be a problem with record locking after a user retrieves a row and attempts to perform an update. The README points you at the location of a patch that can alleviate this condition before you experience it.

INSTALLATION RULE #2
*Before logging a TAR with Worldwide
Support, browse the Oracle8 README files.
You may be surprised (as the four of us have
been from time to time!) at the wealth of
information contained therein.*

VLDB
*With Oracle's attention to very large
information repositories, as time marches on,
we suggest paying extra attention to these
README files looking for issues related to
management of VLDBs.*

Hardware and Software Requirements

Oracle8 for Windows NT requires a strong server, and we think you will be
happiest with a Pentium Pro, nothing less. Table 1-1 details suggested
requirements.

NOTE
*We strongly recommend 64 megabytes, if not
128, for an Oracle8 for Windows NT server.
Naturally when the 64-bit Intel microprocessor
arrives and people make the migration to NT, the
amount of memory on the server will increase.*

Disk Space

Many hours of installation have been lost due to inadequate disk space.
Make sure up front that you have the needed disk space. Regardless of what
the installation guidelines for disk space needs are, make sure you have

Server	Client (NT or Windows 9x)
100 percent IBM compatible with Pentium processor	100 percent IBM compatible with a 486 or more powerful processor
48 megabytes of RAM	16 megabtyes minimum with 48 megabytes for Enterprise Manager
Windows NT compatible Network Interface Card (NIC)	NIC
CD-ROM drive	CD-ROM drive
245 megabytes disk space at a minimum	25 megabytes at a minimum with an extra 25 megabytes when using Enterprise Manager
Windows NT Server or Workstation 4.0	Windows NT Server or Workstation 4.0 or Windows 9x
Netscape Navigator 3 or Internet Exporer 3 for viewing online documentation	Netscape Navigator 3 or Internet Exporer 3 for viewing online documentation

TABLE I-I. *Hardware and Software Requirements*

additional disk space available. A lot of times, product features, new utilities, and extra README files have been added. Each one of these items is not large in itself but when added up become a substantial amount. The documentation, on the other hand, may not have been updated to indicate the additional needed space. An hour into the installation process, you find it aborting, due to insufficient disk space.

INSTALLATION RULE #3
Make sure you have enough disk space up front. Many installs fail due to the lack of adequate disk space.

After an installation on Windows NT, using the typical installation with the starter database and the documentation on disk rather than CD, the **dir/s** command from a DOS window produced the following output:

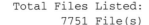

```
     Total Files Listed:
          7751 File(s)        276,907,239 bytes
                              775,323,648 bytes free
```

INSTALLATION RULE #4
Overallocate your disk space needs for the installation process (the requirements Oracle suggests plus an extra 20 percent). Many times, the installation guidelines are low. Better to be safe than sorry.

Starter Database or No Starter Database

Whether you install Oracle8 on a Windows NT or some flavor of UNIX, you can ascertain the success of the installation easily when you ask to create this starter database. The starter database on NT consumes upwards of 100 megabytes of disk space. After an installation activity, it is wise to close and open the database manually to ensure the work ran without error.

INSTALLATION RULE #5
Even if you are never going to use the starter database, let the Oracle8 installer create and open one for you.

INSTALLATION RULE #6
Using Server Manager (the command is **svrmgr30** *from a DOS window), shut down, then start up the starter database to ensure 100 percent that Oracle8 is functioning properly.*

NLS Considerations

NLS stands for National Language Support; Oracle8 and its predecessors support a wide variety of languages and, in some cases, dialects within those languages. For example, the French Canadian support is handled a bit differently than the support of the "same" language in France. One of the hardest things to ensure correct handling of is the storage of accented characters in other languages other than English. You must exercise caution when creating an Oracle8 database. Many DBAs are used to the Oracle7 default character set of USASCII7. When issuing a **create database** statement manually in Server Manager or using the Database Assistant with

Oracle8, ensure the character set value is properly defined along the lines of WE8DEC or a suitable equivalent.

Setting NLS_LANG

This environment variable means something to Oracle as the users interact with the database. After selecting a language near the start of an installation, the language of choice controls the value set for NLS_LANG, made up of the following three components.

- **Language** Specifies the language and its conventions for displaying messages, day name, and month name. For example, when this is set to FRENCH, the month April is displayed as AVR and May is displayed as MAI instead of APR and MAY.

- **Territory** Specifies the territory and its conventions for calculating week and day numbers.

- **Character set** Controls the character set used for displaying messages. This component can be crucial when clients in Quebec interact with Oracle8 to ensure the name "Thérien" is properly displayed rather than "Thirien" or, worse yet, "Therien".

As mentioned previously, Oracle8 supports many different dialects within the same language. Table 1-2 shows how NLS_LANG is set based on the choices you make during the installation process.

Language of Choice	NLS_LANG
Brazilian Portuguese	brazilian_portuguese_brazil.we8iso8859p1
Portuguese	portuguese_portugal.we8iso8859p1
Latin American Spanish	latin_american_spanish_america.we8iso8859p1
Spanish	spanish_spain.we8iso8859p1
Simplified Chinese	simplified_chinese_china.zhs16gbk
Traditional Chinese	traditional_chinese_taiwan.zht16big5

TABLE 1-2.   *Sample of Dialects Within the Same Language*

NLS Entries in the Initialization Parameter File

There are a handful of entries in the Oracle 8.0.3 initialization parameter file that need mentioning. The first impacts the default date display format, the second impacts how it is shown by default.

- ■ **NLS_DATE_FORMAT** The default date display is DD-MON-YY. Common values for this entry are DD/MM/YY to show August 12, 1998, as 12/08/98, YY/MM/DD to show the same date as 98/08/12, or even Mon-DD-YYYY to show Aug-12-1998.

- ■ **NLS_TERRITORY** This determines the following characteristics of data as it is displayed:

  - ■ Date format

  - ■ Decimal character and group separator

  - ■ Local currency symbol

  - ■ ISO currency symbol

  - ■ Week start day

  - ■ Credit and debit symbol

  - ■ ISO week flag

  - ■ List separator

Territory Message Files

If you want to do some cleanup after your Oracle8 installation completes, the information shown in Table 1-3 will help isolate what can be erased. These files could be found in the DBS, CORE40, RDBMS80, PLSQL80, NLSRTL33, PRO80, NET80, OTT80, or PLUS80 subdirectories.

INSTALLATION RULE #7
On many platforms it is quicker and easier to install All Languages. Consider wading through the assortment of message file directories using Table 1-2 and do some cleanup afterwards if you are not licensed for or are not using other languages.

us	American
ar	Arabic
bn	Bengali
ptb	Brazilian Portuguese
bg	Bulgarian
frc	Canadian French
ca	Catalan
hr	Croatian
cs	Czech
dk	Danish
nl	Dutch
eg	Egyptian
gb	English
et	Estonian
sf	Finnish
f	French
din	German Din
d	German
el	Greek
iw	Hebrew
hu	Hungarian
is	Icelandic
i	Italian
ja	Japanese
ko	Korean
esa	Latin American Spanish
lv	Latvian
lt	Lithuanian
ms	Malay
esm	Mexican Spanish
n	Norwegian

TABLE 1-3. *Territory Message File Characters*

pl	Polish
pt	Portuguese
ro	Romanian
ru	Russian
zhs	Simplified Chinese
sk	Slovak
sl	Slovenian
e	Spanish
s	Swedish
th	Thai
zht	Traditional Chinese
tr	Turkish
uk	Ukrainian
vn	Vietnamese

TABLE 1-3. *Territory Message File Characters* (continued)

In most locations around the globe, you are automatically licensed for English and one other language with the base Oracle8 Server product. In Canada, for example, you also automatically receive support for French. In China you may end up with a license that includes Simple Chinese; if you are looking at using languages other than English, consult your friendly neighborhood Oracle office.

Privileges (O/S Level)

Many Oracle installations fail due to inadequate operating system privileges. To avoid these problems during the installation process, we prefer to install Oracle software with a privilege-rich account. Then, after the installation process is complete, we refer to the installation guide and set privilege levels to those in the installation guide. This may seem backwards to you, but in our many years of Oracle experience, this works. We don't waste time during the installation process struggling with privileges. Calling Oracle support with the statement, "I finished installing Oracle with the system account, and everything was working until I set my privileges to those listed in the installation guide," gets much quicker resolution.

INSTALLATION RULE #8

When you have the luxury, install Oracle with an account that is overly rich in privileges (i.e., NT = administrator, UNIX = root, VMS = SYSTEM). Once you have it working, set the account privileges to those listed in the installation guide for your platform and operating system.

Another common privilege problem concerns file access privileges. To avoid file access issues, it is best to have Oracle own its directories and all its files. It is quite common to see installations having problems writing to the directory because the system staff forgot to set Oracle as the owner of the entire directory tree. Make sure every directory and file is owned by the account you installed the Oracle software from.

INSTALLATION RULE #9

Oracle should be the owner of its own directory structure. This includes being a member of the same group.

Privileges (Within the Database)

Oracle has two database accounts where the infrastructure is loaded—the SYS and the SYSTEM account. Note the following points about the infrastructure:

- The initial SYS schema is created by the **create database** statement.

- The data dictionary required to operate the Oracle8 database is set up as catalog.sql runs from the SYS account.

- The structures that support the procedural features are set up in catproc.sql.

■ The default password for the SYS account is CHANGE_ON_INSTALL.

■ The default password for the SYSTEM account is MANAGER.

When you begin an install, make sure these database accounts are reset to the original passwords, even though a lot of the newer software asks you for the current passwords for these accounts during the install. Too many installs fail because some old routine used during the install process assumes the password for SYSTEM is MANAGER.

INSTALLATION RULE #10

When installing some third-party software, reset the SYS account password to CHANGE_ON_INSTALL. Reset the SYSTEM account password to MANAGER. Much of the software still assumes that the passwords are set to these defaults. After the installation process, remember to change your SYSTEM and SYS passwords.

Viewing Objects in the SYS Schema

Oracle8 restricts database users from viewing the objects in the SYS schema. This means that users can **select** information from the dictionary views but not **describe** them. In order to imitate the functionality of Oracle7, there are two things that need attention:

■ O7_DICTIONARY_ACCESSIBILITY is intended to be used for migration from Oracle7 to Oracle8. Restrictions on objects in the SYS schema exist when the parameter is set to FALSE. For example, the privilege SELECT ANY TABLE would allow the recipient to view data in any table except those in the SYS schema.

■ Users (or groups of users in roles) can be given access to the system tables by being enrolled in the SELECT_CATALOG_ROLE created in the catalog.sql script mentioned previously.

SYSOPER and SYSDBA Privileges

Oracle8 implements the same security blanket on secure operations with the database—specifically start up and shut down, using the system privileges SYSOPER and SYSDBA. There are a few components in place to support the proliferation of this security mechanism. Oracle maintains an operating system password file with the Oracle8 login names of users permitted to perform these operations. In order to get the database up and running and available to the user community, you must be fluent in how this works. Let's look at the components:

- A password file created using the ORAPWD80 utility, whose herald is shown in the next listing, followed by a call to the utility using the correct number of parameters:

```
C:\WINNT\PROFILES\ABBEYM\DESKTOP>orapwd80
Usage: orapwd file=<fname> password=<password> entries=<users>
  where
     file - name of password file (mand),
     password - password for SYS and INTERNAL (mand),
     entries - maximum number of distinct DBA and OPERs (opt),
  There are no spaces around the equal-to (=) character.
C:\WINNT\PROFILES\ABBEYM\DESKTOP> orapwd80 file=\orant\database\passwd.ora
                                   password=oracle entries=12
```

- An entry in the initialization parameter file for REMOTE_LOGIN_ PASSWORD_FILE where its value can be one of the following:

   - **NONE** No secure connections are allowed over nonsecure connections (normally, but not limited to, using Oracle's SQL*Net or Net8 mechanism).

NOTE
We have had difficulty even starting and shutting down a database with the value for this parameter set to NONE. We are able to **connect internal***, but receive an error "ORA-01031 insufficient privileges" out of line mode Server Manager and an equivalent message from the OEM Instance Manager when trying to connect as sysoper or sysdba.*

- **EXCLUSIVE** SYSOPER and SYSDBA connections permitted by users SYS and INTERNAL by default. The privileges can be given out to any users permitted to connect to the database.

- **SHARED** The password file can be used by more than one instance on the same machine. The caveat of this value is that no users can be added to the password file, and only SYS and INTERNAL are permitted to perform secure database operations.

INSTALLATION RULE #11
*You must be connected as sysoper or sysdba
to start up or shut down an Oracle8 database.*

Installation Defaults
Oracle8 release 8.0.3 is delivered with REMOTE_LOGIN_PASSWORD_
FILE=SHARED. If you see that this is going to cause you problems, you must:

- Shut down the database using Instance Manager or Server Manager

- Edit the initialization parameter file, changing the entry's value to EXCLUSIVE

- Add one or more users to the password file using the ORAPWD80 utility

- Restart the database

Suppose you give secure connection privileges to user SHAUNAG. When you want to perform remote secure operations or simply shut down or start up, you would connect to the database using the command **connect shaunag as sysoper** or **connect shaunag as sysdba** and be prompted for the secure password.

INSTALLATION RULE #12
*Create a secure account to perform privileged
operations and stay away from haphazard
login as the SYS user.*

SHARED_POOL_SIZE Pitfall

The suggested SHARED_POOL_SIZE is not always adequate. We have had a few occasions where using the default SHARED_POOL_SIZE recommendation has caused the installation to fail. So, based on this experience, we increase the SHARED_POOL_SIZE parameter during installation.

INSTALLATION RULE #13
Increase the default SHARED_POOL_SIZE (an initialization parameter file entry) during the installation process. If it's too small, it will cause your installation to fail. Set it to twice the suggested default.

Proper Sizing of the Shared Pool

When sizing the shared pool, you must be aware of the type of application(s) your Oracle8 database will support. For example, a very common exercise is deploying Designer/2000 on a Windows NT database. When you browse the installation notes to prepare for the work, you will notice that you need to set the SHARED_POOL_SIZE entry to at least 18000000. The Designer/2000 product is very package intensive and, during the installation of the product, must go through compilation of this code which requires gobs of shared pool space. The installation of Oracle8 will work with a smaller pool size, but the setup of a repository for Designer/2000 will fail if you stick with the Server default for this parameter.

VLDB
Very large shared pool sizes for a database of this size should be coupled with a very large data cache (controlled by the initialization parameter file entry db_block_buffers) to provide optimum throughput.

Installation Log

Every Oracle installation session asks you to specify a log file for the installation session. If the same name is chosen, the installation log is appended to the same file each time. After the installation is completed, even if the installation process informs you that all went well, you must review this log to ensure it finished successfully. Even though the install process told you all was well, don't believe it till you see it for yourself.

In this log, you will typically see the error ORA-00942: Table or view does not exist. This particular error should be ignored. It is just informing you the installation process tried to drop a table, but it could not succeed because the table was not there. This is okay, because the first time you install a product, none of the database objects exist.

If you do not have the patience to review the installation logs (this can be a very tedious process), then here is a quick way to search the installation log file for errors. In VMS, the command is:

```
search error.log/win=10 error
```

and in UNIX it is:

```
grep -i ORA- error.log
```

 INSTALLATION RULE #14
Don't assume your installation worked correctly, even if the installation process reports back that it was successful. It is the responsibility of the installer to inspect ALL installation logs to verify all went well.

 INSTALLATION RULE #15
To expedite the search, use a system search utility such as more/grep (UNIX) or search/win (VMS).

File Structure

Once you have installed the Oracle software, you should give some thought to the database file layout. This part of the discussion is not about how you separate the database files for performance reasons (that is covered in Chapter 3), but how you name the file structures to make day-to-day maintenance easier.

Directory	Physical Device (Size)
/u01 or Disk01:[oracle]	Device01 (2Gb)
/u02 or Disk02:[oracle]	Device02 (2Gb)
/u03 or Disk03:[oracle]	Device03 (2Gb)

TABLE 1-4. *Disk Layout Example: One Device per Directory*

Remember, when your site's system manager initializes a disk, there are many options. We do not recommend having your system manager merge multiple physical drives into one logical drive, even if your O/S system allows this.

The first important point to make is that one device equals one directory point. For example, if you have three physical disks, we recommend you instruct your site's system manager to allocate the devices as shown in Table 1-4. This is more flexible and optimal than creating one mount point that is a combination of the three drives, as shown in Table 1-5.

INSTALLATION RULE #16
Map your directory structure to physical devices (e.g., if you have five disks, create five directory points). We do not recommend creating large logical drives.

Directory	Physical Device (Size)
/u01 or Disk01:[oracle]	Device01 (2Gb)
	Device02 (2Gb)
	Device03 (2Gb)

TABLE 1-5. *Disk Layout Example: Multiple Devices per Directory*

Another situation we see quite often is sites taking a two-gigabyte device and breaking it up into three partitions or directories. For example:

```
/sys (500MB)
/data (1g)
/indexes (500MB)
```

It is much simpler and cleaner to have one directory point pointing to the whole physical device. Thus, when placing a file on /u01, obviously it is also being placed on the same physical device as the /data and /indexes directory. We find partitioning disks sometimes limits your view of the world. For disks that are going to be used exclusively to hold Oracle database files, do not partition the disk into separate directories.

INSTALLATION RULE #17
Allocate an entire device to hold Oracle datafiles. Do not partition it into smaller logical devices.

The second point concerns how you allocate space for a large tablespace—one that might take up the entire physical device. For example, if you have a tablespace that is two gigabytes in size and you have a physical device that can hold two gigabytes, then your first instinct may be to allocate space for the tablespace as shown in Figure 1-3. As you can see, the DBA has created a very large tablespace with one datafile of two gigabytes. In theory, this sounds like the easiest way to manage the tablespace; in practice, this is not the case. We have a better alternative.

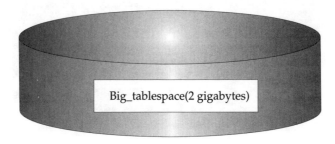

FIGURE 1-3. *Tablespace with one two-gigabyte datafile*

As you can see in Figure 1-4, we allocate space for the tablespace in four datafiles, each 500MB. Compared to Figure 1-3, where the tablespace resides in one datafile of two gigabytes, the setup in Figure 1-4 has numerous advantages:

- Many UNIX systems still have trouble backing up a single file over one gigabyte in size. Backup recovery issues are always a major concern.

- When using multiple equal-sized datafiles, you only need to create the first, then add others as your space requirements increase. By creating the first 500MB datafile initially, you save time when backing up the tablespace that resides in that single file.

- By creating a tablespace in multiple files, you can balance the I/O to that tablespace, if necessary, by moving one datafile to another device. Part of the output of utlbstat and utlestat, as discussed in Chapter 3, reports I/O by database file.

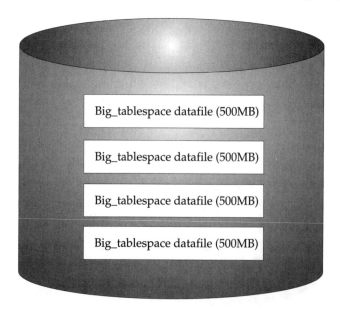

FIGURE 1-4. *Equally sized datafiles making up a tablespace*

By having the database tablespace in smaller, more manageable pieces, you have the option of separating the tablespace's datafiles onto separate devices. The alternative is the setup shown in Figure 1-4. Using that approach, you are forced to go through detailed analysis to determine which database objects are causing the heavy I/O load. Then you would have to drop and re-create those objects on other devices. This is a very time-consuming process.

INSTALLATION RULE #18
Lay out your large tablespaces into small manageable sections.

INSTALLATION RULE #19
Many UNIX backup systems still have problems dealing with datafiles over one gigabyte. We recommend all Oracle datafiles be under one gigabyte (1,073,741,824 bytes).

The third point concerns standardizing your datafile sizes. Make it easy to swap a datafile from one physical device to another. For example, if you have very large tablespaces on two physical devices, make the datafile sizes standard, as shown in Figure 1-5.

Imagine you are tuning the database and you run the utlbstat/utlestat report (discussed in detail in Chapter 6). From that report, you determine that to help balance I/O, you should swap Tablespace A datafile 3 with Tablespace B datafile 4. If your tablespace's datafiles are a standard size, this becomes a very easy task. You know that a datafile from one disk is equal in size to the datafile on another disk.

INSTALLATION RULE #20
Allocate a tablespace's physical datafiles in standard sizes. This will make swapping the datafiles a very easy task when you begin the tuning cycle for I/O balancing.

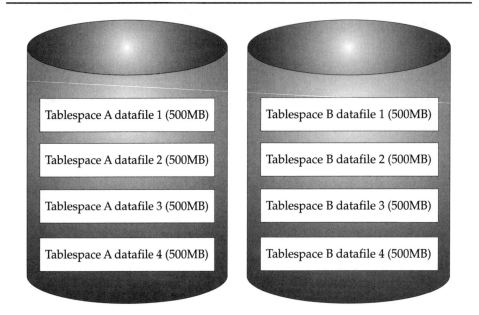

FIGURE 1-5.   *Equally sized datafiles in every tablespace*

Our fourth point deals with not complicating your directory structure. For example, many sites have the following:

```
t:\prod\appl_catscan\catp1.dbf
t:\prod\appl_nurse\nursep1.dbf
t:\prod\/appl_doctor\doctorp1.dbf
t:\training\appl_catscan\catt1.dbf
t:\training\appl_nurse\nurset1.dbf
t:\test\appl_doctor\doctort1.dbf
```

In this case, on the physical device mapped to t:, a file structure is created based on the type of database application. There are three databases (Production, Test, and Training) and three applications (Catscans, Nurses, and Doctors). Segregating the datafiles this way overly complicates the directory structure and limits your ability to see what's going on. We recommend an alternative approach:

```
t:\oradbf\catprod1.dbf
t:\oradbf\nurseprod1.dbf
t:\oradbf\doctorprod1.dbf
```

```
t:\oradbf\cattrn1.dbf
t:\oradbf\nursetrn1.dbf
t:\oradbf\doctortst1.dbf
```

Place all your datafiles into a directory called oradbf, naming the file such that the database name can be gleaned from the file name itself (e.g. the text "trn" means training and "tst" means test). Rather than artificially separating datafiles into separate directories, place them all together. Then, when you move a database file onto that device, you will see every other database file it will be in contention with, regardless of the database. When you are looking for all database files on a particular disk, you have only one location to look at. When you are developing backup schemes, you write a generic backup program that searches every physical device on the system, looking at the oradbf directory.

You can apply the same technique to exports. Create an export directory; whenever you do an export, it should be placed in the export directory. Then create a generic export job that runs every night, backing up any file that is placed into the export directory.

INSTALLATION RULE #21
A database file is a database file. Place them all on a central directory for that disk.

Database Creation Issues

When you create an Oracle database, you need to make a few choices up front that, if done incorrectly, can cost you. The following sections will go over some of these choices. The listings we show are from line mode Server Manager. Figures 1-6 and 1-7 show where this information can be specified using the Oracle8 Database Assistant.

NOTE
The dialog in the Database Assistant provides for two single-membered redo log groups. To add additional groups or members, you can use the OEM Backup Manager through the Logfile menu options.

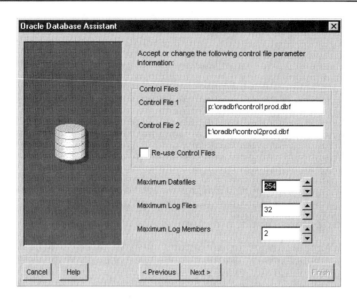

FIGURE 1-6. *Specifying maxdatafiles*

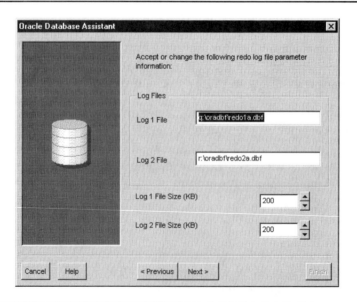

FIGURE 1-7. *Specifying redo log groups and members*

maxdatafiles

The first and most critical, in our opinion, is the choice you make for the **maxdatafiles** parameter when your database is created (refer to the "Oracle Limits" section in Chapter 7). The maximum setting for this parameter is based upon your operating system. Set this value as high as possible. Over time your database will grow (planned and unplanned), and you will need a lot more datafiles than you ever anticipated. The default setting for this parameter is too low, and the cost to increase it is a larger control file. Here's an example:

```
create database prod
...
datafile 't:\oradbf\systemprod1.dbf' size 50MB
...
maxdatafiles 255;
```

INSTALLATION RULE #22
Set **maxdatafiles** to a very high number. Too many sites use the default and run out. The default is too low.

Redo Logs

You should always mirror your redo logs. Redo logs are a single point of failure. If you lose your redo log, you lose your entire database. So, when you create the database, make sure each redo log has a mirror partner.

INSTALLATION RULE #23
Redo logs are a single point of failure for the database: if you lose one, you may lose your entire database and have to restore a copy from a previous backup. To protect yourself, mirror your redo logs.

During database creation, we recommend that you have at least three redo log groups (with Oracle8, we speak of redo log groups that can be made up of one or more members). The following listing shows how to set this up when you create a database. After this code is run, you will have three redo log groups with two members each.

```
SVRMGR> create database PROD
    2> logfile group 1
    3>        ('p:\oradbf\redo1a.dbf', 'q:\oradbf\redo1b.dbf') size 10MB,
    4> logfile group 2
    5>        ('q:\oradbf\redo2a.dbf', 'r:\oradbf\redo2b.dbf') size 10MB,
    6> logfile group 3
    7>        ('r:\oradbf\redo3a.dbf', 'p:\oradbf\redo3b.dbf') size 10MB
    8> datafile 't:\oradbf\systemprod1.dbf' size 50MB
    9> maxdatafiles 255;
Statement processed.
SVRMGR>
```

Log History

Oracle8 maintains a record of redo logs with information about the sequence number used by each redo log, the first system change number (or *SCN*) in each log, and the last system change number registered in the log. For the purposes of planning disaster recovery, we suggest planning for more than the default rows in V$LOG_HISTORY by increasing the value for the **maxloghistory** in the **create database** statement.

INSTALLATION RULE #24
Set the **maxloghistory** *value somewhere between 100 and 200 when your database is created.*

Redo Log Group Members

It's all fine and dandy to plan for multimembered redo log groups, but unless you specify a different value, Oracle8 by default only allows two members per redo log group. This can be changed by increasing the value for **maxlogmembers** as a database is created. There are operating system limits on many platforms that control the maximum number of members for each redo log group.

INSTALLATION RULE #25
Enter a value for **maxlogmembers** *equal to the number of devices upon which you place your redo log groups.*

Tablespace Configuration

Each database should minimally have the following five tablespaces specified:

■ **SYSTEM** This is where all the information owned by SYS should belong. No other user should have the ability to create objects here.

■ **ROLLBACK** This is where your rollback segments should be placed. Before all updates can complete, they must be recorded in the rollback segments. Only rollback segments should go in this tablespace. It should have a very generous default storage clause associated with it. For example:

```
create tablespace rollback_segs
datafile 's:\oradbf\rollprod1.dbf' size 100MB
default storage (initial 500K next 500K pctincrease 0);
```

■ **TEMP** This is where all user temporary space needs are met for **group by** clauses, **order by** clauses, and so on. This tablespace should not contain any objects other than those that Oracle creates and drops internally when processing your SQL statements.

■ **TOOLS** This is where all your database tool objects should be installed. Typically, the tools are objects owned by the system account, for example, the Oracle Forms tables or the Oracle Report tables.

■ **USERS** This is where users should place their own individual tables. It should have a very low default storage clause. If a user does not specify a size, we assume they want a very small size. For example:

```
create tablespace users
datafile 'f:\oradbf\userprod1.dbf' size 50MB
default storage (initial 10K next 10K pctincrease 0);
```

Set it small by default; if users need more space, they should preallocate it up front. Use this as the base installation for any Oracle database. From there, you can add additional tablespaces based on need. The point is, no matter how many physical disks you have or how many users, you should still segregate your basic database into this standard design.

Remember, if your SYSTEM tablespace fills up, your database stops. A frozen database is not a tuned database. By segregating the database this way up front, it paves the way for better performance.

Initialization Parameter File Sizing

Oracle does a very good job of giving you a starting point for your initialization parameter file. We go into great detail on fine-tuning your initialization parameter file in Chapter 5. But when you look at the Oracle default initialization parameter file, remember: small is the number of users, not the size of the database.

INSTALLATION RULE #26
In the default initialization parameter file, small means number of users and not database size.

Oracle Reports

When you install Oracle Reports, it asks if you want central or local table definition. Always choose central. You do not want to be in the business of supporting a thousand users' individual copies of these tables.

INSTALLATION RULE #27
Always choose central table support when installing Oracle Reports. Local table support is a DBA nightmare.

Control Files

Control files contain information your database uses to recover itself and maintain its integrity. If you lose your control files, you are in serious trouble. Because the cost of each control file in terms of disk usage is so small, we strongly suggest, from day one, you create a minimum of three control files on different drives.

INSTALLATION RULE #28
Each database should have a minimum of three control files. Place the control files on separate physical devices.

With Oracle, you can name most any object any way you want. Use the ability to name objects as a tool. For example, call the control file

CONTROL01.DBF or, in the case of multiple databases, CONTROLP1.DBF and CONTROLT1.DBF, where P stands for production and T stands for test.

Scripts

When you install and create a database, do everything through scripts. This includes the creation of all rollback segments, tablespace, indexes, and so on. It will make your life much easier and it will guarantee consistency. All scripts should follow the following format:

```
/* this is the create tablespace script for the production database */
spool script_name.lis
set echo on
create tablespace temp datafile 'd:\oradbf\temp01.dbf' size 50m
default storage (initial 100k next 100k pctincrease 2);
/*  */
create tablespace user_data datafile 'e:\oradbf\user01.dbf' size 100m
default storage (initial 10k next 10k pctincrease 0);
spool off
```

The spool commands make sure you are able to go back later and see how the file ran. The command **set echo on** makes sure you see every SQL statement run. The use of a script makes database creation much easier.

Non-default Entries in the Initialization Parameter File

After the database has been created, shut down, and restarted, it is wise to look at the alert trace file written by Oracle8. Look for nonstandard parameter values and decide which, if any, should be set back to the installation default. The next listing shows some output from one of these alert files:

```
System parameters with non-default values:
    processes               = 50
    shared_pool_size        = 3000000
    control_files           = T:\oradbf\ctl1tst.ora, T:\oradbf\ctl2tst.ora
    db_block_buffers        = 200
    db_block_size           = 2048
    compatible              = 8.0.3.0.0
    log_buffer              = 8192
    log_checkpoint_interval = 8000
```

```
log_checkpoint_timeout   = 0
db_files                 = 1020
db_file_multiblock_read_count= 8
dml_locks                = 100
sequence_cache_entries   = 10
sequence_cache_hash_buckets= 10
remote_login_passwordfile= SHARED
sort_area_size           = 65536
db_name                  = tst
background_dump_dest      = C:\ORANT\rdbms80\trace
user_dump_dest           = C:\ORANT\rdbms80\trace
max_dump_file_size       = 10240
```

Products Completeness Check

This section deals with some issues after an upgrade, not a fresh installation. Some readers may find this material helpful after a fresh installation as well. Our experience has shown that it is a good idea to take the upgrade process one step further. When the information box appears telling you that the installer has successfully completed its work, we recommend doing the following—better safe than sorry!

Oracle8 Server Heralds

After an orainst session where the Oracle Server is upgraded, invoke the following server components and inspect the heralds they display. Each herald on its own is significant, as well as the consistency between each one. A sure sign of there being something wrong would be if one product reported the presence of PL/SQL version 8.0.3 and another version 8.0.2.

Server Manager

The herald should display the correct version numbers for the Server and Server Manager. The following listing reports on these two version numbers:

```
C:\WINNT\PROFILES\ABBEYM\DESKTOP> svrmgr30
Oracle Server Manager Release 3.0.3.0.0 - Production
(c) Copyright 1997, Oracle Corporation.  All Rights Reserved.
Oracle8 Enterprise Edition Release 8.0.3.0.0 - Production
With the Partitioning and Objects options
PL/SQL Release 8.0.3.0.0 - Production
SVRMGR>
```

Export and Import

Invoke these two utilities after the installation and verify their version numbers. The output should resemble the following:

```
C:\WINNT\PROFILES\ABBEYM\DESKTOP> imp80
Import: Release 8.0.3.0.0 - Production on Thu Aug 14 8:18:1 1999
(c) Copyright 1997 Oracle Corporation.  All rights reserved.
Username: system
Password:
Connected to: Oracle8 Enterprise Edition Release 8.0.3.0.0 - Production
With the Partitioning and Objects options
PL/SQL Release 8.0.3.0.0 - Production
C:\WINNT\PROFILES\ABBEYM\DESKTOP>
C:\WINNT\PROFILES\ABBEYM\DESKTOP> exp80
Export: Release 8.0.3.0.0 - Production on Thu Aug 14 8:19:8 1999
(c) Copyright 1997 Oracle Corporation.  All rights reserved.
Username: system
Password:
Connected to: Oracle8 Enterprise Edition Release 8.0.3.0.0 - Production
With the Partitioning and Objects options
PL/SQL Release 8.0.3.0.0 - Production
```

SQL*Plus

When logging onto the Oracle database, the herald reports the Oracle Server version number, the server components in the kernel, and the version of PL/SQL. The following herald is displayed when entering SQL*Plus.

```
SQL*Plus: Release 8.0.3.0.0 - Production on Thu Aug 14 8:21:1 1999
(c) Copyright 1997 Oracle Corporation.  All rights reserved.
Connected to:
Oracle8 Enterprise Edition Release 8.0.3.0.0 - Production
With the Partitioning and Objects options
PL/SQL Release 8.0.3.0.0 - Production
```

From time to time, DBAs report the following display when logging into SQL*Plus after a Server upgrade:

```
SQL*Plus: Release 8.0.3.0.0 - Production on Thu Aug 14 8:21:1 1999
(c) Copyright 1997 Oracle Corporation.  All rights reserved.
Connected to:
Oracle8 Enterprise Edition Release 8.0.3.0.0 - Production
With the Partitioning and Objects options
```

Note the message about PL/SQL is missing—a sure sign that something went wrong during the installation. To fix the problem, log into SQL*Plus as user SYS and run the command:

```
@?/rdbms80/admin/catproc
```

NOTE

This is NOT a normal occurrence and is very rare. We know of no situations where it happened in Windows NT; most reports we have heard are on some flavor of a UNIX machine.

Correct Behavior of PL/SQL

A few packages must be created successfully in order for PL/SQL to function properly. If, for whatever reason, a package vital to PL/SQL was not properly created, the following type of error message will be encountered when trying to run anything in PL/SQL:

```
SQL> begin
  2    declare x number;
  3      begin
  4        x := 9;
  5      end;
  6    end;
  7  /
ERROR:
ORA-06553: PLS-213: package STANDARD not accessible
begin
*
ERROR at line 1:
ORA-06553: PLS-213: package STANDARD not accessible
```

Do not take for granted that PL/SQL packages such as standard were properly created; it is your job to verify that they were successfully compiled after an upgrade.

Database Triggers, Stored Procedures, Functions, and Packages

Most installations use some form of these PL/SQL blocks stored in the database. Before performing an upgrade, it is wise to log onto SQL*Plus as each owner of these types of code and run a script to create another program to recompile all this code after the upgrade.

Triggers

The following script writes a SQL*Plus program that can be run to recompile all your triggers.

```
/* ------------------------------------------------- */
/* This program assumes you are logged in as the     */
/* owner of the tables with triggers associated with */
/* them. This is important, since DBA privileged     */
/* users may experience problems compiling other     */
/* user's code.                                       */
/* ------------------------------------------------- */
set pages 0 feed off echo off trimsp on
spool trgcomp.sql
prompt spool trgcomp
prompt set echo on feed on
select 'alter trigger '||trigger_name||' compile;'
  from user_triggers;
prompt spool off
spool off
```

This will leave you with a file called trgcomp.sql for the current user. After the upgrade, log into SQL*Plus as that user, and run trgcomp.sql. If user bnnj owned a number of triggers, part of the output from this program would resemble the following listing:

```
alter TRIGGER GEO_MAINT compile;
alter TRIGGER ED_LOCK compile;
alter TRIGGER EVENT_CREATE compile;
alter TRIGGER MAKE_SEGMENTS compile;
```

When you run trgcomp.sql, it will produce an output file called trgcomp.lst. Before the upgrade exercise is deemed successful, look in this file for the text created with compilation errors. This is a sign that something did not compile properly.

Procedures, Packages, and Functions

The following script writes a SQL*Plus program that can be run to recompile all your procedures, packages, and functions.

```
/* --------------------------------------------- */
/* Using the USER_SOURCE view, create a script   */
/* to recompile all procedures, functions, and   */
/* packages. Notice we exclude the TYPE of        */
/* PACKAGE BODY since compiling a PACKAGE also    */
/* compiles its BODY at the same time.            */
/* --------------------------------------------- */
set pages 0 feed off echo off
spool ppfcomp.sql
prompt spool ppfcomp
prompt set echo on feed on
select distinct 'alter '||type||' '||name||' compile;'
  from user_source
 where type <> 'PACKAGE BODY';
prompt spool off
spool off
```

Go through the same exercise with the output from this program; the file here will be called ppfcomp.lst. For user sys, part of the output from this program would resemble the following listing:

```
alter PACKAGE DBMS_REFRESH compile;
alter PACKAGE DBMS_UTILITY compile;
alter PACKAGE DIANA compile;
alter PACKAGE DIUTIL compile;
alter PACKAGE PIDL compile;
alter PACKAGE STANDARD compile;
```

Database Links Supported by Net8

After the upgrade, it is wise to test all your database links. They were built using syntax similar to the following, which assumes there is a service descriptor called PROD:

```
SQL> create public database link to_prod
  2     connect to dblink identified by dblink
  3     using 'prod';
Database link created.
SQL>
```

Since a DUAL table exists in every database, after your upgrade completes, run the following SQL*Plus script to look at DUAL in each database accessible remotely:

```
/* ------------------------------------------------ */
/* This program assumes you have been granted access */
/* to the DBA_SYNONYMS view owned by Oracle user SYS */
/* and that you have write access to the current     */
/* directory.                                         */
/* ------------------------------------------------ */
set echo off pages 0 feed off
spool remotes.sql
select 'select * from dual@'||db_link||
  from sys.dba_db_links
 where owner = 'PUBLIC';
spool off
set echo on
spool remotes
```

The output from this program will be written to a file called remotes.lst (the file name is always remotes but the file name extension may differ on your operating system). There should be no Oracle errors reported. If the output file is clean, the Net8 upgrade did not raise any unexpected errors with your database links.

Leftovers from Relinking the Server

In some environments on some platforms, if you have relinked the Oracle Server, Oracle has taken the previous versions of Oracle, exp, and imp and saved a copy with the letter O tagged on the end. The extra space taken up by these O-files is significant. Simply remove these files with the command **rm *O** or your operating system command.

NOTE
This should not occur on the Windows NT platform.

Other Extraneous Files

Those who have used the installer are familiar with the Available Products screen; this is where you select the products you wish to install or upgrade from a list of what is available. You travel around the product list products, pressing the spacebar to highlight those you wish to install. After selecting the products, you start the process by TABing over to the OK button and pressing ENTER. Many times we find after orainst is finished its work, we are left with an assortment of files that belong to products we did not ask to have installed.

NOTE
This should not occur on the Windows NT platform.

Third-Party Products

All too many times, installations using third-party products find themselves unable to use these products after an upgrade to the Oracle Server. The vendors of these products and Oracle do their best to ensure each knows what the other is up to, but sometimes something slips through the cracks. For example, at one point the contents of a library called libcore.a changed, and some vendors were caught off guard. Oracle had taken some information out of this library and created a new one called libnlsrtl. It is best to speak with vendors prior to the Oracle Server upgrade. Many have a special release of their product that is designed to run with the version of the Oracle Server to which you are moving. A few years ago, when Oracle7 was first released, a few vendors' products were not available with the major new Server release. Installers who were unaware of this found themselves unable to use some products until the vendor was ready for Oracle7.

Before moving on, let's look at the checklist shown in Table 1-6 that you should look over after leaving orainst before you sit back, slap your hands together, and say to yourself, "That was not too bad!!"

Activity	Pre	Post
Study README.doc	*	*
Oracle Server and SQL*Plus heralds		*
Presence of PL/SQL in the kernel		*
Correct behavior of PL/SQL		*
Create script to re-create all database triggers	*	
Recompile all database triggers		*
Create script to re-create all stored objects	*	
Recompile all stored objects		*
Version and presence of Server Manager, export, and import		*
What's new and what is no longer part of INIT.ORA	*	*
Net8 listener process		*
Leftovers from installing the Server		*
Extraneous and/or unwanted products		*
Behavior of third-party products		*

TABLE 1-6.   *Pre-/Post-installation Checklist*

Let's Tune It

It has been our experience over the years with Oracle that installing the software can be frustrating at times. We fondly remember the stories we tell one another and problems we have experienced ourselves during installation. Armed with the issues we have discussed in this chapter, we are confident you will make informed decisions when installing Oracle that will pay off down the road. Now that Oracle is properly installed, you are ready to start tuning!

■ Take the time to read the README files Oracle delivers.

■ Ensure that you have an abundance of disk space available during the install—at least the amount you are told to have, plus an extra 20 percent.

- Install from CD-ROM. It offers the most flexible installation environment and does not use as much disk space as tape.

- Plan the distribution of the database files to take advantage of all the disk drives you have at your disposal.

- Keep all Oracle database files under 1 gigabyte (1,073,741,824 bytes).

- Have at least three control files, each placed on a different drive.

- Your database should minimally consist of a SYSTEM, ROLLBACK, TEMP, TOOLS, and USERS tablespace.

- A completeness check on product consistency should be performed after a software upgrade.

- It is wise to recompile all stored objects after an upgrade, including triggers.

- Check the usability of your database links after an upgrade.

Oracle7.x Specifics

Please note the following points organized by the headings for some sections throughout this chapter:

- "README File" Applicable to Oracle7.x.

- "Hardware and Software Requirements" Naturally, the software requirements pertain only to Oracle8. The hardware requirements for Oracle 7.x may be a wee bit lighter. Refer to the appropriate installation guides.

- "Disk Space" Applies to Oracle7.x as does the Starter Database section, even though it uses Oracle8 as an example.

- "NLS Considerations" All material applies to Oracle 7.x though there may not be as many territory message files as shown in Table 1-3.

- "Privileges (O/S Level)" Applies to release 7.x.x.

- "Viewing Objects in the SYS Schema" Not applicable to any release of Oracle7 since access to this schema is automatic without any intervention.

■ "SYSOPER and SYSDBA Privileges"   Does not apply to 7.0.x, but does for 7.1.x, 7.2.x, and 7.3.x.

■ "SHARED_POOL_SIZE Pitfall, Installation Log, File Structure"   All apply to 7.x.x.

■ "Database Creation Issues"   Applicable across the board in 7.x.x.

■ "Products Completeness Check"   Applicable to all 7.x releases.

CHAPTER
2

Memory/CPU

he amount of computer main memory and its efficient usage by Oracle contribute to the tuning process, and understanding some of the workings of memory will help you tune the database. In addition, the processing power of your database is strongly influenced by the computer's CPU. In fact, most operations performed by the software running on your machine require work to be done by the CPU. In terms of tuning the Oracle database, the size and processing power of the CPU will affect the job of tending to online systems throughput. This chapter will discuss memory management issues and explain what resides in memory. We will also discuss the assortment of buffers that occupy main memory, and we will provide some hints on buffer sizing. We will discuss managing your current CPU, assessing the load on your CPU, and ways to maximize your CPU using some of the new Oracle8 features.

Windows NT Performance Monitor

Throughout this section, and in others, the Performance Monitor on the Windows NT operating system will be mentioned. This is not an Oracle product but a product that comes with the Windows NT operating system. This product is used to monitor the operations and performance of the Windows NT operating system. If Oracle is running on a Windows NT platform, this product should be familiar to the people that are responsible for tuning Oracle. Because of this, a brief overview of the product will be done here with a specific slant to monitoring the Oracle environment.

Oracle8 for Windows NT comes with its own configuration of the Windows NT Performance Monitor. It is the same as the operating system Performance Monitor except that it is preloaded with a few of the Oracle8 database performance elements. To access the Oracle8 Performance Monitor, choose Start|Programs|Oracle for Windows NT|Oracle8 Performance Monitor. Figure 2-1 show the Oracle8 Performance Monitor when it first comes up.

Use the Add to Chart option from the Edit menu to add or change performance elements to the chart. Figure 2-2 show the screen for this option.

There are a number of items on the screen that you should be concerned about. The first item is Computer. This is used to select the Windows NT computer upon which Performance Monitoring is desired; it

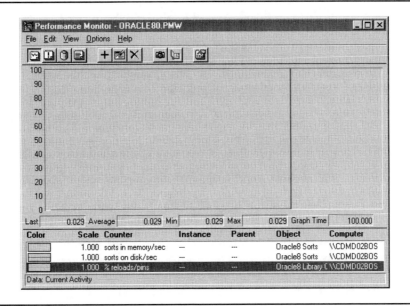

FIGURE 2-1. *Performance Monitor startup*

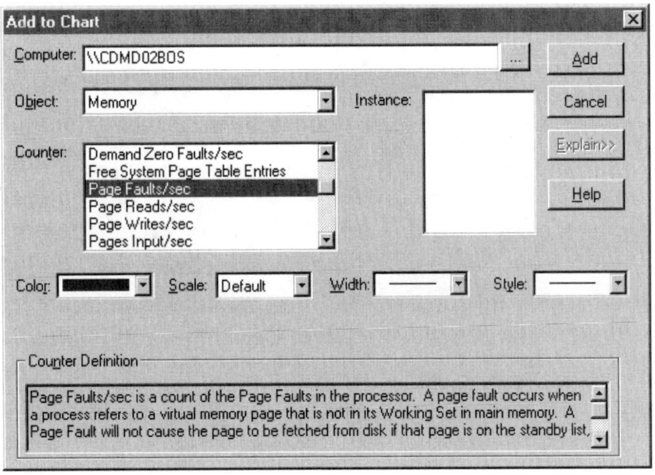

FIGURE 2-2. *Add to Chart*

defaults to the computer that the Performance Monitor is running on. The button to the right with the ellipses (...) lets you browse the network for other computers that can be monitored. The next item is Object. This item identifies a class of performance elements that can be monitored. For example, Figure 2-2 shows the Memory object. Next, the Counter object lists specific elements with the Object that can be monitored. The Instance field lists a specific occurrence of the counter if one exists. The Add button adds the Instance of the Counter for the Object to the chart. The Explain button toggles turning on and off the Counter Definition field found at the bottom of Figure 2-2. Figure 2-3 show the Chart Options window that is accessed from Options|Chart menu. This window is used to change characteristics about the chart. One key field here is the Update Time. This option is used for the sample rate on the chart. The interval is the number of seconds between sampling, and the chart holds 100 samples.

Figure 2-4 show the Performance Monitor at work with various counters selected. This was taken at the time of a full database export. As you can see from the chart the *% Processor Time* counter is quite volatile as the export is happening. This is expected due to the CPU requirements that the export process demands. The solid vertical bar that goes through the entire graph is the current point in time. There is a spike in the *Page Faults* right before this vertical bar, which is right before the export started. You can

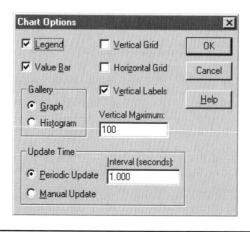

FIGURE 2-3.   *Chart Options*

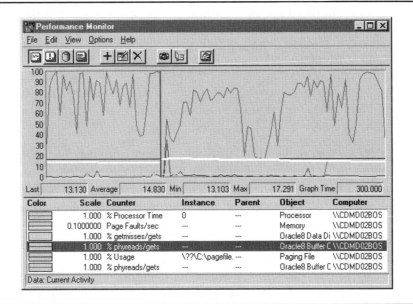

FIGURE 2-4.   *Performance Monitor output*

also see the *% Processor Time* also started to be volatile at that time. This is caused by the fact that the system was not being used prior to the export.

The Performance Monitor is a useful graphics tool that should be used consistently during the tuning process.

Background Processes

Some Oracle8 Server and user processes consume chunks of memory. When an Oracle instance is started, an assortment of background processes is spawned to support the database activities. They run unattended, and take care of resource management and requests for database information as your applications run. The following processes reside in memory and support the activities of an Oracle instance.

- *Process monitor (PMON)*   This is the process that performs recovery when a user process fails. PMON cleans up after aborted user processes and signals Oracle of the death of the user process. Resources are freed up after this information is passed to Oracle, and any locks that were held by the process are released. PMON also checks on the dispatcher and server processes and restarts them if they have failed.

■ *System monitor (SMON)* This is responsible for instance recovery (if needed) when the database is started up. SMON releases any resource requests that the user processes no longer require. In addition SMON coalesces free extents within the database to make free space contiguous and easier to allocate.

■ *Database writer (DBWR)* This takes information out of the buffers and writes it to the database files. (Buffers in the buffer cache are referred to as *dirty* when they contain information that needs to be written to disk by DBWR.) Due to the architecture of the Oracle processes, DBWR ensures that user activities are always able to find free buffers to drop information into. Oracle decides what information to keep in main memory based on least-recently-used, or LRU, logic; blocks containing frequently used information are kept in the buffer cache. Memory access is much faster than disk I/O. Oracle uses write-ahead logging so that the DBWR does not need to write blocks when a transaction commits. This way DBWR can perform its writes in batch with high efficiency. For the most part, DBWR writes only when more data needs to read into the system global area and there is an insufficient number of database buffers free.

■ *Log writer process (LGWR)* This is responsible for writing information from the redo log buffer to the online redo logs. Oracle writes information about all activity against the database to the online redo logs. LGWR writes to the redo log buffers, flushes information to the redo logs when a transaction commits, then reuses the buffers.

■ *Checkpoint process (CKPT)* This is responsible for checkpoint activities. *Checkpointing*, which occurs at predetermined times, is when Oracle writes information from memory to its assortment of database files. While the database is performing a checkpoint, system processing can halt until the checkpoint completes.

■ *Archiver process (ARCH)* This is responsible for copying redo logs to an archive destination when a database is running in

ARCHIVELOG mode. When using this mode, Oracle makes copies of redo logs in a secondary location before reusing the log file for recording of subsequent transactions.

MEMORY/CPU RULE #1

Always run your Oracle8 databases in ARCHIVELOG mode to provide for the best protection against media failure. This also allows you to write consistent backups of the database while it is open and running.

■ *Recoverer process (RECO)* If you use the distributed option with Oracle, this process handles the resolution of problems with distributed transactions. Oracle will support update activities on a remote database and such features as *location transparency,* where tables involved in applications may reside on different nodes of a network. It is brought up by ensuring that the initialization parameter file entry DISTRIBUTED_TRANSACTIONS is set to a value greater than zero.

NOTE

If you set the initialization parameter DISTRIBUTED_TRANSACTIONS to 0 while running Oracle with the distributed option, you will not be permitted to perform any distributed transactions, and the RECO process will not be started.

■ *Dispatcher processes (Dnnn)* If you are using the multithreaded server configuration, you'll find a number of these processes. There is at least one dispatcher process for every communication protocol in use. Each dispatcher process is responsible for routing requests from a connected user process to available shared server processes and returning the response back to the appropriate user process.

■ *Lock processes (LCKn)* If you are using the Oracle Parallel Server option, you'll find a number of these processes, which are used for inter-instance locking.

If you have implemented parallel query processing, you will find a number of processes starting with *P000* that do the parallelization of SQL queries. Chapter 5 discusses parallelization in detail, and should be consulted for further information.

If you are using replication and you are a master site, you'll find one or more *(SNPn) process(es)*. These processes are used as simple administration for most advanced replication environments that are configured to propagate data automatically. The following two initialization parameter file entries control the SNP background process setting for each server.

- JOB_QUEUE_PROCESSES specifies the number of SNPn background processes per Oracle instance.

- JOB_QUEUE_INTERVAL specifies, in seconds, the interval between wake-ups for the SNP background processes on a server.

Trace Files and Instance Alert Files

Any and all of the background processes, when present in your configuration, will produce trace files. *Trace files* are written by Oracle automatically and contain information about user sessions. At the head of each trace file is information that can be used to identify the instance that produced the file. There are date and time stamps to help match each trace file to the user session that produced it.

Normally, trace file names are built with the process acronym (e.g., ARCH), the process ID of that background process, and the extension .trc. They are found in the directory specified in the initialization parameter file by the BACKGROUND_DUMP_DEST parameter.

MEMORY/CPU RULE #2
DBAs are encouraged to browse these trace files periodically and, especially in the case of the alert logs, to do some cleanup. These alert trace files grow forever until someone manually edits them and reduces their size.

Oracle writes events to the alert log files. Part of the tuning process involves inspecting these files from time to time and looking for abnormal situations. Deal with these errors before they prevent normal database operations. Periodically, you may want to examine and then delete some or all of these files. The events recorded in them are simply for your information. Some of the messages, similar to those shown in the next listing, are informative and require no attention.

```
Thread 1 cannot allocate new log, sequence 35
Checkpoint not complete
   Current log# 1 seq# 35 mem# 0: D:\ORANT\DATABASE\LOG2ORCL.ORA
Thread 1 advanced to log sequence 36
   Current log# 2 seq# 36 mem# 0: D:\ORANT\DATABASE\LOG1ORCL.ORA
```

As discussed earlier, Oracle takes information from the log buffers and dumps it to disk. Before Oracle will reuse an online redo log, all information from the buffers destined for that log must be written. If Oracle wants to switch the active redo log group and LGWR has not done its work, Oracle will not be able to switch to the new group, and you'll see an error message like the one shown in the next listing. This situation may require your attention. See the section "The Redo Log Buffer Cache" later in this chapter for more details.

```
Wed Mar 26 15:19:19 1999
Thread 1 cannot allocate new log, sequence 683
Checkpoint not complete
```

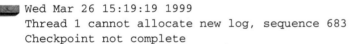

MEMORY/CPU RULE #3
Inspect instance alert log files for error messages regarding online redo log groups. It is the easiest way to determine whether you have enough redo log files for your database. If Oracle cannot reuse a redo log because cleanup is not yet completed, you may need more redo logs.

Every time the instance is started, Oracle lists, in the alert file, all nondefault values for initialization parameter file entries. Using this list, along with the discussion in Chapter 5, you can adjust some of these nondefault parameters as part of the tuning process. Nondefault parameters are not necessarily a problem—some of them are there to support your configuration. We suggest that you be aware (using trace file output shown in the next listing) of what initialization parameter file entries are nondefaults.

```
Starting up ORACLE RDBMS Version: 8.0.3.0.0.
System parameters with non-default values:
    processes               = 59
    timed_statistics        = TRUE
    shared_pool_size        = 10000000
    control_files           = D:\ORANT\DATABASE\ctl1orcl.ora
    db_block_size           = 2048
    log_buffer              = 8192
    log_checkpoint_interval = 10000
    db_files                = 1024
    rollback_segments       = MONSTER, RB1, RB2, RB3, RB4, RB5, RB6, RB7
    sequence_cache_hash_buckets= 10
    remote_login_passwordfile= SHARED
    global_names            = TRUE
    distributed_lock_timeout = 300
    distributed_transactions = 5
    db_name                 = oracle
    text_enable             = TRUE
    job_queue_processes     = 2
    job_queue_interval      = 10
    background_dump_dest     = %RDBMS80%\trace
    user_dump_dest          = %RDBMS80%\trace
    max_dump_file_size      = 10240
```

When you use an existing initialization parameter file as a skeleton to start up a new instance, make sure that the nondefault parameters stay that way for the new database as well. For example, in the previous trace file listing, the TIMED_STATISTICS parameter is set to TRUE to support collection of buffer statistics, as discussed in the section "The Database Buffer Cache" found later in this chapter. As well, the ROLLBACK_SEGMENTS parameter is set to MONSTER. Chapters 3 and 5 discuss rollback segments and the initialization parameter file in more detail.

The SGA

The *system global area* (*SGA*) is a segment of memory allocated to Oracle that contains data and control information particular to an Oracle instance.

Sizing of the SGA is partially a hit-and-miss exercise. You will notice that some parameters in the initialization parameter file have a profound effect on the size of the SGA. The initialization parameter file parameters DB_BLOCK_BUFFERS (the number of buffers dedicated to the database buffer cache) and SHARED_POOL_SIZE (the number of bytes allocated to the shared SQL area) are the major contributors to the size of the SGA. Refer to the discussion in Chapter 8 on how to take advantage of the shared SQL area. The amount of memory allocated to the SGA based on the value of DB_BLOCK_BUFFERS depends on the Oracle block size you use. For example, suppose that 32,768 bytes are allocated for these buffers using a 2K (2,048 bytes) block size; if you increase the block size to 4K (4,096 bytes), the database buffer memory requirement will swell to 65,536 bytes without adjusting the DB_BLOCK_BUFFERS entry in the initialization parameter file. Specific recommendation about the size of the SGA is given later in the section "How Much Memory Is Enough?".

Paging and Swapping

Paging involves moving portions of an application or process out to secondary storage to free up real memory space. *Swapping* involves copying entire processes from memory to secondary storage. Disk drives and an assortment of high-speed storage devices are used for these secondary devices. Your job is to ensure the memory structures used by Oracle can fit into real memory. A number of operating systems requires a contiguous chunk of main memory to start Oracle. During the tuning process, you need to monitor the amount of paging and swapping on your system. The operating system may decide to page out portions of the SGA to make room for new processes or existing processes it deems to be in more need of main memory. You may find that without adequate computer memory, the time slice of CPU each user gets may be used up by swapping and paging, and the applications may appear to be doing nothing else. Swap-space utilization is assessed using a number of operating system-dependent utilities. For example, Figure 2-5 shows the Windows NT Performance Monitor; notice that about 20 percent of the available memory on the machine is being used and that the paging/second peaks at about 40 when an Oracle instance is being started.

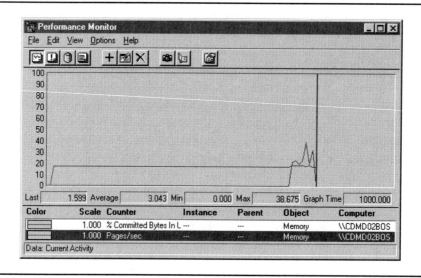

FIGURE 2-5. *Performance Monitor paging activity*

Memory Requirements

When tuning memory and ensuring that enough memory resides on your machine, you should ask what the size requirements are of the programs in memory and what they are doing. These are the same questions you ask yourself regardless of the hardware with which you use Oracle. The programs you use to get answers to these hardware-independent questions are hardware-dependent. The example used in this section is based on a Compaq Proliant machine running Windows NT version 4.0. This environment uses a two-task architecture with client front-end processes utilizing Net8 for access and a back-end shadow process that does the actual work against the database.

Step 1: Requirements Without Including the SGA

The first step is to assess the memory requirements of the database and tools, excluding the SGA. A Windows NT database server should be just that, a database server. It should not be used for any file and print servers.

The only processes running on the machine should be directly involved in the support of the Oracle8 Server.

Figure 2-6 shows the output from the PMON command on a Windows NT machine. It shows the processes that are running on the machine with specific information related to each process. At the top is the total memory on the machine (261560K) and the available memory (156820K), with a typical set of programs running that would be there in an Oracle production environment.

Using this information, you can estimate the base amount of main memory required to support this configuration. For example, 604 bytes are required to support the Performance Monitor process. This also includes the SGA memory requirements, which are discussed in the next section.

Step 2: Assessing the SGA Memory Requirements

The simplest way to see the SGA memory requirements is through the SQL Worksheet interface tool. This tool enables you to enter SQL statements, PL/SQL code, and DBA commands dynamically, and run scripts stored as files. Connect as **internal** with the internal password. Enter **show sga** into

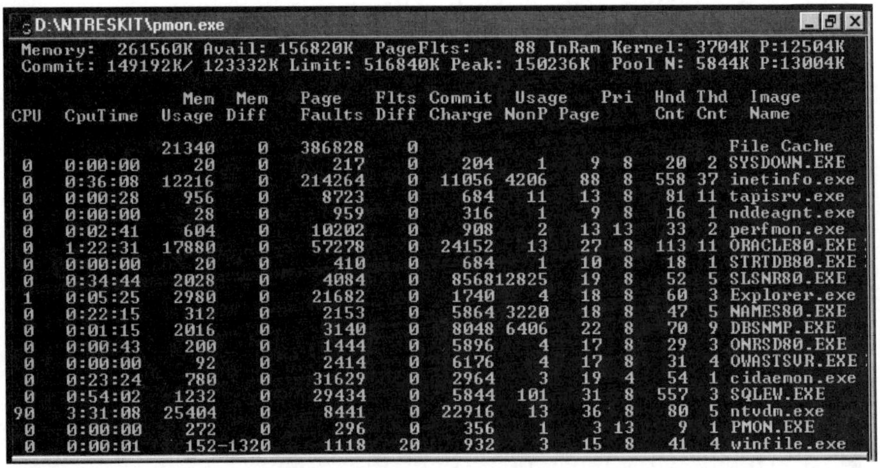

```
D:\NTRESKIT\pmon.exe                                              _ |@|X
Memory:  261560K Avail: 156820K  PageFlts:     88 InRam Kernel: 3704K P:12504K
Commit: 149192K/ 123332K Limit: 516840K Peak: 150236K  Pool N: 5844K P:13004K

           Mem  Mem   Page  Flts Commit  Usage   Pri  Hnd Thd  Image
CPU  CpuTime Usage Diff  Faults Diff Charge NonP Page      Cnt Cnt  Name

            21340    0  386828    0                            File Cache
  0  0:00:00    20    0     217    0     204    1    9  8   20  2 SYSDOWN.EXE
  0  0:36:08 12216    0  214264    0   11056 4206   88  8  558 37 inetinfo.exe
  0  0:00:28   956    0    8723    0     684   11   13  8   81 11 tapisrv.exe
  0  0:00:00    28    0     959    0     316    1    9  8   16  1 nddeagnt.exe
  0  0:02:41   604    0   10202    0     908    2   13 13   33  2 perfmon.exe
  0  1:22:31 17880    0   57278    0   24152   13   27  8  113 11 ORACLE80.EXE
  0  0:00:00    20    0     410    0     684    1   10  8   18  1 STRTDB80.EXE
  0  0:34:44  2028    0    4084    0 856812825   19  8   52  5 SLSNR80.EXE
  1  0:05:25  2980    0   21682    0    1740    4   18  8   60  3 Explorer.exe
  0  0:22:15   312    0    2153    0    5864 3220   18  8   47  5 NAMES80.EXE
  0  0:01:15  2016    0    3140    0    8048 6406   22  8   70  9 DBSNMP.EXE
  0  0:00:43   200    0    1444    0    5896    4   17  8   29  3 ONRSD80.EXE
  0  0:00:00    92    0    2414    0    6176    4   17  8   31  4 OWASTSUR.EXE
  0  0:23:24   780    0   31629    0    2964    3   19  4   54  1 cidaemon.exe
  0  0:54:02  1232    0   29434    0    5844  101   31  8  557  3 SQLEW.EXE
 90  3:31:08 25404    0    8441    0   22916   13   36  8   80  5 ntvdm.exe
  0  0:00:00   272    0     296    0     356    1    3 13    9  1 PMON.EXE
  0  0:00:01   152-1320  1118   20     932    3   15  8   41  4 winfile.exe
```

FIGURE 2-6.   *Windows NT pmon.exe output*

the worksheet and click on the execute icon. The output is similar to that shown here:

```
Oracle8 Release 8.0.3.0.0 - Production
With the Partitioning and Objects options
PL/SQL Release 8.0.3.0.0 - Production
SQLWKS> show sga
Total System Global Area      11726376 bytes
Fixed Size                       46136 bytes
Variable Size                 11053552 bytes
Database Buffers                102400 bytes
Redo Buffers                    524288 bytes
```

From the information shown above and Figure 2-6, this system will consume 81,985,064 bytes, or roughly 78MB of memory (261,560K total—192,948K free, which is 68,612K or 70,258,688 used; add to this the 11,726,376 to get 81,985,064). Of course, your configuration and resultant memory requirements will be different. After going through the steps outlined in this section, you will end up with a realistic estimate of your memory requirements. Even though your hardware and configuration may be different, the process will be the same.

How Much Memory Is Enough?

Using the figure computed in the previous section, the sample system needs at least 78MB main memory for itself. When trying to decide memory size, you need to consider the assortment of other memory consumers that live and breathe on your computer. Speak with the person in your office who is responsible for the computer on which Oracle runs. You must assess the additional space requirements for the following:

- The operating system itself

- The assortment of support mechanisms for that operating system

- The network of operating system buffers

- The software that coexists with Oracle on your machine

- The Oracle databases that coexist on your machine

- The memory overhead per user on the system

- The operating system overhead for supporting the read and write requests of all of those users

A comfortable figure to live with for the amount of total memory needed is one that is roughly three times the one calculated for the support of your Oracle systems. Given the different combinations of concurrent application software that run on your machine, you may find a different figure for your purposes. Although three times is the suggested minimum, the figure could be higher if there are a large number (more than 60) of concurrent users.

The Shared Pool

The shared pool portion of the SGA is made up of the library cache, the dictionary cache, and some user and server session information. When we look at tuning memory with Oracle8, the shared pool is one of the biggest consumers. Let's look at some components that consume space in the shared pool.

The Library Cache

This cache contains parsed and executable SQL statements. For every SQL statement Oracle processes, there is a shared part and a private part. The shared portion of the SGA for every SQL statement is that amount of memory in the shared pool that contains the following components of each statement:

- *Parse tree* A representation of the results of parsing a SQL statement (the parse phase of statement processing is discussed in Chapter 7)

- *Execution plan* A roadmap Oracle builds containing the plan of how a statement will be run (it is written after each SQL statement is optimized)

The private part has two components:

- The persistent portion that occupies space in the SGA for the life of every cursor associated with a SQL statement

- The runtime portion that is acquired when a SQL statement executes, and is released when the statement completes

To make efficient use of the space allocated to the SGA, you should close cursors when you are done with them to free up memory allocated for this runtime portion.

An important key to tuning the SGA is ensuring that the library cache is large enough so Oracle can keep parsed and executable statements in the shared pool. There are two ways to look at the library cache performance. One way is to use the Windows NT Performance Monitor. You would want to add the % reloads/pins counter from the Oracle8 Library Cache object as shown is Figure 2-7.

The other way is to look in the V$LIBRARYCACHE data dictionary view. Both of these methods help to assess the performance of the library cache at its current size. The next listing illustrates the second option. A PIN indicates a cache hit (read from memory) and a RELOAD indicates a cache miss (read from disk).

```
SQL> select sum(pins) "Pins", sum(reloads) "Reloads",
  2            sum(reloads)/(sum(pins)+sum(reloads))*100
  3            "Percentage"
  4  from v$librarycache;
     Pins   Reloads Percentage
--------- --------- ----------
    77926       107  .13712147
SQL>
```

The values in the PINS and RELOADS columns and their relationship in this dynamic performance table are a good indicator of whether the current size may be the optimal size of the library cache in the SGA. The

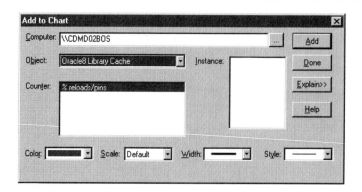

FIGURE 2-7.   *Oracle8 library cache*

RELOADS value should be as close to 0 as possible. Any ratio above 1 percent indicates that the library cache hit rate is too low; a corrective action is required. Increasing this hit rate is accomplished by increasing the size of the shared pool. Using the information from the previous listing, for every 77,926 PINS there were 107 RELOADS; thus a ratio of about 0.1 percent. A figure this low indicates a healthy library cache in the SGA.

The Dictionary Cache

The dictionary cache contains data dictionary information pertaining to segments in the database (e.g., indexes, sequences, and tables), file space availability (for acquisition of space by object creation and extension), and object privileges. Dictionary information is moved out of the cache when space is required for newly required information. Looking at the *hit rate* (the ratio of reads satisfied in memory compared to those going to disk) for entries in the dictionary cache gives you an idea of the efficiency of this cache. This information, again, can be obtained in two ways. One is to use the Windows NT Performance Monitor. You would want to add the % getmisses/gets counter from the Oracle8 Data Dictionary Cache object as shown in Figure 2-8.

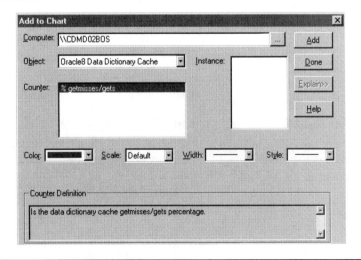

FIGURE 2-8. *Oracle8 Data Dictionary Cache object*

The other way is to use the following code that reports on the dictionary cache by entry. The *miss rate* is calculated as misses divided by the sum of gets and misses and is shown as a percentage.

```
SQL> col "Percentage miss" format 990.00
SQL> col "Gets" format 999,999,990
SQL> col "Misses" format 999,999,990
SQL> select unique parameter "Cache entry",
  2              gets "Gets",                /*Read from memory*/
  3              getmisses "Misses",         /*read from disk*/
  4         getmisses/(gets+getmisses)*100 "Percentage miss"
  5      from v$rowcache
  6    where gets+getmisses <> 0;
Cache entry                          Gets      Misses Percentage miss
--------------------------------- ----------- ----------- ---------------
dc_constraints                        516         259           33.42
dc_files                               11           6           35.29
dc_free_extents                     1,220         270           18.12
dc_object_ids                       1,401         296           17.44
dc_objects                          6,574         605            8.43
dc_profiles                            20           1            4.76
dc_rollback_segments                2,144          19            0.88
dc_segments                         2,126         224            9.53
dc_sequences                           10           4           28.57
dc_synonyms                            43           9           17.31
dc_tablespace_quotas                1,166           2            0.17
dc_tablespaces                      1,740           5            0.29
dc_used_extents                       368         246           40.07
dc_user_grants                      2,079          20            0.95
dc_usernames                        1,957          11            0.56
dc_users                            3,273          23            0.70
SQL>
```

A well-tuned database should report an average dictionary cache hit ratio of over 90 percent. The percentages for the entries **dc_user_grants** and **dc_users**, used during almost all SQL statement processing, should be well under 5 percent each. Notice in the listing how the values for these two are 0.95 percent, and 0.70 percent, respectively. The query shown in the next listing will do just that.

```
SQL> select (1 - (sum(getmisses)/
  2              (sum(gets)+sum(getmisses))))*100 "Hit rate"
```

```
  3   from v$rowcache;
 Hit rate
 ---------
 92.496717
 SQL>
```

What you have to do during the tuning exercise is ensure that adequate space is available in the pool.

 MEMORY/CPU RULE #4
You will need to tweak the size of the shared pool for an Oracle8 fresh install to ensure there is adequate space in the shared pool to allow Oracle to fine-tune the caches in the shared pool.

This is done by increasing the value in the SHARED_POOL_SIZE entry in the initialization parameter file. The determination of the size of the shared pool is not an exact science. There are many factors that come into place such as the number of concurrent users, the extent of the use of stored procedures, the use of private synonyms and grants over public ones, and the consistency of SQL code writing.

The Database Buffer Cache

Oracle needs to read and write data to the database buffer cache during operations. A *cache hit* means the information required is already in memory; a *cache miss* means Oracle must perform disk I/O to satisfy a request. The secret when sizing the database buffer cache is to keep the cache misses to a minimum.

The initialization parameter file entry DB_BLOCK_BUFFERS controls the size of the database block buffer cache. The Performance Monitor can be used to look at the efficiency of the buffer cache. You would want to add the % phyread/gets counter from the Oracle8 Buffer Cache object as shown in Figure 2-9.

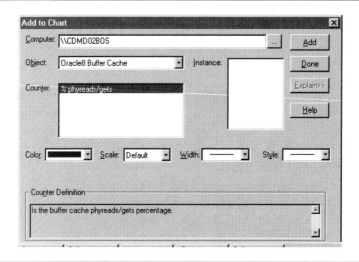

FIGURE 2-9. *Buffer cache gets/misses*

NOTE
*Not all changes to your initialization parameter file require you to bring the database down and up. There is now the **alter session** or **alter system**; however, DB_BLOCK_BUFFERS is one that necessitates restarting the database to activate.*

The Redo Log Buffer Cache

The redo log buffer cache holds information destined for the online redo logs (redo logs were defined at the start of this chapter). During most database operations, the LGWR background process writes efficiently so that space is always available in this cache for new redo entries. Since the redo log buffer is a segment of shared memory, Oracle manages this buffer cache using latches. Latches are to memory as locks are to data: *latches* are simple, low-level serialization mechanisms to protect shared data structures in the SGA. They are acquired for very short periods of time to work with shared structures in memory. The *redo allocation latch* manages requests for space in the redo log buffer cache. The maximum size of a redo entry that can be copied using this latch is determined by the initialization parameter file parameter LOG_SMALL_ENTRY_MAX_SIZE. On multi-CPU systems, redo entries exceeding this maximum are copied and protected during that copy by a redo copy latch. On single-CPU systems, all entries are copied using the redo allocation latch.

It is important to the tuning process to ensure that there are no wait conditions in the movement of information into and out of the redo log buffer cache. Wait situations are detected using the V$LATCH performance table owned by SYS and can be queried as shown here:

```
SQL> select substr(name,1,20) "Latch",
  2            sum(gets) "WTW Gets",
  3            sum(misses) "WTW Misses",
  4            sum(immediate_gets)  "IMM Gets",
  5            sum(immediate_misses)  "IMM Misses"
  6    from v$latch where name like 'redo%'
  7  group by name;
Latch                WTW Gets WTW Misses  IMM Gets IMM Misses
-------------------- --------- ---------- --------- ----------
redo allocation         72248         15         0          0
redo copy                   0          0         0          0
SQL>
```

As you see above, of 72,248 willing-to-wait requests to copy entries into the redo log buffer, 15 were not satisfied. No immediate requests were issued during the time slice the query refers to. Oracle decides internally whether to issue a willing-to-wait or an immediate request. If the immediate_misses are more than one percent of the immediate_gets (not the case in the code above) or the misses are more than one percent of the gets (also not the case in this example), there may be contention for the redo allocation and/or the redo copy latch. The reduction and removal of this contention are part of the memory tuning process.

 MEMORY/CPU RULE #5
On multiprocessor machines, the initialization parameter file entry LOG_SIMULTANEOUS_ COPIES should be set to twice the number of CPUs. This will help reduce any potential contention for the redo copy latch.

Using the Performance Monitor the number of redo log space requests can be Monitored. You would want to add the redo log space requests counter from the Oracle8 Redo Log Buffer object as shown in Figure 2-10.

Figure 2-11 shows the Performance Monitor running while it is measuring the Library Cache, Data Dictionary Cache, Buffer Cache, and the Redo Log Buffers. On the right of the graph you can see that the redo log space request counter jumped from 0 to about 30 and remained there. The measurement was taken at a time when an update was issued and was still pending. The other counters were basically stable, indicating that the Library, Data Dictionary, and Buffer Cache(s) already held all the information needed to process this update.

Multithreaded Server

In two-task environments where server work is done on behalf of the user by a dedicated process (commonly referred to as the *shadow process*), you can bring up a pool of server processes to be shared by users. This is called a *multithreaded server*, commonly referred to as *MTS*. These shared server processes can conserve main memory. Without MTS, a dedicated server process supports the user process, and it sits in limbo until user requests require server process activity. With MTS, idle user processes sit alone until server activity is requested. Requests for server actions are routed to the database via a request queue. Responses from that queue are satisfied and the

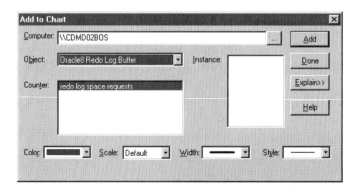

FIGURE 2-10. *Adding redo log space counter*

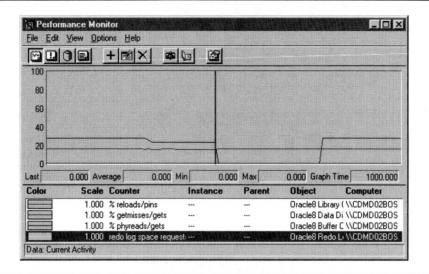

FIGURE 2-11. *Output after adding desired counters*

results are sent back to the requesting user process through a response queue. One or more dispatchers take care of the processing of server requests.

Starting MTS

Following are the steps for bringing up the processes to support the multithreaded server. Steps 1 and 4 describe some Net8 issues. Steps 2 and 3 change some initialization parameter file entries, then shut down and restart the database to take advantage of these entries' new values.

1. Use the configuration tool supplied by Oracle (the Net8 Administrator's Guide documents use of this tool) to build the three support files—listener.ora, tnsnames.ora, and sqlnet.ora. Even though these files are required for using Net8 without MTS, you will probably not already have these files built. Most people end up starting work with Net8 in a two-task environment when first looking at MTS.

2. Make necessary entries in the initialization parameter file (see the next section for details).

3. Shut down, then start up the database.

4. Start up the Net8 listener service using the command Services section of the Control Panel.

When steps 1 through 4 are performed successfully, you will have the multithreaded server running and awaiting user connections.

Changes to the Initialization Parameter File

The MTS parameters listed in Table 2-1 need to be entered in your database startup file to bring up the multithreaded server.

Parameter Name	Meaning and Value(s)
mts_dispatchers	This defines the number of dispatchers to initiate as well as the protocol. The text must be enclosed in double quotes (" "). Example: mts_dispatchers = "tcp,2" mts_dispatchers = "ipc,2"
mts_max_dispatchers	This is the maximum number of dispatchers the database will support. Using the previous example, you code mts_max_dispatchers = 4
mts_servers	This is the number of shared server processes to bring up when the database is started.
mts_service	This is the name of the service. It is recommended that you set it to the same value as the value entered for **db_name** in the initialization parameter file.
mts_max_servers	This controls the maximum number of concurrent shared server processes. Oracle spawns shared processes over and above the number in mts_servers up to the number specified here. The default for this parameter is 10.
mts_listener_address	This defines configuration information of the operating system process that awaits user connections using MTS.

TABLE 2-1.   *Multithreaded Server (MTS) Parameters*

The status of the listener for Net8 can be checked by using the command lsnrctl80 status. The output from this command is shown here:

```
LSNRCTL80 for 32-bit Windows: Version 8.0.3.0.0 - Production on 05-AUG-99
19:28:33
(c) Copyright 1997 Oracle Corporation.  All rights reserved.
Connecting to (ADDRESS=(PROTOCOL=IPC)(KEY=oracle.world))
STATUS of the LISTENER
------------------------
Alias                   LISTENER
Version                 TNSLSNR80 for 32-bit Windows: Version 8.0.3.0.0 -
Production
Start Date              04-AUG-99 11:57:36
Uptime                  1 days 7 hr. 30 min. 57 sec
Trace Level             off
Security                ON
SNMP                    OFF
Listener Parameter File D:\ORANT\NET80\admin\listener.ora
Listener Log File       D:\ORANT\NET80\log\listener.log
Services Summary...
   ORCL         has 1 service handler(s)
   extproc         has 1 service handler(s)
The command completed successfully
```

MEMORY/CPU RULE #5

When using MTS there is an additional requirement of 1K per user for the SHARED_POOL_SIZE for storing information about the connections between the user processes, dispatchers, and servers.

As with all Oracle tuning options there are trade-offs. If your system is constrained by memory then using MTS might be a good option. This will allow multiple users to shared-server processes. But then again if you are stretching the limits on the size of your shared pool you might not be able to use the MTS option. Each installation is unique and an option that works for one might not work for another. The tuning process is a never-ending adventure.

SORT_AREA_SIZE

SORT_AREA_SIZE in the initialization parameter file controls the allocation of chunks of memory for sorting activities. Sorting is explicitly requested by programs or implicitly done by Oracle. It is desirable to do as much sorting as possible in memory—memory sort work is much faster than work done on disk. Index creation and ORDER BY statements in SQL may benefit from an increased value in this parameter. Most environments use a 64K default, but this may be raised by the DBA. You can look at the sort activities of your database using the V$SYSSTAT dynamic performance dictionary view; the following listing provides an example:

```
SQL> select name,value
  2    from v$sysstat
  3   where name like '%sort%';
NAME                                                              VALUE
----------------------------------------------------------- ---------
sorts (memory)                                                     4077
sorts (disk)                                                          2
sorts (rows)                                                      43789
SQL>
```

The listing shows .05 percent of the sorts (2 sorts out of 4077 sorts total) required work done to disk. Your application should be running for a sufficient time (no less than two or three working days at least) to obtain representative counts for normal database activities.

Another way to look at the performance of the SORT_AREA_SIZE is through the Performance Monitor. You would want to add the sorts in memory/sec and sorts on disk/sec counters from the Oracle8 Sorts object as shown in Figure 2-12.

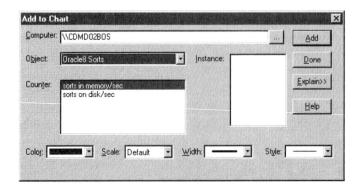

FIGURE 2-12.   *Sorts by type counter*

Figure 2-13 show the Performance Monitor running while it is measuring memory counters on the system. This gives a good overall picture of the memory utilization on the machine. One counter has periodic spikes. This is the *Pages/sec* counter. Since the Oracle database is the only process running on this machine, the smaller spikes are caused by the background Oracle processes doing their job, while the large spike is due to a large user sort being executed.

Favoring CPU

The past few years have seen major advances in CPU power. Vendors continue to produce machines with stronger and stronger CPUs; some machines have multiple CPUs working in parallel and sharing the processing. (This should not be confused with the Oracle8 parallel server option, in which loosely coupled computers, such as the DEC VAX cluster, share a disk but have their own memory.) Oracle, along with the other vendors, has realized that the CPU has grown exponentially while some of the other computer components have not. The smart software manufacturers favor CPU, the smart network administrators favor CPU, and

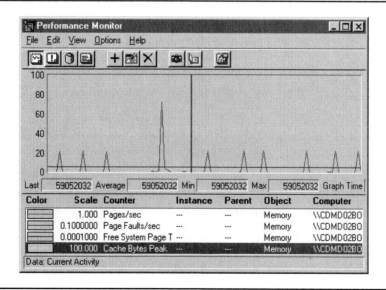

FIGURE 2-13. *Measuring memory counters*

therefore smart DBAs favor CPU to ensure that their applications run faster and sooner.

In addition, with products such as the Oracle parallel query option that came out with release 7.1, Oracle can partition the processing of a query over a specified number of query processes. The direction of the industry is clear. Why is the bulk of the IBM mainframe environment downsizing today? One reason: economics. Reengineering your applications, buying new hardware, and porting your applications to that new environment are all getting cheaper; cost benefits will be realized in two years. This is why the classic legacy systems are disappearing. As system professionals, you strive to get the most out of your applications (at the least cost). The best bang for the buck is by capitalizing on new technology—in the CPU arena for the quickest gain.

CPU technology has produced more and more powerful machines in relatively short time periods. Applications that ran on 486 processors can run twice as fast on the Pentium and maybe three times faster on the Pentium Pro—simply by upgrading the CPU. CPU is cheap and getting cheaper. With emerging CPU technology, bigger and better CPUs can get the work done in a fraction of the time. Oracle technology is moving in a direction that takes advantage of parallel processing. Queries run in a fraction of the time using multiple CPUs. A 16-minute query running in under 30 seconds, on a massively parallel processor with a bank of 20 to 30 CPUs, is not unheard of. In light of this, when we speak of CPU in this chapter, the same discussion points apply to computers with more than one CPU.

Computer manufacturers are building the new-generation computers with multiple processors. Manufacturers have two basic ways to build a machine with more than one processor: shared-memory symmetrical multiprocessors and massively parallel processors.

SMP

The *symmetrical multiprocessor* (SMP) architecture involves more than one CPU utilizing common memory and I/O. The operating system runs concurrently as one system image across multiple CPUs. The operating system provides scheduling so that tasks execute on all CPUs in a symmetrical fashion. There is no single control processor. Each processor executes tasks off a common execution queue. State-of-the-art SMP systems have up to 64 processors (e.g., Cray CS6400); the average SMP has eight to 32 CPUs.

MPP

The *massively parallel processor* (MPP) is somewhat different than the SMP. MPPs are composed of nodes that are connected via a high-speed interconnect mechanism. An MPP node consists of a processor, local memory, and sometimes local I/O. The interprocessor communications and transfers to nonlocally attached I/O are much faster than with SMP machines. Unlike SMP machines, there is no single copy of the operating system controlling work flow or scheduling across nodes. The operating system as such appears to be running independent operating systems on each node. Typically, there is no scheduling provided by the operating system. Task scheduling across nodes is provided by applications or other software that do not exist in the SMP environment. The state-of-the-art MPP can have 4,096 or more processors. Machines with 32 to 512 nodes are commonplace.

The advantage of MPP over SMP is quite simple. Every computer has a piece of hardware called the *system bus,* where interprocess communication takes place. The two-way transfer of information from disk to memory and memory to disk is done on this bus. When you put more than about 32 processors on a common system bus, the bus itself becomes a bottleneck. This means that most SMPs won't be able to take advantage of all of the I/O or CPUs, as they will spend most of their time fighting for the bus. MPPs do not have this problem, because they have local memory as well as global or local high-speed I/O.

Most MPPs also have the characteristic of *scalability,* which means that as you add nodes, each additional node comes with additional memory, additional I/O bandwidth, as well as additional computer horsepower. The machine actually gets faster as you add nodes, with no shared items to become bottlenecks. The same principle applies when operations can be broken down into a set of smaller tasks that can be run independently.

Parallel Query in Oracle8

Oracle's commitment to multiprocessor machines is obvious, based on the number of parallel options that have come out since release 7.1. With the parallel query option, and multi-CPU machines, you can take advantage of the ability to process queries using many query server processes running against multiple CPUs. Clearly, Oracle, like the other vendors, favors CPU for the reasons described in the previous section. The end result of using the parallel query with more than one CPU is faster processing. The processing of queries in parallel is referred to as *query parallelization*. Since this feature relates directly to CPU, we discuss it briefly in this chapter, and again in Chapter 5 dedicated totally to parallelization.

Prior to parallel query processing, an SQL statement was processed by a single server process. SQL statement processing with parallel query is handled the following way. (The first step is the same, with or without the parallel query option.)

1. SQL statements are parsed and, if no matching statement is already in the shared pool, an execution plan is determined (for a discussion of SQL statement processing and using the shared pool, refer to Chapter 8).

2. Oracle determines that the statement is a candidate for parallel processing, as long as both of the following conditions are met:

   ■ The statement must contain a simple **select**, or contain an **update**, **delete**, **insert**, or **create** table using a subquery.

   ■ One or more full-table scans must be in the execution plan determined for the statement.

3. Once it is determined that the statement can be processed in parallel, a query coordinator server process is invoked to manage the parallel processing.

4. The query coordinator dispatches a number of query servers to handle the processing, the number of query processes being determined by a combination of the following:

   ■ Hints embedded in the SQL statement (if present)

   ■ Data dictionary information on the table(s) involved in the parallel process (parallel processing-associated keywords can be used when tables are created or modified)

   ■ A number of initialization parameter file entries that determine the number of parallel query server processes that have been invoked. The number of query server processes used to perform a single operation is referred to as the *degree of parallelism*.

5. The processing to satisfy the parallel query is partitioned among the query server processes, i.e., the workload is shared.

6. The results from the query server processes are merged and returned to the user process in the form of query results.

When parallel query processing is done on multi-CPU machines, the benefits become obvious. The throughput of online queries can increase many times over. Allowing simultaneous processing of portions of a query can dramatically reduce a query's time to completion. Oracle believes the parallel query option will result in the biggest benefits on the following systems.

■ Symmetrical multiprocessor (SMP) or massively parallel processor (MPP) systems

■ Systems with high I/O bandwidth (that is, many datafiles on many different disk drives)

■ Systems with underutilized or intermittently used CPUs (for example, systems where CPU usage is typically less than 30 percent)

■ Systems with sufficient memory to devote to sort space for queries

Other operations that can be parallelized with Oracle8 include

■ Parallel DML statements (i.e. **insert, update, delete**)

■ Parallel recovery

■ Parallel propagation of deferred transactions when using Advanced Replication

Oracle is committed to parallel processing and will no doubt be adding more parallel-aware features to the core product. A more detailed description of the parallel process in discussed in Chapter 5.

How Busy Is Your CPU?

One of the goals of this chapter is to show you how to maximize existing CPU and plan for the turnkey gains that will occur with each new generation of CPU. The example used in this section is based on a Compaq Proliant machine running Windows NT version 4.0.

A starting point is to assess the load on the machine at various times during the day (or predefined times over a series of days). When you have a handle on who is doing what on your machine and when, you can then proceed to ensure your CPU is doing the most efficient job given its processing power. The ability of your CPU to provide acceptable performance for your systems is fundamental to the tuning process. Your operating environment (the mixture of online and background processing) may require some adjustment to maximize the processing power of your CPU. Some suggestions will follow to get you started on a regimen to use your CPU effectively.

Assessing CPU Busy

First, you need the information to decide if your CPU is large enough to support your configuration. At that point, you can prepare a report card on your CPU and use its recommendations to influence your plans for future upgrades (if and when required). Three components need to be assessed to help you get an idea of how much work your CPU has to do on an Oracle server machine:

1. CPU requirements and utilization during busy time periods

2. CPU requirements and utilization during quiet periods

3. The balance between the CPU of the portions dedicated to Oracle and system support services

The following series of exercises you will go through to assess CPU utilization is hardware-independent.

You might think the CPU is not powerful enough to handle the Oracle systems. As we will discuss in Chapter 8, efficient SQL statements run faster than statements that have not been optimized. The results of the following exercise may uncover the need for application tuning. Follow the recommendations in Chapter 8 and the explanations here to assess CPU performance. The following is broken down into three section to correspond to the numbered items above.

CPU Requirements and Utilization During Busy Time Periods

You will now begin to assemble information about your operating environment. One of the steps in the tuning process is finding out how much work your CPU is being asked to do. Application and database tuning are directly linked, because a poorly tuned set of applications will use more CPU and consume more resources. Finding what your CPU has to contend with can be accomplished by gathering statistics on the five components that were introduced in the previous section.

MEMORY/CPU RULE #6

Assess the demands placed on the CPU by the users during busy time periods.

Select a series of times during the day or over a period of a few days. Collect statistics on the number of processes on the machine. Figure 2-14 (which is Figure 2-6 repeated here), shows the activity on the machine at the start of the exercise at 11:27 A.M. Late morning is a good time, because the users in both the eastern and western regions have been up for a

```
D:\NTRESKIT\pmon.exe                                                    _ 5 X
Memory:   261560K Avail: 156820K  PageFlts:    88 InRam Kernel: 3704K P:12504K
Commit: 149192K/ 123332K Limit: 516840K Peak: 150236K  Pool N: 5844K P:13004K

            Mem  Mem    Page   Flts Commit  Usage      Pri  Hnd Thd  Image
CPU  CpuTime Usage Diff  Faults Diff Charge NonP Page       Cnt Cnt  Name

            21340    0  386828    0                             File Cache
 0   0:00:00    20    0     217    0    204    1    9   8   20   2 SYSDOWN.EXE
 0   0:36:08 12216    0  214264    0  11056 4206   88   8  558  37 inetinfo.exe
 0   0:00:28   956    0    8723    0    684   11   13   8   81  11 tapisrv.exe
 0   0:00:00    28    0     959    0    316    1    9   8   16   1 nddeagnt.exe
 0   0:02:41   604    0   10202    0    908    2   13  13   33   2 perfmon.exe
 0   1:22:31 17880    0   57278    0  24152   13   27   8  113  11 ORACLE80.EXE
 0   0:00:00    20    0     410    0    684    1   10   8   18   1 STRTDB80.EXE
 0   0:34:44  2028    0    4084    0 8568 12825  19   8   52   5 SLSNR80.EXE
 1   0:05:25  2980    0   21682    0   1740    4   18   8   60   3 Explorer.exe
 0   0:22:15   312    0    2153    0   5864 3220   18   8   47   5 NAMES80.EXE
 0   0:01:15  2016    0    3140    0   8048 6406   22   8   70   9 DBSNMP.EXE
 0   0:00:43   200    0    1444    0   5896    4   17   8   29   3 ONRSD80.EXE
 0   0:00:00    92    0    2414    0   6176    4   17   8   31   4 OWASTSVR.EXE
 0   0:23:24   780    0   31629    0   2964    3   19   4   54   1 cidaemon.exe
 0   0:54:02  1232    0   29434    0   5844  101   31   8  557   3 SQLEW.EXE
90   3:31:08 25404    0    8441    0  22916   13   36   8   80   5 ntvdm.exe
 0   0:00:00   272    0     296    0    356    1    3  13    9   1 PMON.EXE
 0   0:00:01 152-1320   1118   20    932    3   15   8   41   4 winfile.exe
```

FIGURE 2-14. *pmon.exe output at 11:27 A.M.*

number of hours. Figure 2-15 shows the activity at 1:27 P.M. Snapshot #1 is the time period up to 11:27 A.M. Shapshot #2 is the time period up to 1:27 P.M. These screens were collected using the command from the **Run** option from the Start Menu on Windows NT.

From examining the output, we can begin to assess how busy the users are and the amount of resources they are consuming for their server processes. The following assumptions are made for the purpose of this exercise based on the statistics from the listing of Oracle server processes:

- The listing shows Oracle server processes, identified by "ORACLE80.EXE, STRTDB80.EXE AND SLSNR80.EXE".

- A fixed number of concurrent users connected during the interval.

Table 2-2 shows the CPU utilization of the selected processes running for the interval. For each interval, the CPU time used in minutes and seconds is shown.

For the three Oracle processes running throughout interval #1, the average CPU busy time to support their server processes was 20 percent (obtained from the Performance Monitor). Keeping in mind the nature of the other activities on your machine, this seems like an insignificant

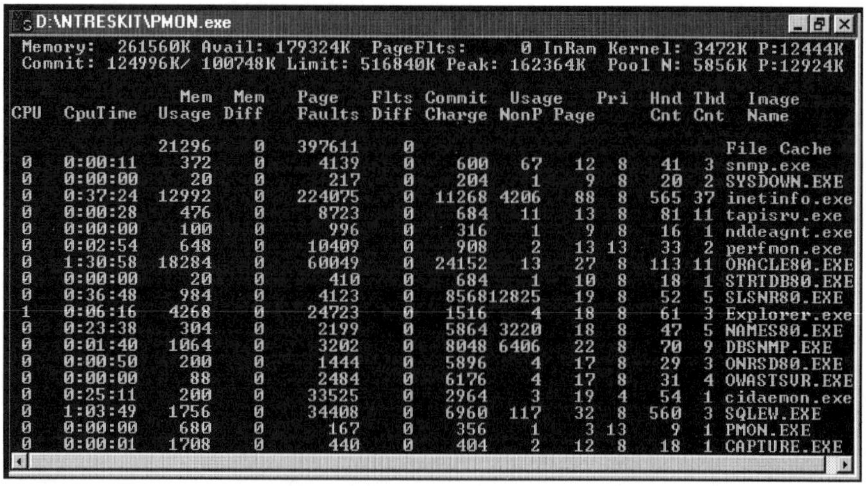

```
D:\NTRESKIT\PMON.exe                                               _ |8|X
Memory:  261560K Avail: 179324K  PageFlts:        0 InRam Kernel: 3472K P:12444K
Commit: 124996K/ 100748K Limit: 516840K Peak: 162364K  Pool N: 5856K P:12924K

          Mem  Mem    Page  Flts Commit  Usage   Pri  Hnd Thd  Image
CPU  CpuTime  Usage Diff  Faults Diff Charge NonP Page      Cnt Cnt  Name
          21296    0  397611    0                           File Cache
0   0:00:11    372    0    4139    0    600   67   12   8    41   3 snmp.exe
0   0:00:00     20    0     217    0    204    1    9   8    20   2 SYSDOWN.EXE
0   0:37:24  12992    0  224075    0  11268 4206   88   8   565  37 inetinfo.exe
0   0:00:28    476    0    8723    0    684   11   13   8    81  11 tapisrv.exe
0   0:00:00    100    0     996    0    316    1    9   8    16   1 nddeagnt.exe
0   0:02:54    648    0   10409    0    908    2   13  13    33   2 perfmon.exe
0   1:30:58  18284    0   60049    0  24152   13   27   8   113  11 ORACLE80.EXE
0   0:00:00     20    0     410    0    684    1   10   8    18   1 STRTDB80.EXE
0   0:36:48    984    0    4123    0 85681 2825   19   8    52   5 SLSNR80.EXE
1   0:06:16   4268    0   24723    0   1516    4   18   8    61   3 Explorer.exe
0   0:23:38    304    0    2199    0   5864 3220   18   8    47   5 NAMES80.EXE
0   0:01:40   1064    0    3202    0   8048 6406   22   8    70   9 DBSNMP.EXE
0   0:00:50    200    0    1444    0   5896    4   17   8    29   3 ONRSD80.EXE
0   0:00:00     88    0    2484    0   6176    4   17   8    31   4 OWASTSUR.EXE
0   0:25:11    200    0   33525    0   2964    3   19   4    54   1 cidaemon.exe
0   1:03:49   1756    0   34408    0   6960  117   32   8   560   3 SQLEW.EXE
0   0:00:00    680    0     167    0    356    1    3  13     9   1 PMON.EXE
0   0:00:01   1708    0     440    0    404    2   12   8    18   1 CAPTURE.EXE
```

FIGURE 2-15.   *pmon.exe output at 1:27 P.M.*

Process	Interval #1 CPU HH:MM:SS	Interval #2 CPU HH:MM:SS	Difference CPU HH:MM:SS
ORACLE80	01:22:31	01:30:58	00:18:27
STRTDB80	00:00:00	00:00:00	00:00:00
SLSNR80	00:34:44	00:36:48	00:02:04

TABLE 2-2.   *CPU Utilization at Two Time Points*

amount, but it can be misleading if you do not look at all other consumers of CPU time. Use your operating system utilities, at predefined periods during the business day, to track the output of CPU monitoring.

CPU Requirements and Utilization During Quiet Periods

The user processes, which show up as Oracle thread users, use varying amounts of CPU time during peak periods. The consumption is heavily dependent on what the user processes are doing. Given the time slice that concurrent user processes get of CPU time, user connect time far exceeds CPU utilization during busy time periods.

MEMORY/CPU RULE #7
Assess the demands placed on the CPU by the users during not-so-busy time periods (evenings and weekends).

The output in Figure 2-16 was generated at 10:35 P.M. on a quiet machine at the end of a full database export. No other users were on the machine, so the whole CPU was at the disposal of whatever Oracle processes required. Notice how Oracle contributed to the use of between 0 percent and 60 percent of the available CPU processing power. While the export was going on, Oracle contributed to the use of between 40 percent and 60 percent processing utilization; after the export completed, Oracle's contribution reduced to zero. Not surprisingly, the CPU is required to process the export on an entire database. Bear in mind that an export entails single table queries. With the joining of multiple tables, it is realistic

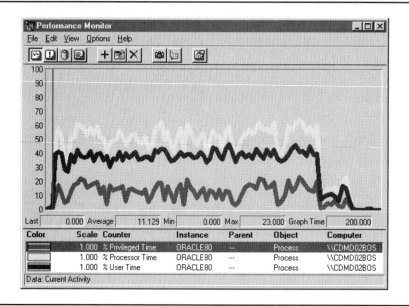

FIGURE 2-16. *Monitoring ORACLE80.EXE process*

to assume that the CPU requirements for a join between large objects will be higher than queries on single tables. Figure 2-17 gives an explanation of the counters that appear in Figure 2-16.

CPU Balance—Oracle Versus System Support Services

During quiet times, Oracle will use as much CPU as is available. When it does not have to share CPU with other consumers, statements in programs

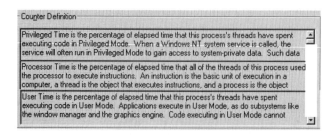

FIGURE 2-17. *Counter explanations*

are processed according to their efficiency. CPU consumption for Oracle user requirements can run as high as 100 percent when the computer is otherwise idle.

MEMORY/CPU RULE #8
Assess the balance between CPU time required to support user processes versus system services.

Because the CPU can only handle either Oracle support or system support one request at a time, knowing the balance between the amount of time dedicated to each is part of the process. In Figure 2-18, CPU usage was reported for both the processor and the ORACLE80 process during a short normal time span.

The graph shows that the ORACLE80 process is using between 10 and 20 percent at peak times while the processor itself is running between 30

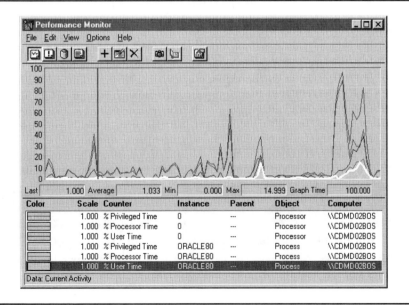

FIGURE 2-18. *CPU usage in a short time period*

and 100 percent at the same time. It also shows that when the ORACLE80 process is not utilizing the CPU, the processor is mostly idle. These results indicate a healthy balance between user and system utilization.

We call this a healthy balance since the percentages for the ORACLE80 process are directly proportional to the percentages for the processor itself, and the processor are fairly idle when not servicing the ORACLE80 process. This means the CPU is spending more time servicing user requests than performing system support.

Conclusions Drawn from the Example

To summarize the findings of the above exercise, you can draw the following conclusions and make recommendations.

CPU Is More than Adequate

Based on the output, this machine's CPU is easily meeting the resource requests of the Oracle database engine, Oracle user application processes, and processes supporting non-Oracle activities. During the business day, there are a great deal of users on the machine making little or no CPU resource requests. More users are idle during the day than those doing transactions against or reporting on the database. During quiet times, Oracle uses as much CPU as it can find. This is a healthy situation since a dedicated CPU speeds up processing of requests and maximizes the power of the computer. The operating system configuration easily supports the databases on this machine. The balance between CPU utilization for system support and user support indicates a correctly sized CPU. Do not consider a CPU upgrade; it is not necessary.

Session Monitoring

Monitor CPU utilization on a regular basis and ensure reporting is done during presumed heaviest user access. Because memory and basic support services are required for support of a great deal of idle sessions, a session monitor process should be put in place to kill unnecessary user sessions after a 20-minute period of terminal inactivity. This could be done at the operating system level, by using Oracle8 profiles as discussed in this chapter or by using the timeout option in Net8.

CPU Too Small

Once you go through the exercises described in the preceding sections, you may realize that your results point to a completely different set of findings. The following guidelines are designed to encourage continued attention, to recognize indicators that may point to problems with the size of your CPU.

- More than 50 percent of CPU utilization is dedicated to support of system services as opposed to satisfying user process requests.

- Transactions seem to be never-ending. After ensuring your applications are tuned, it is possible that the time slice each user gets of CPU may be performing excessive paging and swapping instead of actual processing.

- There is very little (less than 5 percent) CPU idle time even when the activity level on the machine is low. Even though the users are not doing much processing, the CPU is busy.

- If your memory is limited and your SORT_AREA_SIZE is at the default, a CPU that is too small may be overburdened with the I/O requests necessary to perform sorting to disk. Look at disk and memory sort statistics discussed earlier in this chapter.

- Sometime you may be tempted to adjust the priority of the Oracle background processes to compensate for a small CPU. The hope is that if the Oracle processes have a higher priority, the CPU will process user session requests faster due to the increased priority given to Oracle. Increasing the priority of Oracle processes may keep user processes from acquiring an adequate slice of the CPU to get their work accomplished. Reducing the priority of Oracle processes can result in the database writer, for example, never getting an opportunity to write data to disk. Problems may occur when priorities are mismatched between Oracle and user processes.

Maximizing CPU Power

You are encouraged to develop a regimen in which nothing that can run in off-hours is allowed to run during the day. Many installations insist that reports must be produced immediately, and the information contained in them must be 100 percent current. A great deal of reporting that is done with online systems can be canned and run at night. By making this clear to system owners as new systems are developed, you end up giving your CPU a break during its most hectic processing periods—the classic 9:00 to 5:00 working day. You need to convince your users that online data entry systems will perform better when as much reporting work as possible is done at night. The higher up the management chain, the higher the level of summary reporting needed. Summary reporting collects massive amounts of detail transaction data and rolls it up to help management with issues concerning planning, budget control, and resource allocation. Factors that help in tuning CPU utilization are listed at the end of this chapter.

Session Control

Oracle now permits more system and session control from within Oracle than was ever possible before. Moving more and more session control under Oracle's umbrella allows you to have more tools at your disposal that help you maximize the power of your CPU. Restricting access to the database and removing unwanted sessions, as described in the following sections, have operating system security as well as Oracle-based security in place for protection.

Restricting Access

With Oracle, you may want to restrict access to the database during special processing periods to allow high-profile jobs to have the machine to themselves. Ensure that the scheduling of programs run in off-hours does not interfere with your mission-critical applications.

For example, let's say that you work in a government telecommunications installation that bills clients on the first and fifteenth days of each month. You cannot afford to have the billing detail job abort—no bills translates to lost income. This application needs the CPU's undivided attention.

With Oracle8, you can restrict access without having to restart the database. Restricting access is accomplished via the command

```
SQL> alter system enable restricted session;
System altered.
SQL>
```

Restoring the database to normal unrestricted access is accomplished via the command

```
SQL> alter system disable restricted session;
System altered.
SQL>
```

While the database is operating in restricted mode, users without restricted session access capabilities who attempt to connect receive the following error message:

```
ORA-01035: ORACLE only available to users with RESTRICTED SESSION privilege
```

NOTE
Users without the restricted access capability logged on when the system access is changed to restricted can stay connected but will be unable to reconnect.

The restricted access capability is given to and taken away from users as a system privilege with the following command.

```
SQL> -- Give restricted access to FINANCE
SQL> grant restricted access to finance;
Grant succeeded.
SQL> -- Take it away
SQL> revoke restricted access from finance;
Revoke succeeded.
SQL>
```

Removing Unwanted Sessions

Periodically, for an assortment of reasons, user sessions are aborted and the operating system does not clean up when the user signs off. You need to detect the existence of these aborted sessions, then clean up after them to free up any resources they have obtained and still may be using.

Using Instance Manager, runaway sessions can be terminated using graphical point and click. If the Instance Manager is not available, other Oracle tools such as SQL*Plus can be used with the command **alter system kill session**. The command requires two arguments: the session number and the serial number of the process to be killed. It should be noted that care must be taken when killing the session. A number of instances have occurred when a killed process keeps running. This is a known Oracle bug. The only way to completely remove the process, then, is to shut down the database using the Abort option.

Killing the Session Using Instance Manager

Kill a session using the Instance Manager is done by performing these five steps:

1. Connect to the database.

2. Go to the tree on the left and open up SESSIONS.

3. Select the session to kill by highlighting it in the tree.

4. Verify that this is the correct session by the information listed on the right.

5. Choose Session from the Main menu, then Disconnect.

Looking at the Instance Manager Session window in Figure 2-19, notice that one session belongs to the Oracle user name DD0269. This is the session that needs to be killed.

Using Profiles

With Oracle, you may use profiles to limit resource utilization for database users. A *profile* is a set of resource limits. Profiles can aid you when maximizing utilization of the CPU. By default, users are assigned the profile DEFAULT when they are first set up as database users. The dictionary view dba_profiles owned by Oracle user SYS contains information about the limits, if any, placed on resource consumption by defined profiles. Profiles can be created using the Security Manager.

The parameters that are available are CPU/Session, CPU/Call, Connect Time, Idle Time, Concurrent Connections, Reads/Session, Reads/Call, Private SGA, and Composite Limit. Even though only two options mention CPU, the other options have an effect on CPU utilization. To help tune your database, consider setting a nondefault profile for some of your

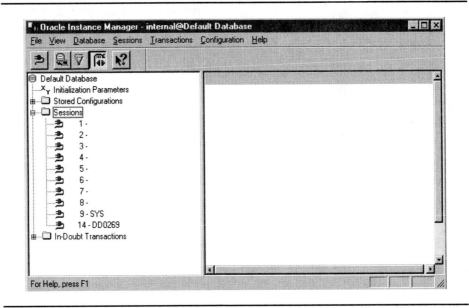

FIGURE 2-19.   *Killing a session in the Instance Manager*

applications. You know your users better than anyone else—your financial
application users may have extraordinary processing requirements that
dictate the following profile. For security reasons, you may restrict them to
one concurrent session per user. This is the SQL code that is used to create
the FINUSERS profile:

```
SQL> create profile finusers limit
        cpu_per_session        20
        sessions_per_user       1
        idle_time              30;
Profile created.
SQL>
```

Users assigned the FINUSERS profile will be allowed 20 minutes of CPU
time per session, one concurrent session per user, and a keyboard inactivity
time of 30 minutes before being logged off Oracle. Because all other resource
limits were not mentioned in the statement, they remain the default.

Your personnel application may have short session requirements with very little CPU needs. The human resources profile could be created using this statement:

```
SQL> create profile humanres limit
     cpu_per_session       20
     idle_time              8;
Profile created.
SQL>
```

Users assigned the HUMANRES profile will be allowed 20 minutes of CPU time per session and a keyboard inactivity time of eight minutes before being logged off Oracle. Again, because all other resource limits were not mentioned in the statement, they remain the default.

Tuning the CPU requires limiting who can do what within your applications. The secret is to maximize the efficient utilization of existing CPU.

Let's Tune It

Because operations in computer memory are the fastest, ensuring that they are used efficiently contributes to Oracle performance. It is your responsibility to help Oracle manage its memory resources efficiently. The following points summarize the recommendations from this chapter.

- Inspect the instance alert files regularly to be aware of any error conditions being raised by Oracle.

- If the DB_BLOCK_SIZE parameter is changed in the initialization parameter file and the database is recreated, the DB_BLOCK_BUFFER parameter will need adjusting for the database buffers to use the same amount of memory (e.g., if the block size is changed from 2,048 to 4,096, the DB_BLOCK_BUFFER parameter should be halved).

- In two-task architecture environments, look at the multithreaded server (MTS) to conserve memory. You may consider MTS as well when users are logged into applications and initiate infrequent server requests due to long periods of terminal inactivity.

■ Monitor the hit rate in the library cache. Adjustments to the SHARED_POOL_SIZE parameter in the initialization parameter file should be considered if the hit ratio is low (less than 80 percent).

■ Monitor the hit rate in the dictionary cache. The SHARED_POOL_SIZE parameter may need adjusting if this hit rate is low (less than 80 percent).

■ Monitor the ratio of misses against gets in the redo log buffer cache by looking at the V$LATCH dictionary view. If the misses are more than 1 percent of the gets, the result may be contention for the redo latches (copy latch and/or allocation latch, depending on the number of CPUs on your system).

■ When changing the initialization parameter file parameter SORT_AREA_SIZE, weigh the impact of the additional memory requests that will be given for ALL instance sort requests against the reported gain of a larger work space for sorting. With a large SORT_AREA_SIZE, requests for memory work space for sort activities will request the parameter value—for example, 640K—to sort two rows that may be returned from a query.

■ If more than 25 percent of sort requests require disk space (using V$SYSSTAT), consider increasing the initialization parameter file parameter SORT_AREA_SIZE.

■ If possible, leave your database up 24 hours a day. The library cache and dictionary cache must be filled each time the database is restarted. In the midst of filling these caches, the miss ratio will skyrocket. If your database is not up all the time, code some SQL statements to force loading of these caches after the database is brought up.

In summary, assess the demands on your existing configuration. See how the CPU is meeting busy and slow time periods processing in your applications. Take advantage of the features highlighted in this chapter and become familiar with the Oracle8 session control mechanisms we have discussed. The first four points below highlight five entries in the initialization parameter file. Adjusting these entries as suggested can help the CPU tuning exercise.

- Allocate as much real memory as possible to the shared pool and database buffers (SHARED_POOL_SIZE and DB_BLOCK_BUFFERS entries in the initialization parameter file) to permit as much work as possible to be done in memory. Work done in memory rather than disk does not use as much CPU.

- Set the initialization parameter file SEQUENCE_CACHE_ENTRIES high (the default is 10—try setting it to 1,000).

- Allocate more than the default amount of memory to do sorting (SORT_AREA_SIZE entry in the initialization parameter file); memory sorts not requiring I/O use much less CPU.

- On multi-CPU machines, increase the initialization parameter file entry LOG_SIMULTANEOUS_COPIES to allow one process per CPU to copy entries into the redo log buffers.

- Minimize I/O at all costs to free up CPU (e.g., a good number-crunching mainframe that is I/O-bound has no time to do any processing when the CPU is so tied up with I/O requests).

- Maximize availability of CPU power by distributing the load over the business day and night.

- Embark on a methodical assessment of your CPU before considering upgrades.

- Run reporting jobs during quiet hours; perhaps trade enhancements to existing systems for the approval to can jobs to run overnight (the old "enhancements cookie trick").

- If you need to back up your data during the day, try doing it between 11:30 A.M. and 1:00 P.M.—these hours tend to be the most quiet during the business day.

- Encourage users to minimize session idle time. Consider implementing a process to kill idle sessions after a predefined time of keyboard inactivity.

- Look at implementing Oracle8 profiles.

- Leave your database up 24 hours a day—precious time is lost when a database has to be closed for system backups.

■ Try to keep current with Oracle versions. Performance enhancements are built into each release of the database engine.

■ Use governors programmed into some of the Oracle tools to limit CPU consumption of the suite of ad hoc end-user query tools (one is built into Data Query 3.0 and later, for example).

■ Keep your users out of SQL*Plus, where they can, after mastering the syntax, submit the famous join of two 300,000 row tables without specifying enough join conditions (commonly referred to as the "query from h...").

■ Hide the operating system from your users. Implement a captive machine environment where users enter applications at once when logging onto their machine if you are utilizing server based applications.

Oracle7.x Specifics

Please note the following points organized by the headings for some sections throughout this chapter:

■ "Windows NT Performance Monitor" Not available with Oracle 7.x.

■ "Background Processes" The checkpoint process in Oracle 7.x needs to be explicitly started by including the parameter CHECKPOINT_PROCESS = TRUE in the parameter initialization file.

■ "Trace Files and Instance Alert Files" All this information is applicable to Oracle 7.x.

■ "The SGA" All this information is applicable to Oracle 7.x.

■ "Paging and Swapping" All this information is applicable to Oracle 7.x.

■ "Memory Requirements" SQL Worksheet is an interface tool in Enterprise Manager, which may not be available with all Oracle 7.x versions. Server Manager should be used instead.

■ "How Much Memory is Enough?" All this information is applicable to Oracle 7.x.

■ "The Shared Pool" All this information is applicable to Oracle 7.x.

■ "The Database Buffer Cache" All this information is applicable to Oracle 7.x.

■ "The Redo Log Buffer Cache" All this information is applicable to Oracle 7.x.

■ "Multithreaded Server" Oracle 7.x uses SQL*Net, which is the equivalent of Net8 in Oracle 8.x.

■ "SORT_AREA_SIZE" All this information is applicable to Oracle 7.x.

■ "Favoring CPU" All this information is applicable to Oracle 7.x.

■ "Parallel Query in Oracle8" Oracle 7.x does not parallelize DML statements, recovery, or the propagation of deferred transactions.

■ "How Busy Is Your CPU?" All this information is applicable to Oracle 7.x.

■ "Maximizing CPU Power" All this information is applicable to Oracle 7.x.

■ "Session Control" Instance Manager is an interface tool in Enterprise Manager, which may not be available with all Oracle 7.x versions. Server Manager should be used instead.

CHAPTER

3

I/O

/O (input/output) is one of the most important aspects of a database's performance. If you think about what a database is—an organizer, receiver, and dispenser of information—then obviously the major function of a database will be reading and writing information to disk. Designing the layout and attributes of your database objects (i.e., tablespaces, tables, indexes, redo logs, temporary segments, and rollback segments) to get the fastest reading and writing of information is crucial. In addition, I/O is one of the most expensive tasks a computer can be requested to do. Even though CPUs become a hundred times faster each year, I/O has not kept up the pace. This chapter will cover these I/O issues.

NOTE
We present some theory, explanations, and formulae throughout this chapter. The explanations have been over-simplified and are designed to give you a flavor of what Oracle does when an activity is initiated. The formulae, their results, and the recommendations we make are intended to be used as guidelines as you wade through I/O issues and make design and storage decisions as you go.

Accessing the DBA and V$ Views Owned by SYS

There are a number of DBA and V$ dynamic performance views belonging to Oracle user SYS mentioned in this chapter. The V$ views are called dynamic performance since they are not fixed views, and the information they contain is not saved each time the database is shut down. When an Oracle instance is started, there is a great deal of information in the data dictionary that is automatically loaded into the V$ views (e.g., the full name and location of all datafiles). You may not automatically have access to these DBA and V$ views without granting privileges on the views while connected to the Oracle8 Server as user SYS. Before we begin, the following code can be used to grant **select** on these views to avoid the frustration of following the text of this chapter and then being told an object does not exist.

```
-- Create a role that has the right to look at the V$ and DBA views
create role vddba;
set echo off pagesize 0 feedback off linesize 200 trimspool on
spool vddba.sql
select 'grant select on '||view_name||' to vddba;' -- *****
  from user_views
 where view_name like 'V%'
    or view_name like 'DBA%';
spool off
set echo on feed on
spool vddba
start vddba
spool off
```

Note how the recipient of the grants is the role VDDBA rather than any specific user name. If you have no problem with giving everybody access to the V$ and DBA views, do not create the role; simply give the grants out to public. If you do this, the line in the previous listing highlighted with the asterisks becomes:

```
select 'grant select on '||view_name||' to public;'
```

The Slow Link in the Chain

I/O operations are among the slowest and most time consuming performed by a database management system. Oracle8 reads all information into memory before making it available to a user session. Likewise, at predetermined times, Oracle writes data from memory to its database data files. Back when many of us worked with large mainframe computers, we used to impress our friends by calling a disk pack a *DASD*, or direct access storage device. We spoke of three factors that affected the speed with which data could be read from and written back to disk:

■ **Seek time** Measurement of the amount of time required for the read/write heads to be positioned over the spot on the disk where the desired data resides. Think of a disk platter as a phonograph record and the position as the middle of track three on side one.

- **Rotational delay** Measurement of the time required to rotate the platter once the heads are properly positioned to bring the spot where the data begins under the heads.

- **Data transfer** Measurement of the time taken to move the data off the disk, bound for memory and system processing.

The technology has changed manyfold, but the theory remains basically the same. In this chapter, we are going to look at many Oracle8 specifics that can be applied across all platforms upon which the software operates. Implementing object relational technology, keeping true relational theory in mind at all times, involves a series of decisions that contributes to the I/O efficiency of your Oracle8-based systems.

VLDB
The overhead for movement of data to and from the disk drives is especially significant with the volume of data stored in very large repositories.

Table and Index Segments

The first objects in your database that will be discussed are the table and index segments. To start with the basics, data is stored in the database in objects called tables. A *table* can be thought of as a spreadsheet, with rows and columns of information that are called *records* and *fields* in the database. A table holds one type of information in fields that have specific formats. Whenever a request is made to the database to read or write data, a record is either read from a table or written to a table.

The other important object in the database is the index. *Indexes* are objects that contain information from selected field(s) in a table stored in sorted order, plus a pointer to where the actual record of information is stored. Indexes are used for speeding up the reading of information in the tables, much like the index to a book. The fastest way to locate information in the database is to scan the index and then proceed directly to that page.

It helps to conceptualize an index as a mini copy of the table. The index contains selective column values and pointers to where the data resides. Suppose a STATE table contained 50 records identified by values in the STATE_NAME column. If the STATE_NAME column is not indexed, then a full table scan of all 50 records would be required to find all occurrences of the state name requested. This would involve reading all columns for all records in the table.

If the STATE_NAME column is indexed, then a search would be performed just on the index structure, which only has the STATE_NAME column and a data pointer in it. Less data is read and the index data is sorted. Oracle is intelligent enough to know that when it passes an entry that is alphabetically after the requested name, it does not have to search any further. Oracle reads data in 2 kilobyte (2K) blocks, so the number of 2K blocks that have to be read for the index is significantly less than the number of blocks that have to be read for the entire table. The amount of data read at a time (2K in the previous sentence) depends on the Oracle block size that was used when the database was created. The DB_BLOCK_SIZE entry in the initialization parameter file shows your current block size. You may see values there from 512 (one-half K) up to 16,384 (16K). The fewer blocks read, the faster the dataset is returned.

VLDB

With large volumes of data, we recommend setting the Oracle data block size to your operating system maximum (usually 8K or 16K). Consult the release notes on your platform for details about the data block size range.

We will now look at the first example of the processing involved to retrieve a column value from a table using an index. This and subsequent queries refer to the PEOPLE table shown here:

SSN	VARCHAR2(9)
FNAME	VARCHAR2(30)
LNAME	VARCHAR2(30)

and the following ADDRESS sample table:

SSN	VARCHAR2(9)
ADDRESS	VARCHAR2(30)
ADDRESS_TYPE	VARCHAR2(4)

Let us examine the steps when a request is made for a person's name from a table by giving that person's social security number. The social security number has an index on it.

```
select fname, lname
  from people
 where ssn = '123456789';
```

Once this SQL statement is issued, the following steps are taken to return the qualifying set of rows:

1. The Oracle Server looks in the data dictionary tables to see that the table PEOPLE exists.

2. Data dictionary tables are examined to see if the user making the request has access to read the requested information.

3. Data dictionary tables are examined again to see if the fields FNAME, LNAME, and SSN exist in the PEOPLE table.

4. Data dictionary tables are examined for a third time to see if the field used in the WHERE clause, SSN, is indexed.

5. The index object for the SSN field in the PEOPLE table is read to find a match on the requested SSN.

6. When a match is found, the ROWID of the requested row of data is obtained.

NOTE
The format of the ROWID has changed dramatically from Oracle7 to Oracle8. Beware of situations where you may be depending on the Oracle7 ROWID format in any DBA-related routines that may run as part of your backups.

7. Armed with the ROWID, Oracle reads the data row using the ROWID as the locator of the desired information.

NOTE
*Oracle8 allows you to store data in an
index-organized table defined with the
organization index keywords. We discuss this
in the next section of this chapter called
"Index-organized Tables." Points 6 and 7 in the
last list do not apply for this type of table.*

As you can see, the process of reading one record of data from the
database is decomposed into many steps, and the preceding list of steps
is not even complete. Oracle brings all information that it reads into
memory in order to use it. Oracle's memory management, as discussed
in Chapter 2, operates on two basic principles:

1. Oracle will keep as much information in memory as there
   is room.

2. When Oracle runs out of room in memory and needs to add data,
   it flushes from its memory the items that have been there the longest
   without being accessed. This is called an *LRU* algorithm, which
   stands for *least recently used*. You will hear this acronym all over
   Oracle technical material.

If the PEOPLE table is being accessed constantly and the data dictionary
cache is tuned properly, then all the data dictionary reads described earlier
are reads from memory and not from disk. Therefore, the only reads that are
actually being done from disk in the PEOPLE table example are the index
and table reads. The "Table and Index Splitting" and the "Table and Index
Disk Striping" sections later in this chapter deal with how to tune the reads
from these segments to optimize the speed of disk reads.

Index-organized Tables

As we discussed in the last section, in most situations, you create a table
segment and a corresponding index segment for most data stored in the
Oracle8 repository. Data in an index-organized table is grouped according

to their primary key column values. Using the more traditional table segment with matching index segment in pre-Oracle8 times, the data and index resembled the entries shown in Table 3-1.

Table 3-2 shows the index-organized feature for the same data content and structure.

Why Use Index-organized Tables

While tuning the Oracle8 Server, you should consider using index-organized tables for the following reasons:

■ Access by primary key is faster than the traditional approach when matching by equality or range searches as in:

```
select blah_blah
  from index_only_table
 where primary_key_col_1 = 212299    -- equality
   and primary_key_col_2 = 99;
select blah_blah
  from index_only_table
 where primary_key_col_1 between 212299 and 231222  -- range search
   and primary_key_col_2 = 99;
```

Data Segment

ROWID	Key Attribute 1	Key Attribute 2	Non-key Attribute 1
AAAACsAABAAAATmAAA	128877	12	Wrangler
AAAACsAABAAAATmAAB	129981	298	Levi's
AAAACsAABAAAATmAAC	212299	99	Zellers

Index Segment

ROWID	Key Attribute 1	Key Attribute 2
AAAACsAABAAAATmAAA	128877	12
AAAACsAABAAAATmAAB	129981	298
AAAACsAABAAAATmAAC	212299	99

TABLE 3-1. *Traditional Data and Index Segments*

Key Attribute 1	Key Attribute 2	Non-key Attribute 1
128877	12	Wrangler
129981	298	Levi's
212299	99	Zellers

TABLE 3-2. *Index-organized Representation*

■ As data is inserted, updated, and deleted, Oracle need not maintain the data segment and the index segment simultaneously, thereby speeding maintenance operations.

I/O RULE #1
Index-organized tables cannot be used in distributed processing (involving remote database links accessing a database other than the one to which you are connected) and cannot be replicated using Oracle8's Advanced Replication feature.

Let's have a brief look at how one of these tables is defined, study the new keywords and their meaning, and then cover some suggestions on the types of applications that may benefit from their use.

Building an Index-organized Table

An index-organized table is created using the following syntax in SQL*Plus, Server Manager, or the SQL Worksheet:

```
SQL*Plus: Release 8.0.3.0.0 - Production on Wed Jul 30 8:19:23 1999
(c) Copyright 1997 Oracle Corporation.  All rights reserved.
Connected to:
Oracle8 Enterprise Edition Release 8.0.3.0.0 - Production
With the Partitioning and Objects options
SQL> create table toc_jind
  2    (toc_id number,
```

```
3       toc_locator varchar2(2),
4       toc_component varchar2(10),
5       toc_desc varchar2(600),
6  constraint toc_jind_pk primary key (toc_id))
7  organization index tablespace fm_iot
8  pctthreshold 20
9  overflow tablespace ov_fm_iot;
Table created.
SQL>
```

Using the line numbers displayed in the **create** statement, inspect the code for the following important points:

- **Line 6** Note that the primary key must be defined with the table creation; error ORA-25175: no PRIMARY KEY constraint found will be raised if this portion is omitted. You cannot specify any storage parameters with the primary key definition.

- **Line 7** Since there is no corresponding table segment for this index-organized table, there are three places to store the index-organized tablespace:

  - In a tablespace dedicated to storage of non-index-organized tables in the same schema (e.g., MY_DATA_1).

  - In a tablespace dedicated to storage of indexes belonging to non-index-organized tables in the same schema (e.g., MY_INDEX_1).

  - In a tablespace dedicated to index-organized tables (e.g., MY_IOT_TS).

- **Lines 8 and 9** This number represents a percent of the Oracle block size. When the length of a row (i.e., key and non-key column data) exceeds this figure, the non-key column data is migrated to the overflow tablespace. Using the toc_jind table (with a pctthreshold of 20) and a block size of 2K (2,048 bytes), rows containing more than 409 bytes (a rough approximation) of data will find their non-key column information in overflow. A pointer is established such that the primary key column data and the non-key data can be retrieved together when required.

I/O RULE #2
Create one or more tablespaces dedicated to storage of index-organized tables and their overflow data. The next section,"Table and Index Splitting," discusses the reasons for this advice.

Information on index-organized table definitions can be found in the USER_TABLES data dictionary view, and the IOT_TYPE column will contain the text IOT or IOT_OVERFLOW; for traditional tables, this column value is null.

Applications That Benefit from Index-organized Tables

Since index-organized tables are brand new (as of Oracle release 8.0.3), time will tell what applications truly benefit from using this new type of storage mechanism. Oracle believes they can enhance performance of information retrieval, spatial, and online analytical processing (*OLAP*) systems. The technical community will attest to the gain of using index-organized tables as they are tested and ultimately adopted in these and perhaps a number of other specific application types. The OLAP systems are synonymous with data warehouses that nowadays store multiple terabytes of data (where a terabyte equals 1,099,511,627,776 bytes). We believe the nature of data warehouse information retrieval by primary key makes warehousing applications an ideal candidate for index-organized tables.

VLDB
Data warehousing applications with OLAP activity are ideal locations for using index-organized tables.

DML and DDL Differences

DML (data manipulation language) and DDL (data definition language) operations on index-organized tables are exactly the same as traditional table activity. You **select**, **insert**, **update**, and **delete** data as well as **analyze** and **grant** privileges in a similar fashion. You can add foreign key constraints to an index-organized table pointing the column values at primary key values in the referenced table. When deciding whether to use index-organized tables, keep in mind the data retrieval habits of your user community, since you are not able to manually build indexes on these tables. Attempting to do this using the **create index** syntax raises the following error:

 ORA-25182: feature not currently available for index-organized tables

Table and Index Splitting

The first rule with table and index objects is to split the indexes from their tables, putting your table data on one disk and your index data on another disk. The way this is accomplished is to always create separate tablespaces for table data and index data. A *tablespace* is one or more data files grouped together to hold Oracle data. When users store data in Oracle, it is placed in a tablespace in which that user has been given the right to occupy space. The *system tablespace* is where Oracle stores all data dictionary information.

I/O RULE #3
Always create separate tablespaces for your tables and indexes and never put objects that are not part of the core Oracle system in the system tablespace.

NOTE
Watch out for some third-party products that end up putting their objects in the system tablespace. With intervention, some allow you to place them elsewhere.

The index tablespace and its corresponding data tablespace should be created on separate disks. Objects (i.e., tables and indexes) are placed in specific tablespaces in the **create** statement. The reasoning is to allow the disk head on one disk to read the index information while the disk head on the other disk reads the table data. Both reads happen faster because one disk head is on the index and the other is on the table data. If the objects were on the same disk, the disk head would need to reposition itself from the index extent to the data extent between the index read and the data read. (An *extent* is a contiguous section of disk space within a tablespace that holds only one object.) This can dramatically decrease the throughput of data in a system.

I/O RULE #4
*Ensure that data tablespaces
and index tablespaces reside on
separate disk drives.*

Along with splitting tables and their indexes on separate disks, there can also be a need to avoid having different tables on the same disk. For example, if two tables are to be accessed at the same time, it would improve performance to have each table on a separate disk. This also applies to indexes where, if an SQL statement would be using two indexes at the same time, it would improve performance to have each index on a separate disk.

The following listing contains three objects that will need to be read from the database. A request is made to display the name and home address of a person whose SSN is known. The name is in one table while the address is in another. The SSN column in the Person table has an index on it.

```
select fname, lname, address
   from person, address
 where ssn = '123-45-0269'
   and person.ssn = address.ssn
   and address_type = 'HOME'
```

The first object is the SSN index on the PEOPLE table, the second object is the PEOPLE table, and the third object is the ADDRESS table. If possible, the three objects that need to be read for one request should be placed on three different disks. In addition, if there is a concatenated index on the SSN and ADDRESS_TYPE from the ADDRESS table, now a fourth object is being read.

Taken to its logical conclusion, you would have only one object in a tablespace and only one tablespace on a disk. Unfortunately, this is neither practical nor totally beneficial. The way the data in your database is to be used must be understood in order to form a comprehensive data placement strategy. Objects that are to be accessed in one statement very frequently should be spread out over separate tablespaces and separate disks to minimize disk contention.

I/O RULE #5
Know how your data is to be accessed by the end users.

I/O RULE #6
Whenever possible, place objects that are most often referenced simultaneously and frequently on separate disks.

Table and Index Disk Striping

The previous section assumed only one user accessing the data in the database. When you add to this picture multiple users accessing different data for the same objects, you start running into I/O contention caused by the number of users—not by hardware limitation. *I/O contention* happens when a resource (e.g., a disk head, a specific data block, or an I/O channel) is being used by one process and another process needs to use that resource but must wait for the first process to finish.

If two users are accessing data from the PEOPLE table and ADDRESS table, both users' disk heads are moving around to access pieces of information. If the object is small, this is not a problem. But if the object is large, then this could increase the read time on each object. When an object in your database is large, it may be useful to place the object on multiple disks. This procedure is called *disk striping*. Disk striping is accomplished by estimating the size of the tablespace that will hold the object and dividing it evenly into multiple datafiles located on different disks. The object is then sized to the datafile size and spread over the files in multiple extents. Disk striping allows the data for one object to be spread over multiple disks, making it possible to simultaneously access data from the same object on different disks.

I/O RULE #7
When your database contains large objects that will have users concurrently accessing different data elements, striping the object over multiple disks is helpful.

VLDB
Use caution when sizing some multimillion row tables on certain operating system platforms, due to limitations placed on the size of a database file. This limit is dictated by the operating system, not by Oracle.

Manual Extent Allocation to Stripe a Table

Extent allocation can be done manually to ensure that a frequently accessed table is spread amongst a number of disks. Suppose we want to load data into an ADDRESS table—2,500,000 or so rows with an average row length of 280 bytes. Thus, we can estimate that the table will consume 700,000,000 bytes, or roughly 680 megabytes, of database space. We want to create the table, allocating the necessary space for the initial amount of data, and a buffer of roughly 20 percent for expansion. In the next two sections, we will look at striping the ADDRESS table first in a dedicated tablespace, then in a tablespace that contains multiple tables.

When a Tablespace Is Dedicated to One Table

The following tablespace has been successfully created to hold the ADDRESS table:

```
SQL> create tablespace nt_prd_data datafile
  2      'c:\orant\database\ntpd_1.dbf' size 200m,
  3      'd:\orant\database\ntpd_2.dbf' size 200m,
  4      'e:\orant\database\ntpd_3.dbf' size 200m,
  5      'h:\orant\database\ntpd_4.dbf' size 200m;
  6  default storage (initial 20m next 20m pctincrease 0);
Tablespace created.
SQL>
```

When we create the ADDRESS table, we ask for four extents at creation time, each just a little bit less than the actual size of each datafile. Oracle can acquire up to 200 megabytes of space in each extent; therefore, by requesting four extents as the table is created, Oracle allocates additional space one extent at a time in each of the datafiles that make up the tablespace. The table creation is shown in the next listing:

```
create table address (
    address_id          number,
    street_id           number,
    address_type_id     number,
...
...
    rural_ind           varchar2(1))
storage (initial 199m next 199m minextents 4 pctincrease 0)
tablespace nt_prd_data;
```

We now need to discover where the initial extent was placed to figure out where to put the other extents. We first get a list of all the FILE_IDs, then look at DBA_EXTENTS to find out where the ADDRESS table's initial extent resides. Now when we issue the following query, we find there is one extent in each datafile allocated when the tablespace was created.

```
SQL> select extent_id,file_id
  2    from dba_extents
  3   where segment_name = 'ADDRESS';
EXTENT_ID    FILE_ID
---------- ----------
        0          7
        1          5
        2          6
        3          8
4 rows selected.
```

When a Tablespace Contains Multiple Tables

This exercise is a little bit different from the previous one. Here we ask for one extent as the ADDRESS table is created (we requested four extents previously), then manually allocate space for the next three extents. Let's create the table, giving it the desired initial request of 199 megabytes.

```
create table address (
    address_id              number,
    street_id               number,
    address_type_id         number,
...
...
    rural_ind               varchar2(1))
storage (initial 199m next 199m pctincrease 0)
tablespace nt_prd_data;
```

Once the table is created, we can find out in which file the initial extent was placed as shown in the next listing. We obtain the FILE_IDs of the datafiles making up the NT_PRD_DATA tablespace, then look at DBA_EXTENTS to find out where the ADDRESS table's initial extent resides.

```
SQL> select file_name,file_id
  2    from dba_data_files
  3    order by 2;
FILE_NAME                                    FILE_ID
---------------------------------------- ----------
C:\ORANT\DATABASE\SYS1ORCL.ORA                  1
C:\ORANT\DATABASE\USR1ORCL.ORA                  2
D:\ORANT\DATABASE\RBS1ORCL.ORA                  3
H:\ORANT\DATABASE\TMP1ORCL.ORA                  4
C:\ORANT\DATABASE\NTPD_1.DBF                     5
D:\ORANT\DATABASE\NTPD_2.DBF                     6
E:\ORANT\DATABASE\NTPD_3.DBF                     7
H:\ORANT\DATABASE\NTPD_4.DBF                     8
8 rows selected.
SQL> select segment_name,file_id
  2    from dba_extents
  3    where segment_name = 'ADDRESS';
SEGMENT_NAME                                 FILE_ID
---------------------------------------- ----------
ADDRESS                                          7
```

We now know that the ADDRESS table resides in the NTPD_3.DBF file in the E:\ORANT\DATABASE directory. Let's now allocate the remaining three extents to consume the additional space for loading the rows into ADDRESS:

```
SQL> alter table address allocate extent
  2     (size 199m datafile 'C:\ORANT\DATABASE\NTPD_1.DBF');
Table altered.
SQL> alter table address allocate extent
  2     (size 199m datafile 'D:\ORANT\DATABASE\NTPD_2.DBF');
Table altered.
SQL> alter table address allocate extent
  2     (size 199m datafile 'H:\ORANT\DATABASE\NTPD_4.DBF');
Table altered.
SQL>
```

To complete this exercise, let's look in the DBA_EXTENTS view to see where the extents are positioned:

```
SQL> select extent_id,file_id
  2     from dba_extents
  3     where segment_name = 'ADDRESS';
 EXTENT_ID     FILE_ID
---------- ----------
         0           7
         1           5
         2           6
         3           8
4 rows selected.
SQL>
```

Row Migration and Row Chaining

As tables are created in the Oracle8 Server, we strive to allocate space and control subsequent space consumption so that once a row is inserted in the database, all the data belonging to that row stays in the same block. Suppose with a 4K (4,096 bytes) block size, the **pctfree** parameter has been set to 20. Remember, this parameter controls the percentage of space in each data block reserved for row updates. If an alphanumeric column contains the text "BARNEY" at row creation time and finds the column value updated to "BARNEY IS A VERY PURPLE FUZZY CHARACTER", the increased size of the row consumes the part of the block set aside by this **pctfree** keyword. One's tuning efforts strive to reduce the following two phenomena:

■ Migrating a row, which happens when the amount of data in an existing row grows, and the row can no longer be accommodated within the current block where it resides. Oracle will hunt for a data block that can hold the updated row and migrate the row.

■ Row chaining, which occurs when records are updated, and the data can neither fit in its current block nor be migrated to another single block with enough free space. Oracle will break the row into pieces and store its column values in different blocks.

The logic that dictates the behavior of migration and chaining can be summed up like so:

```
if a row's column values are updated
    if the amount of data in the row increases
        if there is enough space to accommodate the new amount in current block
            update the row in place
        else
            if there is another block allocated to the table with room
                migrate the row to that block
            else
                break the row into pieces creating a chained row
            end if
        end if
    end if
end if
```

Row chaining and row migration are costly from a tuning perspective, since there is increased I/O for both row updates that lead to migration and chaining, as well as queries that read rows that are in pieces.

I/O RULE #8
Keep row chaining to a minimum by periodically reporting on and fixing rows that have been chained after being updated.

VLDB
Detection and fixing row chaining is especially important when working with very large information repositories.

Detecting and Fixing Row Chaining

To detect row chaining, issue the following command from SQL*Plus, using our ADDRESS table as an example:

```
analyze table address list chained rows;
```

NOTE
Before this statement will complete successfully, the CHAINED_ROWS table must be created and be accessible to the user running the **analyze** *command.*

The CHAINED_ROWS table creation is shown in the next listing (there is an SQL program called utlchain.sql in the \orant\rdbms80\admin folder in Windows NT to create this object).

```
create table chained_rows (
    owner_name          varchar2(30),
    table_name          varchar2(30),
    cluster_name        varchar2(30),
    partition_name      varchar2(30),
    head_rowid          rowid,
    analyze_timestamp   date);
```

It is then a matter of looking at the contents of the CHAINED_ROWS table and, if chaining exists, the query **select table_name,head_rowid from chained_rows where table_name = 'ADDRESS';** will produce output similar to the following:

```
TABLE_NAME                       HEAD_ROWID
-------------------------------- --------------------
ADDRESS                          AAAACsAABAAAATmAAD
ADDRESS                          AAAACsAABAAAATmAAE
```

You then proceed using code similar to the following:

```
SQL> -- Make a copy of the chained rows in a holding table
SQL> create table add_chained as
  2    select *
  3      from address
```

```
  4     where rowid in
  5          (select head_rowid
  6             from chained_rows
  7             where table_name = 'ADDRESS');
Table created.
SQL> -- Delete chained rows from ADDRESS
SQL> delete address
  2     where rowid in
  3          (select head_rowid
  4             from chained_rows
  5             where table_name = 'ADDRESS');
2 rows deleted.
SQL> -- Move rows back in to ADDRESS
SQL> insert into address
  2     select * from add_chained;
2 rows created.
SQL> -- Drop the intermediate table
SQL> drop table add_chained;
Table dropped.
SQL>
```

You can also look in the V$SYSSTAT dictionary view for the figure sitting in the VALUE column where the NAME column equals "table fetch continued row". A non-zero number here indicates there are some reads against chained rows. We now move on to a very important and mandatory player in the I/O game—rollback segments.

Rollback Segments

A *rollback segment* is a database object that holds information when a user does a data manipulation action (i.e., **insert**, **update**, or **delete**), so that this action can be rolled back if needed. When an action is *rolled back,* any changes (issued by **update**, **delete**, or **insert** statements) to data are removed, and the data is returned to the state it was in before the statement was issued.

If your system is a heavy online transaction system, then the rollback segments are very important. A rollback segment needs to be able to hold enough information so that users can perform the needed data manipulation actions. If your system is multiuser, it must also hold the information for all concurrent actions to avoid user actions interfering with each other.

When an action needs rollback space, it uses the next available rollback segment in your system and uses an extent in that segment. A transaction in Oracle is not allowed to span multiple rollback segments. Therefore, if the rollback segment assigned to your transaction runs out of space, Oracle will attempt to extend that rollback segment in the tablespace where it is located. Because of this, you should never use a rollback segment (besides the system rollback segment) in the system tablespace. If the rollback segment being extended is located in the system tablespace, it can cause fragmentation in that tablespace, or it may fill up the system tablespace.

Rollback tablespaces should be created to hold the rollback segments. If your system is a heavy transaction-based system, you should have at least two rollback tablespaces, and these tablespaces should be located on separate disks. To reduce contention for rollback headers, multiple rollback segments should be in each rollback tablespace. *Contention for rollback headers* occurs when transactions trigger requests for buffers for rollback segment blocks, and those buffers are still busy with previous transaction rollback information.

To control the use of the rollback segments, they must be specified in the initialization parameter file. The order that Oracle assigns rollback segments to transactions is the same as the order that they are listed in the initialization parameter file. For this reason, you should interleaf the order of the rollback segments so that the first one is in one tablespace, the next one is in the other, and so on. In this way, while one transaction is processed, the next one uses a rollback segment in the other tablespace located on the other disk, thereby reducing disk head contention and distributing the I/O requests across these disks.

I/O RULE #9
Create at least two user-defined rollback tablespaces on separate disks to hold your rollback segments.

I/O RULE #10
Order the rollback segments in the initialization parameter file so that they toggle between multiple disks.

For example, Disk #1 contains one rollback tablespace with the following rollback segments: rbs01, rbs02, rbs03, rbs04. Disk #2 contains another rollback tablespace with the following rollback segments: rbs05, rbs06, rbs07, rbs08. Your initial instinct may be to order the rollback segments in the initialization parameter file as the following:

```
rollback_segments = (rbs01, rbs02, rbs03, rbs04, rbs05, rbs06, rbs07, rbs08)
```

This order would not accomplish the interleaving desired of the tablespaces. The statement in the initialization parameter file should be the following instead:

```
rollback_segments = (rbs01, rbs05, rbs02, rbs06...)
```

If you can predict that some transactions will have a large amount of rollback information, you should consider creating one rollback segment larger than all the others. Then, when this type of transaction is about to start, you can specify in the code to use the large rollback segment. This way, you can control the haphazard expansion of rollback segments that can sometimes happen. When a transaction causes arbitrary rollback segments to expand, it will fill up the tablespace that the rollback segment is on and cause the transaction to be aborted.

Reducing Fragmentation

Fragmentation of tablespaces occurs when objects they contain extend themselves, and there are no adjacent blocks available in the same extent. Oracle allocates space in blocks, and adjacent chunks of blocks are referred to as *contiguous space*. If there is no contiguous space available, Oracle acquires space elsewhere in the datafile(s) associated with the tablespace. When reading data from tables that are fragmented, there can be extra overhead involved since the disk read-write head must move to another spot over the disk platter to perform the operation. The tuning exercise is hindered when tablespaces become fragmented as a result of the additional read/write head movement we spoke of toward the start of this chapter.

The data dictionary, which is stored in the system tablespace, is read constantly and should be as efficient as possible. When a tablespace runs out of contiguous space, it needs to be expanded (i.e., extra space added with an additional datafile) or reorganized (i.e., the data it contains is moved out, the tablespace re-created, and the data moved back in). In most situations, this can be done using Oracle8 export and import, though the Tablespace Manager in the Oracle Enterprise Manager (affectionately called *OEM*) can be used as well.

NOTE
The Tablespace Manager is part of the Performance Pack, an add-on to the off-the-shelf OEM product sold over and above the base Oracle8 product.

The Tablespace Manager interface involves the familiar point-and-click and fill in the blanks exercise. Open up the Tablespace Manager by clicking its icon in the Oracle Enterprise Manager folder. The main console is shown in Figure 3-1.

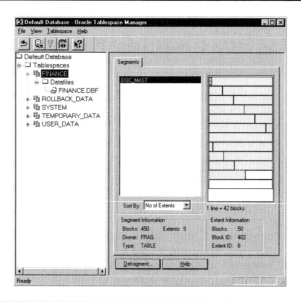

FIGURE 3-1. *Tablespace Manager main console*

NOTE
Defragmenting a table involves submitting a job through the OEM scheduling system. Thus, the Enterprise Manager console must be running and should be invoked before starting the defragmentation exercise.

Expand the Tablespaces list, then double-click a tablespace name to bring up a screen similar to that shown in Figure 3-2. We use the FINANCE tablespace with the DOC_MASTER table as shown.

Notice the diagram where the extents are represented in addition to some segment and extent information. The exercise here is to collapse the twelve extents into one. To start, click Defragment to bring up the first Defragmentation Wizard page as shown in Figure 3-3.

For this example, we have chosen to submit the job to do the defragmentation immediately. We therefore bypass page two of the wizard and go directly to page three as shown in Figure 3-4.

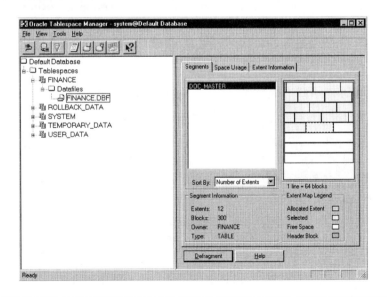

FIGURE 3-2. *DOC_MASTER table extent display*

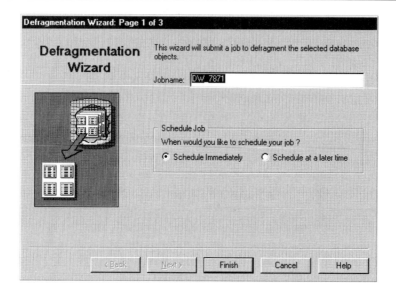

FIGURE 3-3. *First page of the Defragmentation Wizard*

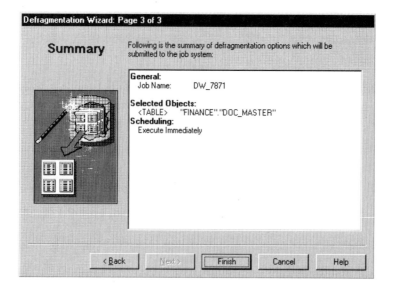

FIGURE 3-4. *Third page of the wizard displaying job information*

Click Finish to begin submitting the job, and you receive a message about the job having been committed. You are then returned to the Tablespace manager console.

NOTE
The job will only be successfully submitted if you have a service defined in the OEM scheduling system. Details about setup and configuration of services are available in the OEM hard-copy or online documentation.

This reorganization is not easy to do with the system tablespace. In fact, the **create database** activity followed by re-creation of the data dictionary is the only way to do this for the system tablespace. This difficulty in reorganizing the system tablespace is the biggest reason to keep only system information in the system tablespace.

I/O RULE #11
Monitor the allocation of extents and intervene when objects become fragmented.

I/O RULE #12
Objects that have more than one extent are candidates for reorganizing; ones that have more than five extents should be rebuilt at the earliest convenience.

Coalescing Free Space

Coalescing is the act of combining adjacent chunks of free space into one large chunk. It is done by the pmon background process as the database operates, but it can also be done manually as we are about to discuss. The data dictionary view DBA_FREE_SPACE keeps track of space available by tablespace and datafile. The following query looks at free space in the SYSTEM tablespace made up of two separate datafiles:

```
-- We recommend ordering as we do below to be able to inspect
-- the output looking for what are adjacent chunks of free space.
select file_id, block_id, blocks, bytes
  from dba_free_space
 where tablespace_name = 'SYSTEM'
 order by 1,2;
```

Let's study the output from this query and a few rules that can be applied to coalescing free space.

	a	b	c	d
	FILE_ID	**BLOCK_ID**	**BLOCKS**	**BYTES**
1	1	1801	75	153600
2	1	1876	175	358400
3	1	5107	525	1075200
4	2	5632	600	1228800
5	2	6232	2055	4208640

As long as the correct ordering is done, the following logic can determine the outcome of a coalescing activity:

```
if BLOCK_ID + BLOCKS (from one row) = BLOCK_ID (from next row)
    if FILE_ID (from one row) = FILE_ID (from next row)
        the space is contiguous and can be coalesced
    end if
end if
```

Thus, since cell b1+c1=b2 and a1=a2, the space in bytes in d1 and d2 can be collapsed during the coalesce activity. Following on, b2+c2<>b3, and therefore the space in d3 will stay on its own. Watch out for the caveat introduced with rows 3 and 4. Notice that b3+c3=b4, however a3<>a4; this means the free space pieces are in different database files and cannot be combined. Free space can be coalesced manually using the following syntax against the SYSTEM tablespace queried previously

```
SQL> alter tablespace system coalesce;
Tablespace altered.
SQL> select file_id, block_id, blocks, bytes
  2    from dba_free_space
  3   where tablespace_name = 'SYSTEM'
```

```
 4    order by 1,2;
FILE_ID    BLOCK_ID        BLOCKS        BYTES
-------  -----------   ------------  ------------
      1         1801           250        512000
      1         5107           525       1075200
      2         5632          2655       5437440
```

Temporary Segments

Temporary segments are objects in the database that are used during a transaction in order to complete the transaction. For example, if a query is issued that requires the result set to be sorted, temporary segments may be used to do the sorting. Temporary segments may be used during index creation to sort the index values.

The location of a user's newly created temporary segment is determined by the **create user** statement. In this statement, a user is assigned a tablespace that will hold his or her temporary segments. Do not leave it as the default, which is the system tablespace. You should create at least one temporary tablespace that will be used for the exclusive use of temporary segments. This tablespace should be assigned to users as their temporary tablespace. If you foresee considerable use of temporary segments by many users at the same time, then you would do better to create multiple temporary tablespaces and then distribute the assignment of users to the tablespaces evenly.

I/O RULE #13
Create at least one tablespace whose exclusive use will be for temporary segments.

Dedicated Temporary Tablespaces

When sort activity needs disk space in addition to what can be accomplished in memory, it is best to use a tablespace dedicated to temporary segments. The default status when a tablespace is created is PERMANENT, and the dedicated type is set using the TEMPORARY keyword as the tablespace is created or altered. Inspect the following listing to see the syntax:

```
SQL> create tablespace temp_tst datafile
   2        'f:\orant\database\temp1.dbf' size 100m,
   3        'f:\orant\database\temp1.dbf' size 100m,
   4        'f:\orant\database\temp1.dbf' size 100m
   5  temporary;
Tablespace created.
SQL>
```

From then on, or until the status is changed, attempting to place a table in the TEMP_TST tablespace will generate the following error:

```
ORA-02195: Attempt to create PERMANENT object in a TEMPORARY tablespace
```

The tablespace must be altered to **permanent** in order for this operation to succeed. When a tablespace is temporary, one sort segment is cached and the normal mechanisms that control sorting to disk are bypassed. This can affect the throughput of sort operations.

IO RULE #14
*Create the temporary tablespace as type
TEMPORARY to improve the performance
of sorts to disk.*

Redo Logs

Redo logs are the transaction logs that record every database manipulation action that takes place, as it takes place, indicating if it is committed or rolled back. You need to have at least two redo log groups for your system to work, because when one log group becomes full, Oracle automatically switches to the next redo log group. If the system is a heavy transaction-oriented system, the redo logs are constantly being written to. Oracle's high performance can be partly attributed to the fact that it does not write changes to the database directly to the database but to the redo logs. The information is written to the actual database files by the DBWR process when a checkpoint occurs (refer to discussion of background processes in Chapter 2). The frequency of the checkpoints is determined by the LOG_CHECKPOINT_INTERVAL parameter in the initialization parameter file.

The batch size has a direct correlation to the length of time your Oracle system takes to come up after it closes abnormally. Oracle needs to apply all changes that were committed and roll back any changes that did not get committed since the last checkpoint as a database is starting up.

Since only one redo log group is active at a time, there is not a compelling need to separate your redo log groups on different disks. The one exception is if you have your Oracle database running in ARCHIVELOG mode. What this means is that you are having Oracle make a file copy of the redo log to an archive area when the log becomes full, so that your database can be recovered from the last backup.

But because the redo logs are constantly being written to, they should be separated from your other objects and tablespaces. Therefore, if the hardware exists, your redo logs should be on a disk that contains objects that are not being read or written to often. That is, they should be on a separate disk from all database objects.

I/O RULE #15
Put your redo logs on a disk that has a low incidence of reads and writes.

Multiplexed Redo Logs

We have mentioned the concept of redo log groups. Redo log groups are made up of members, where each group has the same number of equally sized members and each member on its own is the same size. The maximum number of members per group is operating system dependent. There are two main reasons why redo log groups should have multiple members:

- There is no single point of failure. If, for example, one member of each group resides in H:\ORANT\DATABASE\REDO, with other members elsewhere on drives G: and D:, a disk failure on H: will not cause the database to come down. Oracle will not shut itself down as long as it can write to one member of a redo log group when that group becomes active.

- If running in ARCHIVELOG mode, Oracle will archive a member from a redo log group and, if it finds something wrong with the member it's trying to archive, will go on to another member in the same group.

I/O RULE #16
*Have more than two redo log groups for each
Oracle instance, placing members of each
group on different devices whenever possible.*

We recommend using a descriptive name for your redo log group
members.

I/O RULE #17
*Embed the Oracle system identifier, group
number, and member number of each redo
log group member's file name.*

Applying this rule to a system whose identifier is emsp, we recommend
the following naming convention for three redo log groups with three
members each:

- Group 1 is made up members log1g1_emsp.log, log2g1_emsp.log,
  and log3g1_emsp.log.

- Group 2 is made up members log1g2_emsp.log, log2g2_emsp.log,
  and log3g2_emsp.log.

- Group 3 is made up members log1g3_emsp.log, log2g3_emsp.log,
  and log3g3_emsp.log.

The following three data dictionary views tell you all you want to know
about the active redo log groups and members.

```
SQL> desc v_$logfile
 Name                            Null?    Type
 ------------------------------- -------- ----
 GROUP#                                   NUMBER
 STATUS                                   VARCHAR2(7)
 MEMBER                                   VARCHAR2(513)
SQL> desc v_$log_history
```

```
Name                            Null?    Type
------------------------------- -------- ----
   RECID                                 NUMBER
   STAMP                                 NUMBER
   THREAD#                               NUMBER
   SEQUENCE#                             NUMBER
   FIRST_CHANGE#                         NUMBER
   FIRST_TIME                            DATE
   NEXT_CHANGE#                          NUMBER
SQL> desc v_$archived_log
Name                            Null?    Type
------------------------------- -------- ----
   RECID                                 NUMBER
   STAMP                                 NUMBER
   NAME                                  VARCHAR2(513)
   THREAD#                               NUMBER
   SEQUENCE#                             NUMBER
   RESETLOGS_CHANGE#                     NUMBER
   RESETLOGS_TIME                        DATE
   FIRST_CHANGE#                         NUMBER
   FIRST_TIME                            DATE
   NEXT_CHANGE#                          NUMBER
   NEXT_TIME                             DATE
   BLOCKS                                NUMBER
   BLOCK_SIZE                            NUMBER
   ARCHIVED                              VARCHAR2(3)
   DELETED                               VARCHAR2(3)
   COMPLETION_TIME                       DATE
```

Disk Controllers

Many disk systems have *disk controllers,* which are hardware devices that control the actions of one or more disks. These controllers can also create a bottleneck in your system. You must be aware of which disks are controlled by which controllers. A controller can control the I/O of more than one disk, so, for example, requests made to two disks under one controller result in a decrease in performance while the controller services both disk requests. In addition to putting objects on separate disks being accessed at the same time, you should also make sure that they are on disks controlled by different disk controllers.

If optimal separation for disk controllers is not possible, at least try to distribute the I/O evenly over the controllers. This helps eliminate the degradation of performance due to a heavy request load on a specific disk controller.

Hot Spots

Throughout this chapter, one point cannot be stressed enough: you should distribute your I/O as evenly as possible across as many disks as possible and as many disk controllers as possible. This is easier said than done. The primary objective is to know the application(s) that will be using the data. Find out which objects are most likely to be accessed in conjunction with each other. Separate objects out into separate tablespaces from the beginning. Taking the time to separate objects properly at the beginning is easier than having to move objects around later.

Once your system is created and your users have gotten up to speed with the system, Oracle provides a number of tools to look at the I/O by objects, usually files. These tools help point out hot spots. *Hot spots* are the files within the Oracle database that are most heavily read or written to. In this section, we will discuss hot spot detection by datafile, then by object.

Hot Spots by Datafile

There are three ways we use to monitor and detect hot spots by datafile: V$FILESTAT, Enterprise Manager Performance Pack, and utlbstat/utlestat.

V$FILESTAT Monitoring

We recommend that you become familiar with using the following data dictionary view when looking at I/O balancing and detection of hot spots:

```
SQL> desc v_$filestat
 Name                             Null?    Type
 -------------------------------- -------- ----
 FILE#                                     NUMBER
 PHYRDS                                    NUMBER
 PHYWRTS                                   NUMBER
 PHYBLKRD                                  NUMBER
 PHYBLKWRT                                 NUMBER
 READTIM                                   NUMBER
 WRITETIM                                  NUMBER
```

A query against this view using the physical reads and physical writes
will give you an idea of your I/O balancing. This is shown in the next listing
(the numbers 1-6 on the right side of the output are not part of the query
output; they are there for the analysis that follows).

```
SQL> select name, phyrds, phywrts
  2     from v$datafile a, v$filestat b    -- Join will get the name
                                           -- of each datafile
  3   where a.file# = b.file#;
NAME                                       PHYRDS     PHYWRTS
------------------------------------------ ---------- ----------
C:\ORANT\DATABASE\SYS1ORCL.ORA              11706         573       1
C:\ORANT\DATABASE\USR1ORCL.ORA               9021        8109       2
H:\ORANT\DATABASE\RBS1ORCL.ORA                667        1199       3
G:\ORANT\DATABASE\TMP1ORCL.ORA                349        1288       4
I:\ORANT\DATABASE\FY9697.DBF                43889           0       5
O:\ORANT\DATABASE\FY9798.DBF                29888       21112       6
```

Before moving on to looking at I/O balance within the OEM
Performance Pack, let's interpret the output from the previous listing. This is
a flavor of what you need to go through when analyzing the distribution of
I/O between all your database datafiles.

1. **Lines 3 and 4**   The rollback tablespace and the temporary
   tablespace are on different disk drives.

2. **Lines 5 and 6**   The two fiscal year (fy) dependent datafiles are on
   different drives as well.

3. **Line 5**   Without knowing the nature of the activity against the
   FY9697.DBF datafile, one could easily wonder why the users are
   not saving information back to the database in that file. As it turns
   out, the data in the FY9697.DBF file is not being updated since the
   tablespace it holds is running in read-only mode. The fiscal year
   96/97 data is historical and is not being changed any more! This
   leads to another rule for I/O and balancing in particular.

I/O RULE #18
*Know your applications and the nature of
the user community activity before you run
out and make some hasty changes to try
and relieve what appears to be an I/O
balancing problem.*

Performance Pack Monitoring

Within the OEM Performance Pack, you can view the I/O for all selected files. Using this facility, you can observe both the cumulative and current read and write activity by file. By analyzing this information, you can pinpoint which files are used most heavily, making sure that they are on separate disks and separate disk controllers.

If just one or a few files seem to be seeing a majority of I/O activity, the objects in these files should be looked at closely. If the files contain multiple objects, you should try to separate out these objects either into new files or in existing files that have very low I/O activity on them. If the file contains only one object, then you should consider striping that object. As discussed earlier in this chapter, striping is the process of using multiple files to store an object, in the hope that the I/O can then be distributed among the striped files located on separate disks.

utlbstat/utlestat Monitoring

Oracle provides another tool that is of great assistance in determining I/O by file: the UTLBstat/UTLEstat facility (which will be explained in greater detail in Chapter 5). It is mentioned here because of its relevance to I/O. The utlbstat.sql and utlstat.sql scripts collect database information at different times and compare the two sets of information in a report. Part of this facility is a read/write report by both datafile and tablespace. This report points out hot spots for both reads and writes within your system. The next listing gives an example of the file I/O output from UTLBstat/UTLEstat. The output has been edited, cutting out all columns except physical reads and writes.

TS	FILE_NAME	PHYS_READS	PHYS_WRITES
AP	/tunafsh9/prdxy/ap01.dbf	34673	523
APX	/tunafsh10/prdxy/apx01.dbf	6808	501
AR	/tunafsh9/prdxy/ar01.dbf	3	0
CONV	/tunafsh2/prdxy/conv01.dbf	1236	369
FA	/tunafsh11/prdxy/fa01.dbf	18916	14
FAX	/tunafsh12/prdxy/fax01.dbf	24804	33
FND	/tunafsh13/prdxy/fnd01.dbf	16815	731
FNDX	/tunafsh14/prdxy/fndx01.dbf	5640	1921
GL	/tunafsh7/prdxy/gl01.dbf	66061	239

```
GL        /tunafsh7/prdxy/gl02.dbf          3743        45
GLX       /tunafsh8/prdxy/glx01.dbf        16873       713
HR        /tunafsh13/prdxy/hr01.dbf        13895        99
HR        /tunafsh13/prdxy/hr02.dbf         1824        23
HRX       /tunafsh14/prdxy/hrx01.dbf        1839       188
HRX       /tunafsh14/prdxy/hrx02.dbf         258        21
PO        /tunafsh9/prdxy/po01.dbf         12089       583
POX       /tunafsh10/prdxy/pox01.dbf        3081      1081
RBS       /tunafsh5/prdxy/rbs01.dbf          177      2822
RBS1      /tunafsh6/prdxy/rbs101.dbf          34       616
SYSTEM    /tunafsh1/prdxy/system01.dbf      8502      1024
SYSTEM    /tunafsh1/prdxy/system02.dbf      6948       340
TEMP      /tunafsh11/prdxy/temp03.dbf         17      1064
TEMP      /tunafsh12/prdxy/temp02.dbf         20      3081
TEMP      /tunafsh14/prdxy/temp01.dbf         10       228
```

Based on a total 244,266 reads and 16,259 writes, Table 3-3 summarizes by device.

Device	% Reads	% Writes
1	6	8
2	1	2
5	0	17
6	0	4
7	29	1
8	7	4
9	19	7
10	4	10
11	8	7
12	10	19
13	14	5
14	3	14

TABLE 3-3. *Read and Write Operations by Device*

From examining the statistics in the PHYS READS (data read from the database files) and PHYS WRITES columns (data written to the database files), we notice the following and can begin to draw some conclusions leading to some initial recommendations for load balancing:

1. The application the database supports is primarily retrieval-based since the reads account for 94 percent of the I/O activity and writes a mere 6 percent.

2. Almost one fifth of the read activities are to device #9, containing the AR, PO, and AP tablespaces. This device should be monitored as a potential I/O hot spot. In the future, armed with further evidence, we may consider striping some objects in the AP tablespace since it accounts for three times more reads than PO.

3. More than one quarter of the read activities are to device #7, containing the GL tablespace. This device should be monitored as well. Access by object may be required to determine just what is being hit the most.

4. Almost one fifth of the write activity is done to device #12, containing TEMP and the FAX tablespaces. This makes sense, since the temporary segment and an index tablespace are expected to be high write activity as rows are retrieved/sorted and data modified and created.

Hot Spots by Object

Detection of high-activity objects in the Oracle8 database conjures up visions of what has become one of the most dreaded words to so many DBAs—AUDIT. Oracle8 allows you to set up a wide range of auditing activities to permit tracking of instance activity such as the number of connections by time period all the way to select activity against individual objects. Auditing puts a bad taste in many DBA's mouths. Table 3-4 outlines some potential problems with auditing and offers a way around for anyone feeling it is problematic.

Problem/Question	Workaround/Explanation
The performance hit of auditing is unknown and therefore too scary to consider.	The hit is well under 5 percent, though heavy auditing activity will inevitably have a larger impact. When deciding what and when to audit, take this into consideration.
The volume of audit information will blow up the SYSTEM tablespace.	Be smart! Move data regularly out of SYSTEM or, better still, move it into summary format in another tablespace and wipe SYS.AUD$ table nightly.

TABLE 3-4.   *Common Complaints About Auditing*

The DBA_AUDIT_OBJECT view owned by SYS is where object access audit information is stored. The columns in bold and italics are the ones we use to audit object access:

```
SQL> desc dba_audit_object
 Name                            Null?    Type
 ------------------------------- -------- ----
 OS_USERNAME                              VARCHAR2(255)
 USERNAME                                 VARCHAR2(30)
 USERHOST                                 VARCHAR2(128)
 TERMINAL                                 VARCHAR2(255)
 TIMESTAMP                       NOT NULL DATE
 OWNER                                    VARCHAR2(30)
 OBJ_NAME                                 VARCHAR2(128)
 ACTION_NAME                              VARCHAR2(27)
 NEW_OWNER                                VARCHAR2(30)
 NEW_NAME                                 VARCHAR2(128)
 SES_ACTIONS                              VARCHAR2(19)
 COMMENT_TEXT                             VARCHAR2(4000)
 SESSIONID                       NOT NULL NUMBER
 ENTRYID                         NOT NULL NUMBER
 STATEMENTID                     NOT NULL NUMBER
```

```
RETURNCODE                     NOT NULL NUMBER
PRIV_USED                               VARCHAR2(40)
OBJECT_LABEL                            RAW MLSLABEL
SESSION_LABEL                           RAW MLSLABEL
```

Let's turn on audit by access for the tables owned by BLAIRR:

```
SQL> set pages 0 ver off feed off echo off term off
SQL> spool sch_audit.sql
SQL> select 'audit select on blairr.'||table_name||' by access;'
  2    from sys.dba_tables
  3   where owner = 'BLAIRR';
SQL> spool off
SQL> start sch_audit
```

NOTE
*Before the audit will start to work, you must
set the initialization parameter file entry
audit_trail=true and have the Oracle8 instance
restarted.*

Reporting on Audit Information

Reporting on access by object is a two-step process. Before doing this, you
need to create an audit summary table with the pertinent columns from
DBA_AUDIT_OBJECT, using an SQL statement similar to the following:

```
SQL> create table audit_summary (
  2    owner                   varchar2(30),
  3    obj_name                varchar2(30),
  4    cal_day                 date,
  5    c_access                number);
Table created.
SQL>
```

First, you copy data from DBA_AUDIT_OBJECT into the summary table,
grouping by object and calendar day. Next, you delete audit rows from
SYS.AUD$ for days prior to the current day. Use code resembling the
following to accomplish the desired work:

```
SQL> -- Only copy rows from yesterday ... any earlier data will have been
SQL> -- deleted yesterday by SQL statement after the insert.
SQL> insert into audit_summary
```

```
  2    select owner, obj_name, trunc(timestamp), count(*)
  3      from sys.dba_audit_object
  4     where trunc(timestamp) < trunc(sysdate-1)
  5     group by owner, obj_name, trunc(timestamp);
1210 rows created.
SQL> -- Delete yesterday's data.
SQL> delete sys.aud$
  2    where trunc(timestamp) < trunc(sysdate);
```

Let's look at a report on the summary data before we move on:

```
SQL> select owner, obj_name, cal_day, c_access
  2      from audit_summary
  3     order by cal_day;
OWNER                      OBJ_NAME           CAL_DAY        C_ACCESS
-----------------------    ----------------   -----------    ---------
BLAIRR                     ADDRESS            12-DEC-1999         212
BLAIRR                     ADDRESS            13-DEC-1999         309
BLAIRR                     ADDRESS            14-DEC-1999         322
BLAIRR                     ADDRESS            15-DEC-1999         221
...
...
BLAIRR                     LOCATION           12-DEC-1999        3232
BLAIRR                     LOCATION           13-DEC-1999        3209
BLAIRR                     LOCATION           14-DEC-1999        3210
BLAIRR                     LOCATION           15-DEC-1999        4221
```

An even better way would be using a query that orders the accesses descending and does not worry about the day of the week, as in:

```
SQL> select owner, obj_name, count(*)
  2      from audit_summary
  3     group by owner, obj_name
  4     order by 3 desc;
OWNER                   OBJ_NAME                  COUNT(*)
----------------------  ------------------------  --------
BLAIRR                  LOCATION                    388990
BLAIRR                  PERSON                      230990
...
...
BLAIRR                  ADDRESS                      22981
```

By examining the output from the query, we can easily zero in on the high activity objects and ensure they are somehow placed in different tablespaces on different devices. Before we move on, since we like to practice what we preach, let's show you how to turn off audit by access.

Turning Auditing Off

The following code can be used to turn off audit against the same BLAIRR schema:

```
SQL> set pages 0 ver off feed off echo off term off
SQL> spool sch_noaudit.sql
SQL> select 'noaudit select on blairr.'||table_name||';'
  2    from sys.dba_tables
  3    where owner = 'BLAIRR';
SQL> spool off
SQL> start sch_noaudit
```

I/O RULE #19
Ensure you monitor the size and record count in your SYS audit tables when auditing using Oracle8 and develop a mechanism from day one to wipe the contents daily after moving the information to a summary table.

Proper Table and Index Sizing

The discussion so far has focused on where to put your database objects, which is very important. Equally important is the size these table and index objects are created. The size of the tables and indexes determines the needed size of the tablespaces to hold them, which, in turn, determines which tablespaces can physically fit on how many disks and in which combination.

Another point that should be kept in mind when sizing tables and indexes is the **pctfree** factor, which sets aside a certain percentage of the data block for future use. If the record is to be updated in such a way that NULL fields will be populated or VARCHAR2 fields will have their values updated to a longer value, then a higher **pctfree** factor should be used. But the use of a high **pctfree** factor should be used with caution. The higher the

pctfree, the fewer data rows that can fit into a block. Because Oracle always reads in block increments, the more data per block, the more data is read in one read. Therefore, an accurate determination of the **pctfree** factor of each table and index is important.

The sum of the **pctfree** and the **pctused** must always be less than or equal to 100 and must be chosen so that a block on the free block list does not keep getting switched from available to not available to store data. This will reduce the performance overhead of moving a block on and off the free block list (see Chapter 6 for more on the free block list).

Along with the proper sizing of your database objects (i.e., tables, indexes, and tablespaces) you should also make an effort to standardize this sizing as best as possible. If a tablespace has only one object in it, the database files in the tablespace should be sized as an even increment of the next extent plus the initial extent and an overhead amount (assuming a percent increase of 0). This way, unusable space won't be left in the tablespace.

Sizing Using Formulae

The Oracle8 Server Administrator's Guide (Release 8.0.3) Appendix A provides formulae for the sizing of schema objects. The data and index segments are the segment types you need to size appropriately to provide for:

- Optimal utilization of existing database space

- Optimal packing of information into the Oracle data blocks

- Anticipated growth of the amount of data as the system operates

Let's briefly look at the process to calculate the space required for nonclustered tables (used with permission of Oracle Corporation). *Clustering* is a special storage method that allows you to store tables that are frequently accessed together in the same data block. This reduces the amount of I/O required to retrieve data from these tables during normal system operation. Before embarking on this exercise, we need to get some constant values from the V$TYPE_SIZE and V$PARAMETER dictionary views; the output of two queries showing the desired rows is shown in the next listing.

NOTE
*The query against V$TYPE_SIZE was done
against a Windows NT 4.0 Oracle8 database.
It is possible the values may be different if you
query Oracle8 on some other platform.*

```
SQL> select type, description, type_size
  2    from v$type_size
  3    where type in ('UB1', 'UB2', 'UB4', 'SB2','KCBH',
  4                   'KTBIT','KTBBH','KDBH','KDBT');
TYPE      DESCRIPTION                         TYPE_SIZE
--------  ----------------------------------  ----------
UB1       UNSIGNED BYTE 1                             1
UB2       UNSIGNED BYTE 2                             2
UB4       UNSIGNED BYTE 4                             4
SB2       SIGNED BYTE 2                               2
KCBH      BLOCK COMMON HEADER                        20
KTBIT     TRANSACTION VARIABLE HEADER                24
KTBBH     TRANSACTION FIXED HEADER                   48
KDBH      DATA HEADER                                14
KDBT      TABLE DIRECTORY ENTRY                       4
9 rows selected.
SQL> select value
  2    from v$parameter
  3    where name = 'db_block_size';
VALUE
--------------------------------------------------------
2048
SQL>
```

A quick word on INITRANS before looking at the following formulae.
This keyword controls the number of transaction slots available in the
header portion of each data block to allow concurrent transaction access to
data in the same block. A sample LOCATION table will be used for the
exercise made up of the following columns:

```
Name                             Null?    Type
-------------------------------  -------  ----
LOC_ID                                    NUMBER(6)
LOCATION_NAME                             VARCHAR2(30)
PROVINCE_ID                               VARCHAR2(2)
LOC_TYPE                                  VARCHAR2(2)
```

1. Space available for data (SAD) = data block size - block header size =

   ```
   db_block_size - kcbh - ub4 - ktbbh - (initrans-1) * ktbit - kdbh
   2048 - 20 - 4 - 48 - (2-1) * 24 - 14
   2048 - 20 - 4 - 48 - 24 - 14 = 1938 bytes
   ```

2. Available data space (ADS) =

   ```
   ceil (SAD * (1 - pctfree/100)) - kdbt
   ceil (1938 * (1-20/100)) - 4 [we use a pctfree of 20 for this sample]
   ceil (1938 * .8 ) - 4 = 1551 - 4 = 1547 bytes
   ```

3. Space used per row (SPR) =

   ```
   column size including byte length =
          column size + (1, if column size < 250, else 3)
   -- For all the columns in LOC (assuming the average LOCATION_NAME is
   -- 11 characters
   LOC_ID            6 + 1 =  7
   LOCATION_NAME    30 + 1 = 31
   PROVINCE_ID       2 + 1 =  3
   LOC_TYPE          2 + 1 =  3    For a total of 44 bytes (TCS)
   ```

4. Rowsize (ROWSZ) =

   ```
   3 * ub1 + TCS = 3 * 1 + 44 = 47 bytes
   ```

5. Space used per row (SPROW) =

   ```
   max (ub1 * 3 + ub4 + sb2, ROWSZ) + sb2
   max (1 * 3 + 4 + 2 , 47) + 2 = 49
   max (9 , 47) + 2 = 49 bytes
   ```

6. Number of rows per block (RPB) =

   ```
   floor (ADS / SPROW) = floor (1547/49) = 31 rows per data block
   ```

Armed with the rows per data block, we can then calculate the correct storage parameters for the LOCATION table, knowing there are 390,000 rows to be loaded:

```
SQL> -- Ceil (390000 [rows] / 31 [rows per data block]) = 12581 blocks
SQL> -- 12581 blocks @ 2048 bytes per block = 12581 * 2048 = 25765888 bytes
SQL> -- We allow 20% extra space for record creation bringing the initial
SQL> -- allocation up to 30 megabytes.
```

```
SQL> create table location (
  2   loc_id                   number(6),
  3   location_name            varchar2(30),
  4   province_id              varchar2(2),
  5   loc_type                 varchar2(2))
  6   storage (initial 30m next 4m pctincrease 0);
Table created.
SQL>
```

I/O RULE #20
*When using formulae, keep
in mind the results are a guesstimate, and
assume an average column length (we guessed
the average LOCATION_NAME would be
18 characters) which could produce
erroneous results.*

Sizing Using Existing Data Segments

Another way to properly size tables and indexes is by reading present table
or index storage characteristics and rebuilding the segment based on the
allocations currently in use. Suppose a query against ADD_OWNER's
USER_EXTENTS view yielded the following results:

```
SQL> select segment_name, segment_type, tablespace_name, extent_id,
  2            bytes
  3      from user_extents
  4    where segment_name = 'ADDRESS';
```

SEGMENT_NAME	SEGMENT_TYPE	TABLESPACE_NAME	EXTENT_ID	BYTES
ADDRESS	TABLE	ADDRESS_DATA	0	31457280
ADDRESS	TABLE	ADDRESS_DATA	1	31457280
ADDRESS	TABLE	ADDRESS_DATA	2	31477380
ADDRESS	TABLE	ADDRESS_DATA	3	31457280

```
4 records selected.
SQL>
```

Armed with this output, it is very simple to rebuild the ADDRESS table
by exporting the table, building an SQL script to reset the storage
parameters (with the **indexfile=** parameter), precreating the table with the
fixed storage parameters, then bringing the data back in using import. Using
our ADDRESS table as an example, when the object was originally created,

it was given storage parameters of **initial 30m next 30m pctincrease 0** and, after the exercise building the create script with adjusted parameters, the storage was set up as **initial 120m next 120m pctincrease 0**.

VLDB
When a very large database is used to store information for a data warehouse, this method (i.e., sizing according to the status of existing segments) is the most efficient and easiest way to properly size objects. Periodically, before part or all of the warehouse is refreshed, glean existing extent information from the data dictionary and adjust storage parameters where necessary to reduce extent allocation.

Space—What Is Really Being Used?

Not only must database objects be properly sized, but these objects and the space that they are using must be continually monitored. Once an extent in a tablespace is assigned to a table or index, it would be desirable to know how much of that extent is actually being used by data and how many blocks are empty. There are a number of ways to do this for a table, and there is one way for indexes.

Space Used in a Table—After Initial Load

When data is first placed in an empty table after the load activity, use the SQL*Plus **analyze** command to gather statistics and populate a few data dictionary tables with row information. The DBA_TABLES view owned by SYS is where the information lies that we need for the exercise. The following listing shows the column names we want to inspect cut from a **describe** of SYS.DBA_TABLES:

```
OWNER                              NOT NULL VARCHAR2(30)
TABLE_NAME                         NOT NULL VARCHAR2(30)
...
```

```
NUM_ROWS                               NUMBER
BLOCKS                                 NUMBER
EMPTY_BLOCKS                           NUMBER
...
AVG_ROW_LEN                            NUMBER
...
```

Suppose after analyzing the ADDRESS table, the statistics in Table 3-5 are displayed from this dictionary view. The columns highlighted with three asterisks are used in the next section where we look at the space in use in a table that is not brand new.

I/O RULE #21
The EMPTY_BLOCKS column in the DBA_TABLES view is the number of blocks that have never contained any data since the table was created. Blocks whose rows have been deleted and have become empty are not included in this column value.

Column	Contents	
OWNER	ADD_OWNER	
TABLE_NAME	ADDRESS	
NUM_ROWS	11988293	***
BLOCKS	300000	
EMPTY_BLOCKS	75000	
AVG_ROW_LEN	41	***

TABLE 3-5. *ADDRESS Table Statistics*

This rule is why we specify a brand new table as opposed to one that has been around for a while and undergone significant activity. The next listing shows the work we have discussed so far.

```
SQL> analyze table add_owner.address estimate statistics sample 20 percent;
Table analyzed.
SQL> select empty_blocks
  2    from sys.dba_tables
  3    where owner = 'ADD_OWNER'
  4      and table_name = 'ADDRESS';
    EMPTY_BLOCKS
----------------
           75000
SQL>
```

Armed with this information, we can move one step further and figure out roughly how many more rows will fit into ADDRESS given the average row length of 41 bytes using the following formula (assuming a **pctfree** of 20).

```
more_rows = empty_blocks * db_block_size * (100 - pctfree) / 100 / avg_row_len
          = 75000 * 2048 * 80 / 100 / 41 =  2997073
```

NOTE
This is an approximation and must be interpreted as a guideline for the additional rows that will fit into the ADDRESS table.

Space Used in a Table—Any Time During Its Existence

This task differs from the previous since the value in the EMPTY_BLOCKS column cannot be interpreted as we may assume. In other words, suppose the ADDRESS table is analyzed after six months of activity and the

EMPTY_BLOCKS value drops from 75,000 to 43,000. We cannot assume that 43,000 blocks of the 300,000 allocated are empty. We can only deduce that 43,000 blocks have never contained any data. The next listing shows how to estimate the space in use in the ADDRESS table. The listing uses the collection results shown in Table 3-5.

```
space_in_use (SIU) = num_rows * avg_row_len
                   =  11988293 * 41 = 491520013 bytes
space_allocated (SA) = blocks * db_block_size
                     = 300000 * 2048 =  614400000 bytes
more_rows = (SA - SIU) * (100 - pctfree) / 100 / avg_row_len
          = (614400000 - 491520013) * 80 / 100 / 41 =  2397658
```

Before we move on to look at space usage for indexes, let's look at the difference between the two figures calculated in the last two sections. We estimated the ADDRESS table after its initial load (using the value in EMPTY_BLOCKS) would hold an additional 3 million rows, whereas the other method (calculation based on NUM_ROWS, BLOCKS, and AVG_ROW_LEN) left us with a row estimate of 2.4 million rows. We believe the second number is the better one to go by for the following reasons:

- The table, having undergone record creation, update, and deletion, is more than likely not capable of holding as many rows as we may have deduced immediately after creation.

- The theory of space management is one thing, but our experience shows that the implementation of that theory is not as efficient in the real world as the theory itself. Oracle8 does a nice job of packing rows into blocks up to the appropriate value as specified by **pctfree**, but in practice the data uses a bit more space than it does on paper.

Space Used in an Index

For indexes, Oracle provides the same utility, **analyze**, to see how much space is actually being used. The **analyze index** statement with the **validate structure** qualifier is used to check a particular index for consistency. This statement uses the index as its source and can detect the following:

- Invalid index formats or bad index structure

■ Index entries that do not match row data, or a bad index (as when an index entry has no matching row)

During this validation process, two tables are populated that hold information about the index. These tables can be queried and statistical information about the index can be reported. The tables are INDEX_STATS and INDEX_HISTOGRAM. The next listing shows the columns that are in each of these tables and what information is contained in each column:

```
INDEX_STATS
-----------
HEIGHT                    height of the b-tree
BLOCKS                    blocks allocated to the segment
NAME                      name of the index
PARTITION_NAME            name of the index partition, if partitioned
LF_ROWS                   number of leaf rows (values in the index)
LF_BLKS                   number of leaf blocks in the b-tree
LF_ROWS_LEN               sum of the lengths of all the leaf rows
LF_BLK_LEN                useable space in a leaf block
BR_ROWS                   number of branch rows
BR_BLKS                   number of branch blocks in the b-tree
BR_ROWS_LEN               sum of the lengths of all the branch blocks in the
                          b-tree
BR_BLK_LEN                useable space in a branch block
DEL_LF_ROWS               number of deleted leaf rows in the index
DEL_LF_ROWS_LEN           total length of all deleted rows in the index
DISTINCT_KEYS             number of distinct keys in the index
MOST_REPEATED_KEY         how many times the most repeated key is repeated
BTREE_SPACE               total space currently allocated in the b-tree
USED_SPACE                total space that is currently being used in the
                          b-tree
PCT_USED                  percent of space allocated in the b-tree that is
                          being used
ROWS_PER_KEY              average number of rows per distinct key
BLKS_GETS_PER_ACCESS      Expected number of consistent mode block gets per
                          row. This assumes that a row chosen at random from
                          the table is being searched for using the index

INDEX_HISTOGRAM
---------------
REPEAT_COUNT              number of times that a key is repeated
KEYS_WITH_REPEAT_COUNT    number of keys that are repeated REPEAT_COUNT
```

By querying the two tables, you can determine statistical information about the index. The actual space in use can be found in the PCT_USED column with the following query and the sample output in the next listing:

```
SQL> select pct_used
  2  from index_stats;
    PCT_USED
------------
          92
SQL>
```

Based on the activity of the underlying table, you can then decide whether the index needs more space or should be reorganized. The fast index rebuild, discussed in the next section, is the best way to rebuild an index; indexes can easily be rebuilt using export and SQL*Plus as well, which is discussed afterwards.

Fast Index Rebuild

Oracle8 permits quick reorganization of indexes. Before this new facility existed, the only way to rebuild an index was by using export and import of the table the index referred to or dropping and then re-creating the index using standard SQL. Indexes become badly fragmented just as tables do, but their management is easier using the following SQL statement:

```
alter index sample_index_name rebuild;
```

Oracle reads the existing index segment, building a fresh copy of the index. It does not access the data segment during the rebuild.

I/O RULE #22
*When rebuilding an index with the **alter index ... rebuild** command, the data that the index relates to cannot be modified while the index is being rewritten. Timeout Oracle errors will be raised if the data segment is not quiet during the rebuild exercise.*

Rebuilding Index Using Export/SQL*Plus

One way to rebuild an index is to extract the index creation statement from the Oracle8 data dictionary using the export program. Using Windows NT as an example, the next listing shows a batch file that can be used to extract the index creation statement with the proper storage parameters:

```
rem * Index extract statement program
rem * MASI Inc.  August 1999
rem
rem  By specifying rows=n, export extracts no data, just the SQL statements
rem  required to recreate all aspects of the table's characteristics.
exp80 userid=add_owner/abc123 tables=address rows=n file=addr_nr
rem  With the export complete, we now read the dump file and put the index
rem  creation statements in an SQL file to be run in SQL*Plus.
imp80 userid=add_owner/abc123 file=addr_nr fully indexfile=addr_ind.sql
```

When this batch file completes, the addr_ind.sql script will contain the table create and index create statements that can then be passed to SQL*Plus. The file will require some attention if you want it to run error free by using your favorite text editor and cutting out all lines that contain the **connect** command or a number followed by the text "rows" (not all indexfile files contain this second line). A few lines from addr_ind.sql are shown in the next listing. Cut or comment out the line that is bolded. The index being re-created must be dropped before addr_ind.sql can be run.

```
...
...
REM   MAXTRANS 255 LOGGING STORAGE(INITIAL 317440 NEXT 102400 MINEXTENTS 1
REM   MAXEXTENTS 2147483645 PCTINCREASE 0 FREELISTS 1 FREELIST GROUPS 1
REM   BUFFER_POOL DEFAULT) TABLESPACE "ADDRESS_DATA" ;
CONNECT ADDRESS;
CREATE INDEX "ADD_OWNER"."ADDRESS_1" ON "ADDRESS" ("LOC_ID" ) PCTFREE 10
INITRANS 2 MAXTRANS 255 STORAGE (INITIAL 71680 NEXT 36864 MINEXTENTS 1 MAXEXTENTS
121 PCTINCREASE 50 FREELISTS 1 FREELIST GROUPS 1 BUFFER_POOL DEFAULT)
TABLESPACE "ADDRESS_INDEX" LOGGING ;
```

Reclaiming Space in Indexes for Deleted Rows

When rows are deleted from Oracle8 tables, the index entries pointing at those rows are marked, but the space the index entry consumed is not reused until the index is rebuilt. To investigate the amount of deleted leaf rows consuming space, let's look at a table that was previously created and then altered to add a primary key:

```
SQL> create table test_dlf (
  2        test_dlf_id      number(5),
  3        tdlf_desce       varchar2(20),
  4        tdlf_descf       varchar2(20));
Table created.
SQL> alter table test_dlf add constraint test_dlf_pk primary
  2        key (test_dlf_id) using index;
Table altered.
```

The following SQL can be used to look at the DEL_LF_ROWS count in the primary key index:

```
SQL> analyze index test_dlf_pk validate structure;
Index analyzed.
SQL> select del_lf_rows from index_stats;
DEL_LF_ROWS
-----------
          0
```

After the table has undergone activity with some deletions, the same code displays the following results:

```
SQL> analyze index test_dlf_pk validate structure;
Index analyzed.
SQL> select del_lf_rows from index_stats;
DEL_LF_ROWS
-----------
        981
```

Using the fast index rebuild discussed in the previous section, the deleted leaf row entries can be reclaimed using the SQL statement

```
SQL> alter index test_dlf_pk rebuild;
Index altered.
```

Miscellaneous Tuning of Space Allocation and I/O

Just before closing this chapter in the journey, let's cover a few miscellaneous tuning issues that enable the Oracle8 DBA to do a more efficient job of space management—so closely related to what can mushroom into significant I/O bottlenecks if not attended to.

Reclaiming Unused Space

Often we allocate huge amounts of space for some objects and then, down the road, realize they have shrunk to a row count that requires significantly less space. Our experience has shown this often happens as user requirements change in reporting databases (datamarts and data warehouses) when the user community decides to do lots of aggregation and summarization on what used to be very detailed data. Suppose there is a hierarchy of geographical areas for drill-down using an end-user query tool—continent, country, quadrant, region, sector, city, district, and, finally, outlet. In June 1997, the user community needs information broken down and stored at the outlet level; in February 1998, they are happy with city. The table originally contained 1,080,000 rows and occupied 40 megabytes of database space for data and 110 for indexes. In February 1998, the table is found to have 77,000 rows on the average, using 5 megabytes for data and 11 for indexes. Along comes the following SQL statement:

```
alter table used_to_be_humungous deallocate unused;
```

It gets better. The smart DBA may decide that the user community's expectations are a moving target and, in order to plan for the inevitable change of heart, decides to keep some of the unused space. The DBA includes the KEEP section and the statement becomes:

```
alter table used_to_be_humungous deallocate unused keep XXXX;
```

A few words about the KEEP keyword before we move on. The space quantity mentioned after KEEP (measured in bytes, kilobytes, or megabytes) tells Oracle8 to keep that amount of unallocated space; it does not tell Oracle8 to keep that amount of absolute space. Suppose a table has three extents—extent 1 is 2 megabytes and occupied, extent 2 is 2 megabytes and 50 percent full, and extent 3 is sized at 2 megabytes and totally empty. With the statement **alter table blah_blah_blah deallocate unused keep 1m;**, the second extent stays at 2 megabytes. Its first megabyte of space contains data, and the **alter table** statement instructs Oracle8 to keep 1 megabyte of the unused space.

Striping Using Partitioning

With Oracle8 and the partitioning option, off-the-shelf SQL can be used to manually stripe a table or index by primary key range. Chapter 4 is dedicated to partitioning which, for many DBAs managing very large databases, will become second nature to optimal space management. Partitioning alone is a feature that will end up convincing many installations to make the move to Oracle8.

VLDB
As you will see in Chapter 4, partitioning alone is one of the best ways to handle the management of very large databases.

Tweaking pctfree to Stripe a Table or Index

Another trick you can use to stripe an object is by fiddling with the **pctfree** value as the object is loaded. Suppose the ADDRESS table was designed to have a **pctfree** value of 20, meaning that 20 percent of the data space in each block will be reserved for updates to existing rows. Expecting a 50 percent growth rate over the first year, the ADDRESS table, sitting in a database with a 2K (2,048 bytes) data block, sets aside roughly 400 bytes for row updates. Let's issue the following statement before the table is loaded with data:

```
SQL> alter table address pctfree 50;
Table altered.
```

Now about 1,000 bytes of each data block will be allocated for row updates, meaning the load will not pack the row as full and Oracle will be forced to spread the data into many more empty blocks. The exercise will inevitably cause the segment to span more than one datafile, which is the object of the exercise in the first place. When the table is loaded, issue the following command to reset the value for **pctfree**:

```
alter table address pctfree 20;
```

I/O RULE #23
When striping an object by altering the value of **pctfree***, be sure you set it back to its proper value before turning on access to the user community.*

pctused and the Free List

Oracle maintains a list of data blocks that are candidates for row insertion in memory. The free list entries are by table, and the inclusion of a data block's address is governed by logic that resembles the following.

```
if amount of data in block falls below pctused
    place data block on free list
else
    data block is full and can receive no more rows
end if
```

Sometimes we set **pctused** artificially high and **pctfree** artificially low hoping Oracle will pack the block to the maximum. Often we have seen a table create with **pctfree 0 pctused 99**. This can prove to be an I/O nightmare and can cause a drop in performance when the situation exists for many, many tables. Let's look at the ADDRESS table with an average row length of 41 bytes. Using the 99 percent figure (pretending all 2,048 bytes are available for data storage—which we know is not really the case), a block would be marked as eligible for row creation when 2,028 bytes are occupied, or roughly 20 bytes are still available. This is not enough to hold the average row, and Oracle will do the following when trying to create a row:

1. Search the block IDs on the free list for one that can accommodate the new row.

2. If one is found, it will insert the row and, if the occupied space is still below the figure mentioned in the table's **pctused**, leave the block on the free list.

3. If it does not find one, it will look through the data dictionary for the location of a data block capable of accepting the new data.

We have a formula we use to ensure this situation does not occur.

NOTE
The figure 501 was calculated for the
ADDRESS table in the "Sizing Using Formulae"
section of this chapter.

```
pctused = floor ((available_space - length_1_row) / data_block_size * 100)
        = floor((1501 - 41 ) / 2048 * 100)
        = floor(1460 / 2048 * 100) = 71 percent
```

I/O RULE #24
Use a value for **pctused** *such that a data block*
does not appear on the free list that is unable
to accept a row at record creation time.

Modifying SQL.BSQ

SQL.BSQ is a file sitting in \ORANT\RDBMS80\ADMIN on a Windows NT machine running Oracle8. When you create a new database, the SQL **create database** statement reads this file as it defines the system tablespace and some objects crucial to starting the database for the subsequent setup. There is one table in particular whose storage parameters you should consider changing before a database is created. The OBJ$ table records the existence of every object in the database. Its contents are read continually as Oracle operates, and fragmentation of the table can be a performance hit. OBJ$ is created with **storage (initial 10k next 10k maxextents unlimited pctincrease 0)**. With large databases, especially those with thousands of objects, the parameters should be changed to something along the lines of **storage (initial 4m next 4m pctincrease 0)**. The following listing shows how extended this object becomes over time.

```
SQL> select count(*)
  2    from user_extents
  3   where segment_name = 'OBJ$';
  COUNT(*)
----------
        14
SQL> select sum(bytes)
  2    from user_extents
  3   where segment_name = 'OBJ$';
SUM(BYTES)
----------
   7839744
SQL> select count(*)
  2    from obj$;
  COUNT(*)
----------
     63275
SQL>
```

VLDB
The parameters for a large database of a few hundred gigabytes and up to thousands of objects should have **initial 10m next 10m** *to accommodate all the objects in one or two extents.*

Let's Tune It

This chapter dealt with a number of issues relating to I/O for tuning an Oracle database. To summarize, here are the highlights or main points of this chapter:

■ Create separate tablespaces for heavily accessed tables and their indexes and put them on separate disks.

- Never put application or user objects in the system tablespace.

- You can plan your data distribution better by knowing how your users will be accessing the data.

- Place objects that are most often referenced simultaneously and frequently on separate disks.

- Stripe large objects over multiple disks.

- Create user-defined rollback tablespaces to hold rollback segments.

- Put rollback segments in at least two tablespaces and interleaf their order in the initialization parameter file.

- Create at least one tablespace for the exclusive use of temporary segments and assign users this tablespace as their temporary tablespace.

- Put your redo groups/member on disks that have low incidences of reads and writes.

- Distribute your I/O evenly over disk controllers.

- Identify and reduce disk and object hot spots.

- Properly size your tables, indexes, and tablespaces.

- Monitor the space allocated and used by your tables and indexes and make adjustments when necessary.

Oracle7.x Specifics

Please note the following points organized by the headings for some of the sections of this chapter:

- "Accessing the DBA and V$ Views Owned by SYS"   The names of the V$ and DBA views change from release to release, and you will find more views and differences in existing views from Oracle7.x to Oracle8.

- "Table and Index Segments"   The ROWID of the Oracle7.x database is still the BARF (Block Address Row File) format in hexadecimal notation.

■ "Index-organized Tables" This feature is not available in Oracle 7.x.

■ "Manual Extent Allocation to Stripe a Table" All of this syntax is available in 7.x but not 7.0.xx.

■ "Row Migration and Row Chaining" All of this material is applicable to Oracle7.x, but beware of the different format of the ROWID when looking at the contents of the CHAINED_ROWS table.

■ "Rollback Segments" All of this information is applicable to Oracle7.x.

■ "Reducing Fragmentation" This material is applicable to Oracle7.x, though the look and feel of the work with the Tablespace Manager is different with earlier versions of the Oracle Enterprise Manager.

■ "Coalescing Free Space" The **alter tablespace … coalesce;** statement is not available in Oracle 7.0.x, 7.1.x, or 7.2.x.

■ "Temporary Segments" All of this material is applicable to Oracle7.x except the section about dedicated temporary tablespace, which only works in 7.3.x.

■ "Redo Logs" All of this material is applicable to Oracle7.x; the column makeup of the two V$ views may be different between Oracle8 and Oracle7.x.

■ "Hot Spots" All of this information is applicable to Oracle7.x, though, again, you may find the V$ view makeup different with Oracle7.x.

■ "Sizing Using Formulae" These calculations are Oracle8 specific, and the appropriate Oracle7.x Server Administrator's Guide should be consulted for version-specific details.

■ "Space—What Is Really Being Used" This applies to Oracle7.x as well, except for the Fast Index Rebuild section which is not available with releases 7.0.x, 7.1.x, and 7.2.x.

■ "Reclaiming Unused Space" The **alter table … deallocate unused** statement is not available with Oracle7 versions 7.0.x, 7.1.x, or 7.2.x.

■ "Striping Using Partitioning" This is not available at all with any release of Oracle7.

CHAPTER

4

Partitioning

artitioning allows the database administrator to break up large objects into more manageable pieces. Oracle8 Server can store as many as 512 petabytes of data in its repository—or the equivalent of 576,460,752,303,423,488 bytes of information. Numbers this large seem out of reach of our imagination. However, multiterabyte repositories exist today and seem to be growing as we speak. In this chapter of *Oracle8 Tuning*, we are going to cover some theory related to working with partitioned tables. At first, partitioning sounds like a dream come true; don't get us wrong, we think it is. However, as soon as you start working with range partitioning in Oracle8, you will need a baseline understanding of the nuances and idiosyncrasies involved. Without this, you may find the behavior of the Partitioning Option unpredictable. This is not the case, however; stand up, give yourself a shake, and carry on…

Partitioning and the Tuning Process

Availability is a key component in the tuning process. When data is unavailable, the users suffer downtime that affects their ability to go about their day-to-day business. With the increasing size of many databases, the DBA (database administrator) continually finds the need to work with portions of these large information repositories. Partitioning aids the tuning exercise by:

- Allowing you to work with information in one area without affecting the availability of data elsewhere. For example, the DBA can reorganize, defragment, or refresh one partition in a partitioned table without affecting the availability of data resident in the table's other partitions.

- Streamlining the setup of additional ranges of primary key values by simply creating an additional partition. Suppose a company rolls its fiscal year over December 31 and needs to start capturing requisition information for the new year. You simply add a partition to the appropriate table without affecting the availability of data from current and prior fiscal years.

■ Permitting the DBA to make portions of a partitioned table unavailable to users while the partition is being backed up.

VLDB
While this point is true regardless of the size of your Oracle8 database, it becomes even more crucial as the size swells into the multigigabyte, if not terabyte, range.

■ Allowing the DBA to place partitions in different tablespaces in read-only mode. When historical as well as current transaction data resides in the same table, partitioning allows you to flag one or more partitions as read-only to reduce the overhead initiated by Oracle to maintain consistency and integrity.

■ Permitting the cost-based optimizer (*CBO*) to choose efficient access paths at a higher level of granularity than without partitioning. The CBO may decide to do a full table scan on one partition and an index range scan on another when data to satisfy a query lies in different partitions.

Types of Partitioning Available

The concept of partitioning is nothing new to the Oracle database administrator and data architect. Since the dawn of Oracle V6 (circa 1988), we have been able to specify storage parameters to be used when creating objects in the Oracle Server. Many DBAs out there remember the learning curve of coming to grips with newfangled terminology such as:

■ **pctfree** A figure representing the percent of space in each data block that is reserved for updates to existing rows when the update causes existing row column value lengths to increase

■ **pctused** A figure representing the amount of space in each data block that Oracle will attempt to fill with data destined for new rows

■ **initial** The amount of space to be consumed by a table when the first contiguous chunk of space is allocated; the figure is expressed in bytes (e.g., **initial 8388608**), in kilobytes (e.g., **initial 8192K**), or megabytes (e.g., **initial 8M**)

■ **next** The amount of space to be consumed when the table extends itself (or is manually extended by someone with appropriate privileges); the figure is again expressed in bytes, kilobytes, or megabytes

Release 7.3 of the Oracle Server introduced *partition views*. Partition views involve storage of data in multiple tables with exactly the same column names and column attributes, bringing the data together at runtime using a view built with the **union all** construct.

NOTE
Partition views are supported in Oracle8; however, we recommend that you use the partitioning option and its features, which we highlight in this chapter.

Oracle8 has taken partitioning to another level; the mechanisms in the Oracle8 Server partitioning option move partition definitions into what we refer to as "off-the-shelf" SQL. Let's now look at the two ways to partition data residing in the Oracle8 Server.

NOTE
In Chapter 3, we discussed a form of partitioning called striping. The partitioning we discuss in this chapter is much more robust and flexible. It ends up striping an object and achieving the same results as in the I/O chapter.

Range Partitioning

This type of partitioning is the heart of the Oracle8 Server partitioning approach. Prior to range partitioning, a doc_master table would be created using the following code:

```
create table doc_master (
    fy_code                 varchar2(5),
    doc_num                 number(7),
```

```
        doc_type                varchar2(2),
        budget_amt              number(10,2),
        precomm_amt             number(10,2),
        comm_amt                number(10,2),
        exp_amt                 number(10,2))
tablespace doc_master;
```

PARTITIONING RULE # I

The partitioning option must be installed to use the range partitioning discussed in this section. It is vended as an add-on to the base Oracle8 Server product.

VLDB

The partitioning option is a must for very large databases.

With the partitioning option and some prior knowledge of the data destined for the doc_master table, the Oracle8 DBA uses code similar to the following to set up the doc_master table.

```
create table doc_master (
        fy_code         varchar2(5),
        doc_num         number(7),
        doc_type        varchar2(2),
        budget_amt      number(10,2),
        precomm_amt     number(10,2),
        comm_amt        number(10,2),
        exp_amt         number(10,2))
partition by range (fy_code)
   (partition fy_9697 values less than ('9798')
            tablespace ts_9697,
   partition fy_9798 values less than ('9899')
            tablespace ts_9798);
```

Notice how the partitioning is done on the fy_code column values, and the piece holding 9798 data and the piece holding 9899 data are in separate tablespaces. In an ideal world, these tablespaces would reside on different disk drives; most Windows NT servers are set up with multiple devices that are a bonus with the Oracle8 partitioning approach.

Partition Views

Let's picture the same table that's in the previous section and look at the partition view functionality. Setting up the view is a four-step process:

1. Define a separate table for each value of the fy_code column along the lines of:

```
create table document_9697 (
        fy_code                 varchar2(5),
        doc_num                 number(7),
        doc_type                varchar2(2),
        budget_amt              number(10,2),
        precomm_amt             number(10,2),
        comm_amt                number(10,2),
        exp_amt                 number(10,2));
create table document_9798 (
        fy_code                 varchar2(5),
        doc_num                 number(7),
        doc_type                varchar2(2),
        budget_amt              number(10,2),
        precomm_amt             number(10,2),
        comm_amt                number(10,2),
        exp_amt                 number(10,2));
```

2. Place data in each separate table by either:

   ■ moving the data into Oracle using SQL*Loader, keeping in mind that you must use separate input data files for each fiscal year, or

   ■ moving the data from a separate table that holds all fiscal year data with an SQL statement similar to:

```
insert into document_9697
       select * from document_master
         where fy_code = '9697';
insert into document_9798
       select * from document_master
         where fy_code = '9798';
```

3. Create the same series of constraints and indexes on each table that will come together for the partition view.

4. Define the partition view using the special syntax indicated in bold in the following listing:

```
create or replace view doc_master as
select * from document_9697
union all
select * from document_9798
union all
select * from ........ ;
```

Processing Queries Against Partition Views

And now, the magic begins. The optimizer that helps decide how to access the data required to satisfy SQL statements passed to the Server can now do the following when it encounters a partition view:

- Choose a different access path for each separate partition; it could decide to do a full table scan on the document_9697 portion and an index range scan on the document_9798 portion.

- Eliminate partitions that have no qualifying data based on the selection criteria as illustrated in the following code. With a partition view defined and broken up by fiscal year, the optimizer ignores the tables part of the view whose data could not possibly satisfy the requirements of a query.

```
SQL> -- A query where partition elimination could occur on the
SQL> -- FINANCE_HIST partition view partitioned by FY
SQL> select account, sum(amount), sum(item_ct), ...
  2    from finance_hist
  3    where fy = '98/99'
  4    group by account;
ACCOUNT                 AMOUNT        ITEM_CT
------------------- ------------- ------------
ATYH232                 19090.67        8879
...
...
1290 rows selected.
SQL>
```

PARTITIONING RULE # 2

The initialization parameter file entry for PARTITION_VIEWS_ENABLED must be set to TRUE to allow Oracle8 to process these views.

PARTITIONING RULE # 3

COMPATIBLE must be set to 7.3.0 or 8.0.0 to enable processing of partition views.

Enough said. Since the new Oracle8 functionality (i.e., range partitioning) is the best way to partition your data, we won't spend any more time on partition views. In the long and the short run, you will get better performance and easier management capabilities using range partitioning as discussed in the next few sections.

Partitioning Tables

Partitioning theory is nothing new with Oracle8. What is new is the ability to break tables and indexes into partitions using standard SQL, thereby offering the DBA and data administrator more control over what data is stored where. Decisions have to be made when deciding how to partition your data. Haphazard decisions will lead to less than optimal results. Let's start the partitioning journey by looking at some of these decisions and how some factors spring up based on the volume of data to be stored in a partitioned object versus (or sometimes coupled with) access patterns to the data itself.

VLDB

The sheer volume of data stored in some OLTP databases and data warehouses convinces many to favor frequency of access rather than volume within each potential partition when partitioning for this size of repository.

Deciding How to Partition

There are three main ways to choose to partition data:

- **Based on volume of data** Deciding partition range bounds such that roughly the same volume of information resides in each partition

- **Based on the frequency of access to the data** Deciding partition range bounds paying more attention to frequency of access rather than row counts in each partition

- **Based on the makeup of the data elements** Deciding partition range bounds based on the distribution of column values within the partitioning columns. For example, a world-wide information repository that accesses information by country may end up being partitioned by a three-character country code such as FRA (France), IND (India), CHI (China), or CAN (Canada).

The decision need not be a crap shoot; analyze activity and volume of your information and you may be surprised at the amount of useful information you can gather to influence your decision. This makes even more sense if you are upgrading to Oracle8 from a version that did not support table-based range partitioning or if you are looking at this mechanism after using the more conventional Oracle8 storage facility. Suppose a sales history table's access pattern and record count resemble Table 4-1. We tracked 810,964 accesses to the table with a record count of 110,621 over a 15-day period.

By looking at the information in Table 4-1, we can see that, using either approach, buckets 1 and 4 are accessed the most, whereas buckets 2 and 3 contain the most rows. Based on the access percentages, it is tempting to try lumping according to Table 4-2 or, if favoring row count, to balance by Table 4-3.

This leaves us in an interesting dilemma which conjures up clichés like "six of one, half dozen of the other"! We lean towards balancing range partitioning by access percent, but there is another compelling rule that governs the choice of how to partition, which leads us into our next two rules about how to partition.

Bucket	Primary Key Range	Accesses	%	Rows	%
1	100000-299999	216,290	27	14,990	14
2	300000-499999	103,999	13	28,011	25
3	500000-699999	82,909	10	31,291	28
4	700000-899999	220,211	27	13,431	12
5	900000-999999	187,555	23	22,898	21

TABLE 4-1. *Access and Row Count by Primary Key Range*

PARTITIONING RULE #4
Weigh the frequency of access for the skew of column values when deciding how to choose ranges for partition keys.

PARTITIONING RULE #5
When collapsing buckets during the partition key analysis exercise, you can only combine adjacent buckets.

Let's spend a little time on rule #5. Using the bucket ranges shown in Table 4-1, if we were to partition based on the row count percentages hoping to get roughly the same number in each bucket, we suggest collapsing buckets 1 and 4 into the new bucket 1. Impossible! If this were the case, the bucket ranges would be as shown in Table 4-4.

New Bucket # (Old #)	% Access	% Row Count
1	27	14
2 (2 + 3)	23	53
3 (4)	27	12
4(5)	23	21

TABLE 4-2. *Balancing Favoring Access %*

New Bucket # (Old #)	% Access	% Row Count
1 (1 + 4)	54	26
2 (2)	13	25
3	10	28
4(5)	23	21

TABLE 4-3. *Balancing Favoring Row Count*

This situation cannot be, since the second pocket of primary keys in bucket 1 is larger than the boundaries defined for bucket 2. Before looking at how Oracle8 places rows in partitions based on the partition key definition, let's present a few more rules.

PARTITIONING RULE #6
The values mentioned in the **range** *portion of the partition definition statement must list ascending values in a single-column partition key.*

PARTITIONING RULE #7
All the figures mentioned as boundary column values in the **range** *portion of the partition definition need not list ascending values in a multicolumn partition key (you will see this in action based on the contents of Table 4-5 later in this chapter).*

New Bucket	Primary Key Range	
1	100000-299999	700000-899999
2	300000-499999	
3	500000-699999	
4	900000-999999	

TABLE 4-4. *Impossible Range Boundary*

Using the theory and results of the examination of primary key values in the SALES table, let's define it using the **range** values we discovered, then look at the table's space allocation.

```
SQL> create table sales (
  2      sales_id          number,
  3      cust_id           number(6),
  4      other_col1        varchar2(20),
  5      other_col2        varchar2(20),
  6      other_col3        varchar2(20),
  7      other_col4        varchar2(20),
  8      other_col5        varchar2(20),
  9      od_flag           varchar2(1))
 10      storage (initial 240m next 240m pctincrease 0)
 11      partition by range (cust_id)
 12        (partition part1 values less than (299999) tablespace sales_p1,
 13          partition part2 values less than (699999) tablespace sales_p2,
 14          partition part3 values less than (899999) tablespace sales_p3,
 15          partition part4 values less than (999999) tablespace sales_p4);
Table created.
SQL> select *
  2      from user_extents
  3      where segment_name = 'SALES';
```

SEGMENT_NA	PARTITION_	SEGMENT_TYPE	TABLESPACE	EXTENT_ID	BYTES	BLOCKS
SALES	PART2	TABLE PARTITION	SALES_P2	0	251658240	122880
SALES	PART3	TABLE PARTITION	SALES_P3	0	251658240	122880
SALES	PART4	TABLE PARTITION	SALES_P4	0	251658240	122880
SALES	PART1	TABLE PARTITION	SALES_P1	0	251658240	122880

There are a few important points about the above listing:

- We have encountered a new SEGMENT_TYPE of TABLE PARTITION.

- Each partition has grabbed a value equal to the initial extent mentioned in the table's **storage** definition section.

- Each partition acts like a separate table since it has an initial EXTENT_ID of 0.

Without knowledge of what you are up against with space allocation using Oracle8's partitioned table mechanism, any tuning efforts you have gone through may be wasted. Picture the following scenario that could request 1200 percent of the space you really wanted. You go through an exercise of figuring out the average row size of a large table based on the expected number of rows and the **pctused** and **pctfree** values, decide the table needs 240 megabtyes (or 251,658,240 bytes) based on **initial 240MB next 240MB**. You also pat yourself on the back since you did such a good job of analyzing partition range values, not to mention the awesome work you did figuring out you should set up 12 partitions. You know what's coming next—each of the partitions grabs four 60 megabyte extents (for a total of 2,880 megabytes) and you sit there wondering why your disks are all sitting at 90 percent capacity instead of the expected 58 percent. Can't happen here, you say, but guess what? The four SALES_Pn tablespaces were created with **autoextend on** using the following SQL statements:

```
SQL> create tablespace sales_p1 datafile 'd:\orant\database\sales_p1.dbf'
  2          size 60m reuse autoextend on next 60m maxsize 500m
  3          default storage (initial 60m next 60m pctincrease 0);
Tablespace created.
SQL> create tablespace sales_p2 datafile 'f:\orant\database\sales_p2.dbf'
  2          size 60m reuse autoextend on next 60m maxsize 500m
  3          default storage (initial 60m next 60m pctincrease 0);
Tablespace created.
SQL> create tablespace sales_p3 datafile 'h:\orant\database\sales_p3.dbf'
  2          size 60m reuse autoextend on next 60m maxsize 500m
  3          default storage (initial 60m next 60m pctincrease 0);
Tablespace created.
SQL> create tablespace sales_p4 datafile 'o:\orant\database\sales_p4.dbf'
  2          size 60m reuse autoextend on next 60m maxsize 500m
  3          default storage (initial 60m next 60m pctincrease 0);
Tablespace created.
```

In Which Partition Do I Belong?

After painstakingly analyzing the partitioning approach, you need to be sure that the correct data is going to end up in the expected partition. Let's first look at how Oracle8 places data in a partition defined with a single-column partition key; then we'll look at the same theory for a multicolumn partition key.

Single Column Partition Key

As you code the value for each partition as part of the **range** portion of the **create** or **alter** statement, there are a few points worth noting.

- Rows with partition keys less than the range boundary will end up in that partition.

- Rows with partition keys equal to the range boundary will end up in the partition defined by the next immediately higher range.

- If you hard-code an upper range boundary, an attempt to insert a row with a partition key beyond the hard-coded boundary will generate an error:

```
ERROR at line 1:
ORA-14400: inserted partition key is beyond highest legal partition key
```

- If you attempt to update a row that would necessitate its being placed in a different partition, you will generate an error:

```
ERROR at line 1:
ORA-14402: updating partition key column would cause a partition change
```

- The range boundary for a partition cannot be changed using the **alter partition** command without using the **split partition** helper.

Before moving on to discuss placement of rows where there is a multicolumn partition key, let's sum up placement for single column partition keys with a rule.

PARTITIONING RULE #8
When rows are loaded into a partitioned table with a single-column partition key, a row's partition key column value must be less than the range boundary for a partition to qualify for placement in that partition.

Now we will have a look at the placement of rows in a partition key with more than one column.

Multicolumn Partition Key

In this case, the values in all the columns that make up the partition key are taken into consideration. Suppose a three-column key is built on (**fy_code, cust_num, region**). Table 4-5 shows the partition range definitions. We have defined the rows and columns with numbers and letters to allow us to point to specific cells in the ensuing discussion.

Table 4-6 shows values for the three partition key columns and where rows with those values will be placed.

This leads us into two final rules about placement of data in a partitioned table.

PARTITIONING RULE #9
When loading rows into a partitioned table with a multicolumn partition key, Oracle8 moves from left to right looking at the values in the partition key columns.

Oracle places rows in partitions based on the following logic. For the purpose of this listing, let's suppose a partition key is built on two columns,

	A	B	C	D
	Partition	**fy_code**	**cust_num**	**Region**
1	p1	1997	1200	B
2	p2	1997	9000	F
3	p3	1997	99999	Z
4	p4	1998	99999	Z
5	p5	1999	29999	A
6	p6	1999	99999	Z

TABLE 4-5. *Partition Range Definitions—Multicolumn Partition Key*

Fy_code	cust_num	Region	Partition Used	Why
1997	9000	E	p2	1997 = B2 9000 = C2 E < 2D, and as long as one partition key column value is less than that column's range boundary, the row ends up in that partition
1999	12000	Z	p5	1999 = B5 12000 < C5 qualifying row for p5
1999	999	Z	p5	1999 = B5 999 < C5 qualifying row for p5
1997	9000	F	p3	1997 = B2 9000 = C2 F = D2 and therefore all three column values are NOT less than the range boundaries for p2, so the row qualifies for p3
1999	1	A	p5	1999 = B5 1 < C5 qualifying row for p5

TABLE 4-6. *Column Values for Multicolumn Partition Key*

and the row we are trying to place has partition key column values indicated by cv1 and cv2. As well, the partition ranges for the last partition are defined, as all yours should be, by (**maxvalue,maxvalue**).

```
partition_found = FALSE
partition_num = 1
starting with first column in first partition key
loop until partition_found = TRUE
   if partition key (partition_num) = (maxvalue,maxvalue) then
      partition_found = TRUE
   elsif cv1 > column 1 in partition (partition_num) key then
      go on to next partition
   elsif cv1 = column 1 in partition (partition_num) key then
      if cv2 >= column 2 in partition (partition_num) key then
         go on to next partition
      else
```

```
        place row in partition (partition_num)
        partition_found = TRUE
      end if
    end if
    add 1 to partition_num
end loop
```

Placement of Data in Partitioned Objects

The optimal way to partition a table is by splitting its partitions among more than one tablespace. Once you decide which column(s) will be used for the range partitioning, you name the tablespace for each partition, create the properly sized tablespaces, then create the partitioned table. Keep in mind that a tablespace can be made up of one or more datafiles, whereas a datafile can belong to one and only one tablespace. The following listing shows the creation of three tablespaces to hold the CUSTOMER table:

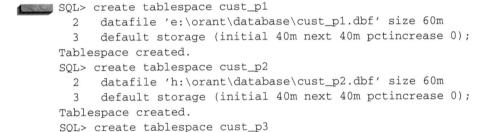

```
SQL> create tablespace cust_p1
  2    datafile 'e:\orant\database\cust_p1.dbf' size 60m
  3    default storage (initial 40m next 40m pctincrease 0);
Tablespace created.
SQL> create tablespace cust_p2
  2    datafile 'h:\orant\database\cust_p2.dbf' size 60m
  3    default storage (initial 40m next 40m pctincrease 0);
Tablespace created.
SQL> create tablespace cust_p3
  2    datafile 'j:\orant\database\cust_p3.dbf' size 60m
  3    default storage (initial 40m next 40m pctincrease 0);
Tablespace created.
```

PARTITIONING RULE #10

The owner of a partitioned object must have space quota assigned for all the tablespaces within which the table or index resides.

PARTITIONING RULE #11

*When attempting to span multiple tablespaces with a partitioned table, code the **tablespace {ts_name}** to ensure each partition is placed in the correct tablespace. Do not rely on the owner's default tablespace.*

Tablespaces for Partitioned Objects

Even though most of the time each tablespace holding data in a partitioned object is the same size, this is not mandatory. When doing access-based data distribution, you may find one partition with significantly more rows than another. If this comes up, there is no reason why, for example, the partitions can't be sized at 100 megabytes for the former and 70 megabytes for the latter.

We cannot stress enough how important it is to name tablespaces for partitioned objects with some meaningful name, maximum 30 characters, at the Oracle level and the operating system level. We would like to suggest the following convention for both levels of naming, although the adoption and following of a convention are more important than the convention itself:

- Choose a name for each tablespace made up of some form of the table name, using the suffix _DATA or _INDEX. Embed the characters _PRT somewhere in the name. Using the SALES tables as an example, the first data tablespace would be named SALES_PRT1_DATA and the thirteenth index tablespace would be named SALES_PRT13_INDEX.

- Choose a name for each datafile for each tablespace that resembles the internal Oracle tablespace name. Again for SALES, the first data tablespace datafile could be called SLS_P1D.DBF and the thirteenth index tablespace datafile could be SLS_P13I.DBF.

VLDB
Be creative but proactive as well when naming tablespaces for very large databases. Sometimes these repositories contain hundreds of tablespaces, and many DBAs out there know the hoops you must go through to rename a tablespace.

Working with Partitions and Their Tablespaces

In this section, we are going to look at the syntax of a handful of operations you are used to performing with nonpartitioned tables, as well as a few unique to partitioned objects. This is a very simple high-level summary of working with partitioned tables. Full details can be browsed in the "Managing Partitioned Tables and Indexes" chapter of the *Oracle8 Server Administrator's Guide*. First, let's look at some operations with the files that make up a partitioned table.

NOTE
*Many of these operations can be accomplished from one of the interfaces in the Oracle Enterprise Manager. The syntax we highlight here can be used from SQL*Plus or Server Manager.*

Operations with Datafiles Holding Partitioned Objects

You will find yourself performing normal routine maintenance with datafiles and tablespaces that hold partition tables. The following items illustrate how some of this is done with members of a partitioned table.

■ **Moving a datafile** This is accomplished the same way as with any other tablespace. On Windows NT, you will get a sharing violation if you attempt to rename a file while Oracle8 is running. You need to accomplish the task with the database mounted but not open, using the **alter database rename file ...;** syntax.

■ **Adding space to a tablespace** This is done the same way as any tablespace, using the **alter tablespace {ts_name} add datafile ...;** syntax.

■ **Dropping a tablespace** Given a tablespace that holds a piece of a partitioned table, when the piece is no longer needed, the tablespace can be dropped by first deleting the data from the partition where the tablespace resides, using the **alter table {table_name} truncate partition {partition_name};** statement. Next, you drop the partition with the **alter table drop partition {partition_name};** syntax. Lastly, you drop the tablespace with the usual **drop tablespace ...;** command.

Operations with Partitions Themselves

Some of this syntax is new to Oracle8. As soon as you start working with and storing data in partitioned objects, much of this syntax will become part of your DBA repertoire.

■ **Moving a partition** When the need arises, you can move a partition from one tablespace to another with the statement **alter table {table_name} move partition {partition_name} tablespace {new_ts_name};**.

■ **Adding a partition** This can be done when you need to add a partition to an existing partitioned table with the range boundary of the new partition at the high end of the last existing partition. If the range boundary of the new partition is not at this high end, you must use the **alter table {table_name} split partition {partition_name} ...;** convention.

■ **Dropping a partition** When this is done, if the partition contains any data, the data will be wiped from the table without warning. Note that an attempt to drop the last remaining partition will generate the following error:

```
ERROR at line 1:
ORA-14083: cannot drop the only partition of a partitioned table
```

■ **Splitting a partition** This is accomplished with the following syntax:

```
SQL> alter table purchase split partition cust_p2 at (555555,1997,44)
  2  into (partition cust_p1a,
  3        partition cust_p1b);
Table altered.
SQL>
```

Note the following about the partition keys that end up being defined for the two partitions created by the split:

1. The first partition assumes range boundaries defined in the **at** portion of the **split partition** section (i.e., 55555,1997,44).

2. The second partition assumes the old partition range boundaries (i.e., 555555,1997,66).

■ **Renaming a partition**   This is common after a partition has been split and the names of the old partitions are no longer meaningful.

■ **Partition exchanging**   This allows one to convert an existing partition in a partitioned table to a regular table or vice versa. The statement resembles **alter table {table_name} exchange partition {partition_name} with {un_partitioned_table};**.

Partitioned Indexes

This topic is closely related to the table partitioning discussed throughout the previous section. The simplest and, in some opinions, the most efficient way to partition indexes is to have a 1:1 match between table and index partitions. Thus, partition key values less than 999 end up in p1 with their own index, as do key values less than **maxvalue** that end up with their own index. Before getting started, however, we need to discuss the concept of **global** and **local** indexes.

Global Indexes

This index type for a partitioned table is the same as regular indexes on nonpartitioned tables. Global indexes that are themselves partitioned may contain key values for columns from more than one partition in the table's data segment. A global index is set up using code similar to the following:

```
SQL> -- The following assumes that the cust_ip1, cust_ip2, and cust_ip3
SQL> -- tablespaces have been created and the user has quota in place.
SQL> -- Remember that the table is partitioned using a multicolumn
SQL> -- partition key, whereas the index partitioning is global and set
SQL> -- up differently.
SQL> create index purchase_1 on purchase (cust_num) global
  2  partition by range (cust_num)
  3    (partition values less than (555555)
```

```
    4                  tablespace cust_ip1,
    5       partition values less than (555557)
    6                  tablespace cust_ip2,
    7       partition values less than (maxvalue)
    8                  tablespace cust_ip3);
Index created.
SQL>
```

A global index is **prefixed** if the left-most indexed column is the same as the left-most partitioning column. For example, if a global partitioned index is built on (fy_code, cust_num) and the **partition by range (fy_code)** defines how to partition, the index is prefixed since the fy_code column is the left-most in both the index and the partition key. If the **partition by range (cust_num)** were used instead, the global index would be nonprefixed.

PARTITIONING RULE #12
The highest range boundary for a global index must contain the keyword **maxvalue** *to ensure the index will be able to accommodate all possible column values from the underlying table.*

Local Indexes

With this indexing approach, all keys in an index partition refer only to rows in a single underlying table partition. If you built a local index on the table partition range boundaries shown in Table 4-5, that index would have the same number of partitions with exactly the same range boundaries as the underlying table. A query against the USER_PART_KEY_COLUMNS confirms the fact that the table partition key and the local index partition key are the same.

```
SQL> select * from user_part_key_columns;
NAME                            COLUMN_NAME                     COLUMN_POSITION
------------------------------  ------------------------------  ---------------
CUSTOMER                        FY_CODE                                       1
CUSTOMER                        CUST_NUM                                      2
CUSTOMER                        REGION                                        3
CUSTOMER_1                      FY_CODE                                       1
CUSTOMER_1                      CUST_NUM                                      2
CUSTOMER_1                      REGION                                        3
6 records selected.
SQL>
```

The data dictionary views USER_TAB_PARTITIONS and USER_IND_PARTITIONS contain range boundary information. Let's look at the view for the object in Table 4-5:

```
SQL> select partition_name,high_value
  2    from user_tab_partitions
  3    order by 1;
PARTITION_NAME                HIGH_VALUE
------------------------      ------------------------------------
P1                            1997, 1200, 'B'
P2                            1997, 9000, 'F'
P3                            1997, 99999, 'Z'
P4                            1998, 10000, 'Z'
P5                            1999, 29999, 'A'
P6                            1999, 99999, 'A'
SQL> select partition_name,high_value
  2    from user_ind_partitions
  3    order by 1;
PARTITION_NAME                HIGH_VALUE
------------------------      ------------------------------------
P1                            1997, 1200, 'B'
P2                            1997, 9000, 'F'
P3                            1997, 99999, 'Z'
P4                            1998, 10000, 'Z'
P5                            1999, 29999, 'A'
P6                            1999, 99999, 'A'
```

Common Operations with Partitioned Objects

Most of the operations you have performed with your nonpartitioned tables and indexes can be run against a partition of a partitioned object. Let's have a look at some of these activities.

Statistic Collection

You will soon find yourself in a situation where you have added a partition to an existing partitioned table or loaded a partition with a significant amount of new data. To collect new statistics for the cost-based optimizer, the extended table partition syntax is used as shown in the next listing. The same options and syntax conventions apply to using the **analyze** command with partitions as with the whole table.

```
SQL> analyze table purchase partition (cust_p1) compute statistics;
Table analyzed.
SQL>
```

In the case of indexes, you will use the **analyze** statement a little differently than with nonpartitioned indexes. Suppose a local nonprefixed index has been set up using the following syntax:

```
SQL> create index purchase_cnum on purchase (cust_num) local;
Index created.
SQL>
```

Since the PURCHASE table is partitioned, the **local** keyword causes Oracle to create a separate index partition for each data partition with exactly the same partition boundaries. To analyze all pieces in a local index, use the following statement:

```
SQL> analyze index purchase_cnum compute statistics;
Index analyzed.
SQL>
```

To collect statistics on single partition of a partitioned index, use the next statement:

```
SQL> analyze index purcase_cnum partition (p4) compute statistics;
Index analyzed.
SQL>
```

The results of the analysis are stored in the USER_TAB_PARTITIONS and the USER_PART_COL_STATISTICS data dictionary views shown in the next listing, with the major columns of interest bolded:

```
SQL> desc sys.user_tab_partitions
 Name                             Null?     Type
 -------------------------------- --------- ----
 TABLE_NAME                       NOT NULL  VARCHAR2(30)
 PARTITION_NAME                             VARCHAR2(30)
 HIGH_VALUE                                 LONG
 HIGH_VALUE_LENGTH                NOT NULL  NUMBER
 PARTITION_POSITION               NOT NULL  NUMBER
 TABLESPACE_NAME                  NOT NULL  VARCHAR2(30)
 PCT_FREE                         NOT NULL  NUMBER
 PCT_USED                         NOT NULL  NUMBER
 INI_TRANS                        NOT NULL  NUMBER
```

```
MAX_TRANS                             NOT NULL NUMBER
INITIAL_EXTENT                                 NUMBER
NEXT_EXTENT                                    NUMBER
MIN_EXTENT                            NOT NULL NUMBER
MAX_EXTENT                            NOT NULL NUMBER
PCT_INCREASE                          NOT NULL NUMBER
FREELISTS                                      NUMBER
FREELIST_GROUPS                                NUMBER
LOGGING                                        VARCHAR2(3)
NUM_ROWS                                       NUMBER
BLOCKS                                         NUMBER
EMPTY_BLOCKS                                   NUMBER
AVG_SPACE                                      NUMBER
CHAIN_CNT                                      NUMBER
AVG_ROW_LEN                                    NUMBER
SAMPLE_SIZE                                    NUMBER
LAST_ANALYZED                                  DATE
BUFFER_POOL                                    VARCHAR2(7)
SQL> desc sys.user_part_col_statistics
Name                           Null?    Type
------------------------------ -------- ----
TABLE_NAME                     NOT NULL VARCHAR2(30)
PARTITION_NAME                          VARCHAR2(30)
COLUMN_NAME                             VARCHAR2(30)
NUM_DISTINCT                            NUMBER
LOW_VALUE                               RAW(32)
HIGH_VALUE                              RAW(32)
DENSITY                                 NUMBER
NUM_NULLS                               NUMBER
NUM_BUCKETS                             NUMBER
SAMPLE_SIZE                             NUMBER
LAST_ANALYZED                          DATE
```

PARTITIONING RULE #13

Analyze partitioned tables by partition instead of by the combination of the partitions together.

VLDB

When loading information into a table partition, rule #13 makes even more sense due to the sheer volume of data involved in such large repositories.

Partition-based Export and Import

The partitioning implementation is fully supported by export and import. With Oracle8, the source of an export and the target of an import can be a partition as well as a table. Let's briefly look at using the two tools through the OEM Data Manager, using partitions rather than tables.

Partition Level Export

After opening up the OEM console and invoking the Data Manager, you will be presented with the Data Manager's main console. Click Data on the menu bar, then select Export as shown in Figure 4-1.

From there, you are presented with the first of seven screens in the Export Wizard. The first screen is administrative, where you specify:

1. The target of the export operation, be it on the local machine via exp80 command or on a remote server via Oracle's job scheduling mechanism.

2. The name and location of the file created by export.

3. If a remote machine via scheduling is selected, the choice of when to schedule the export to be carried out.

Click Next to carry on to the wizard's second screen. In the Object Selection area, expand Default Database, then Users, then the desired username, then Tables, then the desired table name, then Partitions. You are then presented with a list of partitions. Highlight the desired partition, then click Finish to complete the exercise. This is shown in Figure 4-2.

NOTE
There are seven screens to the Export Wizard; we only highlight the first two to illustrate a partition-based export.

Sometimes you may end up exporting partitions and tables belonging to different users at the same time. You can transfer elements from the Selected Objects part of the screen to the Available Objects using the right arrow in the middle of the screen or by drag-and-drop from one window to

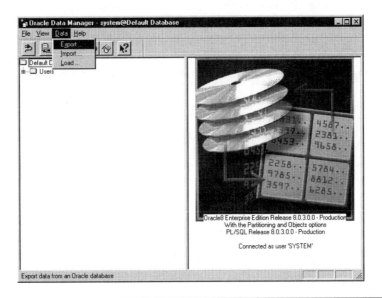

FIGURE 4-1. *Starting export in the Data Manager*

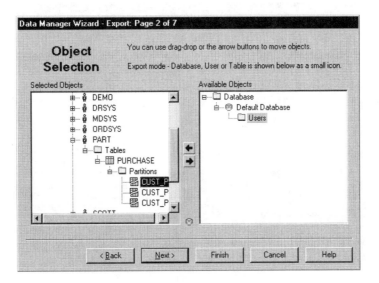

FIGURE 4-2. *Partition selection in Export Wizard dialog*

the other. An export of objects belonging to more than one user is shown in Figure 4-3.

If you choose to use the line-mode interface to export, the following listing shows the command line and the output produced by **exp80**, showing the table_name:partition_name convention highlighted in bold:

```
C:\WINNT\PROFILES\ABBEYM\DESKTOP> exp80 userid=part/part tables=purchase:cust_p1
Export: Release 8.0.3.0.0 - Production on Mon Aug 30 10:11:46 1999
(c) Copyright 1997 Oracle Corporation.  All rights reserved.
Connected to: Oracle8 Enterprise Edition Release 8.0.3.0.0 - Production
With the Partitioning and Objects options
PL/SQL Release 8.0.3.0.0 - Production
Export done in WE8ISO8859P1 character set and WE8ISO8859P1 NCHAR character set
About to export specified tables via Conventional Path ...
. . exporting table                      PURCHASE
. . exporting partition                     CUST_P1      23990 rows exported
Export terminated successfully without warnings.
```

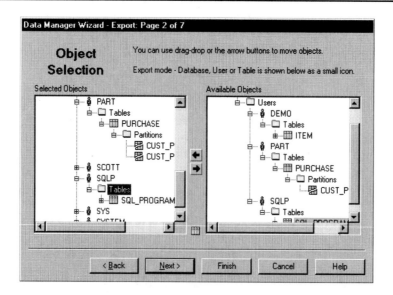

FIGURE 4-3. *Exporting objects from more than one user*

Partition Level Import

Using the line-mode import program **imp80**, the command to bring in a partition is shown in the next listing. The same rules apply to partition-based import as to those used to perform a table-level import.

```
C:\WINNT\PROFILES\ABBEYM\DESKTOP>imp80 userid=part/part tables=purchase:cust_p1
ignore=y
Import: Release 8.0.3.0.0 - Production on Mon Aug 11 10:55:54 1997
(c) Copyright 1997 Oracle Corporation.  All rights reserved.
Connected to: Oracle8 Enterprise Edition Release 8.0.3.0.0 - Production
With the Partitioning and Objects options
PL/SQL Release 8.0.3.0.0 - Production
Export file created by EXPORT:V08.00.03 via conventional path
. importing PART's objects into PART
. . importing partition           "PURCHASE":"CUST_P1"      23990 rows imported
Import terminated successfully without warnings.
C:\WINNT\PROFILES\ABBEYM\DESKTOP>
```

Partition Level SQL*Loader

Readers familiar with SQL*Loader are fluent with the syntax for the control file fed to SQL*Loader. The next listing shows the syntax for the target partition in the control file, with the change bolded.

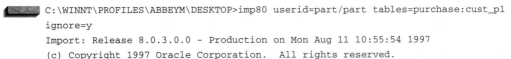

```
load data
infile 'c:\purchase.dat'
into table purchase partition (cust_p1)
(po_num position (1:5) char,
 ...
 ... )
```

Loading data into the partition of a table opens a whole new can of worms, since the partition key definition can restrict what data is allowed to lie in each partition.

PARTITIONING RULE #14

*Pay special attention to the log file written by SQL*Loader when loading a partitioned table; the rejected row count can be affected by data that lies outside of the target partition key values.*

To illustrate, suppose the partition key is defined using two columns with partition range boundaries of ('N',1998) and ('R',2000). A row in the input file with data ('P',1998) destined for partition one will be rejected, as it is out of range for this partition. The following error is written to the log file as the session runs:

```
ORA-14400: inserted partition key is beyond highest legal partition key
```

Converting a Partition View to a Partitioned Table

Many installations are using partition views as a result of the work they did with Oracle 7.3.x. As you migrate to Oracle8 and design more and more applications with partitioned objects, you can use the **exchange** command with the **alter table** to convert partition views to partitioned tables. Examine the following simple example to see how this is done:

```
SQL> -- All this is already in place supporting partition views.
SQL> -- Create the tables to be part of the partition view.
SQL> create table purchase_lt555 (
  2         po_num      number,
  3         cust_num    number) tablespace purchase_low;
Table created.
SQL> create table purchase_gte555 (
  2         po_num      number,
  3         cust_num    number) tablespace purchase_high;
Table created.
SQL> -- Create rows in these 2 tables. Those whose PO_NUM < 555 are
SQL> -- in PURCHASE_LT555, the others in PURCHASE_GTE555.
SQL> insert into purchase_lt555 values (323,15);
1 row created.
SQL> insert into purchase_lt555 values (324,25);
1 row created.
SQL> insert into purchase_lt555 values (325,35);
1 row created.
SQL> insert into purchase_lt555 values (221,45);
1 row created.
SQL> insert into purchase_lt555 values (245,55);
1 row created.
SQL> insert into purchase_gte555 values (623,65);
1 row created.
SQL> insert into purchase_gte555 values (724,75);
1 row created.
```

```
SQL> insert into purchase_gte555 values (825,85);
1 row created.
SQL> insert into purchase_gte555 values (821,95);
1 row created.
SQL> insert into purchase_gte555 values (945,35);
1 row created.
SQL> -- Create the partition view.
SQL> create or replace view purchase_pv as
  2    select * from purchase_lt555
  3  union all
  4    select * from purchase_gte555;
View created.
SQL> -- Define the partitioned table.
SQL> drop table purchase;
Table dropped.
SQL> create table purchase (
  2        po_num      number,
  3        cust_num    number)
  4  partition by range (po_num)
  5      (partition pur_1 values less than (555)
  6                          tablespace purchase_low,
  7       partition pur_2 values less than (maxvalue)
  8                          tablespace purchase_high);
Table created.
SQL> -- Let's do the exchange.
SQL> alter table purchase exchange partition pur_1
  2        with table purchase_lt555;
Table altered.
SQL> alter table purchase exchange partition pur_2
  2        with table purchase_gte555;
Table altered.
SQL> -- Let's look at the outcome.
SQL> select *
  2    from purchase partition (pur_1);

    PO_NUM    CUST_NUM
---------- ----------
       323          15
       324          25
       325          35
       221          45
       245          55
SQL> select *
  2    from purchase partition (pur_2);
```

```
      PO_NUM    CUST_NUM

      ----------  ----------
         623           65
         724           75
         825           85
         821           95
         945           35
SQL>
```

When this completes, the data that used to reside in the PURCHASE_LT555 table is in the PUR_1 partition of the PURCHASE partitioned table, and the data that used to reside in the PURCHASE_GTE555 table is in the PUR_2 partition of PURCHASE.

Partition Maintenance and Global Indexes

When working with pieces of a partitioned table that has a global index, maintenance operations cause the index to be flagged as unusable. Inspect the following code to see how the problem comes up:

```
SQL> -- This becomes a global index since GLOBAL is the default.
SQL> create index purchase_1 on purchase (po_num);
SQL> alter table purchase drop partition pur_2;
Table altered.
SQL> select * from purchase where po_num < 444;
select * from purchase where po_num < 444
                *
ERROR at line 1:
ORA-01502: index 'PART.PURCHASE_1' or partition of such index is in unusable
          state
```

PARTITIONING RULE #15
After partition maintenance, any global indexes on the partitioned object must be rebuilt or recreated. Until one of these operations is carried out, the global index is marked unusable.

Based on the information in rule #15, let's wind up our discussion of partitioning with the Oracle8 Server with one last rule (which is more of a recommendation).

PARTITIONING RULE #16
We like local indexes more than global indexes since they make the management of partitioned objects easier and enhance the availability of data in those objects.

Our prejudice is based on the following two reasons:

- When working with partitions (e.g., splitting or dropping), the local indexes in the unaffected partitions as well as their underlying data partitions are available and usable.

- The definition of each local index partition is exactly the same as its corresponding data partition. A query against USER_TAB_PARTITIONS and USER_IND_PARTITIONS will yield identical results in the HIGH_VALUE column. The matching of index and data portions of partitioned objects is turnkey.

Let's Tune It

Partitioning is the best and really the only way to manage large volumes of data. The mechanisms we have discussed in this chapter provide a robust method for breaking up large objects into more manageable chunks. Let's summarize before moving on:

- Some form of partitioning provides for optimal storage of and access to information in the Oracle8 Server repository.

- Partitioning allows for the selection of different access paths by the cost-based optimizer to get at partitioned data to satisfy user requests for information.

- Partition elimination involves pruning partitions whose partition range boundaries do not contain any data that qualifies for query results.

- The decision to partition or not partition is very closely coupled with the amount of parallelization you implement in your Oracle8 Server. Chapter 5 discusses issues related to parallelization; parallelization and partitioning together will give you the best bang for your tuning dollar.

- A prefixed index is one that is built using the left-most column of the partition key as the left-most column in the index.

- A nonprefixed index is one whose left-most column is not the same as the left-most column in the partition key.

- Global indexes contain entries whose values can span more than one partition in a partitioned table.

- When a partitioned index range boundary's values match the underlying partitioned table range boundaries, the index should be flagged **local** rather than **global**.

- Local indexes are automatically partitioned exactly the same as the data segments to which they refer.

- Local indexes permit the DBA to work with one or more segments of a partitioned table without affecting the availability of data in nonaffected partitions.

- By placing partitions for a partitioned table in separate tablespaces, the DBA can back up portions of a partitioned table without touching the whole table at once.

- The easiest and most efficient way to place partitions is by placing each partition in a separate tablespace and the tablespaces themselves on different disk drives whenever possible.

- A partition key can be made up of up to 16 columns in a partitioned table.

- A bitmap index can not be partitioned. This index approach builds an index that contains a value of 0 or 1 for each column value in each row in the table upon which it is being built. We mention bitmap indexes in Chapter 9.

- The partition-extended syntax (e.g., purchase partition [p1]) is not supported in PL/SQL version 8. One way to use this convention in PL/SQL is to reference a view that is built using the partition extended syntax. This is shown in the next listing:

```
SQL> create or replace view po_97 as
  2      select *
  3         from purchase partition (pur_97);
```

```
View created.
SQL> begin
  2     declare dummy number;
  3     begin
  4       select count(*) into dummy from po_97;
  5     end;
  6  end;
  7  /
PL/SQL procedure successfully completed.
```

- ■ An index-organized table, as discussed in Chapter 2, cannot be partitioned.

- ■ Partition locks are more restrictive than row level locks but not as restrictive as table locks.

- ■ When you add a partition to or split an existing partition in an existing table, Oracle names any indexes generated as a result of the activity starting with the text SYS_P as a prefix. After an add or split activity, look at the Oracle-generated index name and rename the index partition to something more meaningful. The name PV_DEC98 will mean a lot more to you somewhere down the road than the Oracle-assigned name SYS_P992.

- ■ When an activity performed on a partitioned object places an index in an index unusable state, the index must be rebuilt or recreated before the data in the table is accessible.

Oracle7.x Specifics

The "Partitioning and the Tuning Process" section of this chapter is applicable to all versions of Oracle7.x. The "Partition Views" section of "Types of Partitioning Available" is applicable to Oracle7.3.x but not 7.2.x, 7.1.x, or 7.0.x. The balance of the chapter is Oracle8 specific.

CHAPTER
5

Parallelism

arallelism, symmetry, equivalence—these words and
concepts all have something in common. They demonstrate
how the total exceeds the sum of its parts. Goalies may be
able to stop every shot aimed at them, but without the rest
of the team, a goalie is powerless to win without a great
deal of luck. In the world of computers, this concept is applicable in terms
of parallelism. Parallel processing allows a great computer with a whole
team of CPUs to work together to create an even greater computational
power. Parallel processing has existed for many years but, with Oracle8,
the power of multiple processors and servers takes advantage of a computer
topology that can further empower the database to increase application and
server productivity.

The question is: What do I need to be able to take advantage of these
parallelism features incorporated within Oracle8? First you need a
computer, but will any computer do? Possibly. As long as the computer can
support multiple CPUs and you have bought, configured, and installed
these CPUs, you have the opportunity to enter into the parallel query
world. In today's world, this means that you would require a machine and
operating system that supports two or more processors and an operating
system that can address and share processing among these processors.
These machines share memory and disks but spread their processing power
among the numerous CPUs. The reason that parallel process provides us
with so much of a performance boost is that we often run into processing
bottlenecks, as opposed to I/O bottlenecks. By implementing solutions that
use the Parallel Query feature, you will start to experience new problems.
You may then find that I/O is a bottleneck, since the CPUs will now be
hungry for more information at a rate that the system had not experienced
during serial operation execution. In this chapter of *Oracle8 Tuning*, we
will discuss how best to use the parallel query feature, how best to
implement it, and what to do to ensure that you are using this feature at an
optimal level.

Parallel Query Processing

The processing of information using multiple processors requires the
Oracle8 Parallel Query feature. Parallel Query allows SQL statements to
utilize share processing across these processors simultaneously. When
processing SQL on a machine that has only a single processor, all SQL will

execute within a single process. Parallel Query allows statements to be divided and use multiple processes, resulting in quicker completion of the statement.

This discussion is limited to the Parallel Query and does not include the use and configuration of the Parallel Server Option. The Parallel Server Option relates to the linking of multiple database servers together, whereas the Parallel Query option can be implemented on a single server that contains multiple processors.

Parallel Query provides significant performance gains for databases that contain large amounts of data. The types of systems that gain the most from parallel operations include:

- SMP (symmetric multiprocessor), MPP (massively parallel processor machines), and clusters

- High I/O capacity machines (many disks and multiple disk controllers)

- Underutilized CPUs (less than 25 percent CPU busy)

- A system with a large memory capacity

For a definition of SMP and MPP machines, refer to the "SMP" and "MPP" sections in Chapter 2 under "Favoring CPU." If you have a machine that has all of these characteristics, then you are a candidate for implementing parallel processing within your Oracle database. The types of databases that provide the greatest benefit from parallelism are:

- Very large databases (*VLDBs*)

- Data warehouses

- Financial applications

NOTE
Oracle does support parallelization with Oracle Cooperative Applications. If you would like to implement parallelization in your Oracle Financials applications, you have to do it at the operating system level.

VLDB

Multi-CPU machines should always be considered, if not insisted on, for VLDB applications. Although the hardware costs are higher, this is one investment that you should make. So, become friends with your Acquisition Manager and make sure you get your VLDB parallelized.

Generally, the parallel query feature is most useful when the queries require a great deal of time to complete and when a large number of rows are processed. These database applications share a number of common characteristics, the most common being size. These applications are also information intensive. The amount of storage required is very large and, to maximize the retrieval of the information, the parallel query feature spreads the SQL among the active CPUs. This load sharing is performed by efficiently splitting up a request over the many processors running on the system. As noted previously, by working as a team, the goal of completing an operation can be reached sooner and require a smaller amount of effort.

At execution time, Oracle works together with the server's multiple processors to distribute the database operation statement. Interestingly enough, the splitting of work by the parallel query engine is dynamic; if there are any changes to the server's configuration, they will be adapted to by Oracle at the time of the statement request.

It is important to note that the gains you can expect from parallel query if your system is already heavily loaded will be reduced. Ensure that your server has the available cycles for implementing a large, information-intensive database. Also, verify that you have optimized your current CPU usage, disks, and disk controllers before embarking on a parallelism initiative.

The SQL statements and database functions that benefit from parallelization with parallel query are the following:

- **select** statements

- **not in** statements

- **group by** statements

- **create table** ... **as select** ... statements

- **create index**
- nested subqueries in **insert**, **update**, and **delete** statements
- **update** statements
- **delete** statements
- **rebuild index**
- parallel data loading with SQL*Loader
- parallel replication
- **alter table move partition**
- **alter table split partition**
- star transformation

The proper use of these statements, together with the configuration of the database, will provide results in a more timely manner.

Oracle will parallelize operations in the following ways:

- When DML and DDL parallelize by block ranges
- When operations access partitioned tables and indexes
- When executing parallelism by parallel query server processes

The database parallelizes the SQL statement at execution time. At this time, it divides the table or index into ranges of database blocks and then executes on these ranges in parallel. This processing on the ranges is performed by ROWID, and each statement will access the information in parallel for a high and low range of ROWIDs. In the case of partitioned data, the information is not accessed by this range but by the defined partitions. The information is queried by a set of ROWIDs from within each partition, and no scan can overlap two partitions.

NOTE

We discussed indexed-organized tables in Chapter 3. The parallel processing that is done against these objects is based on their primary keys rather than ROWID.

Partitions are excellent candidates for parallel execution, as these data sets can be easily divided into smaller working groups to allow for efficient information interrogation. Basically, each partition becomes a candidate for assignment to an individual parallel query server process. In some cases, the number of parallel processes may be less than the number of partitions; this is due to system limits or table attributes. This is not a problem since a parallel query server process can access multiple partitions. If you access only a single partition during the statement execution, the optimizer will understand not to perform the statement in parallel and will perform the statement serially. Inserts are parallelized during execution as they will be divided among the parallel query server processes.

VLDB

Almost every operation performed on a VLDB is a candidate for parallel optimization.

Look and Feel of Parallel Query

The parallel query feature has a number of different server processes that manage and execute the processing of SQL statements. The first is the query coordinator (P000 process). This process decides how to distribute the SQL statement among one or many parallel query server processes. The other processes can be identified as they will appear as Pxxx in the process list. The values of xxx will be the numerical identifier of the parallel query server process, starting with 1 and continuing to the maximum number set by the database configuration. Thus, a configuration with five parallel query server processes will show processes P000, P001, P002, P003, and P004. Configuration and installation of the parallel query feature requires no intervention, since it is part of the base product. By setting the appropriate parameters in your initialization parameter file, you can utilize the parallel features of Oracle8.

NOTE

This is true with Oracle8 and a number of releases of Oracle7, as documented at the end of this chapter.

The Initialization Parameter File Parallel Style

The configuration of parallel query is a balance of optimizing SQL and configuring the database so that it maximizes the effectiveness of its parallel query server processes. In order to optimize the database configuration, we will investigate some initialization parameter file entries and suggest how best to set these values to optimize parallel SQL execution.

When the database starts and the appropriate entries are set in the initialization parameter file, Oracle will create a number of parallel query server processes that may be addressed by the query coordinator. These parallel processes become available for use in order to perform parallel operations. Once assigned to an operation, these processes will be retained by the operation until its completion. Once completed, the operation will release the parallel query server process to be available to the next operation. In order to maximize these processes, we must look at preparing the database. Let's look at these parameters.

PARALLEL_MIN_SERVERS

This parameter specifies the minimum number of parallel query server processes that will be initiated by the database at the time of instance startup. To optimize the parallel query server processes for normal database operations, the DBA should consider setting the number of PARALLEL_MIN_SERVERS to the formula shown in the next listing:

```
PARALLEL_MIN_SERVERS = the likely number of simultaneous parallel operations
```

By reviewing the information contained in the V$PQ_SYSSTAT data dictionary view, you can identify whether the value you have set is too low or too high. The data you are interested in sits in the STATISTIC column with values shown in the next listing:

```
STATISTIC                       VALUE
------------------------------  ----------
Servers Busy                         0
Servers Idle                         0
```

You are looking for these values to indicate if we have over-committed or under-committed our parallel query server processes.

PARALLEL_MAX_SERVERS

This parameter specifies the maximum number of parallel query server processes that will be spawned when required. At times, when the volume of concurrent operations exceeds the number of current parallel query processes currently running, the query coordinator will start other parallel query server processes up to the number specified in this parameter.

To optimize the parallel query server processes for normal database operations, you should consider setting the number of PARALLEL_MAX_SERVERS to the formula shown in the next listing. The formula is expanded to show the value for a two CPU machine with 30 concurrent users.

```
PARALLEL_MAX_SERVERS = 2 * # of CPUs * # of concurrent users
                     = 2 * 4 * 30 = 240
```

When all parallel query server processes are in use and the maximum number of processes has been reached, the parallel query coordinator will react to the request for processes in excess of PARALLEL_MAX_SERVERS by either switching to serial processing or returning an error if involved in a replication role.

PARALLEL_SERVER_IDLE_TIME

When the parallel query coordinator starts processes beyond the initial number started based on the PARALLEL_MIN_SERVERS parameter, the stopping of these additional processes will be based on this parameter. This period is defined as the time from which the number of query processes exceeds that set by the minimum number of parallel query server processes and has not been utilized for a period in time by any current operations.

OPTIMIZER_PERCENT_PARALLEL

This parameter determines how aggressively the cost-based optimizer (*CBO*) will try to parallelize an operation. By default, the value is set to 0, so the optimizer will not consider parallelization when determining the best execution plan. You will need to decide how aggressive you want the optimizer to be when it comes to determining the best balance between the execution and parallelization of an operation. The higher that this value is set, up to a maximum of 100, the harder the CBO will work to optimize parallel execution. This will determine a plan to minimize execution time based on parallel processing. The optimal setting for this value is shown in the next listing:

```
OPTIMIZER_PERCENT_PARALLEL = 100/number of concurrent users
```

When determining if parallel execution is being performed, ensure that the value is set to 100. This will force the operation into a parallel plan unless a serial plan is faster. Remember that when the value is set lower, the optimizer will favor indexes; when the value is set higher, the optimizer will favor full table scans.

NOTE
If you are using the rule-based optimizer in your database, most of the discussions in this chapter about parallelization do not apply to your facility.

SHARED_POOL_SIZE
The shared pool size must be reviewed. The shared pool is used by the parallel processors to send messages back and forth to each other. The reason for the increase in the pool is that parallel operations require execution plans that require twice as much space as serial plans. To optimize your shared pool, we recommend that you consider the following formula when determining your shared pool size; our example uses a buffer size of 2K on a machine with a current shared pool entry of 20000000, PARALLEL_MAX_SERVERS of 16, and 8 CPUs.

```
SHARED_POOL_SIZE =
   current value + ((3 * message buffer size ) * (CPUs + 2) *
PARALLEL_MAX_SERVERS)
               = 20000000 + ((3 * 2048) * (8 + 2) * 16)
                 20000000 + 6144 * 10 * 16 = 20000000 + 983040 = 20983040
```

The message buffer is used by the operating system to communicate within a process. The size of the message buffer is dependent upon your operating system—it is usually defined as either 2K or 4K. Check with your system administrator to find out what the buffer size is for your configuration.

ALWAYS_ANTI_JOIN

This parameter is important when the SQL operation uses the **not in**
operator. By setting this parameter, you can tell your database to use
parallel functionality when performing anti-joins. By default, **not in** is
evaluated as a (sequential) correlated subquery when the parameter is
set to NESTED_LOOPS. Instead, Oracle will perform a hash-join that will
execute in parallel. To tell the database to do parallel hashing, set the
parameter as follows:

```
ALWAYS_ANTI_JOIN = hash
```

The next SQL statement is an example of the familiar **not in** construct
that the CBO with Oracle8 will react to with the ALWAYS_ANTI_JOIN
entry set to HASH. Note the HASH_AJ hint:

```
select *
   from individual
 where lastname like 'KERZNER%'
   and office_id is not null
   and office_id not in
       (select /*+ hash_aj */ office
          from national_office
        where office_id is not null
          and role = 'SENATORS');
```

The above operation performs a hash anti-join, since it uses the hint
HASH_AJ. By setting the parameter in the database to HASH, we can make
Oracle always perform the HASH anti-join; in our parallel world, this is
what we want to see.

ROW_LOCKING

This parameter tells the database whether to acquire row level locks during
an update operation. The parameter should be set as follows:

```
ROW_LOCKING = ALWAYS
```

By selecting ALWAYS or DEFAULT (they are the same), you tell the
database only to get row locks when the table is being updated. If your
database is set to INTENT, then locks are acquired when you perform a
select for update. This may appear to be fine, but by setting the parameter
to INTENT, all insert, updates, and deletes will performed serially.

COMPATIBLE

This parameter tells the database to use the latest features available within Oracle8. We mention this here to remind you to set the value so you can get all the parallel features available. The parameter should be set as shown in the next listing:

```
COMPATIBLE = 8.0.0
```

The optimization of the database is an exercise in trial and error. In order to see how well your settings for the database have improved or worsened performance, monitor the database after making a change to your initialization parameter file. We discuss the Performance Pack in Chapter 9; use tools such as the Performance Manager to assess the effectiveness of changes you may be making in the initialization parameter file. Keep testing and changing your values and see if you can find measurable improvement to your parallel operations.

Parallel Execution

The execution of all SQL statements goes through the same process when the database has been configured with the parallel query:

1. The statement is parsed.

2. If the statement is a candidate for parallelization, the optimizer determines the execution plan of the statement.

3. The query coordinator determines the method for parallelization of the operation.

What determines the amount of parallelization is the existence of at least one full table scan or index scan in the execution plan. Oracle8 now allows us to utilize parallelism during operations that perform index range scans of a partitioned index and full index scans. To find out if your SQL is a candidate for parallelism, you may evaluate the SQL statement with **explain plan**.

Many times the CBO selects a full table scan for many SQL statements; full table scans are ideal candidates, as they can greatly benefit from parallelization. Even when indexes are used, one can improve the performance by telling the coordinator to use parallel index processing. To tell the query coordinator to initiate parallel processing, you use hints as discussed in the next few sections.

PARALLEL Hint

The **parallel** hint (make sure you spell it right!) allows you to tell the query coordinator how many concurrent parallel query server processes should be used for the parallel operation. The four main operations, **select**, **insert**, **update**, and **delete,** can all take advantage of this hint. Remember that you must identify the table to be parallelized at a minimum. If you do not identify the degree of parallelism or the server instances, the optimizer will set them to the default in the database. If any values exceed those set in the database, the hint will be ignored. The next listing is an example of how this hint is used.

```
select /*+ parallel (product,4) */ date_range, product, unit_price
   from product;
```

NOTE
If you have been using the **parallel** *hint in Oracle7, then you need to know that you will be required to change these to* **parallel_index** *in cases where SQL statements operate on indexes.*

PARALLEL_INDEX Hint

To access information in a table via an index range scans of a partitioned index, the **parallel_index** hint should be used. This hint tells the query coordinator to spread the index scan across multiple parallel query server processes. The next listing shows the format of this hint (for a table being read), where DOP stands for degree of parallelism.

```
/*+ parallel_index (tablename, DOP, parallel server instance split) */
select /*+ parallel_index (product,4) */ date_range, product, unit_price
   from product;
```

The format of the **parallel_index** hint (for an index being scanned) is shown next:

```
/*+ parallel_index (indexname, DOP, parallel server instance split) */
select /*+ parallel_index (date_range_index,4) */ date_range,
       product, unit_price
  from product;
```

NOPARALLEL Hint

When you do not want to use the parallel processing of a **select** statement, the hint **noparallel** is available. This hint disables any default parallel processing the query coordinator may attempt to initiate. This hint is the same as saying: /*+ **parallel** (tablename, 1,1) */. The format of this hint is shown in the next listing:

```
/*+ noparallel (tablename) */

select /*+ noparallel */ date_range, product, unit_price
  from product;
```

APPEND and NOAPPEND Hints

The **append** hint is used when you are only appending data onto the end of a table. So, if your operation requires you to always add data to a table, the **append** hint may be the best choice. This hint should be used only when the function is inserting data into an existing table; for other types of inserts, the **parallel** hint may provide more flexibility. The **noappend** hint overrides the **append** hint. The format of the APPEND hint is shown next:

```
/*+ append*/
```

Parallel SQL Statements

The performance of information manipulation and retrieval has always been and will continue to be an issue to everyone who has had their computer tied up doing the endless query. You must remember the update that started Monday and ended when the computer crashed three days later. Oracle7 and Oracle8 have provided us with new strategies to improve the performance of our SQL statements. Remember that SQL that is poorly formatted and configured will still run poorly, but if the code is written efficiently, parallelism will improve performance.

Manual parallel processing is a derivative of the parallel query feature. Our years of experience in parallelism recently helped us achieve a goal at a major bank's data warehouse project to start a dream sequence. We created six separate processes that addressed a key value range in a 10,000,000 row table and started these six wonderfully written programs. This program then allowed the Oracle Server to distribute the processing among the multiple parallel query processes on the server. The moral of this dream: anyone can perform manual parallel processing. Was this the best solution? By spreading out the processes among the many processors, we were able to achieve the overall performance required for the task. The question then becomes: What was the trade-off versus serial processing of the same task?

The greatest advantage to us was that we could get the transactions per second required to complete this task in our lifetime. But even with parallel hints, the programs would still not provide the performance required.

For every battle won there is a cost; based on the perceived and estimated cost, decisions need to be made. Let's look at what influences decisions:

- Will the separation of tasks provide significant performance increases?

- Do we have enough processes to manage the multiple tasks that will be started?

- If one process fails, does it affect the other processes? Every process will need the ability to be restarted, and no other process will need to depend on another parallel process.

- Can we separate the information with a reasonable amount of work?

- Is this requirement a candidate for manual parallelism?

If we look at all of the above considerations, what makes an operation a better candidate for parallel execution? Let's weigh a few items that will help you decide on parallel execution:

■ Performance increase is always a factor in determining the way to approach the problem. What performance increase can you expect by enabling parallelism? This question is one that we are often asked and a difficult one to define. If every increase of 2 percent is considered a major benefit to your organization, then we must do everything possible to improve performance. If your organization requires a 25 percent improvement, then the choices are not as clear. In this case, the parallelism approach may satisfy both schools of thought and should be considered for all performance reviews.

■ Available processes are a factor of system capacity. If you have the required number of cycles, more parallel query server processes can be started and a better use of system capacity can be achieved. If you do not have the available capacity but want to pursue this approach, then a hardware augmentation will need to be performed before you embark on further parallelism.

■ Interdependence issues try to find answers to questions such as, "Is it possible to perform a part of the task in isolation without concern for other operations?" as well as, "If a task can be performed without regard for other operations then it would appear to be a better candidate for parallelism."

This leads to the question of what work is required to separate the information to a level where it can be easily manipulated. Oracle8 has almost removed this question from consideration. If you have been diligent and partitioned your data already, this becomes a nonissue. People out there who want to take advantage of partitions and the parallel nature of the information ask themselves if the change is worth the cost. The best answer we can give to you is that using the features that are now available in your database tool kit must always be considered. So should we implement this feature? If your machine supports parallelism, then this option must be considered.

If all else fails, performing manual parallelism may provide the best possible results at the end of the day. During the bank project dream, the choice of manual parallelism generated a 300 percent performance boost. The operation was simple to separate. By implementing the function during the prototyping phase of the project, future iterations will also benefit from this execution choice.

With Oracle8, these considerations are minimized, as Oracle8 supports true parallelism for inserts, updates, and deletes. Parallelism can positively affect almost any SQL statement's execution. We will look at how you can improve your SQL by using parallelism to improve performance.

Is It Getting Hot? Or, What Is the Degree of Parallelism?

When the database parallelizes an SQL statement, it parallelizes this statement over a number of parallel query server processes. The number of parallel query server processes used by an operation is known as the *degree of parallelism*. Without the degree of parallelism, the operation will be performed in serial. If you had wanted that, you would not have purchased 12 new processors and more memory and told everyone it was going to help. By understanding the definition of the degree of parallelism, you can now empower everyone in your organization to use all that new hardware and the new and improved database schema when issuing SQL statements.

The degree of parallelism is defined at the statement level. This is done through the use of embedded hints within the statement or by default within the database. At the time of table or index creation you can specify a default degree of parallelism for the object. By default this may be the number of either disks or CPUs.

There are two types of parallel operations that we must define at this point, as they will affect the degree of parallelism that any operation can perform—intra-operations and inter-operations. These two operations can be performed at the same time during statement execution.

Intra-operations and Inter-operations

The intra-operation is an individual operation that depends only upon itself to complete the task, whereas the inter-operation is dependent upon data flowing between operations. If we look at a **select** statement, we can show how these operations interact:

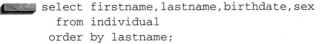
```
select firstname,lastname,birthdate,sex
  from individual
order by lastname;
```

The execution plan of this statement will require the following:

- Full scan of Individual

- **order by** of lastname

The overall query will be handled by a query coordinator. The table scan will be performed by a number of parallel processes that then send the information to a number of sort functions that will organize the details further. If we look at the parallel query server processes, we will see that one group of processes will handle the sort and partitioning of the information (this is an intra-operation function). The information will then be sent to another set of parallel processes (these are inter-operation functions). These processes will then complete and return the information to the parallel query coordinator and then to the user.

In terms of degree of parallelism, we only define the number of intra-operational parallel processes. If possible within the operation, the inter-operation parallelism will result in a doubling of the degree of parallelism.

The Degree of Parallelism within Operations

The balance between too much parallelism and too little is always a concern to us. Luckily, we have a database that is smarter than your average bear. The Oracle query coordinator is that smart. The coordinator determines the degree of parallelism at runtime, based on a number of factors. First, the coordinator looks to see if they are dealing with a smarter than normal programmer who has added hints to their SQL statement. If this has not been done, it will check to see if your DBA was awake when the table or index was created. The coordinator will then look for the object's default degree of parallelism. Once determined, this degree of parallelism will be used by the operation. If you create a table, remember to follow the following format, with the parallel-specific section bolded:

```
SQL> create table individual (
  2      firstname           varchar2(20) not null,
  3      lastname            varchar2(30) not null,
  4      birthdate           date         not null,
  5      gender              varchar2(1)  not null,
  6      initial             varchar2(1),
  7      favorite_beatle     varchar2(6))
  8   parallel (degree 4);
Table created.
SQL>
```

The coordinator will only request the number of parallel query server processes defined by the degree of parallelism. The physical number of processes that the coordinator will be able to get will depend upon how many are available at the time of operation execution.

So now we know how and where the database gets its degree of parallelism, but at some point we will need to tell it what degree of parallelism to use. Therefore, it is necessary to understand how best to tell Oracle what degree of parallelism is defined for a table, index, or hint. By following these rules and selecting the ones that relate to your specific operation, you can define your degree of parallelism, just like the pros:

1. Number of CPUs

2. Number of parallel server operations

3. Number of disks used by a table or index

4. Number of partitions that will be accessed

Suppose you have eight CPUs, but your information is stored on 12 disks. The limiting factor here is CPUs. The degree of parallelism that we should use would be eight.

Although you may request eight parallel query server processes to process your statement, you may not receive this many. Due to limits placed on the database, there may not be a sufficient number of parallel query servers available. If you have defined 25 PARALLEL_MAX_SERVERS, then you can only have 25 parallel processes running. If you exceed this number, Oracle will not spawn additional processes, which will result in some statements being executed in serial mode by the query coordinator. In the case when you have specified the PARALLEL_MIN_PERCENT and the minimum fraction of parallelism is not available, you will receive an error during execution.

By defining the degree of parallelism for an SQL operation, you can profoundly affect the processing of your information. Specify it too high and you may not get processes that you require when you want them. If the value is too low, you may find that your parallel query server processes are not being maximized, resulting in lost performance.

When considering your degree of parallelism, you should by default define it such that it optimizes a majority of operations to maximize the utilization of your I/O and CPU. In some cases, this may not be the best approach, and you may want to override the default degree of parallelism. For example, if your operation requires large amounts of I/O, you may want to increase the degree of parallelism for the operation. If your operation requires a large amount of memory, then you may want to decrease the degree of parallelism. To override the default degree of parallelism, you may decide to incorporate hints into your SQL.

Now that we can define our degree of parallelism, we need to be able to use our knowledge, but where do we use these facts? By using parallelism in your SQL statements, you can increase the performance of many SQL statements. Let's move on to looking at some familiar SQL statements and how they are parallelized.

Familiar SQL Statements Parallel Style

The syntax we are about to feature resembles the conventions you are all used to working with without parallelization. We mentioned before the importance of spelling the word "parallel" correctly; this makes even more sense here since many of the statements we are going to cover will run many times quicker when parallelized. The biggest caveat about using hints can be summed up in the next listing.

```
-- This statement will be parallelized looking for a pool of 4 parallel
-- query server processes.
select col1, col2, col3 /*+ parallel (tab1,4) */ ...
-- This will not be since the word is misspeledd.
select col1, col2, col3 /*+ paralell (tab1,4) */ ...
-- As will this one, since there is an extra space between the leading
-- asterisk and the + sign, thereby violating a stipulation for writing
-- hints
select col1, col2, col3 /* + parallel (tab1,4) */ ...
```

Table Creation

Creating tables can benefit both the creation and the speed of information retrieval from the table. As we showed in the previous section, you can define a table and its degree of parallelism at the time of table creation. This will then benefit everyone who ever retrieves data from the table. When creating a table based on data in another table, we get a double hitter for parallelism. Both **insert** and **select** can be parallelized. If that's not double the fun, then what is?

Each portion of the statement (**insert** and **select**) can have a separately defined degree of parallelism. In the example that follows, we create a table that is aggregated based on information in an operational table. The operational table is partitioned among five different partitions, but no partitioning is being created in the aggregate table. The statement that follows illustrates this type of situation when we have a system that has 20 CPUs:

```
SQL> create table contributions_1997 /*+ parallel (contributions_1997,10) */
  2          as
  3    select indivual_id,sum(income_tax_withholding),
  4            sum(pension_withholding) /*+ parallel (weekly_details,5) */
  5      from weekly_details
  6     where fiscal_year = 1997
  7     group by individual;
Table created.
SQL>
```

In all, the operation will attempt to get 15 parallel query server processes working in a symphony of parallel computing. This is an example of intra-operations and inter-operations—is exactly what parallelism was meant to help.

Physical Design with Oracle8 to Leverage Parallelism

The physical layout and organization of database objects can have a profound effect on the performance that can be achieved. It is so important to consider ideas such as disk striping, partitioning, data file placement, and tablespace organization when creating database objects. Now that we are considering parallelism, it is just as important to consider physical object design when creating your tables and indexes.

When considering the use and implementation of parallelism, you should also consider the physical storage of the objects in the database. We recommend that when creating tablespaces you should create them so that they contain multiple data files. The files contained in each tablespace should be a multiple of the number of CPUs your server contains. So, if we were to create a new tablespace and the server has four CPUs, the tablespace would be created with a minimum of four data files. If we want additional data files, they would be added in multiples of four, so we would go from four data files to eight, 12, 16, and so on. By doing this you will reduce fragmentation and reduce I/O contention.

PARALLELISM RULE #I
Space management of the objects created through or configured for the parallel operations must be carefully planned in order to maximize parallel effectiveness.

Inserts, Updates, and Deletes

The processing of information in parallel has its obvious advantages, as we discussed above. This section attempts to aid in the implementation of parallel DML and DDL by describing the use of parallel inserts, updates, and deletes.

The Parallel Insert

When working with data in a data warehouse database, we are often asked as DBAs and programmers to create a simple aggregate table. The architect tells you the information comes from seven different tables, and says, "Don't worry, most of the tables are indexed," and "Could we please have the resulting table by Monday?" The question that the person who is going to program then needs to ask is, "Which Monday?" Then you remember something you read in an excellent performance tuning book about **insert** and parallelism, so you return to your cubicle to complete your task.

Inserts are performed during three basic situations:

1. Simple insert statement, illustrated by the following:

```
SQL> insert into children_detail values
  2  ('Baila','Abramson','29-SEP-1989','F','Radar');
SQL>
```

2. An **insert** and **create table** based upon a nested **select**, shown next:

```
SQL> insert into children_detail
  2     select firstname, lastname, birthdate, sex
  3        from individual
  4      where type = 'KID';
1289  records created.
SQL>
```

3. An **insert** from a source file using SQL*Loader

We hope you have been paying attention; here comes the test. Which inserts are going to get the most improvement by allowing for parallel processing? The answer is 2 and 3. If you answered 1, please refer to the book *Oracle8: A Beginner's Guide* (Osborne/McGraw-Hill, Oracle Press, 1997) for some additional help, or just continue reading. The first simply performs a single, simple function, just one **insert** and one set of values; single processes gain no benefit from a split. On the other hand, 2 and 3 could deal with large amounts of data, and more processes working together can reach the goal sooner. Just as with **select** statements, an **insert** with one or more nested **select** statements will gain the same parallel advantage. SQL*Loader has been able to perform parallel processing since Oracle7, and this parallel performance is improved with Oracle8. We will discuss SQL*Loader specifics later in this section.

Example 2 shows us the type of format that our simple seven-table join will utilize to create the aggregate table. Although it does not show how to use parallel hints within the SQL statement, the statement below incorporates some of the hints:

```
SQL> insert into children_detail /*+ parallel (children_detail, 4) */
  2     select firstname, lastname, birthdate,
  3            gender, sum(annual_income) /*+ parallel (individual, 6) */
  4      from individual
  5      where type = 'KID'
  6      group by firstname, lastname, birthdate, gender;
239 rows created.
SQL>
```

Notice how we have told the query coordinator that we want to parallelize both the **insert** and the **select** statements. By doing this, we can spread this statement out over even more query processes.

PARALLELISM RULE #2
*When inserting records into a table either with a **create table** or an **insert**, the operation should be performed in parallel if possible. This will greatly enhance I/O and reduce the amount of I/O contention.*

PARALLELISM RULE #3
*Recovery of parallel transactions is dependent upon the operation that is being performed. If you create a table or index using the **nologging** feature, you will disable undo and redo logging. Tread carefully when using **nologging**.*

Parallel Updates and Deletes
The operation of performing an **update** or **delete** in parallel requires the database to be set up with partitions. If, and only if, the tables are partitioned can the operation perform in parallel.

PARALLELISM RULE #4
*You cannot parallelize an **update** or **delete** operation unless the operation affects two or more partitions simultaneously in a partitioned table.*

PARALLELISM RULE #5
Oracle will choose the degree of parallelism based on the degree defined during table creation or as defined by a hint in the SQL statement. The hint will take precedence over the default degree of parallelism, if possible.

The decision to parallelize these statements has more to do with the way your database is prepared, rather than a "should I or shouldn't I?" question. If you define your tables and indexes using partitions, you have allowed for parallel updates and deletes. If you have not set up partitions, then these operations will not be helped by parallelism.

Parallel Indexing

The creation and rebuilding of indexes can be a time consuming operation when dealing with a large volume of information requiring an index. Oracle8 has allowed us to access indexes with hints but, just as important, we can also tell Oracle to create and rebuild an index using parallel processing. In order to parallelize the construction and rebuilding of an index, the PARALLEL hint can be used to optimize this operation. This is extremely important when large amounts of data require indexes to be created. By doing this indexes can be dropped and recreated in a much more efficient manner.

The following example demonstrates how to parallelize the creation of an index:

```
SQL> create index idx_1997_sales_product
  2    on 1997_sales (product_id)
  3    nosort
  4    nologging
  5    parallel (degree 5);
Index created.
SQL>
```

The following example demonstrates how to parallelize the rebuilding of an index:

```
SQL> alter index idx_1997_sales_product rebuild
  2           nologging parallel (degree 5);
Index altered.
SQL>
```

NOTE

PARALLELISM RULE #6 By creating and rebuilding indexes using parallel processing, you will minimize the time required to perform a lengthy task.

Parallel Loading

The ability to load data into the database in parallel can have a huge impact upon the performance of the load operation. Parallel loading can greatly reduce time and resources and provide users with a higher degree of information availability. SQL*Loader supports parallel loading and its benefits for loading large volumes of information efficiently. There are many features of SQL*Loader that improve load performance, such as direct path loads. These loads insert information into the data tables and lower overhead of the loading process. So, when considering loading data into tables, you should always consider whether parallel loading will provide sufficient benefits to allow for performance gains. We will focus our discussion on the impact of parallel loading in this section.

There are three ways in which you can parallelize your loading operations:

- By splitting conventional loads
- By concurrent loading of different objects
- By concurrent loading of data into a single object

If possible, you should try to parallelize the loading of data, but the type of load that is best suited to your environment is the question we will now help you answer. If we look at each of the load types and the characteristics of each, the loading method should become a simpler choice.

Splitting Conventional Loads

Conventional loads simply execute **insert** statements to place information in the database. If we decide that any load can be characterized as a conventional load, how can we parallelize the load in order to make it more efficient?

This type of load would have the following characteristics:

- Single table at a time
- Single partition
- No information restrictions
- Retains all integrity rules

To perform this type of load, we can simply separate the SQL*Loader sessions into separate loads. This can be done by loading multiple files simultaneously. If we look at this type of operation we would see the following commands issued:

```
sqlldr80 userid=jillian/brentford control=tab1.ctl data=01jan.dat parallel=true
sqlldr80 userid=jillian/brentford control=tab1.ctl data=02jan.dat parallel=true
sqlldr80 userid=jillian/brentford control=tab1.ctl data=03jan.dat parallel=true
```

These commands would result in three separate loads that would all ask the system for resources. The same control file is used, as we have specified the unique data file that will be used to supply the data to the database. In the above case, the data is all being loaded into the same table since the control file is the same, but these processes could just as easily be performed for multiple tables.

PARALLELISM RULE #7
*When loading data in parallel into a single table, each loader session will require its own extent during the loading process. So, if you are loading data into a new table, each parallel SQL*Loader session will take an **initial** extent to be used for loading. If you are loading data into an existing table, each session will take a **next** extent if required.*

PARALLELISM RULE #8
*When using parallel loading, SQL*Loader may require that the indexes are rebuilt after the load has completed. This function may be performed in parallel, as we will discuss later in this chapter.*

Concurrent Loading of Different Objects

Another approach is the loading of different objects in parallel. This approach covers direct loading of separate objects and single objects into multiple partitions. These types of loads can benefit from parallel loading in combination with direct path loading, but there are limitations. The characteristics of this type of load include:

- Single or multiple tables
- Multiple partitions of a single table
- Direct path loads
- Referential integrity to be disabled
- Triggers do not to execute

These loads differ mainly in that they are direct path loads and are therefore limited by the constraints imposed by these types of loads. It is also important to note that if you are loading using parallel direct loading, rows are only appended to a table. If you want to **truncate** the table before performing the load, you will need to do this before commencing the load.

If we looked at this type of operation, we would see the following commands issued:

```
sqlload userid=baila/radar control=tab1.ctl data=01jan.dat parallel=true direct=true
sqlload userid=baila/radar control=tab1.ctl data=02jan.dat parallel=true direct=true
sqlload userid=baila/radar control=tab2.ctl data=addr.dat parallel=true direct=true
```

Concurrent Loading into the Same Object

The final type of load is the load where we are performing parallel direct loads of data into the same table or partition. This type of load can provide performance for loading data into a single table, but does not have the additional limitation imposed by direct loads. The characteristics of this type of load include:

- Single table
- Single partition of a single table
- Direct path loads
- Referential integrity to be disabled
- Triggers do not to execute
- Indexes need to be rebuilt after load completes

If we looked at this type of operation, we would see the following commands issued:

```
sqlload userid=pakman/sue control=tab1.ctl data=01jan.dat parallel=true direct=true
sqlload userid=pakman/sue control=tab1.ctl data=02jan.dat parallel=true direct=true
sqlload userid=pakman/sue control=tab1.ctl data=03jan.dat parallel=true direct=true
```

These loads all have the **parallel** option set to **true**. This means that the loads are performed in **parallel**, but each load will be considered a single process. The option tells the database that multiple loads will be performed at the same time.

We also recommended when performing parallel direct loads that each load process inserts data into data files stored on different devices. By running the loads against separate data files, you can maximize I/O. The file can be specified with the **file** keyword in the **options** clause of a SQL*Loader control file. The example of a control file header that follows demonstrates this concept.

```
load data
infile 'susan_decor_sales_0197.dat'
insert into table sales
options (file='/app/data/sales_97.dat')
...
```

The **file** keyword has certain constraints that must be considered when specifying it within the control file.

- For nonpartitioned tables, the data file must be part of the tablespace that contains the table.

- For partitioned tables performing a single partition load, the data file must be in the tablespace that holds the table partition.

- For a full table load of a partitioned table, the file must be in the tablespace that holds all of the partitions. Therefore, all partitions must be contained in a single tablespace.

Parallel Operation Limitations

As with any Oracle feature and product, there are always limitations. These limits are sometimes painful to accept but, at the same time, if we are not aware of them, we can waste time tracking down problems that are limitations. The following summarizes some of the limitations of the Parallel Query feature:

- Parallel DML must be the first and only statement of a transaction, so you will need to issue a **commit** or **rollback** before performing a parallel operation.

- Updates and deletes may only be parallelized on partitioned tables. If the table is not partitioned, the operation will execute serially.

- Tables that contain object column and lob (blob, clob, nclob, and bfile) datatypes cannot be parallelized.

- Index-organized tables may not be parallelized.

- Database triggers are not supported for parallel operations.

- There is no referential integrity support for direct-load **insert**.

- Global indexes are not supported for parallel updates.

- When performing a parallel insert into a nonpartitioned table, the indexes will not be maintained.

- You cannot perform an operation on tables that have self-referential integrity constraints or delete cascade constraints.

- Clustered tables may not have parallel operation performed on them.

When you violate any of these rules, your operation will perform in serial. You will not receive any warnings or any errors. You will only discover the problem by noticing that it did not achieve its anticipated performance benchmark or by viewing the parallel query view tables.

Parallel Performance

In order to evaluate how well we are doing in this parallel world, we recommend that you evaluate and review the performance of your operations. You need to know what to look for and figure out if you can do the parallelization any better. If you can ask the right questions, you should be able to determine if the answers are those that you expect. The following three issues sum up what needs to be looked at:

- What performance is expected
- If the SQL is optimally written and structured
- Whether we are running in parallel or serial

Let's look at each question and what it means and figure out if we can improve the operation.

The question of performance is one that at times can be quite esoteric. Is an acceptable response time three seconds, or one hour? At a recent project, we were able to identify a real performance problem. How did we know? Considering the pilot and another similar project, we were able to see that we were not getting the expected performance. We felt that we should be able to expect at least a result that was four to five times faster than what we were getting. So the investigation began. We looked at everything, from the way the database had been installed (not by us), the methods being used by the operation, and the data that was being accessed. By implementing some changes to the initialization parameter file, optimizing table storage, analyzing the tables and indexes, and, finally, implementing parallel execution, we exceeded our performance expectations. If you can measure it, you may be able to improve it. Being able to quantify your performance expectations is required for determining if you may be having some problems.

The same exercise may be performed if you feel your system and operations have been well tuned. As we know, DBAs are always looking at keeping busy, and performance tuning is an art. By making subtle changes, the DBA could provide you with small performance gains that will allow your system to run at optimal levels longer.

Now that we have determined that the performance we are receiving is not what we desire, we want to start tuning the database and the operations it is performing. The issue of tuning the database will not be discussed here. You should refer to the configuration of the parallel query feature contained earlier in this chapter about tuning the database for the parallel feature. We will need to understand how the operation is executing and to ensure that it is using the parallel query server processes.

To verify that your SQL is executing in parallel, immediately run a query against the V$PQ_SESSTAT and V$PQ_SYSSTAT data dictionary views. You are looking to see that the number of parallel query server processes being used is the number you would expect after reviewing the default degree of parallelism or the hint that you have added to your SQL statement. The following is a sample output from these two views:

```
SQL> select * from v$pq_sesstat;
STATISTIC                        LAST_QUERY SESSION_TOTAL
-------------------------------- ---------- -------------
DML Parallelized                          2             4
Queries Parallelized                      0             0
DFO Trees                                 2             2
Server Thread                             3             0
Allocation Height                         3             0
Allocation Width                          0             0
Local Msgs Sent                          21            50
Distr Msgs Sent                           0             0
Local Msgs Recv'd                        21            50
Distr Msgs Recv'd                         0             0
11 rows selected.
SQL>
```

The information provided by the view shows the details of the last query executed and the cumulative totals for the session. What we are looking for from this view is the number of statements that have been parallelized. We look at the number of DML statements that were parallelized (such as inserts, updates, and deletes). The queries parallelized indicate the number of all other parallel statements.

```
SQL> select * from v$pq_sysstat;
STATISTIC                        VALUE
-------------------------------- ---------
Servers Busy                             5
Servers Idle                             3
Servers Highwater                       16
Server Sessions                          8
Servers Started                          5
Servers Shutdown                         0
Servers Cleaned Up                       0
Queries Initiated                        0
DML Initiated                           20
DFO Trees                                2
Local Msgs Sent                         60
Distr Msgs Sent                          0
Local Msgs Recv'd                       60
Distr Msgs Recv'd                        0
15 rows selected.
SQL>
```

The view V$PQ_SYSSTAT is similar to V$PQ_SESSTAT but deals with the parallel query feature for the entire database instance. The information we are more concerned with is the number of parallel query server processes and idle servers and highwater servers. These will indicate to us the type of usage we are getting from our query processes. If we are finding that we are continually maximizing our parallel query servers but not the CPU usage, this will indicate that we should increase the number of parallel query server processes.

In the case where you find that your "Servers Busy" is always above what you have set for PARALLEL_MIN_SERVERS, and "Servers Started" is continuously growing, you should consider raising this parameter. This will reduce parallel process contention, and the database will not need to continually start new parallel query server processes.

The information contained in the view V$PQ_TQSTAT is also useful, as it will show you the number of rows produced and consumed by each parallel query server process. You are looking for an even distribution of transactions across each parallel query server process.

If you have determined that the problem is due to an uneven distribution of transactions, it is most probably due to your data. If you are performing a join, and the number of distinct values used in the join is less than the degree of parallelism, you will not be maximizing the use of each of the query server processes. The usage pattern that you can expect in a case such as this would be high usage of some processes and no usage in others. To eliminate this problem, you need to rewrite your SQL so that the number of values being used by the joins exceeds the degree of parallelism.

The problems of uneven distribution may also be due to I/O problems. This is where you call your system administrator and start to investigate—or just do it yourself. I/O can be a difficult problem to diagnose but, given time and money, can be solved. I/O contention and bottlenecks may require that you buy new hardware, reorganize existing hardware, rewrite operations, or rearrange your data. You may need to do one or all of these things in order to fix your I/O problems. The question is what to check for to evaluate your I/O situation. This list is by no means complete but should serve as a starting point:

■ Do you have the needed I/O bandwidth? This requires that you have an understanding of and have evaluated the throughput of your disk controllers.

- Is your SQL using a high enough degree of parallelism? Verify that you have optimized the maximum number of parallel servers in your database and that the SQL optimizes your parallel I/O.

- Remember that you can have too much of a good thing, so do not overdo the degree of parallelism. By setting the degree of parallelism too high, you will not be performing all portions of your transaction in parallel—some may be performed in serial.

- Make sure that your system supports parallel query. You should NEVER implement parallel query on a system that contains only one CPU. You will find that this will reduce the performance of your system.

You cannot assume that your operations are being performed in parallel. You may find that at times when you wanted parallel execution you are getting serial execution, so verify that you are getting the results you expect.

The use and implementation of the parallel query feature is something that every installation of Oracle should consider, if at all possible. The benefits that can be garnered will provide a very fast return on investment in both performance increases and optimization of computer resources. So, by optimizing your parallel operations, making your SQL as efficient as possible will allow you to optimize your operational and data warehouse functions. If you have multiple CPUs, the question is whether you can afford *not* to implement these features.

Let's Tune It

To summarize parallelism, its features, how to leverage its power, and using it in real-life situations, inspect the following points as a summary of what we have covered in this chapter:

- Ensure that your hardware will support parallel query feature. Single CPU machines will have performance degraded by using parallel features.

- The best database candidates for parallel usage are data warehouses, VLDB, and large data-intensive applications.

■ Set up the Parallel Query feature by setting appropriate values in the initialization parameter file.

■ Set the initialization parameter file entry PARALLEL_MIN_SERVERS = the likely number of simultaneous parallel operations.

■ Set the initialization parameter file entry PARALLEL_MAX_SERVERS = 2 * # of CPUs * # of concurrent users.

■ Set the initialization parameter file entry OPTIMIZER_PERCENT_PARALLEL = 100/number of concurrent users; this is dependent upon the weight you want to give to parallel processing in the cost-based optimizer.

■ Generally, you will be required to increase the parameter SHARED_POOL_SIZE when using parallelism.

■ Use hints in your SQL operations to tell Oracle to parallelize your operation.

■ **parallel** hints may access data and indexes. When data is accessed by a table scan, use **parallel** hint. When an index scan is used, the PARALLEL_INDEX hint may be used.

■ Don't exceed the maximum number of parallel query server processes available on your machine, or your operation will not execute in parallel.

■ The number of parallel query server processes used by an operation is known as the *degree of parallelism*.

■ Tables can be created with a default degree of parallelism.

■ Hints will take precedence over the default degree of parallelism that has been defined for the table.

■ When creating a table or inserting records based on data in another table, use **parallel** hints in both the **insert** and **select** sections of the SQL command.

■ Create and rebuild indexes using **parallel** hints to reduce the time to perform this lengthy task.

- Use the **parallel** option available in SQL*Loader to improve load performance. By loading using parallelism, you can spread the work for the load among many servers. Be careful when loading a table, as each load process will want to address individual table extents. The result may be a table that has grown larger than expected.

- Use the views V$PQ_SESSTAT, V$PQ_SYSSTAT, and V$PQ_TQSTAT to monitor and tune your implementation of the parallel query features.

Oracle 7.x Specifics

Please note the following points organized by the headings for some sections throughout this chapter:

- "Look and Feel of Parallel Query" With release 7.1., 7.2, and 7.3, verify that the parallel query feature is installed by looking at V$OPTION.

- "Parallel Execution" Only full table scans can be parallelized for Oracle 7 releases 7.1, 7.2, and 7.3. Parallelization was not available with 7.0.x.

- "Familiar SQL Statements Parallel Style" Only parallel influencing hint available with release 7.x.

- "Parallel Loading" The parallel loading feature is supported by release 7.3 with or without the parallel query feature; the parallel query feature must be installed with 7.1 and 7.2. Parallel loading is not available with 7.0.x.

CHAPTER
6

Other Database Issues

he preceding chapters of this book have dealt with the basics: memory, I/O, and CPU. This chapter will deal with other database issues that affect the performance of an Oracle database. First, we'll discuss the entries in the initialization parameter (database parameters) file. The parameters within the initialization parameter file allow optimization of memory structures, database-wide defaults, and user and process default limits. Lock contention is an important consideration in multiuser Oracle systems that handle heavy data manipulation. Oracle gives you out-of-the-box tools which we discuss all over *Oracle8 Tuning*. We'll also discuss tuning of the redo logs in some detail. All these tools can be used to tune an Oracle system and investigate what is happening within the database.

The Initialization Parameter (INIT.ORA) File

There are over 100 entries in the initialization parameter file that you can set if you so desire. Some of these parameters affect performance, while others do not. Many works, including the *Oracle8 Server Reference Manual*, provide a comprehensive list of the parameters that you can set in the initialization parameter file. Not all entries in this file that you can set will be mentioned in this chapter; the parameters discussed here will be broken into two groups:

- Parameters affecting the entire database limits
- Parameters affecting the user or an individual process

There are a number of special characters that can appear in the Initialization Parameter file. Table 6-1 lists the special characters and their meaning.

Some initialization parameters are *dynamic*, that is, they can be modified using the **alter session**, **alter system**, or **alter system deferred** command while an instance is running. Table 6-2 lists the initialization parameters that are alterable with **alter session**. Parameters changed with this command are only valid during the current session. Table 6-3 lists the initialization parameters that are alterable with the **alter system**. Parameters

Character	Description
#	Comment
(	Start of list of values
)	End of list of values
"	Start or end of quoted string
' (single quote)	Start or end of quoted string
=	Separator of keyword or value(s)
, (comma)	Separator of elements
-	Precedes UNIX-style keyword
\	Escape character

TABLE 6-1. *Special Characters in Initialization File*

Alterable Parameter	Alterable Parameter
allow_partial_sn_results	b_tree_bitmaps_plans
db_file_multiblock_read_count	global_names
hash_area_size	hash_multiblock_io_count
max_dump_file_size	nls_currency
nls_date_format	nls_date_language
nls_iso_currency	nls_language
nls_numeric_characters	nls_sort
nls_territory	object_cache_max_size_percent
object_cache_optimal_size	ops_admin_group
optimizer_mode	optimizer_percent_parallel
optimizer_search_limit	parallel_instance_group
prallel_min_percent	partition_view_enabled
plsqlv2_compatibility	remote_dependencies_mode
sort_area_retained_size	sort_area_size
sort_direct_writes	sort_read_fac
sort_write_buffer_size	sort_write_buffers
spin_count	star_transformation_enabled
text_enable	timed_statistics

TABLE 6-2. *Options That Can Be Changed with alter session*

Alterable Parameter	Alterable Parameter
aq_tm_processes	control_file_record_keep_time
db_block_checkpoint_batch	db_block_checksum
db_block_max_dirty_target	db_file_miltiblock_read_count
fixed_date	freeze_db_for_fast_instance_recovery
global_names	hash_multiblock_io_count
license_max_sessions	license_max_users
license_session_warning	log_archive_duplex_destq
log_archive_min_succeed_dest	log_checkpoint_interval
log_checkpoint_timeout	log_small_entry_max_size
max_dump_file_size	mts_dispatchers
mts_servers	ops_admin_group
parallel_instance_group	parallel_transaction_resource_timeout
plsqlv2_compatibility	remote_dependencies_mode
resource_limit	spin_count
text_enabled	time_os_statistics
timed_statisitics	user_dump_dest

TABLE 6-3. *Options That Can Be Changed with alter system*

changed in this fashion are still valid until changed again or the instance goes down.

NOTE
*The **alter system** command does not always change the parameter for the current session, so the **alter session** should be used in addition to it.*

Table 6-4 lists the initialization parameters that are alterable with **alter session deferred**. Parameters changed this way take effect for all future sessions that connect to the database but don't affect the currently connected sessions. (Tables 6-1 through 6-4 used with permission of Oracle Corporation, from the *Oracle8 Server Reference Manual*.)

Alterable Parameter	Alterable Parameter
allow_partial_sn_results	backup_disk_to_slaves
basckup_tape_to_slaves	db_file_direct_to_count
object_cache_max_size_percent	object_cache_optimal_size
sort_area_retained_size	sort_area_size
sort_direct_writes	sort_read_fac
sort_write_buffer_size	sort_write_buffers
transaction_auditing	

TABLE 6-4. *Options That Can Be Changed with alter system deferred Option*

The information in Tables 6-2, 6-3, and 6-4 is provided because a shutdown instance is not a tuned instance. This way, if one of these parameters needs to be changed, it can be done dynamically with shutting down and restarting the instance.

To see the current setting for the parameters in a database listed alphabetically, the following command should be used in Server Manager or the SQL*Worksheet:

```
SQLWKS> show parameters
```

Database-wide Parameters

Database-wide parameters impose limits (for example, set a maximum number of oranges that can be put in the shopping cart) or define a number of entries that Oracle maintains for you (for example, keep five checkout counters active simultaneously in the store). Let's look at those database-wide parameters that affect performance.

CREATE_BITMAP_AREA_SIZE

This specifies the amount of memory allocated for creation of bitmap indexes. Many works, especially *Oracle Data Warehousing* (Corey and Abbey, Oracle Press 1997), explain bitmap indexes and lay out an example of what they look like. The default value is 8MB, though larger values might lead to faster bitmap index creation. From a performance perspective, before changing this entry from the default, all of the following should apply:

1. You support a decision-support database that uses bitmap indexes.

2. You create bitmap indexes on an ongoing basis.

3. You support a database whose contents are primarily static.

4. The cardinality of the columns dictates using bitmap indexes.

Cardinality is a measurement of the number of unique values in a column relative to the number of rows in a table. The GENDER column of a PERSON table is used frequently to illustrate how this cardinality is determined. Suppose PERSON contains 12,909 rows and, surprise surprise, the GENDER column contains either "F" or "M". Determine the cardinality according to the following formula; it is always expressed as a percentage.

```
cardinality = number of possible unique column values / number of rows in table
            = 2 / 12909 * 100 = .0155
```

Thus, GENDER is a candidate for a bitmap index if your data is static and it is commonly mentioned as a selection criterion in SQL statements. Take the same PERSON table with up to 50 values for a state code. Applying the same formula, the result becomes:

```
cardinality =  50 / 12909 * 100 = .39
```

This also makes the ST_CDE column a candidate for a bitmap index upon initial inspection. However, the next rule suggests that this is not the case.

ISSUES RULE #1
If the cardinality of a column is over $1/100^{th}$ of 1 percent (yes that is .01 percent), it is not a candidate for a bitmap index.

Even after making this rule, there have been situations where people reported better performance from a bitmap index than a traditional index when the cardinality is as high as 1 percent. To decide if this applies in your situation, you will have to test the performance of queries using both indexing approaches.

BITMAP_MERGE_AREA_SIZE

This parameter specifies the amount of memory used to merge bitmaps retrieved from a range scan of the index. The default is 1MB, though performance with larger values may improve when multiple bitmap index segments are brought together as query results are assembled.

SHARED_POOL_SIZE

This parameter determines the amount of memory that Oracle uses for its library cache and data dictionary cache. The value is expressed in bytes, commonly even multiples of 1,000,000. These caches are discussed in Chapters 2 and 7. Chapter 2 also discusses the Oracle8 multithreaded server (mts). When you use mts, some user process information is in this pool as well.

The following command and its output can be used to view what part of the memory allocated to the shared pool is free:

```
SQL> select * from v$sgastat where name = 'free memory';
POOL           NAME                             BYTES
-----------    ------------------------------   ----------
shared pool    free memory                         1419576
1 row selected.
SQL>
```

LIBRARY CACHE   The library cache contains shared SQL and PL/SQL information. Ideally, caching commonly used prepared SQL and PL/SQL statements into memory is the goal. A number of statistics are available to help you determine how effectively Oracle is using this cache. Due to the substantial overhead associated with parsing PL/SQL and SQL statements, the goal is to parse once and execute many times. Chapter 8 discusses the phases in the processing of SQL statements (parse, execute, and fetch) and use of the shared pool. Readers who are familiar with Oracle 3GL compilers have probably seen and used the HOLD_CURSOR parameter. Setting the parameter to "Y" instructs Oracle to keep the precompiler SQL statements in the shared pool. Again, the goal is to make the SQL area large enough to hold frequently used SQL statements in memory to avoid reparsing. Interpretation of these statistics will be covered in the section on utlbstat and utlestat later in this chapter.

The entire tuning process of the shared pool is treated extensively in Chapter 8. If the tuning process determines that the shared pool size needs adjustment, this is done in the initialization parameter file.

DATA DICTIONARY CACHE   In Oracle8, the allocation of space to the different structure types in the shared pool is managed by Oracle internal mechanisms. The data dictionary cache contains data dictionary items in memory. The objective is to keep all needed data dictionary information cached so that physical disk access can be minimized. The data dictionary is where Oracle stores all the information required to monitor itself (that is, who owns it, where is it, and how to get it). Before Oracle can return a piece of data to the user, it must first examine the data dictionary. The hit and miss statistics for the data dictionary are presented in the utlbstat/utlestat package that comes with Oracle (see the "utlbstat/utlestat" section later in this chapter).

Table 6-5 gives a list of parameters and what items in the data dictionary they affect. Examining the output from utlbstat/utlestat helps to determine if specific data elements are cached effectively.

The occurrence of the objects in memory is not dependent upon the number of specific objects that have been defined within the database. It is dependent upon the number of objects that are referenced by the users. The standards used to implement systems within an organization help determine the number of objects that end up in memory. For example, if you use *public grants* (everyone who can connect to the database has privileges on objects) and *public synonyms* (a central reference name for all users to refer to an object) for your database objects, then the grants and synonyms needed in the dictionary cache are quite small compared to an organization that grants access by individual users and creates private user synonyms for those objects.

Even though Oracle8 takes care of tuning its own data dictionary cache, we feel it is useful to understand the details of how the DC caches are managed. The bottom line: if you are not pleased with your hit ratio, then you need to increase the initialization parameter file entry SHARED_POOL_SIZE.

SESSION INFORMATION   Session information is used when the database is running Oracle's multithreaded server. Under this mode, Oracle

Parameter	Contains Information About
dc_column_grants	Grants that have been given on columns within tables
dc_columns	Columns that are in the tables in the database
dc_contraints	Constraints that have been defined in the database
dc_database_links	Database links to remote databases that have been defined in the database
dc_files	Files that are defined in the database
dc_free_extents	Chunks of free space that can be used in the database
dc_indexes	Indexes that exist in the database
dc_object_ids	ID number of objects in the database
dc_objects	Objects in the database
dc_profiles	Profiles that have been set up in the database
dc_rollback_segments	Rollback segments that are usable in the database
dc_segments	Segments in the database that are being used
dc_sequence_grants	Grants that have been given to sequence numbers
dc_sequences	Sequence numbers that have been defined in the database
dc_synonyms	Synonyms that have been defined in the database
dc_table_grants	Grants that have been given on the tables in the database
dc_tables	Tables that are in the database
dc_tablspace_quotas	Quotas that have been applied to specific tablespaces
dc_tablespaces	Number of tablespaces
dc_used_extents	Chunks of file space in the database that are currently used
dc_user_grants	Grants that have been given to users in the database
dc_usernames	Usernames that are in the database (e.g., SYS and SYSTEM)
dc_users	Users authorized to connect to the database

TABLE 6-5. *The dc_ Information Slots in the Dictionary Cache*

stores session information in the shared pool rather than in the individual process or user's memory. By looking at the V$SESSTAT and V$STATNAME dictionary views, you can measure the size of session information. The number sitting in the VALUE column from V$SESSTAT shows the number of bytes of memory the process is using. The numbers returned under the

VALUE column can be summed to find out the total amount of memory in use by all running processes. The results are in bytes, and their sum can be helpful when making adjustments to the size of the shared pool. In the following listing, we have shown statistics number 15 (session memory) and 16 (max session memory). We introduced the V$STATNAME view to retrieve the NAME of each STATISTIC# from V$SESSTAT.

```
SQL> select a.sid, b.name,a.value from v$sesstat a, v$statname b
  2 where a.statistic# in (15,16)
  3 and a.statistic# = b.statistic#
  4 order by 1,3;
SID         NAME                    VALUE
----------  ----------------------  ----------
         1  session uga memory      11864
         1  session uga memory max  11864
         2  session uga memory      13232
         2  session uga memory max  13232
         3  session uga memory      11584
         3  session uga memory max  11584
         4  session uga memory      11584
         4  session uga memory max  11584
         5  session uga memory      38488
         5  session uga memory max  38488
         6  session uga memory      32428
         6  session uga memory max  32428
         7  session uga memory      17636
         7  session uga memory max  17636
         8  session uga memory      20496
         8  session uga memory max  20496
         9  session uga memory      24580
         9  session uga memory max  24580
        11  session uga memory      24636
        11  session uga memory max  24636
20 rows selected.
SQL>
```

ISSUES RULE #2

Make the shared pool large enough to eliminate unnecessary reparsing.

ISSUES RULE #3
The shared pool should be large enough to achieve an 80 percent or greater hit ratio on the data dictionary cache. Since the caches are always empty when the database starts up, measure after the database has been primed.

SHARED_POOL_RESERVED Parameters

The two parameters that fall into this category are SHARED_POOL_RESERVED_SIZE and SHARED_POOL_MIN_ALLOC. The former specifies the shared pool space which is reserved for large contiguous requests for shared pool memory. By default this is set to 5 percent of the Shared Pool. A value of 10 percent is recommended by Oracle for most systems.

NOTE
A value of SHARED_POOL_RESERVED_SIZE that is greater than 50 percent of the SHARED_POOL_SIZE will produce Oracle errors.

The SHARED_POOL_RESERVED_MIN_ALLOC controls the allocation of reserved memory. Requests for memory allocations greater than the value of this parameter will allocate space from the reserved list if a chunk of memory of sufficient size is not found on the unreserved shared pool free lists. Before we move on, let's look at some logic that controls allocation of space in the shared pool (reserved and unreserved areas).

NOTE
This logic is designed to give you a flavor of how space is allocated in both areas. It is oversimplified to make the analogy.

```
if requested allocation > shared_pool_reserved_size
   search unreserved free list
   if space found in unreserved area
      allocate space for request in unreserved area
   else
```

```
         return ORA- error
      end if
else
   if requested allocation can be satisfied in unreserved free list
      allocate space for request in unreserved area
   else
      if requested allocation < shared_pool_reserved_min_alloc
         return ORA- error
      else
         if requested allocation can be satisfied in reserved free list
            allocate space for request in reserved area
         else
            return ORA- error
         end if
      end if
   end if
end if
```

Using the information in Table 6-6, let's look at some allocation or error situations. The table assumes SHARED_POOL_RESERVED_SIZE=5000000 and SHARED_POOL_RESERVED_MIN_ALLOC=2500000.

| Request in Bytes | Largest Available | | Result and Reason |
	Unreserved	Reserved	
4000000	6000000	4000000	Unreserved—unreserved has available space and it is searched first.
6000000	800000	4000000	ORA error—the request is too big to qualify for reserved, and there is not enough in unreserved.
1000000	900000	3000000	ORA error—there is space in reserved but the request is below the minimum for which reserved is available; not enough space is available in unreserved either.
4000000	2000000	4500000	Reserved—between the amount for which reserved is available and the maximum that can go in reserved. Enough space exists in reserved to satisfy request.

TABLE 6-6. *Sample Requests and Their Results*

LOG_CHECKPOINT_INTERVAL

This is the number of newly filled redo log file blocks (based on the size of your operating system blocks, not the Oracle block size) that are needed to trigger a checkpoint. If this value is larger than the size of the redo logs, then a checkpoint only occurs when there is a log switch (when the redo log fills up). If the redo logs for your system are large, or the time that Oracle takes to recover using the redo log needs to be shortened, then the value of this parameter should be set to a number smaller than the size of the redo logs. There are two schools of thought about the relationship between checkpoints and redo log switches.

1. Ensure there is no checkpointing between log switches. Checkpoints are too expensive from an I/O perspective to be happening anywhere other than a redo log switch.

2. Allow checkpoints to occur between log switches. Our application is mission critical and, given the size of our redo logs, checkpointing between log switches can reduce instance down time by shortening recovery time.

Let's look at the theory behind implementing each approach.

CHECKPOINTING BETWEEN LOG SWITCHES   This value for LOG_CHECKPOINT_INTERVAL should be set so that checkpoints are spread as evenly as possible through the processing of a redo log. Setting of the parameter is done according to the following formula, using an O/S block size of 512 bytes and a redo log size of 5MB; we want four checkpoints between log switches.

```
LOG_CHECKPOINT_INTERVAL =  size of redo log in bytes /
                           bytes in os block /
                           desired checkpoints between log switches
                        =  5242880 / 512 / 4 = 2560
```

It would make no sense to set LOG_CHECKPOINT_INTERVAL to any value other than 2560 in this scenario. For example, if your redo log were the equivalent of 1,000 O/S blocks, then it would not make sense to set this parameter to 900; the net effect would be a checkpoint once 900 blocks were written, then again when 100 blocks more were written (remember, when a redo log fills up, you have a log switch). If you wish to have checkpoints more often than 1,000 blocks, you should set a value that would evenly space checkpoints throughout the redo log. For example, if your redo log is 1,000 blocks and you set LOG_CHECKPOINT_INTERVAL to 250, you would have four checkpoints per redo log file.

CHECKPOINTING ONLY AT A LOG SWITCH   To ensure a checkpoint only occurs at a log switch, the following formula is used. Not wanting any checkpoints to occur, we cut the last line from the previous formula where we wanted them to occur between switches.

```
LOG_CHECKPOINT_INTERVAL =  CEIL (redo log size in bytes / bytes in os block) + 1)
                        =  CEIL (5242880 / 512 + 1) = 10241
```

Let's do a reality check on this number. Using the value 1,027, the number of bytes of redo that will be written at the value the interval is set is:

```
redo bytes written = 10241 * 512 = 5243392
```

Since this number (5,243,392) is larger than the size of a redo log member (5,242,880), the writing of log_checkpoint_interval_bytes will never get a chance to trigger a checkpoint.

EFFECT OF CHECKPOINTS ON PERFORMANCE   Another factor that determines when checkpointing should be done is the speed of the disk drives. If the disk drives are slow, it takes a longer time to recover using the redo logs. The database writer process also takes a longer time to write an entire redo log. Therefore, to reduce these time delays, perhaps checkpointing should be more frequent. But be careful—a high frequency of checkpoints in an Oracle system can degrade performance. Too frequent checkpoints diminish the benefits of delayed database file writes in batch rather than transaction mode.

As with most tunable parameters, there is no exact science to determine appropriate settings. Experimentation with each Oracle system and with each hardware, file distribution, and user activity configuration is necessary.

The number of occurrences that the DBWR has been notified to do a checkpoint for a given instance is shown using the Performance Pack (part of the Oracle Enterprise Manager discussed in Chapter 9) in the system statistics monitor chart.

The LOG_CHECKPOINT_INTERVAL
parameter should never be set to 0. This
effectively causes internal checkpoints to be
initiated even if a single redo log buffer has
been written since the last request.

ISSUES RULE #4
If the length of system down time must be
reduced at all costs, set the checkpoint interval
to occur at evenly spaced lengths throughout
the logging process. This will reduce the
startup time of the system after a crash.

LOG_CHECKPOINT_TIMEOUT

In considering checkpoints, we should not overlook the parameter
LOG_CHECKPOINT_TIMEOUT. This parameter works on time. The value
forces a checkpoint based on the number of seconds since the last
checkpoint. If you want to guarantee a checkpoint every three minutes, for
example, you would set the value to 180. This parameter is different than
LOG_CHECKPOINT_INTERVAL, which uses the number of buffers filled as
its indicator of when to force a checkpoint.

ISSUES RULE #5
If performance is your concern, set
LOG_CHECKPOINT_TIMEOUT=0 (the
default, which tells Oracle to pay no attention
to time when deciding when to checkpoint).
Set LOG_CHECKPOINT_INTERVAL to a
size greater than the physical redo log file.
Then checkpoints will occur only when the
redo log file fills up.

LOG_ARCHIVE_DUPLEX_DEST

When running a database in ARCHIVELOG mode, Oracle copies redo
logs to the destination specified in the initialization parameter file for

LOG_ARCHIVE_DEST. We have always thought it would be nice if we could have the archiver process write to more than one destination. This can be accomplished with Oracle8 by setting a value for LOG_ARCHIVE_DUPLEX_DEST. Inspect the next listing to see where the archiver will copy redo logs as they are archived.

```
log_archive_dest = f:\prod\arclogs\arc_
log_archive_format = %s.arc
log_archive_duplex_dest = t:\prod\arclogs\duplex\arc_
```

As a member of the redo log group with sequence number 2989 is archived, two files will be created—f:\prod\arclogs\arc_2989.arc and t:\prod\arclogs\duplex\arc_2989.arc. We are happy with this approach since there is no longer a single point of failure.

LOG_CHECKPOINTS_TO_ALERT

The value for this parameter determines whether checkpoint start and finish are logged to the instance alert file. We spoke in the LOG_CHECKPOINT_INTERVAL and LOG_CHECKPOINT_TIMEOUT sections about controlling the frequency of checkpoints based on the amount of redo generated. Setting this parameter to TRUE will cause text similar to the following to appear in the alert file:

```
Tue Aug 26 19:58:09 1999
Beginning database checkpoint by background
Tue Aug 26 19:58:10 1999
Thread 1 advanced to log sequence 3423
  Current log# 1 seq# 3423 mem# 0: /oradata2/rep01/redo01a.log
  Current log# 1 seq# 3423 mem# 1: /oradata3/rep01/redo01b.log
  Current log# 1 seq# 3423 mem# 2: /oradata4/rep01/redo01c.log
Tue Aug 26 19:58:23 1999
Completed database checkpoint by background
Tue Aug 26 22:12:19 1999
Beginning database checkpoint by background
```

Thus, we now know that a checkpoint started at 19:58:09 and completed at 19:58:23, therefore taking 14 seconds. We also know that the next checkpoint began at 22:12:19 or roughly 2 hours and 11 minutes later. There is no easy way to get this information without enabling this feature using this parameter.

ISSUES RULE #6
Set LOG_CHECKPOINTS_TO_ALERT = TRUE
to assist the ongoing tuning process
by providing checkpoint start, end, and
duration information.

DB_BLOCK_BUFFERS

This parameter is the number of database block buffers that are cached in memory. This is your *data* cache, one of the most important parameters you have in the initialization parameter file. Before the introduction of the SHARED_POOL_SIZE parameter in Oracle7, this would have been the most important tunable parameter in the initialization parameter file. Now, it is debatable which is the most important tunable parameter in the parameters file, DB_BLOCK_BUFFERS or the SHARED_POOL_SIZE. Simply stated: Every piece of data a user ever sees first passes through this DB_BLOCK_BUFFERS data cache.

The larger the cache, the more data Oracle can hold in memory; the smaller the cache, the less data Oracle can hold in memory. If the data is not in memory, Oracle issues the needed I/O requests to obtain the data. Remember, I/O is one of the slowest operations a computer can perform. Oracle manages this area using a Least Recently Used (*LRU*) algorithm. This means that if the buffer cache contains a hot data block (in a trading system, an example of a hot data block would be one containing Oracle stock), then, memory permitting, it stays in the cache. If the buffer cache contains a cold data block (in a trading system, it would be a data block holding Sybase stock), then when additional DB_BLOCK_BUFFERS are needed, Oracle will swap the cold blocks out of memory.

To summarize, the larger the number you choose for DB_BLOCK_ BUFFERS, the larger your user data cache. A large data cache is very desirable. In fact, in a perfect world, you might want to make your DB_BLOCK_BUFFERS large enough to hold your entire database. In this situation, the need to go to the actual disk might be eliminated.

We know of two situations where this concept was taken to the limit, and both had very interesting results. In the first situation, with a very large Oracle database on a Pyramid/Nile machine, the DBA had always heard that the larger the System Global Area (SGA), the better. He made changes to the initialization parameter file that caused the SGA to grow to 750MB. It is important that its SHARED_POOL_SIZE and DB_BLOCK_BUFFERS parameters typically account for 90 percent of SGA total size. So, in this case, we had an enormous DB_BLOCK_BUFFERS setting. It was set to 40000 (Pyramid is a 16K block, whereas most UNIX boxes are typically 2K blocks). When we began to evaluate this database, we questioned the need for such a large DB_BLOCK_BUFFERS. When we lowered DB_BLOCK_BUFFERS, we saw database performance increase. We wondered why performance would increase when Oracle no longer had to read its data from disk and it could use main memory.

The solution turned out to be quite simple. Oracle itself was constraining the operation of the system, because the SGA was taking up 75 percent of the available memory. We had induced system paging and swapping by requesting too much memory for the SGA. As we discussed in Chapter 2, paging involves moving portions of an application or process out to secondary storage to free up real memory space. Swapping involves copying entire processes from memory to secondary storage.

ISSUES RULE #7
Remember, Oracle is one of many processes that must all live, share, and breathe all available resources. In addition, the SGA should never take over 50 percent of the available memory.

The interesting problem that came out of this situation was how to determine when DB_BLOCK_BUFFERS is set too high. To determine this, we came up with the following SQL statement. This code must be run from the Oracle SYS account.

```
select decode(state,0,'Free',
                    1, 'Read and Modified',
                    2, 'Read and Not Modified',
                    3, 'Currently Being Read', 'Other'), Count(*)
   from x$bh
 group by decode(state, 0,'Free',
                    1, 'Read and Modified',
                    2, 'Read and Not Modified',
                    3, 'Currently Being Read', 'Other');
```

By looking at the status of the block header, we can determine what they are doing. If they are free, this means that the DB_BLOCK_BUFFERS value is too large—it has leftover blocks that were never used. In the case of DB_BLOCK_BUFFERS set to 40,000, we found quite a few that were never used. This was an interesting twist to an old rule.

ISSUES RULE #8
Set the DB_BLOCK_BUFFERS as high as possible for your operating environment in order to hold as much data in memory as possible. But don't induce excessive operating system paging and swapping. (This goes to show you that every rule, no matter how good, has its exceptions.)

The second situation involved a very large Oracle database on a VAX/VMS 6450 machine. Because the entire machine was dedicated to a single Oracle application, we had the luxury of tuning the entire machine to benefit Oracle. At that time, we had never heard of a VAX/VMS SGA over 32 megabytes, so we decided to look into the pros and cons of doing an SGA larger than 32 megabytes.

The quest for information led us to Mark Porter (rumor has it that Mark is now known as Video LAD), who was then an Oracle kernel developer. We discussed what we were trying to do, and Mark explained that it was possible because the VMS operating system current at the time supported larger *working set sizes* (the amount of memory a VMS system administrator allocates to a user session). This larger working set size now allowed a VMS installation the ability to increase the SGA size over 32 megabytes. So, with Mark's help, we made the necessary system changes to handle a larger SGA and tried it. The most notable change was an increase in the time needed to enter SQL*Plus. After we examined the situation, this made sense. Oracle had to map the requested image to the SGA. The larger the number the SGA was set to, the more work the operating system had to do to invoke SQL*Plus.

By making the decision to go to a larger SGA, we had to live with the trade-off that initial image activation would be slower the first time.

ISSUES RULE #9
Tuning is all about trade-offs. As the DBA, you must constantly struggle with all the available resources and decide what the equitable split is for your situation.

In summary, you need to look at your individual situation and decide what is appropriate for your applications and available memory. As a rule of thumb, we recommend making DB_BLOCK_BUFFERS as large as possible. You do this to minimize I/O, which is a very expensive operation. It is a trade-off that you will find usually makes sense. If the system is strictly a data entry system, with little or no query action, then this trade-off would not make sense. On the other hand, if the system is a reporting system that uses few batch or interactive user processes, it would be best to allocate as much available memory as possible to Oracle so that as much data as possible could be stored in memory to reduce the direct system I/O. In most environments, it's a mix, so we still stand by Issues Rule #8 mentioned earlier.

DB_BLOCK_LRU_EXTENDED_STATISTICS

This parameter enables or disables the compilation of statistics in the x$kcbrbh and the x$kcbcbh tables. Using these tables, you can assess the change in the number of disk accesses that would be gained by increasing the allocation of additional buffers or would be lost by the removal of a portion of buffers. Consult the discussion in Chapter 2 for details.

The use of this statistics-gathering tool has itself an effect on the performance of the database. This parameter should not be turned on in normal operation. It should only be used in a controlled test environment where the negative performance impact will not adversely affect the normal, necessary operations of the database.

In general, we see very few people using this parameter, because it requires starting and stopping the database so that you can get these statistics. In addition, while this parameter is turned on, your database performance is affected.

The utlbstat and utlestat utilities discussed later in this chapter give information on the ratio of times data was found in memory compared to the number of requests for data needed to be satisfied from disk (i.e., the hit ratio). The Enterprise Manager monitor I/O also gives a summary statistic that shows this ratio. These are all excellent ways to determine if DB_BLOCK_BUFFERS is too small.

DB_BLOCK_LRU_STATISTICS

This parameter is set either to TRUE or FALSE. A TRUE setting combined with the DB_BLOCK_LRU_EXTENDED_STATISTICS set to a nonzero value allows monitoring the gain or loss of cache hits from adding or removing buffers from the database block buffer pool.

ISSUES RULE #10
Only use the DB_BLOCK_LRU_STATISTICS to determine if more or less DB_BLOCKS_BUFFERS should be used, and don't use it during normal operations because of the negative impact it has on performance.

DML_LOCKS

This parameter is the maximum number of locks that can be placed on all tables by all users at one time. If you have three users updating five tables, you need 15 DML locks to perform the concurrent operation. If you do not have this parameter set high enough, processing stops and an Oracle error is issued.

Our experience has shown that this parameter should be set artificially high from the start. This parameter has no effect on performance—resetting it involves modifying the initialization parameter file and restarting the database. A closed database is not a tuned database—restarting the database will flush all cache information loaded into memory.

ISSUES RULE #11
Overestimate the number of DML_LOCKS that will be needed, because if you run out, it's a show stopper. Better too many than not enough.

LOG_BUFFER

This parameter is the number of bytes that are allocated to the redo log buffer in the SGA. This area is used when a user is executing a transaction that can be rolled back. Once a transaction is committed or rolled back, the information in the log buffer in the SGA is written to the redo log file. If the Oracle system is processing long transactions or if many in-process transactions will be occurring, this parameter should be increased to reduce the I/O to the redo logs.

ISSUES RULE #12
Size the LOG_BUFFER properly to reduce I/O to the redo logs.

PROCESSES

This parameter defines the maximum number of processes that can simultaneously connect to the Oracle database. The default number of 50 is good only for a very limited system. Keep in mind that the background Oracle processes are included in this number and, if an application is written that spawns processes recursively, all these spawned processes count.

The conservative setting of the parameter is used to limit the number of users, for a business reason or because of hardware/system capacity issues. If limiting users is not a concern, then it is best to overestimate this parameter value.

ISSUES RULE #13
If the objective is to not limit the number of users on the system, overestimate the number of concurrent processes.

One parameter, SESSIONS, is a derived parameter from the PROCESSES parameter. If you are letting Oracle determine the value of this parameter from the PROCESSES parameter, you should have not problems if you change the value for PROCESSES. If you have decided to explicitly set the SESSION parameter in the initialization file, then it needs to be changed any time the value of PROCESSES is changed.

To go along with that, the values of ENQUEUE_RESOURCES and TRANSACTIONS are derived from the value of SESSIONS. The same rules mentioned above for the explicit setting of the SESSION parameter also apply for the explicit setting of the ENQUEUE_RESOURCES and TRANSACTIONS parameters.

ROLLBACK_SEGMENTS

This parameter is the line in the initialization parameter file where all user-created private rollback segments are referenced. For example, the line may read:

```
ROLLBACK_SEGMENTS = (RS1,RS2,RBS_HUGE)
```

We never use public rollback segments. With Oracle, you have the choice between a private or a public rollback segment. A private rollback segment can only be used if referenced in the line above. The advantage to using a private rollback segment is that you have complete control over what segments are acquired by the database instance when started. A public rollback segment is there for the taking. You have no control over which public rollback segments the database instance will acquire.

As we suggested in Chapter 3, never put rollback segments in the same tablespace as your data and indexes. You cannot take a tablespace offline that contains rollback information, because rollback segments are always active. In addition, for performance reasons, you should place your private rollback segments in their own tablespace(s).

One of the major performance gains with Oracle version 6 was its ability to break the I/O barrier concerning updates. This was accomplished by breaking the update into two distinct phases: the undo phase and the commit phase. We will illustrate this point using the example of a banking system.

1. Money Grabbers goes to the local automated teller and requests her bank account balance. Using SQL, the request is the following:

```
select name,account,balance
  from orcl
 where name = 'MONEY GRABBERS'
   and account = '5002300';
```

Table 6-7 shows what values exist in what areas (SGA, rollback, and redo log) as the above SQL is run.

2. Money Grabbers, noticing a bank error of $200 in her favor, decides to make a withdrawal. Using SQL, the transaction is the following:

```
update orcl
set balance = balance-200
  werc name = 'MONEY GRABBERS'
    and  account = '5002300';
```

Table 6-8 shows what values exist in these same three areas after running the **update**.

3. Money Grabbers is told that the machine is working, and the machine then asks, "Do you want to commit the changes you have made?" She responds YES, and the SQL issued is the following:

```
commit_work;
```

Table 6-9 now shows the values held in these three locations after the transaction is committed.

As you can see in Tables 6-7 through 6-9, your rollback segment contains your undo information. Had the machine crashed during the update in Table 6-8, the database would have recovered itself by rolling back or undoing based on what was in the rollback segment. Had the computer crashed after the complete transaction was committed, the database would have recovered using the redo log and rollback segments. What is important here is that the update statement is broken into two distinct phases. The update is no longer a bottleneck affecting system

Location	Account	Name	Balance	Undo/Redo info
SGA	5002300	Money Grabbers	500	null
Rollback	null	null	null	null
Redo Log	null	null	null	null

TABLE 6-7. *Current Account Status at Start*

Location	Account	Name	Balance	Undo/Redo Info
SGA	5002300	Money Grabbers	300	null
Rollback	null	null	null	500
Redo log	null	null	null	null

TABLE 6-8. *Values Stored in Three Locations After Update*

performance. Because the commit was recorded in the redo log, the database doesn't have to record the bank account balance for Money Grabbers immediately back to the database file.

Another benefit of this approach is the fact it allows *hot blocks* (blocks containing data in the midst of being changed) to stay current in memory, because among the rollback segment, the redo log, and the database files, Oracle is able to remain consistent. So if another transaction happened against the same data block, that block would still be in memory even though the database file itself still contains the initial balance. The database maintains its integrity because issuing the statement commit_work; caused Oracle to record the transaction on disk. Oracle uses this mechanism to protect you and your data!

Another benefit of rollback segments has to do with read consistency. Until the rollback segments are overwritten, Oracle has a copy of the database blocks before the update. So a long-running transaction that started before the update would be able to present you a read-consistent view of the database.

Location	Account	Name	Balance	Undo/Redo Info
SGA	5002300	Money Grabbers	300	null
Rollback	null	null	null	null
Redo log	null	null	null	−200

TABLE 6-9. *Values Stored in Three Locations When Transaction Completed and Saved*

ISSUES RULE #14
Always name your rollback segments in the initialization parameter file. Rollback segments named in this file should be private.

ISSUES RULE #15
Always place your rollback segments in their own tablespace.

ISSUES RULE #16
Always create a special rollback segment designed to handle your large transactions (commonly referred to as "the update from h..."). See Chapter 8 for a discussion of **set transaction use rollback segment**.

NOTE
*Once the **commit** is issued, this means that Oracle has written sufficient information to disk to be able to recreate your transaction.*

SEQUENCE_CACHE_ENTRIES

This parameter is the total number of sequence numbers that are cached in the SGA at one time. Setting this number correctly greatly reduces the overhead spent in obtaining sequence numbers. If you create a sequence with the **nocache** option, setting this parameter will have no effect on the sequence.

SESSIONS

This parameter is the number of user and system sessions allowed at one time. This parameter is derived from the value you chose in the initialization parameter file for PROCESSES. Oracle sets this value according to the following formula:

```
SESSIONS = (1.1 * PROCESSES) + 5
```

The extra five is to account for recursive processes. Unless your applications create concurrent recursive sessions, the derived value should be sufficient.

UTL_FILE_DIR

To take advantage of PL/SQL file I/O features, one or more of these entries must be specified. All users can read or write files in the directory specified by the string for this parameter. Simply code one or more of these parameters each followed by a valid directory name.

```
UTL_FILE_DIR = F:\UTL_DIR\PRD1
UTL_FILE_DIR = D:\UTL_DIR\PRD2
UTL_FILE_DIR = K:\UTL_DIR\PRD3
```

Individual User/Process Parameters

The following initialization parameter file entries affect an individual user process. As an example, let's say you have 100 users and you give them 1MB of sort space. Then potentially, if every user is sorting, you would need an additional 100MB of O/S memory above and beyond what the SGA was using.

OPEN_CURSORS

This parameter is the maximum number of cursors a user can have open at one time. Both implicit and explicit cursors are used by processes. Developer/2000 uses cursors constantly to fetch multiple rows into blocks and to do list_values. The setting for OPEN_CURSORS determines the amount of memory a user allocates on an operating system level for handling SQL statements. It's best to have this value set high and let the operating system control the actual amount of real memory a user acquires. If this value is set too low, it will stop Oracle processing. When the operating system controls a user's memory, processing usually does not stop when a user hits the limit. In the VAX/VMS system, the user's memory is paged out. We have found that the VAX/VMS handling of memory allocation is more efficient than setting limits within the Oracle database.

ISSUES RULE #17
*Be generous with the OPEN_CURSORS
parameter, especially in a Developer/2000
application environment. This will be a show
stopper for your application if it is set too low
in the initialization parameter file.*

CLOSED_CACHED_OPEN_CURSORS

This parameter determines whether cursors that are opened and cached
into memory by PL/SQL are automatically closed at each commit. A value
of FALSE allows cursors that are opened by PL/SQL to be held open so that
subsequent executions need not open a new cursor. This can cause
subsequent executions of frequently used cursors to be quicker. A value of
TRUE closes all open cursors at each commit or rollback and frees up the
memory that the cursors were taking up. If cursors are frequently reused,
then setting this value to FALSE should improve performance.

ISSUES RULE #18
*Set the CLOSED_CACHED_OPEN_CURSORS
parameter, especially in a Developer 2000
application environment where cursors
are frequently reused, to FALSE. This will
improve the performance of most
Developer/2000 applications.*

SORT_AREA_SIZE

This is the amount of memory per user process that is allocated for sorting.
When Oracle cannot acquire enough memory to complete the sort in
memory, it completes the process on disk; thus, an inadequate value for
this parameter causes excessive sorts on disk (disk access is very slow
compared to the alternative). Be very careful, however, when being
generous, because the sort area in memory is allocated on a per user basis.

If you are in the process of a full database import, substantial gains can
be made by increasing the value in SORT_AREA_SIZE. Operations such as
index creations require a great deal of sort work space. If your installation
does a lot of nightly batch processing, we recommend increasing this
parameter when there are fewer demands on system memory. Remember,

with Oracle8, you no longer need to restart the database to change this parameter. This parameter can be used dynamically in two ways:

- The **alter session** command will change this parameter just for the current session, which would work well for nightly batch processing.

- The **alter system deferred** command will change this parameter for all subsequent connections to the database.

The second option would need to be used if you are doing an import.

NOTE
*If the **alter system deferred** command is used, remember that the change stays in effect until another **alter system deferred** command is used to modify this parameter or the database is shut down and restarted.*

The V$SYSSTAT table holds information on your sort utilization. Of particular interest are rows with sorts(memory) and sorts(disk) in the NAME column. These two statistics should be examined on a periodic basis when the system has been up and running for a while. By comparing the results from different observations and different times, you can determine if a significant number of sorts are being done on disk and not in memory. If this is the case, then the size of the sort area should be increased.

ISSUES RULE #19
Size your SORT_AREA_SIZE to fit the need of the users. This is a big user of memory and also a big help with performance.

utlbstat and utlestat

Without your spending any additional money, Oracle supplies you with two of the most useful scripts ever created for tuning an Oracle database. They are called utlbstat and utlestat. For those of you who used Oracle way back in version 6, these were previously known as bstat and estat. With these two scripts, you will be able to gather a snapshot of Oracle performance over a given period of time.

utlbstat—An Introduction

The utlbstat component gathers the initial performance statistics. It should not be run immediately after your database has started, or it will skew your results. When a database is first started, none of the system caches are loaded, which is not a realistic picture of a running database. Your goal here is to determine how well your system performs during normal business operations. Statistics that utlbstat gathers are stored in temporary tables. Table 6-10 presents these tables, their source system tables, and a general description.

utlestat—An Introduction

The utlestat component gathers performance statistics at the end of your observation period. The utlestat script must be run at the end of the period for which you want to tune performance. The results of utlestat are placed

Utlbstat Table	Derived from	Description
STATS$DATES	system	Start and end date/time for statistics gathering
STATS$BEGIN_ROLL	v$rollstat	Rollback segment information
STATS$BEGIN_FILE	v$filestat, ts$, v$datafile	Database file information
STATS$BEGIN_STATS	v$sysstat	System statistics
STATS$BEGIN_DC	v$rowcache	System data dictionary information
STATS$BEGIN_LIB	v$librarycache	System library cache information
STATS$BEGIN_LATCH	v$latch	System latch information
STATS$BEGIN_EVENT	v$system_event	Wait events information
STATS$BEGIN_BCK_EVENT	v$session, v$session_event	Background wait events
STATS$BEGIN_WAITSTAT	v$waitstat	Buffer busy wait statistics

TABLE 6-10. *Tables Built by utlbstat*

in the temporary tables. Table 6-11 presents these tables, their source system tables, and a general description.

When utlestat has finished gathering statistics, it then does a comparison of the information that was stored in both sets of temporary tables (utlbstat and utlestat) and stores the differences in another set of temporary tables. Table 6-12 presents the tables that are used for the differences and their sources.

The table of differences as shown in Table 6-12 is then used for utlbstat/utlestat to generate a report of very useful information. An example of this report is gone over section by section later in this chapter. Before we go into details, let's give an example of how to use utlbstat/utlestat.

utlbstat/utlestat Example

Here are the five steps needed to obtain information and arrive at some tuning recommendations:

1. Choose the correct time slice.

2. Check the initialization parameter file.

Utlestat Table	Derived from	Description
STATS$END_EVENT	v$system_event	Wait event information
STATS$END_LATCH	v$latch	System latch information
STATS$END_ROLL	v$rollstat	Rollback segment information
STATS$END_FILE	v$filestat, ts$, v$datafile	Database file information
STATS$END_STATS	v$sysstat	System statistics information
STATS$END_DC	v$rowcache	System data dictionary statistics
STATS$END_LIB	v$librarycache	System library cache information
STATS$END_BCK_EVENT	v$session, v$session_event	Background wait events
STATS$END_WAITSTAT	v$waitstat	Buffer busy wait statistics

TABLE 6-11. *Tables Built by utlestat*

utlestat Difference Table	Source Tables
STATS$STATS	V$STATNAME, STATS$BEGIN(END)_STATS
STATS$LATCHES	V$LATCHNAME, STATS$BEGIN(END)_LATCHES
STATS$EVENTS	STATS$BEGIN(END)_EVENTS
STATS$ROLL	STATS$BEGIN(END)_ROLL
STATS$FILES	STATS$BEGIN(FND)_FILES
STATS$DC	STATS$BEGIN(END)_DC
STATS$BCK_EVENT	STATS$BEGIN(END)_BCK_EVENT
STATS$WAITSTAT	STATS$BEGIN(END)WAITSTAT
STATS$LIB	STATS$BEGIN(END)_LIB

TABLE 6-12.   *utlestat Difference Tables*

3. Turn on utlbstat at the appropriate time.

4. Run utlestat at the end of the time period.

5. Interpret the output.

Choose the Correct Time Slice

The time period you choose must be representative of your work load, or you may corrupt your statistics and make poor tuning choices. For example, if your system is in the process of a major data conversion that would never normally run, then gathering results at that point in time is not going to give you an accurate portrayal of your system's resource needs. On the other hand, running utlbstat/utlestat during recurring peak processing times will give you an excellent view of your performance needs.

Check Initialization Parameter File

In order for all the statistics to be populated during a utlbstat/utlestat session, you must set TIMED_STATISTICS = TRUE in the initialization parameter file. If your database is not running with TIMED_STATISTICS = TRUE, this parameter can be changed using the **alter system** command without having to shut down and restart your database.

Turn on utlbstat at the Appropriate Time

You must run utlbstat from Server Manager, because it does a connect internal to start the collection of statistics. Only some operating system accounts can do connect internal. If you are going to run this set of scripts via another utility, then it is recommended that utlbstat.sql be edited to remove the **connect internal** command at the beginning. What must still be kept in mind is that you need to do connect internal as the user when using another facility to connect to Oracle. Use the following command:

 `SQL> @%RDBMS80%\admin\utlbstat`

Don't forget that the database must have been active for a while, or the results you receive will be skewed. Because the statistics are gathered from the time utlbstat is run until the time utlestat is run, statistics gathered while the Oracle memory structures are being initially populated throws off the statistics. All information is loaded into memory when you first start an Oracle database, and this action would show up in the statistics. Therefore, this utility should be run after a system has been up for a while and has reached some type of equilibrium. Remember, never run utlbstat/utlestat right after the database starts.

Run utlestat at the End of the Time Period

Run the following command to invoke utlestat:

 `SQLWKS> @%RDBMS80%\admin\utlestat`

The output from utlbstat/utlestat is placed in an ASCII file called report.txt.

NOTE
If the database went down between running utlbstat and utlestat, your results are no good, because everything that was in memory before the system went down needs to be reloaded after the system comes back up.

What is unique about these utilities is there is no performance hit on your database except for the few minutes it takes to run each program. All these programs do is gather a snapshot of the system at the start and a snapshot of the system at the end. The results reported in the output are derived from these two points of activity. Without further ado, let's interpret.

Interpret the Output

The output from utlbstat/utlestat contained in the O/S file report.txt will now be gone over a section at a time. We will be highlighting only those areas that in our experience have made a difference.

Library Cache

The following output shows us information about the different types of objects in the library cache:

LIBRARY	GETS	GETHITRATI	PINS	PINHITRATI	RELOADS	INVALIDATI
BODY	3	1	3	1	0	0
CLUSTER	20	1	26	1	0	0
INDEX	0	1	0	1	0	0
OBJECT	0	1	0	1	0	0
PIPE	0	1	0	1	0	0
SQL AREA	90472	.999	184926	.998	198	356
TABLE/PROCED	18467	.985	20342	.963	190	0
TRIGGER	1	1	1	1	0	0

The question that most DBAs have is, "How do I tune it?" Well, this is quite easy. First, you want to minimize reloads. In fact, you should strive to have zero reloads. Remember the golden rule: Parse once, execute many times.

Oracle manages the library cache in much the same way as it does the data cache. When a user issues a new statement, Oracle first determines that it is already in the library cache (Oracle uses a special hashing routine to determine if the statement is already present in the library cache). For example, **commit** would more than likely already be in the cache. In this case, Oracle would just execute the command. In the situation where the procedure is not in the library cache, Oracle attempts to parse the statement and place it into the cache. If there is not enough room in the library cache, then Oracle makes room for the procedure by removing an existing entry. A reload means the removed entry is then rerequested. So, reloads are very bad. It's like doing a job twice that you hated to do the first time. They should never happen in a well-tuned system.

The second situation you look for is low hit ratios on the pinhitratio column and the gethitratio column. Any ratio less than 80 percent is not acceptable. To tune this cache, you just need to increase the SHARED_POOL_SIZE in the initialization parameter file.

ISSUES RULE #20

Reload represents entries in the library cache that were parsed more than once. You should strive for the goal of zero reloads. The solution is to increase the initialization parameter file SHARED_POOL_SIZE parameter.

ISSUES RULE #21

Gethitratio and pinhitratio should always be greater than 80 percent. If you fall below this mark, you should increase the value of SHARED_POOL_SIZE in the initialization parameter file.

System Stats

The next listing shows the first few lines of the system statistics. What's nice about this section is that you are able to get the total amount of activity for the time slice you chose and an overall average for all transactions during the time slice. The information shown lists total system statistics for the time period, broken down by transaction average.

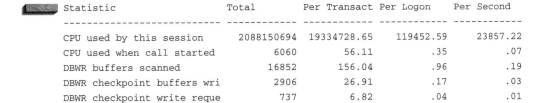

Statistic	Total	Per Transact	Per Logon	Per Second
CPU used by this session	2088150694	19334728.65	119452.59	23857.22
CPU used when call started	6060	56.11	.35	.07
DBWR buffers scanned	16852	156.04	.96	.19
DBWR checkpoint buffers wri	2906	26.91	.17	.03
DBWR checkpoint write reque	737	6.82	.04	.01

DATA CACHE EFFECTIVENESS   Effectiveness can be measured using the above listing. Remember, all data must pass through this cache before it can be accessed by Oracle. To determine the hit ratio, use these simple formulae:

```
LOGICAL READS = CONSISTENT GETS + DB BLOCK GETS
HIT RATIO = (LOGICAL READS - PHYSICAL READS)/LOGICAL READS
```

Now we apply the formulae to the information from the preceding listing:

```
LOGICAL READS   = CONSISTENT GETS + DB BLOCK GETS
(157,694)       = ( 42,533 + 115,161 )
HIT RATIO       = (LOGICAL READS - PHYSICAL READS)/LOGICAL READS
(95.45)         = (157,694 - 7,171)/157,694
```

The result of this calculation gives us a hit ratio of over 95 percent. This means that over 95 percent of all requests were resolved by information residing in the data cache. If this result was less than 80 percent, we would need to increase the value in the DB_BLOCK_BUFFERS entry in the initialization parameter file.

ISSUES RULE #22
Your data cache should have a hit ratio greater than 80 percent.

Events

The following output is for system events that happen within the Oracle system:

Event Name	Count	Total Time	Avg Time
rdbms ipc message	17486	17485887	999.99
SQL*Net message from client	3595	8825822	2455.03
db file sequential read	3898	6211	1.59
db file scattered read	203	2390	11.77
log file switch completion	76	2061	27.12
log file switch (checkpoint inco	12	298	24.83
log file sync	178	89	.5
write complete waits	93	51	.55
free buffer waits	31	36	1.16
buffer busy waits	11	25	2.27
control file sequential read	11	19	1.73
latch free	7	13	1.86
SQL*Net break/reset to client	116	12	.1
SQL*Net message to client	3595	5	0
file identify	1	2	2
file open	22	1	.05

BUFFER BUSY WAIT RATIO   The goal is to eliminate all waits for resources. We use this ratio to determine if there is a problem. Using the statistics from the previous two output listings, you should perform the following calculations:

```
BUFFER BUSY WAITS RATIO    = BUFFER BUSY WAITS/LOGICAL READS
LOGICAL READS              = CONSISTENT GETS + DB BLOCK GETS
```

Now we apply these calculations to the information given above:

```
LOGICAL READS  = CONSISTENT GETS + DB BLOCK GETS
    (157,694) =     ( 42,533 + 115,161 )
 BUFFER BUSY WAITS RATIO    = BUFFER BUSY WAITS/LOGICAL READS
    (.00007)               = (11/157,694)
```

A ratio of greater than 4 percent is a problem. In our example, we are close to 0 percent, which is desirable. If there is a problem, the Oracle8 version of utlestat now captures the information from the V$WAITSTAT table. The following listing shows the output:

```
CLASS              COUNT            TIME
------------------ ---------------- ----------------
data block                    11               25
```

Examining the preceding query, we feel comfortable concluding waits for data blocks are all that occurred. If the waiting that is due to data blocks is excessive (again, over a 4 percent ratio), you need to modify your **freelist** setting (a *freelist* is a list of data blocks that contain free space). So before Oracle inserts rows into a table, it will go to the freelists to find data blocks that have enough free space to accept the insert. Every table has one or more freelists. The value of **freelist** is determined when you first create the table. If you do not specify a **freelist** value, the default is 1.

If the waiting is due to an Undo segment header, the wait is for database buffers containing rollback segment header information. Or, if the waiting is due to Undo block, the wait is for database buffers containing rollback segment data blocks. Remember, before an update can be completed, it must first be recorded in your rollback segment. Contention in this area affects all updates, even updates that were attempted and then aborted. The solution is to add more rollback segments.

ISSUES RULE #23

*If you see data block waits, you need to increase your freelist parameter on heavily inserted tables. You must re-create the table to change an existing freelist setting. When in doubt, we recommend setting the **freelist** to 2 on tables you suspect may become insert bottlenecks.*

ISSUES RULE #24

All resource waits are bad and should be avoided. If you see undo rollback segment waits, then increase the number of private rollback segments your database contains.

SORTS   The system statistics listing above gives very good statistics on your sort usage. The sorts(disk) row tells you how many times you had to sort to disk; that is a sort that could not be handled by the size you specified for the 'SORT_AREA_SIZE parameter in the initialization parameter file. The sorts (memory) row tells you how many times you were able to complete the sort using just memory. We feel that 90 percent or higher of all sorting should be done in memory.

   To eliminate sorts to disk, you should increase the initialization parameter file entry SORT_AREA_SIZE. The larger you make SORT_AREA_SIZE, the larger the sort that can be accomplished by Oracle in memory. Unlike other parameters, this is allocated per user. This is taken from available memory, not from the Oracle SGA area of memory.

CHAINING   When a row spans more than one data block, this can be detected looking at the "table fetch continued row" value. Chaining negatively affects performance. The more chaining found, the poorer the database performs. We recommend eliminating all chained rows. In the system statistics listing above, a total of four chained data blocks were read during the utlbstat/utlestat period; this number is quite small, considering how many total blocks were read. However, we still recommend eliminating all chained rows. With Oracle8 and the **analyze table list chained rows** command, you can detect chaining information in the data dictionary view USER_TABLES.

ENQUEUE WAITS   We like to think of enqueues as locks. When you see waits appearing, this means that Oracle needed another lock but could not obtain it. The solution is to raise the initialization parameter file entry ENQUEUE_RESOURCES. ENQUEUE_RESOURCES represents the number of resources that can be locked by the lock manager.

DATABASE WRITER PROCESS   From the system statistics listing, the DBWR buffers scanned row gives you an excellent overview of the volume of information that has gone through the database writer. This DBWR (database writer process) is discussed in the "Background Processes" section of Chapter 2. The DBWR checkpoints rows give you an excellent indication of how many checkpoints you are doing. The question most DBAs have is, "How do I improve the speed of the database process DBWR?" because DBWR does all the reading and writing to the database files (the checkpoint process only modifies the header of database files if it is enabled in the initialization parameter file).

If you are on an operating system that supports additional database writers, the first thing to do is increase the number of database writers that are activated. Some DBAs are under the misunderstanding that this value is constrained by the number of CPUs your processes have, and this is not correct. The initialization parameter file entry should be based on the number of datafiles your database has. We recommend setting the entry

DB_WRITERS to two per database file. If you suspect that you will need more, then run utlbstat/utlestat and slowly add more.

ISSUES RULE #25
If you are on an operating system that allows multiple DBWR processes (e.g., UNIX), then increase the number of database writers you have.

The other initialization parameter file entry that has a great effect on database writer performance is DB_BLOCK_WRITE_BATCH. The larger the value, the less often the database process is signaled to write. Adjusting this parameter affects how efficient the DBWR will perform.

APPLICATION EFFECTIVENESS   By looking at the table scans (short tables) and table scans (long tables) rows, you can determine how many full table scans your database is doing. A *full table scan* occurs when Oracle does not have an appropriate index to use, and it is forced to read every row in the table. If you intend to process the majority of records, using a full table scan is faster. In most environments, though, we expect to see the majority of the access being done via indexes. So this ratio is used primarily to determine if there is a problem. The formula is as follows:

```
NON-INDEX LOOKUPS RATIO = Table Scans (Long Tables) /
                          Table Scans (Long Tables) +
                          Table Scans (Short Tables)
```

In the system statistics listing, if we apply the formula, we see the following results:

```
Table Scans (Long Table)        =   43
Table Scans (Short Table)       =   542
Non-Index Lookups Ratio  .07  =   43/(43+542)
```

This ratio indicates that 7 percent of all table lookups are full table scans. This is typically a very good situation. If this were over 30 percent and the sample was taken during the day when lots of users were logged on, you should suspect major problems. Chapter 7 discusses how to determine what indexes you need and how effectively they are working.

Average Write Queue Length

This is the average length of the dirty buffer write queue. This
should be compared to the initialization parameter file entry
DB_BLOCK_WRITE_BATCH. If the average write queue length is larger
than the DB_BLOCK_WRITE_BATCH entry, increase the value of
DB_BLOCK_WRITE_BATCH. Also, a quick inspection of the I/O balance
of your disk drives should be made. This could be an indication that one
disk drive is doing most of the work.

```
Average Write Queue Length
--------------------------
 .28648974668275030156815444
```

Tablespace and File I/O

This section of the report gives the information about the physical reads and
writes that are happening to the tablespaces and files that make them up.
Because I/O is one of the slowest operations a computer can perform, the
following listing should prove quite useful.

The interpretation of I/O information was covered in detail in Chapter 3.
Briefly, this information is used to look at the physical reads and writes that
are happening to each file to detect an uneven work load. If an uneven
work load exists, you may need to do one of the following:

- Move one or more database files to another disk to balance the load.

- When a frequently accessed table shares space in a datafile with
  other tables, take the busy table out of the shared datafile and put it
  in its own datafile on another drive.

The goal is to have a database with as balanced a distribution of I/O
as possible.

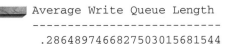

TABLE_SPACE	FILE_NAME	PHYS READS	PHYS BLKS READ	PHYS READ TIME	WRITES	PHYS WRITES	PHYS WRITE WRT TIME	MEGABYTES
ROLLBACK_DATA	D:\...\RBS1ORCL.ORA	918	918	1407	2428	2428	2243	10
ROLLBACK_DATA	D:\...\RBS2ORCL.ORA	558	558	897	1362	1362	1178	52
SYSTEM	D:\...\SYS1ORCL.ORA	1847	3244	3231	427	427	418	42
TEMPORARY_DATA	D:\...\TMP1ORCL.ORA	75	75	0	75	75	0	2

```
USER_DATA      D:\...\USR1ORCL.ORA  420  834 1663   791  791  617    3
USER_DATA      D:\...\USR2ORCL.ORA 1039 1573 2558  1255 1255 1011  524
```

In looking at the above listing, we see a few problems. The largest amount, 38 percent, of all the reads is being done in the SYSTEM tablespace. If the time slice for this observation was when a number of system operations (i.e., grants executed, synonyms created, table or index expansion) were being performed, that would account for this percentage. If not, you need to look into the system tablespace and make sure that there are no user objects, tables, or indexes in the system tablespace. The next heaviest read tablespace, 30 percent of total reads, is the USER_DATA tablespace. This tablespace needs to be looked at to see if some objects could be moved to another tablespace to distribute the I/O.

In summary, use the output above as a quick way to determine your I/O load balance. Remember though, this only shows you Oracle I/O. If other operating system files are on those disks, they will not be accounted for.

ISSUES RULE #26
The utlbstat/utlestat output will only give you the Oracle I/O perspective. Be very careful you don't overlook operating system files that may be on the same device.

ISSUES RULE #27
I/O is a major bottleneck for performance. You should always distribute your I/O as evenly as possible.

Latches

This section of the report (see the following listing) contains information about the latches and the statistics associated with them. Latches are Oracle's method of establishing process ownership of objects that the database needs to use. Think of a latch as a very efficient internal Oracle lock.

LATCH_NAME	GETS	MISSES	HIT_RATIO	SLEEPS	SLEEPS/MISS
Active checkpoint	30950	1	1	1	1
Checkpoint queue 1	60056	3	1	3	1
Token Manager	2422	0	1	0	0
cache buffer handl	2776	0	1	0	0
cache buffers chai	552924	14	1	14	1
cache buffers lru	14103	0	1	0	0
dml lock allocatio	1711	0	1	0	0
enqueue hash chain	14580	0	1	0	0
enqueues	62116	0	1	0	0
ktm global data	291	0	1	0	0
latch wait list	2	0	1	0	0
library cache	1049780	2	1	2	1
library cache load	1132	0	1	0	0
list of block allo	821	0	1	0	0
messages	223018	0	1	0	0
modify parameter v	17481	0	1	0	0
multiblock read ob	924	0	1	0	0
ncodef allocation	1391	0	1	0	0
process allocation	3	0	1	0	0
redo allocation	161272	11	1	11	1
row cache objects	180542	1	1	1	1
sequence cache	2310	0	1	0	0
session allocation	71658	0	1	0	0
session idle bit	125277	0	1	0	0
session switching	1391	0	1	0	0
shared pool	225438	0	1	0	0
sort extent pool	291	0	1	0	0
transaction alloca	3259	0	1	0	0
undo global data	8371	0	1	0	0
user lock	8	0	1	0	0

As can be seen from above, latches are used in a number of different ways. The objective is to have the HIT_RATIO as high as possible: this means that when a latch is requested, it is available. The SLEEPS should be as low as possible: this means a latch was requested and could not be supplied. The process that requested the latch went into a sleep state until the needed resource was available. Sleeps should be avoided.

The following section contains latch information. This information is on latches that processes are not allowed to wait for. If the process cannot get the requested latch, rather than sleep, it times out. The goal is to have the NOWAIT_HIT_RATIO as close to 1 as possible.

LATCH_NAME	NOWAIT_GETS	NOWAIT_MISSES	NOWAIT_HIT_RATIO
Token Manager	5	0	1
cache buffers chai	664672	24	25
cache buffers lru	17010	1	2
latch wait list	2	0	1
library cache	5	0	1
process allocation	3	0	1
row cache objects	5	0	1
vecio buf des	5	0	1

What's important when looking at the above two listings is that access to the redo log buffer is regulated by latches. Two types of latches control access to the redo log buffer—redo allocation latch and redo copy latch.

As updates occur, space is allocated in your redo log buffer using the redo allocation latch. Because there is a single redo allocation latch, only one user can allocate space in the redo log buffer via the redo allocation latch at a time. The most information that can be copied on the redo allocation latch at a time is determined by the initialization parameter file entry LOG_SMALL_ENTRY_MAX_SIZE. If the amount of information to be copied is greater than LOG_SMALL_ENTRY_MAX_SIZE, Oracle escalates up to a redo copy latch. While holding this redo copy latch, the user process will fill the redo log buffer with its information. When the process is done, it then releases the redo copy latch.

If you are on a computer system that has multiple CPUs, then you are allowed to have one redo copy latch per CPU. This is done through the initialization parameter file entry LOG_SIMULTANEOUS_COPIES.

If your hit ratio starts to fall below 85 percent, then you have *latch contention*. If you are having redo allocation latch contention, then make the initialization parameter file entry LOG_SMALL_ENTRY_MAX_SIZE smaller. By making this value smaller, you will cause more activity to happen on the redo copy latches.

ISSUES RULE #28
If you determine you have redo allocation latch contention, make the initialization parameter file entry parameter LOG_SMALL_ENTRY_MAX_SIZE smaller; this will cause Oracle to use more redo copy latches.

If you are having redo copy latch contention, then increase the initialization parameter file entry LOG_SIMULTANEOUS_COPIES. Another way to reduce contention on the redo copy latches is to tell Oracle to prebuild the redo entry. Many times, an Oracle user's redo activity is made up of many small pieces. It can be much more efficient to instruct the database to put all the pieces together before requesting the redo copy latch. You do this through the LOG_ENTRY_PREBUILD_THRESHOLD entry. The default setting is 0.

ISSUES RULE #29
If you have redo copy latch contention, make the initialization parameter file entry LOG_SIMULTANEOUS_COPIES larger. Another alternative is to tell Oracle to prebuild redo entry information before requesting the latch. You do this by setting a value for the LOG_ENTRY_PREBUILD_THRESHOLD entry.

Rollback Segment Information
This information gives you statistics about the rollback segments and their efficiency. Remember, all updates must first become rollback entries.

UNDO SEGMENT	TRANS TBL_GETS	TRANS TBL_WAITS	UNDO BYTES_WRITTEN	SEGMENT SIZE_BYTES	XACTS	SRINKS	WRAPS
0	294	0	0	407552	0	0	0
2	403	0	36094	2199552	0	0	1
3	421	0	49996	2199552	-1	0	1
4	1528	0	1694524	1738752	0	0	34
5	1480	0	2119492	2250752	1	0	43
6	413	0	37542	2301952	0	0	1

7	413	0	48072	509952	0	0	1
8	409	0	40512	151552	0	0	1
18	423	0	52300	110592	0	0	6

Here, the important columns are TRANS_TBL_WAITS and TRANS_TBL_GETS. The ratio of these values should be less than 4 percent, using the following formula:

```
ROLLBACK WAIT RATIO  =  TRANS_TBL_WAITS/TRANS_TBL_GETS * 100
```

If you see rollback contention, you just need to create additional private rollback segments. After creating them, you must reference them in the initialization parameter file entry ROLLBACK_SEGMENTS = ( ). Then alter the new rollback segments online.

ISSUES RULE #30
If you are detecting rollback segment contention, add more rollback segments. When in doubt, add more.

Initialization Parameter File Entries

The section of the report shown here presents a list of all the initialization parameter file entries that have settings other than the default. This is provided for informational purposes, because an analysis of the other information might lead to changes in one of these parameters. It is convenient to have it printed here rather than printing out the file itself.

NAME	VALUE
background_dump_dest	%RDBMS80%\trace
control_files	D:\ORANT\DATABASE\ctl1orcl.ora
db_block_size	2048
db_files	1024
db_name	oracle
distributed_lock_timeout	300
distributed_transactions	5
global_names	TRUE
job_queue_interval	10
job_queue_processes	2
log_buffer	8192
log_checkpoint_interval	10000
max_dump_file_size	10240

```
processes                        59
remote_login_passwordfile        SHARED
rollback_segments                MONSTER, RB1, RB2, RB3, RB4, RB5, RB6,
sequence_cache_hash_buckets      10
shared_pool_size                 10000000
text_enable                      TRUE
timed_statistics                 TRUE
user_dump_dest                   %RDBMS80%\trace
```

Data Dictionary Statistics

This section of the report give the statistics specifically on the data dictionary cache, which is part of the shared SQL area in Oracle8.

NAME	GET_REQS	GET_MISS	SCAN_REQ	SCAN_MIS	MOD_REQS	COUNT	CUR_USAG
dc_tablespaces	22920	0	0	0	0	6	5
dc_free_extents	3279	26	28	0	80	68	24
dc_segments	794	1	0	0	28	614	592
dc_rollback_seg	11098	0	0	0	0	24	20
dc_used_extents	127	28	0	0	28	505	504
dc_users	554	0	0	0	0	29	21
dc_user_grants	224	1	0	0	0	70	20
dc_objects	18938	138	0	0	312	1436	1435
dc_synonyms	216	103	0	0	103	141	134
dc_usernames	619	0	0	0	0	21	16
dc_object_ids	523	103	0	0	103	847	843
dc_sequences	41	0	0	0	39	48	45
dc_profiles	2	0	0	0	0	10	3

The meanings of these parameters and the reason to have them cached in memory was covered earlier in this chapter. Here are the major areas of interest:

- The GET_REQS column shows how many times a particular dictionary type was requested.

- The GET_MISS column shows the number of times the requested item was not found in the cache; if it's not in the cache, then Oracle must go out and get it.

- The CUR_USAG is the number of entries in the cache that are being used. The object is to have GET_MISS and SCAN_MISS as low as possible.

If the miss number is over 10 percent of the gets, then it helps to increase the SHARED_POOL_SIZE entry in the initialization parameter file. Again, you must keep in mind that increasing this parameter does have a direct effect on the size of the SGA and the amount of system memory that is being used by Oracle.

Statistics Gather Times

This section of the report gives the start and stop date and time of the statistics gathering. When utlbstat is run, the date and time is recorded; likewise for utlestat.

```
START_TIME          END_TIME
----------------- ------------------
18-aug-99 17:56:02 19-aug-99 18:14:49
```

ISSUES RULE #31

Run utlbstat/utlestat often with TIMED_STATISTICS = TRUE in the initialization parameter file and examine the output and make changes to the initialization parameter file, the database, or the application, as deemed necessary.

Miscellaneous Tuning Considerations

This leaves us with four remaining areas to wrap up in our discussion of other database issues. Using the rules in this chapter and the assortment of short scripts presented, let's attend to a few loose ends before tying up this chapter. The first issue, related to **pctfree**, was also touched on in Chapter 2 where we discussed I/O, but let's have a look at it again from another slant.

PCTFREE

To avoid wasted storage, many DBAs overallocate pctfree. This can be a real performance mistake. Remember, **pctfree** is room that is reserved within the data block for future updates. Let's say you have a million-row table that has **pctfree** set to 20 percent. After reviewing the application, you determine that this million-row table contains lab results that rarely if ever change. You decide to re-create the table with a **pctfree** of 1. This means that on a million-row table, every I/O request you make will draw 19 percent additional rows, since this room is no longer reserved for future updates. This amounts to a substantial (I/O) performance increase.

On the flip side, you may encounter situations where it makes sense to set **pctfree** to 90. Here is a situation we experienced: we built a budgeting system, and every month we loaded in the detail data. The first three months, all worked well. By the fourth month, our reports ran 50 percent longer. By the sixth month, they ran 200 percent longer. Finally, just as our users were on the verge of a rebellion, we determined what was wrong.

The first month, Oracle packed all the data into the data block as tightly as possible, leaving only 10 percent of the data block free for future updates. The second month, the next data load of budget actuals arrived. Oracle placed it into the **pctfree** area of the data block. The third month, when the budget actuals arrived, Oracle was forced to chain every record, because **pctfree** would not hold the new entries.

The problem here is the dataset was not completely on the initial load. We should have instructed Oracle to set **pctfree** to 90 when we created the table, since we only had 8 percent of the data in the first month.

Tuning Redo Logs

Every instance of the database must have at least two redo logs. These are separate from the data files, which actually store the database data. These redo logs, working in conjunction with the background process LGWR, record all changes made to the database. Another way to think of redo logs is to call them transaction logs. In the event of a database failure, these redo logs can be replayed to bring the database back from a failure.

There are two basic ways you can configure databases concerning redo logs: NOARCHIVELOG mode and ARCHIVELOG mode. The first configuration, NOARCHIVELOG mode, only protects you from instance failure. In this mode, whenever a redo log fills up with a transaction, it switches to the other redo log. In essence, it writes to each one in a circular fashion. Because it could eventually write over some previous transaction log information, NOARCHIVELOG mode will not protect you from media failure. In the ARCHIVELOG mode configuration, the redo logs are used in a circular fashion but with one basic difference: the background process ARCH. Its job is to wake up when a redo log becomes inactive and write its contents out to a system file. In the event of a media failure, you will have a record of every transaction within the database, and you can replay the event to make the database whole.

Because the redo logs have the task of recording every committed transaction (note that transactions can be written to the redo logs before they are committed), you can see what great potential redo logs have to become an impediment to good system performance. Let's take a look at how we can tune the redo logs to help your system gain great system throughput.

REDO LOGS: The I/O Perspective

Whenever you look at system performance, you must look at I/O. It is one of the most expensive operations a computer can perform. One of the major benefits of version 6 was that it eliminated the I/O bottleneck associated with **commit**: it took the process of commit and broke it into numerous I/O streams. For example, if you run the following statement:

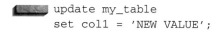

```
update my_table
set col1 = 'NEW VALUE';
```

you have three clear I/O streams:

- As the **update** occurs, it is recorded in the rollback segment. Remember that the rollback segment is used in case the transaction is aborted. If aborted, it will roll the database back to the way it was before you started the update.

- Once you **commit** the transaction, the record of the commit is recorded in the redo log. In the event of system failure, Oracle will be able to recover itself. Think of **commit** as meaning that somewhere a copy of the transaction was written to disk.

- Over time, the database will record the change back onto the datafile. Remember, Oracle does a great job of keeping hot spots (frequently accessed user and dictionary data) in memory.

ISSUES RULE #32
*Always put your redo logs on a separate disk
from your datafiles.*

Redo Logs: Memory Issues

The problem with redo logs is that when a log switch occurs, the SGA is flushed. A log switch occurs when the redo log fills up, and it must switch over to another redo log to record further transactions. Once again, the log switch forces a database checkpoint to occur, which tells Oracle to flush portions of the SGA to ensure system integrity.

The good side of this is that if you have frequent checkpoints and your system crashes, your recovery will be quick. The bad side is that by flushing the SGA, you lose the benefits of keeping hot spots in memory. It is a very expensive process to retrieve information off a disk compared to fetching information out of memory. So, here's what you do: as a rule of thumb, have much larger redo logs. In fact, try to time log switches so that they only happen at lunch and off-hours. If the system were to crash, it might take the database a lot longer to recover, but let's be honest: in a stable environment, the system will very rarely crash. If you can obtain substantial performance gains 360 days out of the year, while two to five times a year the system crashes and takes longer to recover—we can consider that a home run. Major performance gains for minimal risk. Remember, all tuning is specific to your situation. However, here are two general rules that probably apply to 98 percent of all customers who ask, "How do I make sure my log switches happen less often?"

- Make your redo logs a lot bigger.

- Set the initialization parameter file entry LOG_CHECKPOINT_ INTERVAL to a size greater than the redo logs file size and set the LOG_CHECKPOINT_TIMEOUT parameter to 0. By making these two changes, only when the redo log files fill up and cause a log switch will you have a checkpoint. Finally, enable the checkpoint process.

The LOG_CHECKPOINT_INTERVAL parameter forces a checkpoint when a predetermined number of redo log blocks have been written to disk relative to the last database checkpoint.

The LOG_CHECK_POINT_TIMEOUT parameter can be set to force a database checkpoint based on the number of seconds after the previous database checkpoint started.

Here are two SQL statements that are very useful when working with redo logs:

```
SQLWKS> select * from v$log;
    GROUP# THREAD# SEQUENCE# BYTES  MEMBERS ARC STATUS      FIRST_CHAN FIRST_TIM
    ------ ------- --------- ------ ------- --- --------- ---------- ---------
         1       1       373 204800       1 NO  CURRENT       46695 19-AUG-99
         2       1       372 204800       1 NO  INACTIVE      46670 19-AUG-99
    2 rows selected.

SQLWKS> select * from v$logfile;
    GROUP# STATUS  MEMBER
    ------ ------- ----------------------------
         1              D:\ORANT\DATABASE\LOG2ORCL.ORA
         2              D:\ORANT\DATABASE\LOG1ORCL.ORA
    2 rows selected.
SQLWKS>
```

You will need these SQL statements when you are ready to change the redo
log files.

Let's Tune It

This section summarizes the main points of this chapter and is designed for
the DBA who needs to tune the database quickly. Later, when you have
more time, you can go back and read the specifics presented in this
chapter. Following is a number of steps to make your database perform
better, based on situations we see in most environments.

- Increase the initialization parameter file entry
  DB_BLOCK_BUFFERS. This is your data cache. Before a database
  can present, manipulate, or examine a piece of data, it must first
  reside in this cache. The larger the data cache, the more likely the
  Oracle database will have what it needs in memory. The smaller
  the cache, the more likely Oracle will have to issue I/Os to put the
  information in the cache.

- Increase the initialization parameter file entry
  SHARED_POOL_SIZE. This is your library cache and data
  dictionary cache. This is where Oracle stores information it needs
  to manage itself. If the cache is large enough, it will greatly reduce
  the amount of reparsing Oracle has to do or the time it takes to
  manage itself.

- Distribute your I/O stream and separate data from indexes. I/O is one of the most expensive operations a computer can perform. You can't eliminate all I/O, so it is best to be wise about your I/O streams. On the data side, you should separate your data and indexes. On the update side, you should look at separating your rollback segments, redo logs, and archive logs. On the system overhead side, you should separate your system tablespace, your TOOLS tablespace, and your TEMP tablespace.

- Evaluate your index scheme. One of the quickest ways to make Oracle perform well is to add needed indexes. Be generous about this. Also, look for tables that have no indexes.

- Enlarge your redo logs. If you have a very stable environment where the computer very rarely crashes, then think about making your checkpoints occur less often (remember, a checkpoint causes your SGA to be flushed). To do this, make your redo logs a lot bigger. Then set LOG_CHECK_POINT_INTERVAL greater than your redo log size.

- Increase your SORT_AREA_SIZE. Sorting is a major part of life in an Oracle database; try increasing your SORT_AREA_SIZE to eliminate sorting to disk.

Oracle 7.x Specifics

Please note the following points organized by the headings for the same sections throughout this chapter:

- "The Initialization Parameter (INIT.ORA) File"   Contents of Tables 6-2, 6-3, and 6-4 change with each major release of Oracle. The *Server Reference Manual* for your specific Oracle version should be consulted for applicable parameters that fall into these categories for your particular version of Oracle.

- "Database-wide Parameters"   The checkpoint process in Oracle 7.x needs to be explicitly started by including the parameter CHECKPOINT_PROCESS = TRUE in the initialization parameter file.

- "CLOSED_CACHED_OPEN_CURSORS"   New in Oracle 8.x.

- "utlbstat and utlestat" Contents of Tables 6-10, 6-11, and 6-12 have changed with Oracle8.x. bck_event and waitstat tables have been added.

- "Buffer Busy Wait Ratio" This output is not available in Oracle 7.x. It can be obtained by running the following code:

```
select class, sum(count) 'Total Waits'
  from sys.v$waitstat
 where class in ('undo header', undo block', 'data block')
 group by class;
```

- "Miscellaneous Tuning Considerations" All this information is applicable to Oracle 7.x.

CHAPTER
7

Show Stoppers

how stoppers do just that. "Stop the show—something weird is going on! Get the users to log off NOW! The instance has to come down immediately!" The show (your applications) starts to behave in different ways. Previously unseen error situations come up all of a sudden. Experienced DBAs (yes, you, and the four of us as well!) run into this from time to time. In this chapter, we will guide you through some show stopping that can be avoided with knowledge and planning.

This Show Stoppers chapter is a hodgepodge of ideas, situations, and experiences we have all had and would like to share with you—and sometimes it's the little stuff that causes the biggest problems. To illustrate this point, recently on a familiar television network, an emergency room medical documentary mentioned an oddity about trauma medicine. A 25-year-old man was seen with a gunshot wound between the eyes, a bullet embedded in his head. Another man, over 70 years old, fell off the third step of his front porch. The 25-year-old lived, the 70-year-old died. See what we mean?

Let's get started—if the kids are not in bed yet, wait until they are and, oh yeah, put on the kettle, this could be a long night. By careful planning and watching for the things we are talking about, you can have time to have dinner with your family rather than with your system administrator. Right, Glen. The first issue we discuss relates to an issue that occurs when you attempt to store characters from the extended character set in your Oracle8 database.

Working with Data from Extended Character Sets

As you make the move up to Oracle8 and continue to work partially with Oracle7, many of us have run across anomalies with extended characters. We have painstakingly planned movement of data via export and import or through the Data Migration Assistant.

SHOW STOPPER
Database unable to store text containing
information using the extended character set!

Without ensuring the operating system environment is properly set up, it is easy to inadvertently move extended character data out of:

- An Oracle7 database up to Oracle8 and lose all the accented characters

- Another database vendor's repository and have the accents stripped off on the way into Oracle

- Text files containing extended accented characters only to find them stripped when stored in the Oracle repository

Using Windows NT and UNIX examples, let's look at how to ensure this does not happen.

Windows NT

To ensure the Windows NT registry will be able to store extended characters, it is worth inspecting it before moving data into an Oracle8 repository. The easiest way to look in the registry is to go through the Start|Run menu, then enter the command "regedit". This will bring up a display similar to that shown in Figure 7-1.

Proceed to Edit|Find on the menu bar, then enter the text NLS_LANG in the Find dialog box. Leave Keys, Values, and Data checked and ensure Match whole string only is unselected. Click Find Next to begin.

NOTE
You may use the shortcut key combination
CTRL-F rather than the menu bar.

When Windows finds the desired text, you will see a dialog box with the NLS_LANG search string highlighted. If the value requires changing, right-click on the highlighted text to bring up the pop-up menu shown in Figure 7-2.

When the Edit String display appears, enter the new value in the Value data entry area. The three most common values for NLS_LANG are:

- AMERICAN_AMERICA.US7ASCII

- AMERICAN_AMERICA.WE8DEC

- AMERICAN_AMERICA.WE8ISO8859P1

- FRENCH_CANADA.WE8DEC

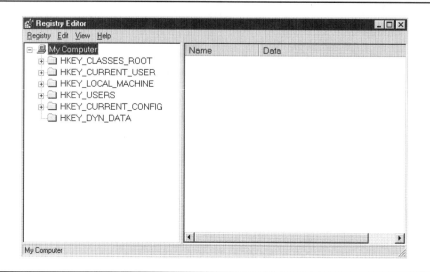

FIGURE 7-1. *NT Registry Editor startup*

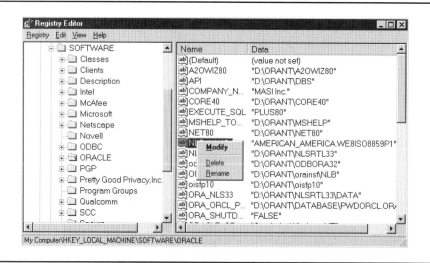

FIGURE 7-2. *Registry Entry pop-up menu*

STOPPERS RULE #1
*We recommend using either of the WE8
character set definitions for all your databases.
This permits storage of normal and extended
characters regardless of your current
requirements; they may change over time and
it is best to be prepared.*

UNIX

The UNIX environment setting for the same variable can be checked and
modified, if necessary, starting with the **env** command. On some UNIX
machines, you may find a few pages of output to the command, so it is best
to enter the following command:

```
/home/oracle --> (prod)
masii> env | grep NLS_LANG
```

Using the UNIX system prompt shown in the previous listing, the output
from the command will either show a value for NLS_LANG or show nothing.

```
/home/oracle> # If defined, the output will be
/home/oracle --> (prod)
masii> env | grep NLS_LANG
NLS_LANG=american_america.we8dec
/home/oracle> # If not defined, the output will be a system prompt since
/home/oracle> # NLS_LANG has no current value
/home/oracle --> (prod)
masii> env | grep NLS_LANG
masii>
```

Depending on the type of UNIX operating system, NLS_LANG is set
using one of the following commands:

- export NLS_LANG= american_america.we8dec

- setenv NLS_LANG american_america.we8dec

- set NLS_LANG= american_america.we8dec

Checking Accented Characters

Regardless of whether your environment needed changing or not, after
completing a move involving accented characters, it is wise to check the

outcome. Once we were in the midst of upgrading a client from V6 to Oracle7 and, as a last step, took the time to look at some text on a data entry screen. To our horror, the text "On doit détruire" had been changed to "On doit ditruire" during the upgrade.

This introduces an interesting concept related to accented characters—you must ascertain whether it is data in the database that is wrong or the way the data is displayed on the client that is the problem. Using the example "On doit détruire" , there are two common anomalies:

■ One where the data is displayed as "On doit detruire"

■ One where the data is displayed as "On doit ditruire"

Upon initial inspection, it appears that the accent has been stripped off the é in the first case and in the second that the é character has been incorrectly interpreted and stored in the database. Using SQL*Plus and the character set on a Windows NT platform, issue a query and inspect the results similar to the following, given that the primary key of the offending row is known to be 213.

```
SQL> -- The offending character is in position 10 in the TEXT_F column
SQL> select ascii(substr(text_f,10,1))
  2     from off_master
  3   where off_id = 213;
ASCII(SUBSTR(TEXT_F,10,1))
-------------------------
                      233

SQL>
```

When looking at the display of extended characters, the following logic is used to determine exactly where the problem exists—on the server or on the client:

```
if the ASCII sequence on the server is 233(é)then
    if the client displays é then
        all is well
    elsif the client displays i or e then
        problem is on the client
    end if
else
    problem is on the server
end if
```

Code of Character in Database	Represents	Displayed	é Stored Correctly	Problem on Server	Client
233	é	é	Y	N	N
233	é	i	Y	N	Y
233	é	e	Y	N	Y
105	i	i	N	Y	?
101	e	e	N	Y	?

TABLE 7-1. *Possible Display for é Character Stored in Database*

Let's look at the information in Table 7-1 before moving on. When the server ASCII code is 233 and the correct character is displayed on the client, there is no problem. On the other hand, when the ASCII code 105 or 101 is displayed on the server, the character has been stripped and must be rectified before the display on the client can be judged. Hence, the question marks in the two cells in the table.

Next we are going to look at a nagging problem that creeps up when working from a client (e.g., NT Workstation 4) on an Oracle database on a Server (e.g., Windows NT).

Client/Server Drive Assignments

Client/server drive assignments can be a headache, especially the differences between those assignments active on the client and those on the server. Picture a scenario where a query showing the name and location of database files yields the results shown in the next listing.

```
SQL> select file_name, tablespace_name
  2    from sys.dba_data_files
  3    order by 1;
FILE_NAME                          TABLESPACE_NAME
------------------------------------------------------
F:\ORANT\DATABASE\CUSTOM_1.ORA     CUSTOM
F:\ORANT\DATABASE\CUSTOM_2.ORA     CUSTOM
F:\ORANT\DATABASE\FINANCE_1.ORA    FINANCE
```

```
H:\ORANT\DATABASE\FINANCE_2.ORA    FINANCE
G:\ORANT\DATABASE\RBS1ORCL.ORA     ROLLBACK
G:\ORANT\DATABASE\SYS1ORCL.ORA     SYSTEM
G:\ORANT\DATABASE\TEMP1ORCL.ORA    TEMPORARY_DATA
```

SHOW STOPPER

*Not enough permission to remove files belonging
to tablespaces that have been dropped!*

Suppose you want to change the size of the ROLLBACK tablespace
datafile, which entails erasing the RBS1ORCL.ORA file on drive G:. Figure
7-3 shows the current drive assignments, with G: assigned to "Dmo on
Hq_fs1". Notice how D: on the client is assigned to a local CD-ROM drive.

The puzzle, in one case, got even more perplexing. We went through
the Map Network Drive dialog box in the Explorer and could not find the
device containing the database files we needed to get to erase
G:\ORANT\DATABASE\RBS1ORCL.ORA. Then we managed to find the
NT administrator, and the drive containing the required database file was

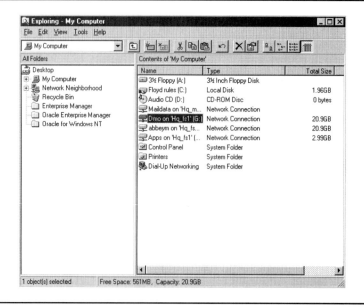

FIGURE 7-3. *Drive assignments on the client*

made available (two and a half hours later). The permissions were set to allow us to remove the rollback segment datafile on drive G:, and all was well.

STOPPERS RULE #2

Ensure you have write permission to network drives before attempting to do any database file maintenance operations that may require erasing files that show up in a query against DBA_DATA_FILES.

Something else we have seen in a Windows NT environment—and this can cause problems elsewhere in a client server configuration—is reassignment of a drive on the server containing Oracle8 database files. Since Oracle (unfortunately) stores logical drive letters in the data dictionary, a system whose drive letters get reassigned requires you to rename the Oracle database files accordingly.

STOPPERS RULE #3

In a client/server environment, when drive letter maintenance is to be done on the server, ensure the Oracle database is shut down normally before the reassignment commences. The affected database files will have to be renamed as Oracle is restarted.

In a number of places in this work we have discussed rebuilding a control file and the CONTROL_FILES entry in the initialization parameter file. If the drive letter upon which any of your control files reside is changed, you will have to edit the parameter file and change this entry. In the next section, we discuss an issue related to rebuilding schemas, a common activity on many reporting or decision support databases.

What Happened to Those Indexes?

A funny thing can happen on the way to a refresh of the whole or part of a data warehouse or reporting database repository. Many of the rebuilds we do of schemas in an Oracle database involve dropping some existing objects and then re-creating those objects before populating them again with new information. Suppose users are, for the most part, satisfied with the performance of the database; after a rebuild of all or part of the database is carried out, the next day they complain that performance is abysmal.

SHOW STOPPER
Database schema missing one or more
crucial indexes dues to Oracle errors upon
index creation!

This show stopper can be the result of many problems:

- Perhaps the database file that contains an index was unavailable when a **create index** statement was encountered, generating the following error:

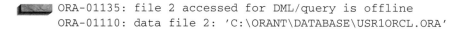

```
ORA-01135: file 2 accessed for DML/query is offline
ORA-01110: data file 2: 'C:\ORANT\DATABASE\USR1ORCL.ORA'
```

- There was not enough space available in the tablespace where the index is supposed to reside, returning one of the table extension errors:

```
ORA-01659: unable to allocate MINEXTENTS beyond 17 in tablespace IND1_TBSP
```

- Someone (and it could not possibly be you) made a typo similar to the following when a new column was added to an existing index, raising an Oracle error similar to the following:

```
SQL> create index naddy_1 on naddy (col1, col2;
               *
ERROR at line: 1
ORA-00907: missing right parenthesis
SQL>
```

STOPPERS RULE #4
Inspect table names, view names, index names,
and column names before and after a schema is
rebuilt to ensure completeness of rebuild.

Great rule, but let's look at a way to do this. The following SQL script creates a spool file whose name is determined by the second parameter passed in. It dumps partial contents of the USER_VIEWS, USER_TABLES, USER_INDEXES, and USER_IND_COLUMNS for the schema in question. It is run beforehand using the command

```
sqlplus @objects STEVE Before
```

and after using the command

```
sqlplus @objects STEVE After
```

producing "Before.lst" and "After.lst".

```
/* ---------------------------------------------------------- */
/*  objects.sql                                               */
/*                                                            */
/*  Display partial contents of 4 USER_ series of views       */
/*  for comparison between before and after rebuild.          */
/*                                                            */
/*  Oracle8 Tuning    Corey & Abbey & Dechichio & Abramson   */
/* ---------------------------------------------------------- */
def sowner="&1"
def timer="&2"
set echo off feed off pages 0 ver off lines 1000 trimsp on
-- Spool file ends up with name of second parameter (i.e.,
-- Before.lst or After.1st.
spool &2
prompt ===== &timer =====
prompt
select table_name
  from sys.dba_tables
 where owner = upper('&&sowner');
select view_name
  from sys.dba_views
 where owner = upper('&&sowner');
select table_name,index_name
  from sys.dba_indexes
 where owner = upper('&&sowner');
select index_name,column_position,column_name
  from sys.dba_ind_columns
 where index_owner = upper('&&sowner')
 order by index_name,column_position;
prompt
spool off
exit
```

The final step is to compare the two listing files looking for discrepancies. There are many shareware products that will allow you to do this on Windows NT, as well as the familiar diff command on UNIX. Sample output from diff is shown in the next listing.

```
1c1
< After
---
> Before
1d0
< AP_INVOICES_1
5c4
< AP_GENERAL_2
---
>
9a9,11
> GL_GOTCHAS_1
> GL_GOTCHAS_2
> GL_BALANCES_N1
```

Differences require investigation. The approach we discuss in the last few paragraphs helps ensure that the schema rebuilds you perform do just what they are intended to do—clone a schema.

In an ideal world, you could set up an environment on your server that would be allowed (by the host operating system) to consume as many resources as it needed. This is not the case on any computer; limits are defined by Oracle8 and the operating system as well, as you will see.

Database Limits vs. Operating System Limits

We know by now that Oracle8 was engineered to support up to 10,000 users with a database that can span over 10 terabytes in size. You would think, with such capabilities, you would not have to worry about the maximum number of data files you can physically have, yet you must. If you don't choose a setting for **maxdatafiles**, a choice is made for you. It is this ability to specify such details in the database configuration that enables you to tune the Oracle8 database to support so many users and such large disk farms. The next listing is our first of two **create database** scripts in this chapter. You see a sample of the many choices you can make just in the **create database** statement itself. Many of the keywords used in this listing have never been coded by seasoned DBAs. Coupled with the many entries in the initialization parameter file, you have a lot of decisions to make, as lines 8 to 16 show.

NOTE
The default entry for **maxdatafiles** *varies from* platform to platform. The details are in the Installation Notes for your operating system.

```
SVRMGR> create database newtest
    2>    controlfile reuse
    3>    datafile 'f:\orant\database\sys1orcl.ora' autoextend on,
    4>               'g:\orant\database\sys2orcl.ora' autoextend on
    5>                  next 10m maxsize unlimited
    6>    logfile group 1 ('diskb:log1.log', 'diskc:log1.log') size 50k,
    7>            group 2 ('diskb:log2.log', 'diskc:log2.log') size 50k
    8>    maxlogfiles 5
    9>    maxloghistory 100
   10>    maxdatafiles 10
   11>    maxinstances 2
   12>    exclusive
   13>    character set we8dec
   14>    national character set ja16sjisfixed
   15>    noarchivelog
   16>    maxlogmembers 4;
Statement processed.
SVRMGR>
```

This ability the database gives you to make all these choices makes a lot of sense if you sit down and think about it. A database that is 100MB in size with three users will not need the same amount of resources needed by a 10 terabyte database with over 10,000 users. These choices you make in the initialization parameter file and **create database** statement are all about managing resources. You are deciding how much resource the database obtains and where it will allocate it. This allows you to tailor the database to your organization's particular needs. As DBAs, we all know that with each choice you make comes a trade-off.

No matter what choices you make though, an Oracle8 database always performs within the limits imposed by your operating system. At the same time, the database will always operate within the limits you set in the initialization parameter file and any limits you chose when you created the initial database. This leads us to Stoppers Rule #5.

STOPPERS RULE # 5
The lowest number specified by operating system restrictions or the Oracle database is the one that counts. In others words, it's the weakest link or lowest value that rules.

For example, if your current operating system limits you to an open file limit of 48, putting

```
db_files = 60
```

in your initialization parameter file or using a **maxdatafiles** value of 54 when creating a database will still only permit you to have 48 files open, and an operating system related error will be raised. Likewise, if your **maxdatafiles** is set to 16, and your operating system permits 64 open files for each user, putting

```
db_files = 32
```

in your initialization parameter file will still only permit you to have 16 datafiles open at the same time.

Some problems you encounter are only temporary. For example, if you inadvertently set **db_files** too low in the initialization parameter file, you can always change it. This does mean stopping the show though. But you can shut down the database, make the necessary corrections, and restart the database. Upon database startup, the new initialization parameter will take effect as long as Stoppers Rule #3 is not violated.

If you found you initially created the database with limits that don't make sense, then use the **alter database** command to correct the situation. But yes, you do have to take the database offline. Remember, the controls files need to be re-created; we look at creating a control file in the "Creating an Instance Control File" section of Chapter 11.

Operating System Limits

Oracle will only operate within the limits laid out by your operating system. When the database tries to exceed a operating system limit, it will fail in its attempt. Let's take a look at a common operating system limit that we see come into play quite a bit.

O/S Limit of Maximum Number of Files Open

Keep in mind that the operating systems' maximum number of files that a user can have open concurrently may impact on the database configuration some point down the road when you least expect it. As your instance (or instances) approaches that number, you will have problems adding more files without intervention by your hardware support personnel. Your database has to be down and stay down while these hardware people do whatever has to be done to increase that number.

For scenario #1, picture a corporate development environment. There are six databases owned by an account called oracle. There are 14 control files, 18 redo log group members, and 46 datafiles all used by that user. Suppose the maximum number of open files dictated by your operating system is 128. Table 7-2 shows the minimum number of files used by Oracle8 (78 open files) for this six-database configuration. With the assortment of *trace files* (files written by Oracle that track system and user activities against the database) and the six instance alert files (each instance maintains its own alert file for system event logging), the 128 limit could be easily exceeded. When it is exceeded you get a show stopper:

SHOW STOPPER
Concurrent open file limit needs adjusting!

Database	Control Files	Redo Logs	Datafiles
dev	3	3	8
tst	2	3	8
uacc	2	3	8
case	3	3	8
proto	2	3	8
prior	2	3	6
Totals	14	18	46

TABLE 7-2. *Files Allocated to Six Oracle Instances*

For scenario #2, consider the following. An Oracle instance is shut down once a week for a full image backup. When the backup completes, the machine is rebooted and Oracle is started. The file limit quota for the process that brings up Oracle is set at 20. The current number of database files, redo logs, trace files, alert file, and control files is 18. It should be noted that as far as the operating system is concerned, an open file is an open file. Therefore all files should be accounted for when setting a limit for an operating system process. During the week, three new database files were created. The operating system did not have a problem with Oracle creating the additional files. What did happen was that when the database was started after the full image backup, it would not come up. The error message was very cryptic. It stated that it could not open a file because it was locked. After about two hours of investigating this problem in the middle of the night with a number of coworkers, we recalled that a number of files were added. The open file quota of the Oracle startup process was checked, and it was discovered to be too low. After increasing it to the operating system maximum, the instance was able to start up without any problem. This time delay can be costly, not to mention frustrating, to the end user.

SHOW STOPPER
Database down an extra two hours after backups; unable to open all its required files!

STOPPERS RULE #6
Be aware of limits that may be placed on the number of open files by your operating system. Work with your hardware personnel to ensure operating system limits are not exceeded by Oracle's requirements.

Operating System Initialization File

Just as Oracle8 has an initialization parameter file, most operating systems have an equivalent file. The setting on this startup file will have a direct effect on the database and its ability to get the resource it needs. You should take time to review this file and note any potential problem areas.

STOPPERS RULE #7
Review the operating system initialization file.
Compare it to the Oracle8 initialization file.
Very common problems have to do with the
number of open files or enqueue locks that
can be obtained. Discuss the entries within
this file with the system manager to see if any
parameters might need adjusting.

Just as the Oracle8 database needs to be restarted for changes to the
initialization to take effect, most operating system initialization file
adjustments require rebooting the computer. As any experienced DBA is
quick to note, any time you do something to the operating system that
necessitates rebooting the system, the system administrator will make sure
you hear about it. They will also make sure every user who is willing to
listen hears about it and that you keep hearing about it every time you want
to make any change, no matter how small. Not only that, you will hear
about it and hear about it and hear about it and hear about it.

SHOW STOPPER
Computer must come down in order for
adjustments to the operating systems parameter
file to take effect. This disrupts all users! This
also creates bad press for the DBAs.

Let's now have a look at another form of limits—those placed on you
and your applications by Oracle8 datatypes—and issues such as the
maximum amount of data each will store coupled with the operations you
are allowed to perform with each.

Oracle8 Datatype Limits

A *datatype* tells an Oracle database what it can and can't do with the
contents stored within the database. For example, you can add, subtract,
and multiply the information stored within the number datatype. On the
other hand, the database would not allow you to add, subtract, or multiply
the contents of the varchar2 datatype. Associated with each datatype are a

set of rules and the capacity of information it can hold. Table 7-3 is a complete list of the most common Oracle8 internal datatypes.

Table 7-3 also indicates how much information each datatype can hold in a single occurrence. These are hard limits. For example, a single field of type CHAR will not hold more than 2,000 bytes. By all accounts you will

Datatype	Details
VARCHAR2(size)	Variable length character string having maximum length size bytes. Maximum size is 4,000 and minimum is 1. You must specify size for a VARCHAR2. *Note: The maximum length of varchar2 was expanded in Oracle8.*
NVARCHAR2(size)	Variable-length character string having maximum length size characters or bytes, depending on the choice of national character set. Maximum size is determined by the number of bytes required to store each character, with an upper limit of 4,000 bytes. You must specify size for NVARCHAR2.
NUMBER(p,s)	Number having precision p and scale s. The precision can range from 1 to 38. The scale can range from -84 to 127.
LONG	Character data of variable length up to 2 gigabytes.
DATE	Valid date range from January 1, 4712 B.C. to December 31, 4712 A.D.
RAW(size)	Raw binary data of length size bytes. Maximum size is 2,000 bytes. You must specify size for a RAW value.
LONG RAW	Raw binary data of variable length up to 2 gigabytes.
ROWID	Hexadecimal string representing the unique address of a row in its table. This datatype is primarily for values returned by the ROWID pseudocolumn. *Note: The extended ROWID in Oracle8 looks different than Oracle7 hexadecimal ROWIDs.*
CHAR(size)	Fixed length character data of length size bytes. Maximum size is 2,000 bytes. Default and minimum size is 1 byte. *Note: The maximum length of CHAR was expanded in Oracle8.*

TABLE 7-3. *Oracle8 Internal Datatype Summary*

Datatype	Details
NCHAR(size)	Fixed-length character data of length size characters or bytes, depending on the choice of national character set. Maximum size is determined by the number of bytes required to store each character, with an upper limit of 2,000 bytes. Default and minimum size is 1 character or 1 byte, depending on the character set.
MLSLABEL	Binary format of an operating system label. This datatype is used with Trusted Oracle.
CLOB	A character large object containing single byte characters. Maximum size is 4 gigabytes. Valid accessible range is 1 to $2^{32} - 1$.
NCLOB	A character large object containing fixed-width multibyte characters. Maximum size is 4 gigabytes. Stores national character set data. Valid accessible range is 1 to $2^{32} - 1$.
BLOB	A binary large object. Maximum size is 4 gigabytes. Valid accessible range is 1 to $2^{32} - 1$.
BFILE	Contains a locator to a large binary file stored outside the database. Enables byte stream I/O access to external LOBs residing on the database server. Maximum size is 4 gigabytes. Valid accessible range is 1 to $2^{32} - 1$.

TABLE 7-3. *Oracle8 Internal Datatype Summary* (continued*)*

most likely never hit these limits, but over the years we have learned that for every new capacity that is added to the database, there is an application out there ready to test it to its fullest. When you exceed these limits, we have experienced very strange problems that are very hard to trace.

STOPPERS RULE #8
Do not try to use a datatype beyond its stated limits. Experience has taught us that when you inadvertently go beyond the limits dictated by each datatype and somehow succeed, funny things happen. In addition, make sure you use datatypes in an appropriate manner.

When you experience problems with datatypes, it is usually code written using the Oracle Call Interface (OCI) such as code written in Pro*C. Even though the database is giving appropriate warnings that the datatype is being used incorrectly, the Pro*C program written to interact with the database ignores the problem. The data somehow gets stored in the database, and then the fun begins. Many times, the database will do a conversion on the data to make it work. This conversion ends up storing data within the database, which wreaks havoc with your applications.

Another variation we have seen is when a Pro*C program is trying to insert a record into a tablespace that is completely full. Yet the Pro*C program ignores the warning it receives that the record was not stored. Many times, these programs are inserting very complicated records into the database that span many different tablespaces and tables, so some of the record is stored and other portions don't make it. The results can be frustrating, especially when you find yourself with hanging relationships.

SHOW STOPPER

Corrupt or missing data will stop your applications!

STOPPERS RULE #9

*Pro*C programs that do not pay very strict attention to datatype size restrictions are a very high risk to the database. Establish very tight standards to ensure they do not pose a risk.*

Other Thoughts

We talked about the datatype having hard capacity limits. There are a few other interesting Oracle8 limits that we would be remiss not to mention:

- Maximum number of datafiles per tablespace is 1022.

- Maximum number of columns in a table is 1000.

- Maximum number of columns per primary key is 16.

- Maximum number of columns in a partition key is 16.

Without delving into the idiosyncrasies of each of these limits—trust us—be aware they exist.

Oracle Limits

One initialization parameter file entry (DB_FILES) and one **create database** parameter (**maxdatafiles**) have an effect on the number of files your instance may acquire. Let's look more closely at these two.

DB_FILES

The most common occurrence is when you try to add a file to your configuration, and you exceed the DB_FILES initialization parameter file entry. DB_FILES can be increased (governed naturally by the operating system limits mentioned above), but the instance has to be shut down and then restarted for the new value to take effect. The need to adjust DB_FILES is a show stopper:

SHOW STOPPER
Database coming down to activate new value
for db_files!

Consider the following real-life scenario we have experienced. Our finance people were attempting to complete a travel claim transaction (underlying table is called TRAV_AUDIT), and were receiving an error indicating that the PRD_IDX index could not allocate space that was needed.

The application is using Developer/2000, and the activity is creating a new index entry in the TRAV_AUDIT_1 index on the TRAV_AUDIT table. For whatever reason, there is not enough space available in the PRD_IDX tablespace to satisfy the request for 1,024 blocks of space (the instance this error message was received on has an Oracle block size of 4K or 4,096 bytes—thus, the error indicates the application is requesting 1024*4096 or 4,194,304 bytes, or just over 4MB). The suggested resolution for this problem is to use the **alter tablespace add datafile** statement to add one or more files to the tablespace indicated or to create the object in another tablespace.

The natural step to take is to add another datafile to the PRD_IDX tablespace by running the command (using Windows NT as an example platform). This command returns an Oracle error. Even though the SQL in the code is syntactically correct and the filename passed to NT is correct, an Oracle error is raised.

```
SQL> alter tablespace prd_idx
  2    add datafile 'f:\orant\database\prdind_2.dbf' size 10M;
alter tablespace prd_idx
                  *
ERROR at line 1:
ORA-01118: cannot add any more database files: limit of 40 exceeded
```

In this case, there was an entry in the initialization parameter file that said

```
db_files = 40
```

That entry was changed to

```
db_files = 60
```

The instance restarted and the extra file was added to the PRD_IDX tablespace.

MAXDATAFILES

A value for this parameter is included when a database is created. Its value affects the size of your instance control file(s)—this control file(s) must be large enough to hold information for all database files. If and when this parameter needs to be increased, you must rebuild your control file. In the "Creating an Instance Control File" section of Chapter 11, we discuss an Oracle feature where you instruct Oracle to make a text copy of the SQL statements required to rebuild the control file. The need to change the value of **maxdatafiles** is a show stopper.

SHOW STOPPER
Database down to rebuild control files!

STOPPERS RULE #10
Set the **maxdatafiles** *parameter in the* **create database** *command to a number that will permit you to double the number of database files your instance uses.*

STOPPERS RULE #11
When **maxdatafiles** *needs to be increased, use*
alter database backup controlfile to trace*, then*
edit that output and re-create your control file.

ENQUEUE_RESOURCES

This initialization parameter controls the number of resources that can be locked by the operating system. Think of enqueues as locks. When you compare them to latches, they are a lot more expensive. We have seen applications fail because they cannot get enough enqueues. The application times out.

STOPPERS RULE #12
Set ENQUEUE_RESOURCES to the number of
tables in your database plus 40 percent;
monitor the number of tables as more
applications come on board, and adjust
ENQUEUE_RESOURCES when required.

This rule reinforces an approach we stick to throughout *Oracle8 Tuning*—be thorough, take the time up front, and be proactive.

Re-creating a Database

If the need arises to perform this activity, you need to prepare yourself beforehand to minimize down time. If you are not prepared, you will have a show stopper.

SHOW STOPPER
Need to re-create a database and the DBA is
unprepared; the process is severely delayed!

The creation of a database becomes much easier with Oracle8 and the Enterprise Manager. Appendix C is dedicated to creating an Oracle8 database on Windows NT using the Database Assistant. The following steps should be used to create a database:

- Back up all existing databases—whenever you are about to create a new database, we strongly recommend that you back up all your existing databases. This includes all database files (i.e., parameter files, datafiles, redo log files, and control files).

- Create parameter files—make a copy of the parameter file that Oracle supplied with the distribution media and give it a new name.

- Edit new parameter files—there are a number of parameters in the Initialization File that are database specific. These should be changed when creating a new instance (i.e., *DB_NAME, DB_DOMAIN, CONTROL_FILES*). Other parameters in the Initialization File should also be looked at and changed appropriately.

- Check the instance identifier for your system—the instance identifier needs to be unique on a machine and should match the name of the database (value of *DB_NAME*).

- Create the database—use the SQL command **create database**, a sample of which is shown in the next listing. After the database is created, there are a few other scripts (catalog, catproc, catldr, and catexp) that we run, the locations of which are platform dependent, though they usually reside in some flavor of the RDBMS80\ADMIN folder.

NOTE
Unlike our first **create database** *script in this chapter, this one has a bare-bones minimum of keywords in the statement where the database is created. This flavor of the* **create** *statement is the one most are familiar with.*

```
C:\WINNT\PROFILES\ABBEYM\DESKTOP> svrmgr30
Oracle Server Manager Release 3.0.3.0.0 - Production
(c) Copyright 1997, Oracle Corporation.  All Rights Reserved.
Oracle8 Enterprise Edition Release 8.0.3.0.0 - Production
With the Partitioning and Objects options
PL/SQL Release 8.0.3.0.0 - Production
```

```
SVRMGR> connect internal
Password:
Connected.
SVRMGR> rem The following command will
SVRMGR> rem     create the SYSTEM tablespace
SVRMGR> rem     create the SYSTEM rollback segment
SVRMGR> rem     create the control files for the database
SVRMGR> rem     create the redo log files for the database
SVRMGR> rem     create the users SYS and SYSTEM
SVRMGR> rem     specify the character set that stores data in the database
SVRMGR> startup nomount
ORACLE instance started.
Total System Global Area       12071016 bytes
Fixed Size                        46136 bytes
Variable Size                  11090992 bytes
Database Buffers                 409600 bytes
Redo Buffers                     524288 bytes
SVRMGR>   create database devel
    2> datafile 'd:\orant\database\sysdev1.dbs'         size 20M
    3> logfile group 1 ('c:\orant\redo\dev_log1a.log',
    4>                   'd:\orant\redo\dev_log1b.log') size 2M,
    5>          group 2 ('d:\orant\redo\dev_log2a.log',
    6>                   'c:\orant\redo\dev_log2b.log') size 2M
    7>    maxdatafiles 40
    8>    character set we8iso8859p1;
Statement processed.
SVRMGR>
```

■ Back up the database—always back up a newly created database. You never know when you may have to go back to it.

We cannot stress enough the importance of adding this skill to your skill set as a DBA. It has been our experience that less than 50 percent of the DBAs out there have ever done this. Now is the time! This leads into our next rule.

STOPPERS RULE #13
Learn how to create a database and practice before you are forced to do so during a real-life emergency.

With the Oracle8 Database Assistant, perhaps the number of DBAs who have never taken the time or who have been forced to go through the process of re-creating a database will decrease. Appendix C of this work is dedicated to the Database Assistant and leads you through a sample session setting up a second instance on Windows NT.

Freelist Contention

As we discuss in a number of places throughout this book, Oracle maintains data dictionary information in memory. This allows almost instantaneous access to information that resides on disk but has been loaded into memory. Some of the information in memory keeps track of the space that is available in the tablespaces for inserting new rows. When tables are created, you can instruct Oracle how much information to keep in memory for blocks that are available for creating records. This is referred to as the *freelist* for the table. When creating a table, the **create table** would look like the following SQL.

```
SQL> create table my_table (seq      number,
  2                         my_key   varchar2(10),
  3                         desc     varchar2(40))
  4                         freelist 12;
Table created.
```

The **freelist** setting of 12 overrides the Oracle default of 1. Whatever this parameter is set to is the number of block IDs that Oracle will maintain in memory that are candidates for record insertion. When Oracle needs space in a table to create a new record, it searches the table's free list in memory until it either finds a block that can hold the new information or runs out of block IDs. If there are no block IDs in memory that can accommodate the new record, Oracle reads more dictionary information from disk. As multiuser applications run, there are many situations where a number of transactions are simultaneously looking for a block to insert data into. This can lead to another show stopper.

SHOW STOPPER
*Excessive disk I/O to satisfy requests for block
IDs to create new rows!*

This bottleneck is called *freelist contention*. Freelist contention occurs when multiple processes are searching the **freelist** at the same time and, when the end of the list is reached, requesting additional information from disk. Minimizing I/O, as we have advised you throughout this book, is one of the biggest contributors to tuning.

You can assess the freelist contention that is going on in your database by looking at the V$WAITSTAT and V$SYSSTAT dictionary views owned by SYS. Use the following queries to compute the percent of the two figures against one another. The first query will tell you how many freelist wait situations have been detected. The second will tell you how many total requests for data have been recorded in the dictionary.

```
SQL> select class, count
  2     from v$waitstat
  3   where class = 'free list';
CLASS                          COUNT
---------------------------    -----
free list                        59
SQL> select name,value
  2     from v$sysstat
  3   where name in ('db_block_gets','consistent gets');
CLASS                          COUNT
---------------------------    -----------
db block gets                  12850
consistent gets                10119
SQL>
```

The result returned in the first query of 59 is then used to compute the percent of requests for data that resulted in a wait for a resource, initiated by not enough **freelist**. Using the queries' results,

```
freelist wait events = (free list count) / (db block gets +
                                        consistent gets) * 100
                = 59 / (12850 + 10119) * 100
                = 59 / 22969 = 0.26
```

This means that less than 1 percent of the requests for data resulted in a **freelist** wait situation.

STOPPERS RULE #14

*If the number of waits for free blocks is greater than 1 percent of the total number of requests, consider increasing the **freelist** parameter on your **insert** and **update** intensive tables.*

We continue to stress the importance of knowing your applications. When you're making adjustments to the **freelist** parameters, you must know which tables are high insert and update, as mentioned in the last rule. To change this parameter for a table, you need to do the following:

1. Export the data from the table with the grants and indexes.

2. Drop the table.

3. Re-create the table with an increased **freelist** parameter.

4. Import the data back into the table ensuring you code IGNORE=Y when you run the import.

NOTE
You should be aware of any foreign key constraints that point to the table you are going to drop. These must be disabled before the drop and then enabled after the import.

Since many users may be accessing a table at the same time your applications run, you need to ensure there are at least enough **freelist** entries to accommodate this concurrent access. This leads us into our next rule.

STOPPERS RULE #15
*Have a sufficient number of **freelist** entries for a table to accommodate the number of concurrent processes that will be inserting data into that table.*

Concurrent user access to the database is fundamental to smooth operations of any Oracle instance.

Runaway Size (PCTINCREASE)

The storage **pctincrease** is used when creating tables, tablespaces, indexes, and clusters. Without fully understanding usage of **pctincrease**, you can create a show stopper.

SHOW STOPPER

*Unpredictable and runaway amounts of space
being eaten up by tables!*

When speaking about this parameter, we need to mention **initial** and
next to discuss the concept of **pctincrease** fully. Starting with version 6 of
Oracle, you were given control over the fine-tuning of space allocation.
Consider the following **create table** statement:

```
SQL> create table my_table (seq      number,
  2                          my_key  varchar2(10),
  3                          desc    varchar2(40))
  4          storage (initial 100K next 100K pctincrease 0);
Table created.
SQL>
```

The three keywords in the parentheses after the word **storage** and their
values are as follows:

- **initial** is the amount of space allocated to a table when created—in
  this case, 100K (102,400 bytes) of space is reserved for data when
  the table is created.

- **next** is the size of the first extent allocated when the table needs
  additional space—here, though not always, it is the same as **initial**.

- **pctincrease** is the percent that each extent (other than the first as
  sized by the **next** value) exceeds the size of the previous extent.

Oracle uses 50 as the default for **pctincrease**. You need to visit that
value when you create tables. The size of extents can grow
exponentially—think of the doubling penny concept. If you were to start
with a single penny and keep doubling it every day, you would be a very
rich person in a remarkably short time period! In a mere 19 days, you
would have over $10,000. Tables 7-4, 7-5, and 7-6 show the size of extents
allocated to three tables with the listed storage parameters. These tables
exist in a database where the Oracle block size is 4K (4,096 bytes).

If the **pctincrease** of a table needs adjusting, issue the command

```
SQL> alter table my_table storage (pctincrease 0);
Table altered.
SQL>
```

Extent id	Extent Size in Bytes
1	12288
2	20480
3	40960
4	61440
5	81920
6	122880
7	184320
8	266240
9	389120

TABLE 7-4. *Extent Sizes for Initial 4K Next 10K and pctincrease 50*

Extent id	Extent Size in Bytes
1	102400
2	163840
3	245760
4	368640
5	532480

TABLE 7-5. *Extent Sizes for Initial 500K Next 100K and pctincrease 50*

Extent id	Extent Size in Bytes
1	102400
2	102400
3	102400
4	102400
5	102400
6	102400
7	102400
8	102400

TABLE 7-6. *Extent Sizes for Initial 100K Next 100K and pctincrease 0*

Naturally, this will take effect with the next extent allocated. Those already used by a table stay as they are. Keep in mind that once an extent is allocated to a table, it belongs to that table for the life of the table. The only time extents are deallocated from a table is when that table is re-created; when a table is dropped, naturally all its reserved space is returned to the pool of free space.

STOPPERS RULE #16
Set the **pctincrease** *to 0 when creating tables.*
Look at existing tables and reset this value to 0.

Situations may arise that have extraordinary space requirements. Say that, for example, according to the formula

```
next extent size = previous extent size * pctincrease / 100
```

you know that a table is going to need 1MB (one megabyte or 1,048,576 bytes) for some new records. Prior to Oracle7, you had to change the **next** value, create the new rows, then change the value back to what it was previously. You can now do the following:

```
alter table my_table allocate extent size 1M;
```

The worry about doing it the old way is if you ever forget to change the storage parameters back to what they used to be, you may continue to grab 1MB rather than the 100K (what the **next** value was before you changed it).

STOPPERS RULE #17
When you require space for a table larger than
the next extent will be, use the SQL statement
alter table allocate extent *rather than*
adjusting the storage parameters for the table.

Next, we have a look at space management of indexes; the space is handled somewhat differently than tables when looking at how space is released when rows are deleted.

Free Space in Indexes

Correct sizing of indexes becomes even more crucial when we discuss how Oracle8 deals with index entries for rows deleted from tables. Oracle8 will not reuse index space in blocks whose corresponding data rows have been deleted. For example, using a 2K block size, say each index entry for a table takes up 50 bytes, and the index has **initrans** set to 2. There are 46 bytes reserved for transaction information, leaving 2,002 bytes for index entries. The index block will hold up to 40 index entries. If 50 percent of the rows a full index block points to are deleted, Oracle will not use the 1,000 bytes freed up. This could lead to another show stopper.

SHOW STOPPER
Runaway space consumption on indexes pointing to tables undergoing high delete activity!

This indicates that you need to monitor the amount of index space dedicated to deleted rows. First, you need to **validate** an index, then look at statistics in the INDEX_STATS dictionary view. Use the following query.

```
SQL> validate index pk_period_dtl;
Index analyzed.
SQL> select lf_rows, lf_rows_len, del_lf_rows, del_lf_rows_len
  2     from index_stats where name = 'PK_PERIOD_DTL';

 LF_ROWS LF_ROWS_LEN DEL_LF_ROWS DEL_LF_ROWS_LEN
-------- ----------- ----------- ---------------
    2589       92340          97            3432
SQL>
```

From examining this output, there are now 2,589 values in the index, whose space consumption in the index amounts to 92,340 bytes. There are 97 slots in the index that used to point to rows that have been deleted, consuming 3,432 bytes of space in the index. Thus, 3.7 percent of the space allocated to the PK_PERIOD_DTL index is taken up by what we call "dead entries." It is wise to monitor the space still consumed by deleted rows in an index and, when a threshold is passed, perform an index rebuild.

STOPPERS RULE #18
When the deleted row space in an index is
over 20 percent of the space being used in the
index, you should drop and re-create the
index to reclaim unused space.

Transaction Space

The **initrans**, **maxtrans**, and **pctfree** parameters control the amount of space that keeps track of transactions against a table. The **initrans** parameter sets aside a certain number of bytes for each transaction slot in each data block that resides in a table.

NOTE
The specific number of bytes is stored in the
V$TYPE_SIZE view as the constant KTBIT. For
this example, we will use 24.

Space is reserved in a data block for data and header information. Data will be loaded into data blocks until it occupies an amount dictated by the **pctfree** entry for each table. If this **pctfree** is set to 40 for a table, Oracle8 will reserve 40 percent of each block (1,638 bytes of a 4,096-byte or 4K block) free for expansion of column values in existing rows. The space left over for expansion of existing records we call the pctfree space. If your applications need to support concurrent access to a table by more than one user, you should increase this **initrans** value. Oracle8 will allocate space in a data block for transactions in these 24-byte slices and will allocate up to the number of slots delineated by **maxtrans**. If **maxtrans** is set too low, you have a show stopper.

SHOW STOPPER
Block contention—transaction space limited in
data blocks!

Using a 2K (2,048 bytes) block size as an example, Oracle8 will initially reserve 24 bytes of transaction space in the header of the data block with the following **create index** statement:

```
SQL>create index my_index on my_table (seq, my_key)
  2    storage (initrans 1 maxtrans 4);
Table created.
SQL>
```

This header is in the same physical location as the block itself. Each block is logically made up of header space and data space. If the my_index index ever needs transaction space for four concurrent transactions, Oracle8 will use the extra three slots, bringing the total transaction space up to 24 bytes. Those 96 bytes are taken from the free data space and, when the slots are no longer needed, they are not deallocated from the header space as unused data space. If a fifth concurrent transaction needed a transaction slot, it queues itself behind a transaction already using one of the slots. It then uses that slot when the previous transaction completes. Thus, if **maxtrans** is set too low, you will get another show stopper.

SHOW STOPPER
Wait time for previous transactions to terminate!

STOPPERS RULE #19
*Set **initrans** high enough at least to accommodate the expected number of concurrent transactions a table experiences.*

STOPPERS RULE #20
*Set **maxtrans** to the value of **initrans** + 2.*

STOPPERS RULE #21
*When raising **initrans** and **maxtrans** for a table, raise it for the data and index components at the same time. After all, inserting a row into a table also requires creation of an additional index entry.*

The next show stopper we have a look at involves running an Oracle8 database in ARCHIVELOG mode and monitoring the amount of space consumed in the directory where the archived redo logs are copied.

ARCHIVELOG Destination Full

We have recommended running your production database in ARCHIVELOG mode. We discuss this concept in a number of places throughout *Oracle8 Tuning*. Oracle makes a copy of redo logs before it reuses them and places that copy in a location specified by the two initialization parameter file entries LOG_ARCHIVE_DEST and LOG_ARCHIVE_FORMAT.

NOTE
We discuss the LOG_ARCHIVE_DUPLEX_ DEST entry in the initialization parameter file in the section of Chapter 6 by the same name.

It is your responsibility to monitor the space on the drive where Oracle writes archived redo logs. If the destination fills to capacity, the next time Oracle tries to archive a redo log, you have a show stopper:

SHOW STOPPER
Archive process unable to complete redo log copy!

This unfortunate situation is evident when users entering SQL*Plus are presented with the Oracle error 00257, meaning:

```
ORA-00257: archiver is stuck. CONNECT INTERNAL only, until freed
Cause: The ARCH process received an error while trying to archive
a redo log file.
If the problem is not resolved soon, the database will stop
executing transactions. The most likely cause of this message
is that the destination device is out of space to store the
redo log file.
```

```
Action: Check the archiver trace file for a detailed description
of the problem. Also, verify that the device specified in the
initialization parameter ARCHIVE_LOG_DEST is set up properly for
archiving.
```

We have found the following reasons for the archive directory to suddenly fill up during normal operating conditions.

■ For some reason, the previous night's backup routine, which is supposed to put archived redo logs out to tape and then erase them, aborted the last time it ran—the step that was supposed to erase them never ran.

■ An application has deleted a large number of rows from a very large table, and the redo log files written by that transaction alone created a very large number of archived redo logs.

■ If your archive log destination drive shares space with other Oracle database files, you may have inadvertently drastically reduced the available space by adding a datafile to a tablespace that resides on that drive.

This leads into our next few rules.

STOPPERS RULE #22
Monitor the available space on the directory that contains your archived redo logs. If its utilization climbs over 90 percent, it may require immediate intervention.

STOPPERS RULE #23
Dedicate enough space in your archive log destination to hold at least two full days of archived redo logs.

STOPPERS RULE #24
Archived redo logs should be backed up every day and deleted afterwards. Do not rely on manual purging of the archived redo log destination.

Picture the following scenario that happened to one of our clients using Oracle on HP-UX. They were having a problem with locking on a few central tables in their application and decided to shut down the database and then restart it at once. Closing and subsequently reopening will cause any locks that were held to be released. When they brought the database up, the very first user who attempted to connect was presented with the secure database logon screen as mentioned previously. They looked at the space utilization on the archive destination, knowing it must be 100 percent. They had filled up this drive a number of times and felt, as we would have, smug in being so quick to recognize the situation. The UNIX *bdf* command reported the utilization of the destination drive was a mere 72 percent. Briefly, this is what had happened (it may not happen to you, but isn't is interesting how easily the show can be stopped?):

■ Oracle is responsible for making the copy of a redo log in the archive destination.

■ There is a UNIX concept (as with most operating systems) of file protection. When Oracle is in the midst of copying the redo log, the file protection is set to 000—this means that no processes are allowed to overwrite the archived redo log until the copying is complete.

■ If the background process ARCH (as discussed in Chapter 2) does not complete the copying, the file protection is left at 000.

■ When the copying completes, the protection of the file is changed to 640, meaning that Oracle can overwrite it if necessary.

■ When the database was first shut down, Oracle had partially archived a redo log but, since the copy was not complete, the file protection for the archived redo log was left at 000.

■ When the database was brought up, one of the first things it did was try to create a complete copy of the archived redo log it had started to create but had not finished.

■ Since it could not overwrite the partially created archived redo log, the database sat in limbo until the partially copied redo log was erased manually.

When the partially copied redo log was erased, Oracle carried on recreating the full copy of the archived redo log, and all was well.

Getting Locked Up by Locks

As discussed in Chapter 6, the initialization parameter file entry DML_LOCKS sets the maximum number of locks that can be placed on all objects by all users at one time. If this entry is set too low, you have a show stopper:

SHOW STOPPER
Applications raising Oracle errors due to too few DML_LOCKS!

We have found through our experience that the default value for this entry is too low and must be raised.

STOPPERS RULE #25
Set DML_LOCKS in your initialization parameter file to the number of concurrent users times 10.

ANSI C Compiler

Oracle8 insists that the appropriate C compiler be used when installing the Server. All too many times, in HP-UX for example, we have tried to relink the server during an installation or upgrade and have been told the ANSI C compiler can not be found.

SHOW STOPPER
Unable to relink Oracle—C compiler incompatible.

The C compiler that is installed by default with many operating systems is not the version that Oracle insists be in place when the Server is relinked. If Oracle finds the incorrect compiler, a Server installation or upgrade will fail and inhibit access to the affected environment.

STOPPERS RULE #26
Get your systems administration people to ensure the correct C compiler is in place if you need to relink the Oracle Server.

In our experience, in most cases, the correct compiler, once located on your operating system vendor's distribution medium, can be put in place easily and in a matter of minutes—interesting how it's the little things that can cause the most problems!

ANSI C Compiler—Back to the Root of the Problem

You can trace the roots of this problem back to the founding fathers and what gave this company its competitive advantage early on. Larry Ellison, Ed Oates, and the late Bob Miner founded Oracle in 1977. As a side note and a great trivia question for your next techie outing, not to mention how impressive it sounds at cocktail parties, the original name for Oracle Corporation was System Development Laboratories. Then, after reading an article published by E.F. Codd in the *IBM Journal of Research and Development* on the theory of relational database management systems, they decided to change the name from System Development Laboratories to (another great trivia question) Relational Software, Incorporated.

The goal of this new firm was to produce a database management system based on the theories of relational database management. In fact, Oracle was able to produce the first RDBMS in 1980 a good four years before IBM released DB2. In order to differentiate Relational Software from the competitor IBM, they decided to offer the RDBMS on a variety of different computers, knowing that IBM would not. Some old Oracle coffee cups have the slogan *Compatibility, Portability, and Connectability* written on them. This slogan summarized Oracle's positioning in the marketplace.

To enable Oracle to run on as many different computers as possible, they chose the C programming language to write the RDBMS in. This decision was a very big gamble—you must remember that back then C was a new toy on the market. As we all know today, the decision to embrace C was the right one. By writing the RDBMS in C, they were able to develop an RDBMS that would run on virtually any box—yes, even a WANG. Even though the RDBMS was written in C, Oracle had to spend a lot of its resources maintaining a different version of the RDBMS in C for every variation a vendor had. This made it painfully clear to Oracle that the earlier a set of industry standards were developed for C, the better it would be for the corporation. They would then be able to reduce the amount of time and effort it took to deploy a new version of the RDBMS. This motivated Oracle to be a very early supporter of the ANSI C standards committee.

Early on, they helped shape the direction of the language and helped promote its adoption. This adoption of ANSI C as an industry standard helped Oracle minimize the amount of effort it took to port and maintain databases for the various hardware platforms. Today, Oracle continues its tradition of supporting and directing industry standards.

Don't Be Afraid to Read the Directions

The four of us were sometimes guilty of never being willing to ask for directions when lost. The result of this fear was that we sometimes spent too much time trying to find our way. Over time, unlike many of our brethren, we have learned that it's acceptable to stop and ask for help—that this is not a sign of weakness but a sign of strength. Far too many times, we see the DBA and developers not taking the time to stop and read the installation or user's guide. This is a sure path to disaster.

SHOW STOPPER
Failure (or stubbornness??) to read the documentation can easily cause the process to be severely delayed!

It's not enough to read the documentation; you must be proactive. We have learned that it is best to look into the directories and search for filenames containing the words *README* or some variation. Reading all pertinent read-me files is critical to avoiding problems. Last minute critical advice and warnings about possible pitfalls or incompatibilities to avoid are always contained within the files. The fact is, many times the documentation is printed weeks before the development code is finished being developed. The documentation CD has improved this situation somewhat, but still the most up-to-date information is always contained in the read-me files.

SHOW STOPPER #27
Always read the README files that come with every Oracle8 installation. Key information and ways to avoid pitfalls are always there.

Our Best Friend Is a Dog

There is a saying that "Man's best friend is a dog," but a DBA's best friend is another DBA. Always ask other DBAs before you begin a new upgrade of the database. Many times, they have learned lessons the hard way and are willing to share the experience. You don't need to get burned by fire to know that you should not stick your hand in it.

SHOW STOPPER #28

*Always ask advice of those who have traveled
the path before you.*

Who Has the Keys to the Castle?

Many a time, we have seen database installations and production databases fail only due to privileges. Make sure you have the necessary privileges before you begin any installation or upgrade.

SHOW STOPPER

*Not enough privileges to perform the task
at hand!*

STOPPERS RULE #29

*If you do not have the privileges you need,
you will waste your time. For example, to
initially install Oracle, you must be able to run
a portion of the installation from the root
account in UNIX.*

The database needs to be king of its castle. Having the right to use it is not the same as owning it. Many times, especially under the UNIX operating system, some system administrators resist having the Oracle account owning all the directories the database files reside in. They insist that making Oracle part of the appropriate group is enough. Eventually, this always results in a failed database. Somehow, the privileges get changed and the database has problems. The two most likely problems are:

1. The database will not start up because the process that initiates the startup cannot write to the database files.

2. The process that tries to archive log files fails because it can't write to the archive destination disk.

Experience has taught us that having the account that owns the Oracle software (be it UNIX, Windows NT, or any other platform) own its own directories avoids a lot of problems.

STOPPERS RULE #30
Have the account that owns the Oracle
software own its own directories and files.

Disk Space Is Cheap, and What About Memory?

When will people learn that disk space is cheap? This is not the 1970s or '80s, when we had to conserve every byte possible. Look at the mess conserving bytes got the industry in. Someone figured out you could save a lot of disk space if you only put in a two-character year instead of a four-character year. This became standard practice in the industry—why not? The year 2000 was so very far away! Well, today, that decision is costing the industry billions.

When you are installing or upgrading to Oracle8, make sure you have plenty of disk space. We have seen more installations and upgrades fail due to a lack of disk space. Don't even begin the process unless you have a lot more than you think.

SHOW STOPPER
Inadequate disk space to complete upgrade
or installation!

STOPPERS RULE #31
Don't begin an Oracle8 installation or upgrade
unless you have enough disk space.

There is an old saying in the real estate business which states "All new home buyers are liars." They tell you they are only going to spend X, but they almost always end up spending X+Y. Well, we also have a saying: all vendors are liars. Oracle and Microsoft have a history of lying to us. Every time Microsoft releases a new version of its software, it requires a lot more memory than stated; every time Oracle releases a new copy of the database, it requires a lot more disk space than the installation manual tells you. Learn from this. If Microsoft informs you it needs 16MB of memory to run, then plan on 32MB of RAM. If Oracle tells you that you need 1 gigabyte of disk space for installation, plan on $1\frac{1}{2}$ or 2. In defense of both companies, we think they only test the code on the most minimal configuration.

SHOW STOPPER
Administrator failed to allow extra disk
requirements over and above what the
vendor suggested.

We Forgot What You Said About Memory

To think that programs used to run in under 64K of memory. Today, that is not the case. Every release of Oracle requires more and more memory. Before you begin any upgrade or installation, make sure you have enough. To quote the Oracle documentation, "Oracle8 requires at least 16 megabytes of RAM for operating a minimum configuration. Full use of Oracle8, particularly use in conjunction with the Oracle product suite of Developer/2000 tools, network utilities, and special applications, requires at least 32 megabytes. See your operating system-specific Oracle documentation for more information on memory requirements specific to your operating system."

SHOW STOPPER
Not enough system memory to support the
Oracle8 instance!

STOPPERS RULE #32
Always make sure you have enough memory
before you begin an installation or upgrade.

You Need Contiguous Free Memory Within the SGA

Another strange twist on ensuring you have enough memory is to make
sure you have enough contiguous memory within the SGA. As Oracle
procedures are loaded into and out of the SGA, they leave chunks of free
space. If an Oracle8 procedure cannot get a chunk of free space to hold it,
the procedure will not load in memory. This will cause your PL/SQL
procedures to fail. This will stop your applications.

SHOW STOPPER
PL/SQL blocks cannot find adequate free
contiguous memory!

STOPPERS RULE #33
If a PL/SQL procedure cannot get enough free
memory within the SGA to load, it will fail.

We discussed the initialization parameter file entries SHARED_POOL_
RESERVED_SIZE and SHARED_POOL_RESERVED_MIN_ALLOC in the
"SHARED_POOL_RESERVED Parameters" section of Chapter 6. These
entries, when set, reserve a minimum and maximum amount of space in
the shared pool portion of the SGA for large PL/SQL blocks of code. Since
Oracle release 7.2, the PL/SQL code has been now broken into smaller
chunks. This means the entire package does not need to be in contiguous
memory, but the smaller pieces do. As a side note, an Oracle8 stored
package can now be up to 80K in size.

Truncate It, Don't Drop It!

Many times when a DBA has to re-create a database or a portion of the
database, they first go out and drop all the contents and then import
recreate everything. Many times, this process does not work or, minimally,
just takes too long.

SHOW STOPPER
*Access to database delayed lengthy amount
of time!*

Use the **truncate** command. It is the quickest way to empty the contents
of a table while maintaining all its relationships.

STOPPERS RULE #34
*Avoid many problems by using **truncate**, not
drop, when emptying the contents of a table.*

The **truncate** command is a double-edged sword. As we suggest in
Stoppers Rule #31, **truncate** is one of our best friends. Imagine the
following scenario:

1. The DBA is asked to wipe the contents of the FINANCE_9697 table.

2. The DBA logs into SQL*Plus as the owner of FINANCE_9697 and
   issues the command shown in the next listing; the cursor sits there
   for two to three minutes, then Oracle returns the message shown.

```
SQL> delete finance_9596;
12908 rows deleted.
SQL>
```

3. The DBA calmly notices the last command, realizes the
   FINANCE_9596 table has been cleared out by mistake, and issues
   the command and receives feedback from Oracle as shown next.

```
SQL> rollback;
Rollback complete.
SQL> select count(*)
  2    from finance_9596;
   COUNT(*)
------------
      12908
SQL>
```

Phew (thanks to Jordan Noah), that was a close one. Many of you know
what's coming next, so here goes. Suppose the three point listing above

used the **truncate** command rather than **delete**. That's right—one cannot roll back a **truncate table** command since Oracle writes nothing about the transaction to the redo logs. The next listing shows how the exercise would play out.

```
SQL> truncate table finance_9596;
Table truncated.
SQL> rollback;
Rollback complete.
SQL> select count(*)
  2    from finance_9596;
    COUNT(*)
------------
           0
```

SHOW STOPPER
DBA made a typo and a table has to be restored from an export or an image backup!

STOPPERS RULE #35
Be careful when truncating tables because there is NO undo generated as there is when one uses the **delete** *command.*

911—Help, I'm in Trouble

Up to now, we have talked about what to do to avoid the show stopping, but what do you do when even the best plans fail? You take it. That's right, you take it. When Murphy's law strikes, you are a victim. If you think it's never going to strike, you are not a victim, you are a fool. So let's discuss how you deal with the unforeseen.

Assess the Situation

We know you are having a problem, but chill out. Everything is relative. It reminds us of a time one of us was working on a trading floor. The database we did all the trades with went down. The head trader came in complaining that they were in the midst of the biggest trade of the year and informed our lead DBA in a very loud, raw manner that he was not happy. This was a hospital, and when the database went down it could affect someone's life. The DBA did not find the traders' noise a hindrance. The point is, every crisis is relative. If you allow yourself to get caught up in it, you will not be able to adequately assess the situation.

STOPPERS RULE #36

Take the time to asses the situation and determine what your real risk is.

Assess the situation and ask yourself the following questions:

1. Is it production, development, or test?

2. Has the database stopped working or is the problem slowing it down?

3. Is it something obvious or something we have seen before?

4. Is it something that can be fixed or is it better to roll the database back to its last backup?

Contact Oracle WorldWide Customer Support

You are paying for Oracle Support, use it. Once you have determined you cannot solve your problem yourself, call in the troops. Get the call out to Oracle support. The sooner the process starts, the quicker you will have resolution. Be smart about how you do it. For example, always keep your own written records when dealing with Oracle Support. Figure 7-4 suggests a sample form you can use; run off some copies of it.

When you call, make sure you give them the needed facts to categorize the problem correctly. If your production database is down, then let them know right away. Always ask them what severity is assigned to the call. If you told them you have a down production database and they assign your call a severity 3, ask them to up the priority. If it's production that is down, make sure they know it. Always determine what is a reasonable response time and hold them to it. The squeaky wheel gets the oil. If production is down and they have not called you back in a reasonable amount of time, call them. After an hour of no response, ask to talk to the duty manager.

```
Oracle Support Call Log

Tar #_____        Severity Assigned to Call _____

Initial Call to Support:_____        Caller:_____

Date/Time of Callback(s): Oracle        Your Organization

                         _____        _____

                         _____        _____

                         _____        _____

                         _____        _____

Problem
Description:_____

            _____

            _____


Resolution:

_____

_____

_____
```

FIGURE 7-4. *Sample form for dealing with Oracle Support*

Trust your instincts when you get an answer. It is very difficult to solve a problem over the phone. If the answer you are getting does not make sense, then you are probably right. Discuss your concerns with the support analysts and explain the issues you have with the answer. Work as a team.

Simon Says

When was the last time any support organization, not just Oracle's, let you down? Why did that happen? Was it because:

- They don't care? They actually do, but put yourself in their place and remind yourself of the last time someone insisted something happen immediately and you couldn't even begin to work on it for a week.

- They don't have enough analysts? This could be the case, but exactly where do we expect them to find these people? Would you rather have many, many technicians who know very little or half the number who know a lot? I think the latter.

- They don't know what they are doing? Oracle8 is a very complex product, and we think it is remarkable Oracle is able to support the product at the technical level they do.

- The support centers get hundreds of calls a day? Perhaps.

We think that all of the above contribute to many people's feelings about the support, but we also want to point out one of the biggest reasons Oracle can be stretched beyond their limits—Simon says "Close your support calls when you no longer need any more answers". If we all did this, you'd be surprised how much more time the support analysts would have on their hands. This leads us into our next show stopper, which is actually a REPPOTS WOHS, or a show stopper in reverse.

 SHOW STOPPER
Support analysts spinning their wheels on calls that should be closed by the customer!

There is no need to spend another second on the call, since the customer has solved the problem and just hasn't gotten around to calling Oracle. You'd be surprised how much further the analysts' time would go if they weren't tied up on nuisance calls.

STOPPERS RULE #37
Close your support calls with Oracle as soon as you have the goods to enable you to solve the problem that led to the request for help.

Use Your Oracle Network

Rather than sit by the phone waiting for some analysts a thousand miles away to solve your problem, keep working the issue. Attend your local users group meetings and keep business cards. Call up other DBAs you think might have encountered the problem and swap ideas. Many times, this is the quickest way to get an answer.

Use the Internet or Other Information Networks

By the year 2000, there will be over 50,000,000 million Internet users. Today, it is already a great source of technical information. If you have a question about a down database or any technical issue, there is a pretty high chance that among the Internet community someone has experienced the problem before. Check out the "Resources on the World Wide Web" section of Chapter 10 for some suggestions of where to get started.

There Are No Magic Bullets

It is a major show stopper: DBAs that do not help themselves. Rather than sit and wait for Oracle to solve all the problems, help yourself. Use people you met in the industry. Use the documentation. Use your common sense, and use the Internet.

Let's Tune It

This chapter is different from others in this book. The material presented affects the ability of Oracle to run uninterrupted. We have presented the theme in a number of spots throughout this book that a down database is not a tuned database. The points we present in this chapter are relevant—they are a series of known situations to watch out for. Being aware of potential problems before they happen to you is part of the tuning approach.

- Ensure the operating system open file limit is high enough to allow Oracle to have more than enough open files to support all database operations.

- Allow enough transaction space (through setting of **initrans** and **maxtrans**) in your data blocks to support concurrent user access.

- Set **pctincrease** for tables to 0 when they are created.

- Know how to reorganize your tables using a combination of export and import.

- Track the space dedicated to deleted rows in your tables' indexes and re-create indexes when the percent is over 20.

- Monitor the disk utilization of the directory that receives your archived redo logs.

- When required, manually allocate large extents to tables that exceed the tables' current storage parameters using **alter table allocate extent** rather than adjusting these parameters beforehand and resetting them after.

- Learn how to create a database and become fluent with the series of SQL scripts that need to be run on a fresh database to set up the data dictionary.

Oracle 7.x Specifics

Please note the following points organized by the headings for some of the sections of this chapter:

- "Working with Data from Extended Character Sets" Applicable to Oracle 7.x.

- "Client/Server Drive Assignments" Applicable to Oracle 7.x.

- "What Happened to Those Indexes?" Applicable to Oracle 7.x.

- "Database Limits vs. Operating System Limits" Applicable to Oracle 7.x.

- "Operating System Limits" Applicable to Oracle 7.x.

- "Oracle8 Datatype Limits" As we have mentioned, the maximum size of some datatypes is expanded in Oracle8, and there are also some new types. The NVARCHAR2, NCHAR, CLOB, NCLOB, BLOB, and BFILE are all new. The format of the ROWID is different.

- "Oracle Limits" Applicable to Oracle 7.x.

- "Re-creating a Database" Applicable to Oracle 7.x, even the **create database** sample. (Keep in mind that the **create database** scripts in other places around *Oracle8 Tuning* will not necessarily work with Oracle 7.x).

- "Freelist Contention" Applicable to Oracle 7.x.

- "Runaway Size (PCTINCREASE)" Applicable to Oracle 7.x.

- "Free Space In Indexes" Applicable to Oracle 7.x.

- "Transaction Space" Applicable to Oracle 7.x.

- "ARCHIVELOG Destination Full" Applicable to Oracle 7.x, except mention of the LOG_ARCHIVE_DUPLEX_DEST initialization parameter file entry.

- "Getting Locked Up by Locks" Applicable to Oracle 7.x.

■ "ANSI C Compiler" Same rule applies to Oracle 7.3.x, but releases 7.2 and 7.1 were more forgiving. It was only at 7.3 that relinking the Server blew up without a proper ANSI C compiler.

■ "Don't Be Afraid to Read the Directions" Applicable to Oracle 7.x.

■ "Who Has the Keys to the Castle?" Applicable to Oracle 7.x.

■ "Disk Space Is Cheap, and What About Memory?" Applicable to Oracle 7.x.

■ "Truncate It, Don't Drop It!" Applicable to Oracle 7.x.

■ "911—Help I'm in Trouble" Applicable to Oracle 7.x (and versions 2, 3, 4, 5, and 6, too!).

CHAPTER
8

Application Tuning

s with all computer programming languages, tuning plays an important role with Oracle. Due to added memory management enhancements with each new version of Oracle, application and program tuning become even more crucial. You need to train yourself to optimize SQL statements, make use of central blocks of code (database triggers, procedures, functions, and packages), investigate declarative integrity, and use the off-the-shelf performance monitoring tools. Incorporating program tuning into ongoing program development and maintenance allows you to code in ways that take advantage of the speed and throughput enhancing routines that Oracle continues to add to the software. DBA and hardware support personnel can tune the database and support hardware; without tuning applications, this effort may be *wasted*.

This chapter will discuss some of the tools at your disposal for tuning your applications. We will highlight some of the rules you should follow when choosing and setting up indexes to speed data retrieval. We will cover forms of generic code that you are encouraged to write to take advantage of the Oracle shared SQL area. Throughout this chapter are references to the *initialization parameter file,* which is a file read by Oracle whenever a database is started.

Oracle8 offers more bells and whistles of which the application developer may take advantage. The **set autotrace on** feature, discussed in its own section in this chapter, assists tuning SQL statements as they are developed. Table 8-1 shows the database objects that will be referenced in some of the application tuning examples in this chapter.

Oracle Enterprise Manager

In a number of places throughout this chapter, we speak of the Oracle Enterprise Manager, affectionately called *OEM,* and the Performance Pack. Back in the early Oracle7 days, we used full-screen SQL*DBA to fulfill our monitoring requirements. A bit later, with the emergence of Server Manager, we used the GUI-based incarnation to do our monitoring. There were a few releases of this product for Windows, but the major monitoring activities were done using an X-type client. GUI Server Manager started to disappear with release 7.3 and is obsolete as of production release 8.0.3.

OEM is the backbone of many secure database activities, made up of a system of management screens such as a Schema Manager, a Storage

Table	Column	Datatype
PEOPLE	pin	number(6)
	pos_id	number(2)
	last_name	varchar2(20)
	first_name	varchar2(20)
PLANT_DETAIL	plant_id	number(2)
	city_id	number(2)
	location	varchar2(20)
SAL_LIMIT	pos_id	number(2)
	sal_cap	number(8,2)
	over_time	varchar2(1)
WORK_CITY	city_id	number(2)
	sdesc	varchar2(20)
	ldesc	varchar2(60)

TABLE 8-1.   *Sample Database Tables*

Manager, and a Data Manager for example. A word of warning about OEM (this warning is not designed to scare you away from OEM or not let any secure database activities be handed off to other personnel when appropriate):

APPLICATION TUNING RULE #1
Be careful when allowing members of the technical community access to the Managers in OEM. Once connected to an instance through an OEM Manager interface, operations normally associated with skilled DBAs can end up in the hands of not-so-skilled users.

Let's expand a bit on this rule before moving on. Often we have seen applications coming on board and, during the roll out, power users and pseudo-DBAs have access to the SYSTEM account on the database where the system resides. This is not a situation we like as DBAs, but, as we all know, office politics rather than our own wishes can take over. Rest assured—these people do not know enough about secure database SQL syntax to do any damage. When we say "secure database SQL syntax", we mean SQL like **drop table** or **alter tablespace** or **grant dba to**. Armed with the SYSTEM password, these people can inadvertently stumble into some very powerful SQL. The OEM Security Manager, for example, builds very powerful SQL, as do most of the managers, through a point-and-click interface. Beware!

The gist of Rule #1 is along the lines of all suggestions you have and will continue to get and give about working with the Oracle8 Server. Use common sense, and allow the drawbridge down only to those who know what they are doing. In this context, the drawbridge crosses a moat (first introduced in *Oracle Data Warehousing,* Corey and Abbey, Oracle Press 1997). The moat protects the castle (i.e., the database) and only those who know how to carry on business in the castle are allowed across the moat. In one of our recent client sites, this concept was referred to as the "Blair Scenario".

The Shared SQL Area

One of the turnkey performance enhancements that came about with Oracle7 and continues with Oracle8 is the creation of an area in the SGA called the *shared pool.* This segment of memory is dedicated to holding parsed and executable SQL statements as well as the dictionary cache (see Chapter 2 for a discussion on this cache). Subsequent statements passed to Oracle are compared against statements in the shared pool. If, according to the following rules, the new statement matches an old statement already in the pool, Oracle executes the compiled statement rather than reprocessing the statement just received. In order to qualify for this matching condition, all three of the next application tuning rules must be true.

APPLICATION TUNING RULE #2
There must be a character-by-character (paying attention to case) match between the statement being examined and the one already in the shared pool.

NOTE
Before this comparison is performed, Oracle applies an internal algorithm using the new statement. It then checks the results against values of statements already in the pool. If the new value matches one already there, the string comparison outlined in Rule #1 is performed.

To illustrate Rule #1, consider the following Oracle statements and why they do or do not qualify.

1. select pin from person where last_name = 'LAU';

2. select PIN from person where last_name = 'LAU';

Statements 1 and 2 do *not* qualify because "pin" is lowercase in 1 and uppercase in 2.

1. select pin from person where last_name = 'LAU';

2. select pin from person where last_name = 'LAU';

Statements 1 and 2 *do* qualify because the case match of both statements is exactly the same.

1. select pin from person where last_name =
'LAU';

2. select pin from person where last_name = 'LAU';

Statements 1 and 2 do *not* qualify because 1 is split over two lines whereas 2 is on a single line.

APPLICATION TUNING RULE #3
The objects being referenced in the new statement are exactly the same as those objects in a statement that has passed the comparison in Rule #1.

NOTE
If an object referenced in a SQL statement in the shared pool is modified, the statement is flagged as invalid. The next time a statement is passed to Oracle that is the same as that invalid statement, the old statement will be replaced by the new since the underlying object has been modified.

For this example, the users have access to the objects in Table 8-2. Consider the statements in Table 8-3 and why they can or cannot be shared between the two users listed in Table 8-2.

Table 8-3 shows that the objects are different. Even though both users have a private synonym sal_limit to refer to the same database table, these individual private synonyms are actually database objects themselves.

APPLICATION TUNING RULE #4
If bind variables are referenced, they must have the same name in both the new and existing statements.

As examples, the first two statements in the following listing are identical, whereas the next two statements are not (even if the different bind variables have the same value at run time).

```
select pin,pos_id,last_name,first_name from people where pin = :blk1.pin;
select pin,pos_id,last_name,first_name from people where pin = :blk1.pin;
select pos_id,sal_cap from sal_limit where over_time = :blk1_ot_ind;
select pos_id,sal_cap from sal_limit where over_time = :blk1_ov_ind;
```

User	Object Name	Accessed via
mcleodmg	sal_limit	private synonym
	work_city	public synonym
	plant_detail	public synonym
kbrazeau	sal_limit	private synonym
	work_city	public synonym
	plant_detail	table_owner

TABLE 8-2. *Sample Database Objects for Two Users*

SQL Statement	Objects Matching	Why
select max(sal_cap) from sal_limit;	NO	Each user has a private synonym **sal_limit**—these are different objects
select count(*) from work_city where sdesc like 'NEW%';	YES	Both users reference **work_city** by the same public synonym—the same object
select a.sdesc, b.location from work_city a, plant_detail b where a.city_id = b.city_id;	NO	User mcleodmg references **plant_detail** by a public synonym whereas user jproudf is the table owner—these are different objects
select * from sal_limit where over_time is not null;	NO	Each user has a private synonym **sal_limit**—these are different objects

TABLE 8-3.   *Object Resolution of SQL Statements*

Monitoring the Shared Pool

As with most monitoring tasks, there are two ways to monitor the shared pool with the SQL and PL/SQL statements resident therein. Knowing what statements are already there assists you in coding SQL that matches. As mentioned in the previous section, by matching your statement to an already existing statement (according to the three rules outlined), you ensure that the one already there is reused. The first way is to use the Performance Manager in OEM; the other way, which many prefer, is using SQL*Worksheet or SQL*Plus. Let's first look at getting the information from OEM.

NOTE
Chapter 9 is dedicated to the Performance Pack, of which the Performance Manager is an integral part.

What's in the Shared Pool—OEM

You can monitor the shared pool using the Performance Pack Tool of the Enterprise Manager. Choose Display|Memory|SQL Area from the Performance Manager main console to bring up a display resembling that shown in Figure 8-1.

Notice how only part of the full SQL Text is displayed. To scroll through the text display, double-click on a row, and then use the arrow keys to move through the text. Table 8-4 explains the columns shown in the SQL Area chart.

Notice the SQL Text column contains PL/SQL blocks as well as SQL statements. The code that begins with the word **declare** is the start of a PL/SQL block. The code segments that start with **select**, **insert**, **update**, or **delete** are straight SQL. The Persistent Memory row in Table 8-4 mentions *cursors*. A cursor is a chunk of memory allocated to process an SQL statement.

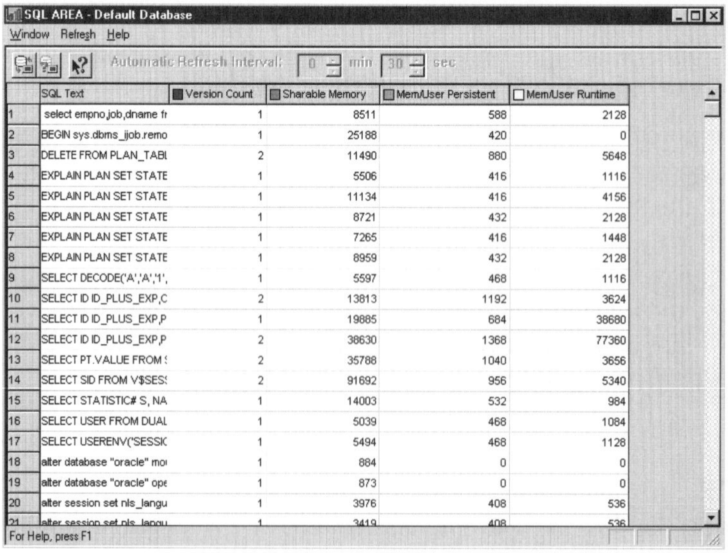

	SQL Text	Version Count	Sharable Memory	Mem/User Persistent	Mem/User Runtime
1	select empno,job,dname fr	1	8511	588	2128
2	BEGIN sys.dbms_ijob.remo	1	25188	420	0
3	DELETE FROM PLAN_TABL	2	11490	880	5648
4	EXPLAIN PLAN SET STATE	1	5506	416	1116
5	EXPLAIN PLAN SET STATE	1	11134	416	4156
6	EXPLAIN PLAN SET STATE	1	8721	432	2128
7	EXPLAIN PLAN SET STATE	1	7265	416	1448
8	EXPLAIN PLAN SET STATE	1	8959	432	2128
9	SELECT DECODE('A','A','1',	1	5597	468	1116
10	SELECT ID ID_PLUS_EXP,C	2	13813	1192	3624
11	SELECT ID ID_PLUS_EXP,P	1	19885	684	38680
12	SELECT ID ID_PLUS_EXP,P	2	38630	1368	77360
13	SELECT PT.VALUE FROM	2	35788	1040	3656
14	SELECT SID FROM V$SES	2	91692	956	5340
15	SELECT STATISTIC# S, NA	1	14003	532	984
16	SELECT USER FROM DUAL	1	5039	468	1084
17	SELECT USERENV('SESSI	1	5494	468	1128
18	alter database "oracle" mo	1	884	0	0
19	alter database "oracle" ope	1	873	0	0
20	alter session set nls_langu	1	3976	408	536
21	alter session set nls_langu	1	3419	408	536

FIGURE 8-1. *The SQL Area chart in Performance Manager*

Column	Meaning
Version Count	If greater than zero, more than one user is using the statement.
Sharable Memory	Indicates the number of bytes shared by users using this statement at the same time.
Persistent Memory	Indicates the number of bytes per user while that user's cursor is open in the shared pool.
Runtime memory	Indicates the number of bytes that is needed per user while the cursor is executing.

TABLE 8-4. *SQL Area Column Contents*

What's in the Shared Pool—Query V$ Views

Peeking into the shared pool can be accomplished using a query like the one shown in the following listing:

```
select b.address,b.sql_text,sorts,users_executing
  from sys.v_$sqlarea a,sys.v_$sqltext b
 where a.hash_value = b.hash_value
 order by b.address,piece,sorts,users_executing;
```

Some readers may already be familiar with the V$SQLAREA dictionary view and queries against its SQL_TEXT column to look at statements in the shared pool. We suggest using the query shown in the previous listing; it allows you to get all the SQL statement text, whereas V_$SQLAREA alone only allows access to 1,000 characters in each statement. By bringing V_$SQLTEXT into the equation, joining on the bolded columns in the previous listing, and introducing the PIECE column underlined in the same listing, we gain access to all the SQL statement text. Let's look at the first few lines of output generated by the query shown in the previous listing.

```
ADDRESS  SQL_TEXT                                    SORTS USERS_EXECUTING
-------- ------------------------------------------- --------- ---------------
0291E218 select b.address,b.sql_text,sorts,users_         4               1
         executing   from sys.v_$
0291E218 sqlarea a,sys.v_$sqltext b  where a.hash        4               1
         _value = b.hash_value  o
```

0291E218	rder by b.address,piece,sorts,users_exec uting	4	1
02ABABE0	begin dbms_output.disable; end;	0	0
02ABC1F8	alter session set nls_language= 'AMERICA N' nls_territory= 'AMERI	0	0
02ABC1F8	CA' nls_currency= '$' nls_iso_currency= 'AMERICA' nls_numeric_ch	0	0
02ABC1F8	aracters= '.,' nls_calendar= 'GREGORIAN' nls_date_format= 'DD-MO	0	0
02ABC1F8	N-YY' nls_date_language= 'AMERICAN' nls _sort= 'BINARY'	0	0

The output may not be pretty, but it works. Look at the statement with ADDRESS 0291E218 and how it is split between the "$" and the "S" that starts SQLAREA. Also, the word "order" is split between the "o" and the "r". When you sue this query, you will get used to this cryptic way of splitting the SQL text.

APPLICATION TUNING RULE #5
Become familiar with some form of shared pool SQL statement monitoring. Knowing what the code in the pool looks like will help you adopt coding conventions. By using conventions similar to statements already in the pool, you can reuse the statements already there.

Tuning the Shared Pool

The shared pool holds shared SQL and PL/SQL statements (referred to as the *library cache*), the data dictionary cache, and information on sessions against the database. The size of the shared pool is dictated by the value in SHARED_POOL_SIZE in the initialization parameter file. DBAs may need to visit the size of the shared pool if they receive ORA-4031 errors (unable to allocate *num* bytes of shared memory *num, num, num*) when Oracle tries to find more space in the shared pool. Statements are placed in the shared pool and flushed according to an LRU (least recently used) algorithm. Even though the parsed form of statements is aged out of the pool, the SQL text remains in dictionary tables in memory for longer time periods (space permitting).

NOTE
*The database must be shut down and restarted
to activate a resize of the shared pool.*

The most common way to monitor library cache activity is by querying
the V$LIBRARYCACHE data dictionary view with code similar to that
shown in the next listing.

```
SQL> select namespace, gets, gethits, gethitratio, pins,
  2         pinhits, pinhitratio
  3    from v$librarycache;
NAMESPACE          GETS   GETHITS GETHITRATIO      PINS   PINHITS PINHITRATIO
--------------- --------- --------- ----------- --------- --------- -----------
SQL AREA           125908    125755  .99878483    254244    253884  .99858404
TABLE/PROCEDURE     25439     25307  .99481112     25896     25648  .99042323
BODY                   11         9  .81818182        11         9  .81818182
TRIGGER                 0         0           1         0         0           1
INDEX                  28         0           0        28         0           0
CLUSTER               163       158  .96932515       228       223  .97807018
OBJECT                  0         0           1         0         0           1
PIPE                    0         0           1         0         0           1
8 rows selected.
SQL>
```

The same output can be obtained by selecting Display|Memory|Library
Cache Details from the Performance Manager main console. Figure 8-2
shows this chart in action.

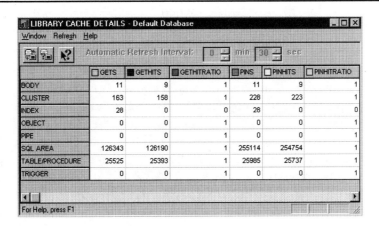

FIGURE 8-2.   *Library cache details chart*

A healthy library cache should report a hit ratio in the SQL_AREA of very close to 100 percent. DBAs find that sizing the shared pool is partially a game of hit and miss. The shared pool size is coded in the initialization parameter file under the SHARED_POOL_SIZE entry. The default is 3.5MB, and the value is in bytes. The library cache holds all shared SQL and PL/SQL statements. Rapid access to this cache is the biggest contributor to shared pool tuning. Statements are loaded and flushed from the pool using the familiar LRU (least recently used) algorithm. Often a summary figure is as informative as the more detailed query shown in the previous listing. This summary query is shown next.

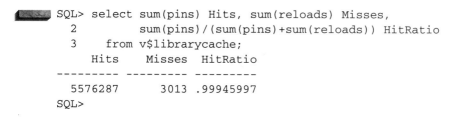

```
SQL> select sum(pins) Hits, sum(reloads) Misses,
  2             sum(pins)/(sum(pins)+sum(reloads)) HitRatio
  3     from v$librarycache;
     Hits    Misses  HitRatio
--------- --------- ---------
  5576287      3013 .99945997
SQL>
```

NOTE
To access the V$ views in the dictionary, user SYS must grant privileges to the database user wanting to use these views. As well, the user must be made a member of the SELECT_ CATALOG_ROLE. The views actually start with V_$, and this real view name rather than the public synonym must be used when the grant is done.

Oracle makes room in the shared pool for new statements when processing a statement that does not match one already there. The initialization parameter file entry CURSOR_SPACE_FOR_TIME affects when a statement in shared SQL can be deallocated from the pool. When set to FALSE (the default), Oracle deallocates space held by a statement in the shared pool even if application cursors using that statement are still open. If the amount of available memory is enough such that the shared pool can be sized to hold all application cursors, you may consider setting this parameter to TRUE. A small amount of time is saved during statement execution when the parameter is set to TRUE. Oracle does not have to search the pool to see if the statement is already there.

Manual Management of the Shared Pool

Objects can be manually pinned in the shared pool in cases where you know a piece of application code is being reused over and over. Oracle supplies the DBMS_SHARED_POOL package, the script to create which lies in RDBMS80\ADMIN. The package is set up in two parts—the first by dbmspool.sql, the second by prvtpool.sql. There are a number of procedures and functions in the package. Let's have a look at viewing the size of objects in the pool, then how to pin or release pieces of SQL code. The package contents are shown in the next listing.

```
SQL> desc dbms_shared_pool
PROCEDURE ABORTED_REQUEST_THRESHOLD
 Argument Name                  Type                    In/Out Default?
 ------------------------------ ----------------------- ------ --------
 THRESHOLD_SIZE                 NUMBER                  IN     DEFAULT
PROCEDURE KEEP
 Argument Name                  Type                    In/Out Default?
 ------------------------------ ----------------------- ------ --------
 NAME                           VARCHAR2                IN     DEFAULT
 FLAG                           CHAR                    IN     DEFAULT
PROCEDURE SIZES
 Argument Name                  Type                    In/Out Default?
 ------------------------------ ----------------------- ------ --------
 MINSIZE                        NUMBER                  IN     DEFAULT
PROCEDURE UNKEEP
 Argument Name                  Type                    In/Out Default?
 ------------------------------ ----------------------- ------ --------
 NAME                           VARCHAR2                IN     DEFAULT
 FLAG                           CHAR                    IN     DEFAULT
```

NOTE
You will probably have to run the code to create the DBMS_SHARED_POOL package, as it is not created during a vanilla install.

Size of Code Segments in the Pool

Before deciding what you may want to pin, run the SIZES procedure in
DBMS_SHARED_POOL to see what is there. The next listing shows output
from the execution of SIZES.

```
SQL> execute dbms_shared_pool.sizes (20)
SIZE(K)  KEPT    NAME
-------  ------  -------------------------------------------------------------
165              SYS.STANDARD                        (PACKAGE)
73               SELECT TO_CHAR(SHARABLE_MEM / 1000 ,'999999') SZ,DECODE(KEPT_VE
ERSIONS,0,'        ',RPAD('YES(' || TO_CHAR(KEPT_VERSIONS)  |
| ')' ,6)) KEEPED,RAWTOHEX(ADDRESS) || ',' || TO_CHAR(HASH
_VALUE)  NAME,SUBSTR(SQL_TEXT,1,354) EXTRA,1 ISCURSOR    FRO
M V$SQLAREA  WHERE SHARABLE_MEM > :b1 * 1000    UNION SELECT
TO_CHAR(SHARABLE_MEM / 1000 ,'999999') SZ,DECODE(KEPT,'
(02998050,473041910)      (CURSOR)
26               select i.obj#,i.ts#,i.file#,i.block#,i.intcols,i.type#,i.flags,
, i.property,i.pctfree$,i.initrans,i.maxtrans,i.blevel,i.le
afcnt,i.distkey, i.lblkkey,i.dblkkey,i.clufac,i.cols,i.anal
yzetime,i.samplesize,i.dataobj#, nvl(i.degree,1),nvl(i.inst
ances,1),i.rowcnt,i.pctthres$,i.indmethod#,i.trunccnt,nvl(c
.unicols,0),nvl(c.deferrable#+c.valid#,0) from ind$ i, (
(02B50F70,2577101735)      (CURSOR)
24               BEGIN sys.dbms_ijob.remove(:job); END;
(02B28704,88643110)        (CURSOR)
24               SYS.STANDARD                        (PACKAGE BODY)
20               SYS.V$SQLAREA                       (VIEW)
20               SYS.X$KGLOB                         (TABLE)
PL/SQL procedure successfully completed.
SQL>
```

The type of SQL is listed in parentheses at the end of the code belonging
to each piece.

NOTE
*To display results from this procedure, you
must issue the **set serveroutput on** command
to liven output to the screen.*

Pinning a Code Segment

The KEEP procedure takes two arguments—the object name and the object
type. Object types are listed in Table 8-5.

Object Type	Represented by
Procedure	P
Cursor	C
Trigger	R
Sequence	Q

TABLE 8-5. *Object Types Passed to the KEEP Procedure*

The next listing shows how the procedure is used. After completion, the KEPT column in the output from running the SIZES procedure will change from null to YES.

```
SQL> execute dbms_shared_pool.keep ('GEO_MAINT','P');
PL/SQL procedure successfully completed.
SQL> execute dbms_shared_pool.sizes (1600)
SIZE(K) KEPT    NAME
------- ------  ------------------------------------------------
1650    YES     GM.GEO_MAINT                    (PACKAGE)
SQL>
```

If the object to be pinned is a cursor, you enter the cursor address shown in the SIZES output, as shown next:

```
SQL> execute dbms_shared_pool.keep ('02998050,473041910','C')
PL/SQL procedure successfully completed.
SQL>
```

A common problem people have with KEEP is specifying the name of an object or a cursor address that does not exist at that time in the shared pool. Inspect the following output showing the error condition raised:

```
SQL> execute dbms_shared_pool.keep ('02998050,473041914','C')
begin dbms_shared_pool.keep ('02998050,473041914','C'); end;
*
ERROR at line 1:
ORA-06570: shared pool object does not exist, cannot be pinned
ORA-06512: at "SYS.DBMS_SHARED_POOL", line 23
ORA-06512: at "SYS.DBMS_SHARED_POOL", line 41
ORA-06512: at line 1
SQL>
```

Releasing a Code Segment

The opposite of KEEP is, surprise surprise, UNKEEP. It works the same way as KEEP, as shown in the next listing. The same type of error is encountered if you try to UNKEEP a piece of code that is not in the shared pool (i.e., the name of an object or a cursor address).

```
SQL>  execute dbms_shared_pool.unkeep ('02998050,473041910','C')
PL/SQL procedure successfully completed.
SQL>
```

NOTE
The cursor address will not stay the same each time a cursor is loaded into the shared pool. Unlike the name of a stored object, it is harder to pin cursors since the address must be obtained yet again to initiate a KEEP or UNKEEP activity.

SQL Statement Processing

The Structured Query Language (SQL) is the basis for all interaction with data in the Oracle database. Regardless of the tool used to communicate with Oracle (SQL*Plus, Developer/2000, Visual Basic, or others), SQL statements are passed to Oracle. After syntax checking, object resolution, and the selection of the most efficient access path, data is fetched and modified and/or displayed for the user.

The first step in processing an SQL statement is the creation of a cursor. Most programmatic interfaces do the creation manually. Subsequent processing of statements involves the following.

  1. During the parse phase, the syntax of the SQL statement is checked and object resolution is determined. Parse locks are obtained, where required, and object privileges are checked. Most, though not all, errors are encountered during this phase. Objects mentioned in a statement must exist in the user's schema or be accessible in a schema belonging to another user. As a last step, the shared pool is examined and, if necessary, the statement is loaded into the pool. Oracle determines the characteristics of the query

results and processes the information to decide on the datatype of the results and the length of column output to be displayed. Oracle looks at the possibility of parallelizing the statement during the determination of the execution plan.

2. During the execute phase, the necessary reads and writes are performed to support the statement being processed. For **select** statements, Oracle implements a *read consistency* approach that ensures data read for assembling of the query results represents the data values in place when the query was received for processing. To illustrate this point, suppose a query fetches rows from a table whose CLASSN column contains the text "IN" and, while the query is being processed, another user issues the statement **update pmast set classn = 'LO' where classn = 'IN' and pid between 100822 and 100900;**. The query reads the PMAST table as though the rows affected by the update still say "IN" for CLASSN. Locks are obtained for **update** and **delete** statements, ensuring data integrity of the information involved in the operation.

3. During the fetch phase, data (if any) that qualifies based on the SQL statement being processed is retrieved, assembled, sorted (if necessary), and displayed as statement output.

After the last row is fetched for the query results, the cursor acquired at the start of processing is closed. Parse is the most expensive (time-consuming and resource-intensive) of the three phases because the most effective execution plan for each SQL statement is constructed, and a search for an identical statement already in the shared pool is performed.

By avoiding the expensive parse phase, your application will run faster. This is why it is important to code SQL statements to take advantage of those already parsed and sitting in the shared pool. This is a large contributor when tuning applications written to interact with the Oracle8 database.

Using Generic Code

Generic code refers to SQL statements that are stored in the database. Every user who needs to process SQL statements while running an application uses a copy of this centralized code. When generic code is processed, it is first fetched from the database and passed to Oracle for processing.

Allowing Oracle to process matching SQL statements enhances performance. Oracle8 triggers and procedures are the most common implementation of central shared code. *Declarative integrity* (building predefined relationships into the dictionary at object creation time) is a form of shared generic code, because the routines initiated by Oracle are always the same. The nature and execution of declarative integrity routines at run time are determined by Oracle and are always identical each time they are invoked.

Declarative Integrity

With declarative integrity, you are encouraged to start using and experimenting with data dictionary-enforced constraints. Data integrity ensures that relationships between values in different database objects are enforced. You code rules for these relationships using SQL during object creation and modification. For example, a business rule may require that when entering a new plant definition into the PLANT_DETAIL table, the CITY_ID entered must already exist in the WORK_CITY table. Doing this programmatically is fine, but to use generic code you should use declarative integrity. Enforcement of declarative integrity is done by non-SQL internal Oracle code, not by SQL in the shared pool. Thus, in a way, it is a form of generic code.

TIP

When converting existing application objects to take advantage of declarative integrity, try disabling the constraints while doing the conversion. Sudden implementation at run time may cause applications to "stop working"! Applications not designed to work with database enforced integrity constraints need careful evaluation before turning this feature on.

With version 6 of Oracle, we sometimes coded declarative integrity when tables were created. With version 6, when applications ran against tables containing declarative integrity definitions, the constraints they defined were not enforced automatically as they ran. Enforcement of constraints was done by you when writing applications—they were implemented programmatically. When we speak of converting existing applications, we refer to an exercise you may go through to move the programmatic enforcement of constraints into Oracle's hands by using declarative integrity. To illustrate this point, consider the following table definition:

```
SQL> create table plant_detail  (
  2         plant_id      number(2),
  3         city_id       number(2) check (city_id < 90),
  4         location      varchar2(20));
Table created.
SQL>
```

Against a version 6 database, the syntax of the declarative integrity in this statement was checked when the table was created. However, as your application ran, it was your responsibility to ensure a CITY_ID of 95 was not saved in the database. With Oracle7, and continuing with Oracle8, a form of generic code is invoked that does the check for you. When you convert existing applications, you take the program segment that does the checking out of your applications and let Oracle do the enforcement.

Database Triggers

Database triggers are event-driven routines that run transparent to applications. They are stored in the data dictionary and are created using the SQL **create trigger** command. They cannot be invoked manually, unlike some other forms of triggers you may be familiar with in various Oracle tool products. Triggers are commonly used for auditing purposes. Some applications write a before-update image of a row when it is changed; prior to database triggers, this procedure had to be done manually. Some triggers are also used to do activity logging. For example, the update activity on a restricted screen can be logged using a database trigger. Using triggers contributes to efficient use of generic code.

NOTE
Developers and object owners need the system privilege CREATE TRIGGER to successfully write database triggers. To execute triggers, you need privileges on the objects to which the trigger belongs.

Procedures and Packages

Procedures accomplish specific tasks for you, and they are a group of SQL and/or PL/SQL statements; they must be invoked manually. *Packages* group related procedures and functions together and allow their storage as a single unit in the database; their SQL text and compiled code are stored in the data dictionary, and executable copies reside in the shared pool. It is possible that frequently used procedures may reside in the SGA forever (so to speak). A number of packages belong to the Oracle user SYS that are automatically loaded when the database is started. For example, the package STANDARD is referenced implicitly by Oracle during processing of most PL/SQL blocks and will always be in the shared pool. A frequently used application that contains many database procedures will more than likely find these procedures always in memory.

Schema of Execution

This is an issue related to procedures, packages, functions, and triggers that can prove a headache to the developer and DBA without mentioning a few issues. Most procedures, packages, functions, and triggers execute under the auspices of the schema that owns the object rather than the schema of the user executing the object. Picture a scenario where a schema named FINANCE has a trigger on a BUDGET table that writes audit rows to a BUDGET_A table when a row is updated. Suppose an application user wants to look at the contents of the BUDGET_A table. Let's log onto SQL*Plus and have some fun, as shown in the next listing.

```
SQL> conn mallia/shauna
Connected.
SQL> desc budget_a
ERROR:
ORA-04043: object budget_a does not exist
SQL> -- Obviously there is no public or private synonym on BUDGET_A, that's why
SQL> -- the error was raised. Let's try again with the account qualifier.
SQL> desc finance.budget_a
ERROR:
ORA-04043: object budget_a does not exist
SQL> -- So why does the following statement work, considering there is a
SQL> -- trigger that fires when the EXP_COMM column in the BUDGET table is
SQL> -- updated??
SQL> update budget
  2     set exp_comm = 1.5*exp_comm
```

```
   3      where line_id = 890
   4          and comp_ind is null;
11  rows  updated.
SQL> rollback;
Rollback complete.
SQL>
```

The **update** statement works, leading into the next application tuning rule:

APPLICATION TUNING RULE #6
*Stored PL/SQL objects execute using the
permissions of the owner of the objects, not
the executor of the object. Understanding this
will ensure your efforts can concentrate on
tuning rather than trying to figure out
explanations for the likes of what is illustrated
in the previous listing.*

The Cost-Based Optimizer (CBO)

An *optimization approach* is an internal mechanism used by Oracle to
figure out the most efficient access path to the data required to satisfy an
SQL statement. The *cost-based optimizer* chooses an execution plan based
on the access path that would produce the best throughput. The execution
plan can be made up of several access paths. When using CBO, you must
gather statistics on your objects to be fed to the optimizer. Let's have a look
at gathering these statistics with the SQL command **analyze**.

APPLICATION TUNING RULE #7
*Do not gather statistics on the SYS schema.
We cannot stress this enough, and we have
seen a number of situations where analyzing
SYS caused performance problems.*

Gathering Statistics

The general format for the **analyze** command is shown in the next listing:

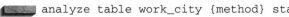
```
analyze table work_city {method} statistics {size of sample}
```

There are two methods through which analysis can be performed—
compute and estimate. When computing statistics, you simply code the
object name followed by the keywords **compute statistics**, as in this listing:

```
SQL> analyze index work_city_1 compute statistics;
Index analyzed.
SQL> analyze table work_city compute statistics;
Table analyzed.
SQL>
```

When estimating statistics, refer to Table 8-6 for details on specifying
the size of the sample to be fed to the collection process.

APPLICATION TUNING RULE #8
When estimating statistics, use the **sample 20
percent** *option. We believe this to be a
significant size that will be truly representative
of the rows in the object.*

APPLICATION TUNING RULE #9
*Estimate statistics with the 20 percent
sample for tables, and compute statistics
for your indexes.*

Statistics can be collected from SQL*Plus using the **analyze** command
or from two PL/SQL procedures owned by SYS. Let's discuss the SQL*Plus
approach first.

Sample Specification	Meaning
none specified	Oracle uses a random sample of 1,064 rows from the table and, if that sample represents 50 percent or more of the rows in the table, statistics are computed rather than estimated.
sample *n* rows	Oracle uses a sample whose size is determined by the value of *n*.
sample *n* percent	Oracle uses a percentage of rows for the sample based on the value specified for *n*.

TABLE 8-6. *Specifying Sample Size When Estimating Statistics*

Scripting the Statistic Collection Process

The following listing shows two SQL statements that can be used to collect statistics for all objects in the database except those belonging to SYS and SYSTEM.

```
/* ------------------------------------------------------------ */
/*  statgath.sql                                                */
/*  Analyze all tables and indexes in the database             */
/* ------------------------------------------------------------ */
set pagesize 0 feedback off trimspool on linesize 999 echo off
spool ana_db.sql
prompt
prompt spool ana_db
prompt
prompt set echo on feedback on
select 'analyze index '||owner||'.'||index_name||
       ' compute statistics;'
  from sys.dba_indexes
 where owner not in ('SYS','SYSTEM');
select 'analyze table '||owner||'.'||table_name||
       ' estimate statistics sample 20 percent;'
  from sys.dba_tables
 where owner not in ('SYS','SYSTEM');
prompt
prompt spool off
spool off
```

APPLICATION TUNING RULE #10

*Create a central account to perform all gathering of statistics. That user does not need the DBA role but should be granted the **analyze any** system privilege to enable the account to analyze objects in any schema.*

Gathering Statistics Using PL/SQL Procedures

DBMS_DDL and DBMS_UTILITY package components can be used in PL/SQL to collect statistics. They belong to SYS and most of the procedures they contain, unlike most other stored objects that execute under the schema of the owner, execute under the schema of the user running the procedure. DBMS_DDL contains a handful of procedures that perform many tasks. Have a look around the RDBMS80\ADMIN directory at the programs that start with the text "dbms". The ANALYZE_OBJECT procedure description is shown next, picked out of the **descr dbms_ddl** command:

```
PROCEDURE ANALYZE_OBJECT
Argument Name                   Type                      In/Out Default?
------------------------------- ------------------------- ------ --------
TYPE                            VARCHAR2                  IN     DEFAULT
SCHEMA                          VARCHAR2                  IN     DEFAULT
NAME                            VARCHAR2                  IN     DEFAULT
METHOD                          VARCHAR2                  IN     DEFAULT
ESTIMATE_ROWS                   NUMBER                    IN     DEFAULT
ESTIMATE_PERCENT                NUMBER                    IN     DEFAULT
METHOD_OPT                      VARCHAR2                  IN     DEFAULT
```

Table 8-7 discusses the arguments passed to this procedure.

The ANALYZE_SCHEMA procedure, part of DBMS_UTILITY, is shown in the next listing. The description of its arguments matches those displayed in Table 8-7.

```
PROCEDURE ANALYZE_SCHEMA
Argument Name                   Type                      In/Out Default?
------------------------------- ------------------------- ------ --------
SCHEMA                          VARCHAR2                  IN/OUT DEFAULT
METHOD                          VARCHAR2                  IN/OUT DEFAULT
ESTIMATE_ROWS                   NUMBER                    IN/OUT DEFAULT
ESTIMATE_PERCENT                NUMBER                    IN/OUT DEFAULT
METHOD_OPT                      VARCHAR2                  IN/OUT DEFAULT
```

Argument	Meaning
type	One of TABLE, CLUSTER, or INDEX
schema	The name of the schema owning the objects being analyzed. If NULL, defaults to the current schema
name	Name of object to analyze
method	Value must be null or ESTIMATE. If the latter, one of the following two arguments should be nonzero
estimate_rows	The row size of the sample
estimate_percent	The percentage of object rows to be used for the collection
method_opt	For building of histograms, the scope of the analysis

TABLE 8-7. *Arguments Passed to ANALYZE_OBJECTS*

Before moving on, let's show a few examples of using these two procedures to collect statistics on objects:

```
SQL> -- Sample 20 percent for table in current schema
SQL> execute dbms_ddl.analyze_object ('TABLE',null,'PHONE','ESTIMATE',
                                null,20);
PL/SQL procedure successfully completed.
SQL> -- Compute for index in current schema
SQL> execute dbms_ddl.analyze_object ('INDEX',null,'PHONE_1','COMPUTE');
PL/SQL procedure successfully completed.
SQL> -- Compute for index belonging to MASON
SQL> execute dbms_ddl.analyze_object ('INDEX','MASON','PHONE_1',
                                'COMPUTE');
PL/SQL procedure successfully completed.
SQL> -- Compute for all objects in current schema - note the word USER, a
SQL> -- system variable containing the username of the session.
SQL> execute dbms_utility.analyze_schema (user,'COMPUTE');
PL/SQL procedure successfully completed.
SQL> -- Estimate sampling 20 percent for schema MORDECAI.
SQL> execute dbms_utility.analyze_schema ('MORDECAI','ESTIMATE',null,20);
PL/SQL procedure successfully completed.
SQL>
```

Developing a Statistic Collection Plan

In the realm of collecting statistics on Oracle8 objects, there are a few questions that arise when you are figuring out a plan of attack for analysis. You need to answer these questions and decide for yourself, or take the recommendations we make in the following few sections.

Objects Needing Analysis

There are essentially two ways to look at what needs to be analyzed—size of tables and nature of application. When we speak of *nature of application*, we mean whether the system is online transaction processing (*OLTP*) or decision support (*DSS*). The two types can differ dramatically based on the static or dynamic nature of the data coupled with the volume of the data. There are essentially three types of tables in OLTP systems; let's look at each type and recommend an approach to analysis:

1. Code tables—contain primarily static data of low volume. These tables, due to their size, should be analyzed often since the small size overrides the static nature of the information.

2. Historical tables—contain static data, with extra information deposited from online transaction tables periodically (e.g., ten months after the close of a fiscal year business). These tables should be analyzed immediately after new data has been added; there is no need to analyze weekly.

3. Transaction tables—contain relatively dynamic data. These tables should be analyzed often as well.

In the DSS environment, there are some history-type tables, no transaction tables, and some code tables. One of many things that separates DSS repositories from OLTP is the static nature of the data. We are not suggesting that data in the data warehouse never changes—portions gets continually refreshed, while some others are loaded and stay that way forever. In a DSS system, all objects require analysis.

Translating "Often"

In most cases, the word "often" is too subjective to provide any value to recommendations. There are two schools of thought when deciding the frequency of analysis.

■ Methodically collect statistics on access patterns and row counts of tables and build a frequency grid indicating a measurement of dynamics of all objects' data. Choose a frequency based on the measurement so that totally dynamic objects are analyzed twice a week, partially dynamic are analyzed once a week, and the rest are analyzed monthly.

■ Pick a time frame based on your intuition, and analyze all objects based on that frequency.

We attend the second school, and have ever since we started working with CBO. This leads us to our last rule on gathering statistics, then we will move on to discussing hints.

APPLICATION TUNING RULE #11
Analyze tables and indexes once a week. We prefer doing it on Friday since it can be the lowest activity business day.

Where Statistics Are Stored

Table and index statistics can be seen in the DBA_TABLES and
DBA_INDEXES views, shown in the next listing. There are partition specific
views for each of these DBA_ objects called DBA_TAB_PARTITIONS and
DBA_IND_PARTITIONS. Column statistics for tables and partitions are
available in DBA_TAB_COL_STATISTICS and DBA_PART_COL_
STATISTICS shown as well in the following listing. Columns of specific
interest in each view description are bolded.

NOTE
*Some of you may be used to looking in
USER_TAB_COLUMNS for statistics. The
information in USER_TAB_COL_STATISTICS is
the same but more concise.*

```
SQL> desc dba_tables
 Name                                  Null?    Type
 ------------------------------------- -------- ----
 OWNER                                 NOT NULL VARCHAR2(30)
 TABLE_NAME                            NOT NULL VARCHAR2(30)
 TABLESPACE_NAME                                VARCHAR2(30)
 CLUSTER_NAME                                   VARCHAR2(30)
 IOT_NAME                                       VARCHAR2(30)
 PCT_FREE                                       NUMBER
 PCT_USED                                       NUMBER
 INI_TRANS                                      NUMBER
 MAX_TRANS                                      NUMBER
 INITIAL_EXTENT                                 NUMBER
 NEXT_EXTENT                                    NUMBER
 MIN_EXTENTS                                    NUMBER
 MAX_EXTENTS                                    NUMBER
 PCT_INCREASE                                   NUMBER
 FREELISTS                                      NUMBER
 FREELIST_GROUPS                                NUMBER
 LOGGING                                        VARCHAR2(3)
 BACKED_UP                                      VARCHAR2(1)
 NUM_ROWS                                       NUMBER
 BLOCKS                                         NUMBER
 EMPTY_BLOCKS                                   NUMBER
 AVG_SPACE                                      NUMBER
 CHAIN_CNT                                      NUMBER
 AVG_ROW_LEN                                    NUMBER
```

```
AVG_SPACE_FREELIST_BLOCKS             NUMBER
NUM_FREELIST_BLOCKS                   NUMBER
DEGREE                                VARCHAR2(10)
INSTANCES                             VARCHAR2(10)
CACHE                                 VARCHAR2(5)
TABLE_LOCK                            VARCHAR2(8)
SAMPLE_SIZE                           NUMBER
LAST_ANALYZED                         DATE
PARTITIONED                           VARCHAR2(3)
IOT_TYPE                              VARCHAR2(12)
TEMPORARY                             VARCHAR2(1)
NESTED                                VARCHAR2(3)
BUFFER_POOL                           VARCHAR2(7)

SQL> desc sys.dba_indexes
 Name                         Null?     Type
 ---------------------------- --------  ----
 OWNER                        NOT NULL VARCHAR2(30)
 INDEX_NAME                   NOT NULL VARCHAR2(30)
 INDEX_TYPE                            VARCHAR2(12)
 TABLE_OWNER                  NOT NULL VARCHAR2(30)
 TABLE_NAME                   NOT NULL VARCHAR2(30)
 TABLE_TYPE                            VARCHAR2(11)
 UNIQUENESS                            VARCHAR2(9)
 TABLESPACE_NAME                       VARCHAR2(30)
 INI_TRANS                             NUMBER
 MAX_TRANS                             NUMBER
 INITIAL_EXTENT                        NUMBER
 NEXT_EXTENT                           NUMBER
 MIN_EXTENTS                           NUMBER
 MAX_EXTENTS                           NUMBER
 PCT_INCREASE                          NUMBER
 PCT_THRESHOLD                         NUMBER
 INCLUDE_COLUMN                        NUMBER
 FREELISTS                             NUMBER
 FREELIST_GROUPS                       NUMBER
 PCT_FREE                              NUMBER
 LOGGING                               VARCHAR2(3)
 BLEVEL                                NUMBER
 LEAF_BLOCKS                           NUMBER
 DISTINCT_KEYS                         NUMBER
 AVG_LEAF_BLOCKS_PER_KEY               NUMBER
 AVG_DATA_BLOCKS_PER_KEY               NUMBER
 CLUSTERING_FACTOR                     NUMBER
 STATUS                                VARCHAR2(8)
```

```
SQL> desc dba_part_col_statistics
 Name                                Null?     Type
 ----------------------------------- --------  ----
 OWNER                               NOT NULL  VARCHAR2(30)
 TABLE_NAME                          NOT NULL  VARCHAR2(30)
 PARTITION_NAME                                VARCHAR2(30)
 COLUMN_NAME                                   VARCHAR2(30)
 NUM_DISTINCT                                  NUMBER
 LOW_VALUE                                     RAW(32)
 HIGH_VALUE                                    RAW(32)
 DENSITY                                       NUMBER
 NUM_NULLS                                     NUMBER
 NUM_BUCKETS                                   NUMBER
 SAMPLE_SIZE                                   NUMBER
 LAST_ANALYZED                                 DATE

SQL> desc dba_tab_col_statistics
 Name                                Null?     Type
 ----------------------------------- --------  ----
 TABLE_NAME                          NOT NULL  VARCHAR2(30)
 COLUMN_NAME                         NOT NULL  VARCHAR2(30)
 NUM_DISTINCT                                  NUMBER
 LOW_VALUE                                     RAW(32)
 HIGH_VALUE                                    RAW(32)
 DENSITY                                       NUMBER
 NUM_NULLS                                     NUMBER
 NUM_BUCKETS                                   NUMBER
 LAST_ANALYZED                                 DATE
 SAMPLE_SIZE                                   NUMBER
SQL>
```

Table 8-8 highlights a few of these columns with some important points related to each that will help you use this information for what it is intended for—to make you more aware of your data.

Using Hints

Hints, the comment text placed immediately after **select**, **update**, or **delete** keywords, can be useful when deciding how to instruct cost-based optimization. SQL statements that contain hints will be treated according to the hint text. You can use either form of SQL comment conventions: the

View Name	Column Name	Notes
dba_tables	empty_blocks	The count here is the number of blocks allocated to a table that have never contained data. If a block contained date in the past but no longer holds any rows, it will not be counted in this value
	avg_row_len	We use this figure multiplied by num_rows to give a very good estimate of the actual space occupied at any point in time.
	sample_size	If table statistics are computed, this column value is 0. If estimated with no sample, this column value is 1064.
user_tab_col_statistics	num_nulls	If there are any null values in a column, this will contain a value. Oracle8 (as did Oracle 7.3) maintains statistics on nulls.
	num_buckets	This column contains a not null value when histograms have been created after using the **analyze** command with the **for all indexed columns** or some similar construct.

TABLE 8-8. *Notes on Views Containing Statistics*

text bounded on either end by the /* and */ characters or preceded by a double dash (--). For example, the comment

```
/*+ first_rows */
```

is the same as

```
--+ first_rows
```

Table 8-9 lists the five most commonly used hints we have run across. In this table, throughput means optimizing to retrieve *all rows* that satisfy the query as quickly as possible. When we speak of the best response time,

Type	Hint(s)	Meaning/Caveats
Goal	all_rows	Optimizes for the best throughput
	first_rows	Optimizes for the best response time; ignores in **delete** and **update** statements (they return no rows) and **select** statements that require assembly of all rows before returning the first
	rule	Uses the rule-based approach; ignores any other hints
Join order	ordered	Joins tables in order they appear in FROM rather than allowing optimizer to choose
Access	index_desc (table index_name)	Index scans in descending order (opposite of the default ascending scan)

TABLE 8-9. *The Five Most Commonly Used Hints*

we mean optimizing to present the *first row* that qualifies for the query as quickly as possible. A query against a view rather than a table is an example of a statement that may assemble all rows before returning the first.

Table 8-10 shows a handful of additional hints used with CBO against the Oracle8 Server that, when used properly, we have found to be the most effective on performance of SQL statements with the cost-based optimizer.

 APPLICATION TUNING RULE #12
*When using object names in hints, the alias rather than the object name must be used if an object alias is used in the **from** clause.*

For example, if the PLANT_DETAIL table is aliased to PD in a query, your hint will have to use the alias PD rather than the actual table name or the hint will be ignored. Since the hint is a special form of a comment, if

Hint	Meaning	Example
full	Tells CBO to do a full table on the table name enclosed in parentheses.	--+ full (city)
rowid	Tells CBO to do a table access by rowid for the table name enclosed in parentheses.	/*+ rowid (location) */
star	Forces a star query plan to be used if possible. A star plan has the largest table in the query last in the join order. The hint applies when there are at least three tables, the large table's concatenated index having at least three columns.	/*+ star */
driving site	Instructs Oracle to use the location of the table mentioned in the hint as the execution site for a distributed query.	/*+ driving_site (city) */
parallel	Tells Oracle to process the query using the number of parallel query server processes on the table specified with the hint.	--+ parallel (city, 4)
noparallel	Tells Oracle to override a parallel specification on the table mentioned in the hint.	/*+ noparallel (city) */

TABLE 8-10.   *Popular Hints and Their Meanings*

syntax is not followed in the hint text, the hint is treated as a comment. Inspect the following listing for situations we have seen:

```
select /*  full (plant_detail) */  -- hint ignored (missing + sign)
...
select --+ parallel (plant_detail, 4)
   from plant_detail pd            -- hint ignored since it does not use alias
...
select /*+ parallel (city, YES) */ -- hint ignored since YES is in a number's
place
```

Programs may contain many SQL statements that use different approaches. Your SQL may end up looking like any of the following:

```
select  /*+ RULE  */ ...
select  /* there is no hint in this statement */ ...
select  /*+ ALL_ROWS  */ ...
```

The first statement forces use of the rule-based optimizer. The second uses the optimizer mode as defined in the initialization parameter file. The third statement uses the cost-based optimizer and chooses the most efficient access path for retrieval of all rows that satisfy the selection criteria.

Optimizer Mode by Session

The OPTIMIZER_MODE entry in the initialization parameter file decides the instance-wide default mode for query optimization. To override this default for a complete session in SQL*Plus, at the top of your program code put the statement

```
alter session set optimizer_goal= {mode_of_desire};
```

This statement remains in effect until the termination of that session or you issue a similar statement that resets to another value. The {mode_of_desire} can be any of the modes listed in Table 8-11.

You can use a combination of session statements and hints in your SQL programs. Your code may look like the following:

```
alter session set optimizer_goal = ALL_ROWS;
select /*+ RULE  : uses rule-based approach */ ...
select /* there is no hint in this statement */ ...
select /*+ FIRST_ROWS */ ...
alter session set optimizer_goal = RULE;
select /* uses rule-based approach for remainder of statements
           without hints */ ...
```

Optimizer Mode	Meaning
RULE	Use the rule-based optimizer
ALL_ROWS	Use the cost-based optimizer approach with the goal of best throughput for all rows that satisfy selection criteria
FIRST_ROWS	Use the cost-based optimizer approach with the goal of best response time for the first row that will be retrieved
CHOOSE	Use the cost-based optimizer approach with the goal choice decided by the optimizer at execution time

TABLE 8-11.   *Goals for Alter Session Command*

explain plan

The **explain plan** tool can prove useful when determining access paths to your data. Using the SQL*Plus command

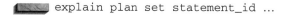
```
explain plan set statement_id ...
```

you insert rows into an object called the PLAN_TABLE. When running this command, you specify an identifier in single quotes to store the explained statement in this table. To accomplish this, perform the following steps:

1. Load the statement. If the statement contains any substitution variables, you will be prompted for them when the statement is run. The word "Explained" appears to indicate successful completion.

2. Run a script to report on the execution plan.

3. Assess the execution plan.

These three steps should be repeated until you are happy with the access path. In the following code, notice the **delete** statement at the top of the script. This ensures that any other statements that may have been loaded into the PLAN_TABLE are not left lying around when you report on the statement you have just loaded. The FLEX_VALUE and FLEX_VALUE_SET_ID columns in the FND_FLEX_VALUES table are indexed. The FLEX_VALUE_SET_NAME and FLEX_VALUE_SET_ID columns from the FND_FLEX_VALUE_SETS table are indexed. The **select** statement takes part of the FLEX_VALUE column value from FND_FLEX_VALUES, along with the English and French description fields.

```
delete plan_table where statement_id = 'ZZ';
explain plan set statement_id = 'ZZ' for
select substr(a.flex_value,1,4) responsibility,
       a.description             edesc,
       c.description             fdesc
  from fnd_flex_values a,
       fnd_flex_value_sets b,
       fnd_flex_values c
 where b.flex_value_set_name = 'RESP'
   and a.flex_value_set_id = b.flex_value_set_id
   and c.flex_value_set_id = b.flex_value_set_id
   and a.flex_value = c.flex_value;
```

The statement now resides in the PLAN_TABLE and can be extracted using the following code:

```
set echo off term off feed off ver off
spool xpl
select decode(id,0,'',
        lpad(' ',2*(level-1))||level||'.'||position)||' '||
        operation||' '||options||' '||object_name||' '||
        object_type||' '||
        decode(id,0,'Cost = '||position) Query_plan
   from plan_table
connect by prior id = parent_id
   and statement_id = upper('&1')
 start with id = 0 and statement_id = upper('&1');
spool off
set term on
prompt
prompt Output from EXPLAIN PLAN is in file called "xpl.lst" . . .
prompt
```

The resulting output from running this code is as follows:

```
QUERY_PLAN
-----------------------------------------------------------------
 SELECT STATEMENT     Cost = 1416
  2.1 NESTED LOOPS
    3.1 NESTED LOOPS
      4.1 TABLE ACCESS BY INDEX ROWID FND_FLEX_VALUE_SETS
        5.1 INDEX RANGE SCAN FND_FLEX_VALUES_SETS_1 NON-UNIQUE
      4.2 TABLE ACCESS BY INDEX ROWID FND_FLEX_VALUES
        5.1 INDEX RANGE SCAN FND_FLEX_VALUES_2 NON-UNIQUE
    3.2 TABLE ACCESS BY INDEX ROWID FND_FLEX_VALUES
      4.1 INDEX RANGE SCAN FND_FLEX_VALUES_1 NON-UNIQUE
```

This output seems cryptic on first examination. Most of this output can be explained by the names of the operations, which are listed in Table 8-12.

Keep in mind that EXPLAIN PLAN is a valuable off-the-shelf tuning aid provided by Oracle. It is useful throughout the development cycle. Programs that have bottlenecks at certain spots can be tuned using this facility. You must own a PLAN_TABLE or have access to one in someone else's schema. When figuring out what indexes to set up based on the requirements of an application, you can see if indexes are actually getting used and check the efficiency of the access path Oracle chooses based on

Line	Operation	Meaning
2.1	NESTED LOOPS	An operation that accepts two sets of rows, an outer set and an inner set. Oracle compares each row of the outer set with each row of the inner set and returns those rows that satisfy a condition
3.1	See 2.1	
3.2	TABLE ACCESS BY INDEX ROWID	A retrieval of a row from a table based on its ROWID
4.1	See 3.2	
5.1	INDEX RANGE SCAN	A retrieval of one or more ROWIDs from an index. Indexes values are scanned in ascending order
4.2	See 4.1	

TABLE 8-12. *Operations and Explanations*

the indexes in place. The first row returned from an ordered query on an execution plan (if explained using a cost-based approach) is the *cost* estimated by Oracle to execute according to those existing indexes. Comparing that cost relative to those with a different set of indexes helps you make tough indexing decisions. The following difficult decisions about indexing can become readily clear after such an exercise.

- Are the existing indexes being used?

- What columns should be put together in composite (concatenated) indexes?

- Would it be more efficient to break up a composite index into multiple single-column indexes?

NOTE
A script called utlxplan.sql creates the PLAN_TABLE table. Its location is usually rdbms80\admin, but it can differ on different machines.

Using set autotrace

Introduced in Oracle release 7.3, this environment command allows you to trace SQL statements on the fly as they are executed. The format of the command is the same as other **set** commands issued in SQL*Plus. Look at the following listing to see a series of these commands passed to Oracle at once.

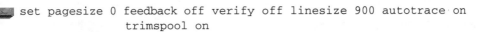

```
set pagesize 0 feedback off verify off linesize 900 autotrace on
                trimspool on
```

NOTE
A user must have access to or own a PLAN_TABLE and be a member of the PLUSTRACE role as discussed in the next section, or the **set autotrace** *will return an Oracle error.*

Inspect the following listing to see what can go wrong as the note suggests:

```
SQL*Plus: Release 8.0.3.0.0 - Production on Wed Sep 3 18:28:44 1999
(c) Copyright 1997 Oracle Corporation.  All rights reserved.
Connected to:
Oracle8 Enterprise Edition Release 8.0.3.0.0 - Production
With the Partitioning and Objects options
PL/SQL Release 8.0.3.0.0 - Production
SQL> set autotrace on
Unable to verify PLAN_TABLE format or existence
Error enabling EXPLAIN report
Cannot find the Session Identifier.  Check PLUSTRACE role is enabled
Error enabling STATISTICS report
SQL>
```

After access to a PLAN_TABLE has been established, there will be no feedback whatsoever from the **set autotrace** command. The command can be shortened to **set autot on**, if you prefer.

BEWARE
You cannot shorten this command to set auto on because that is the abbreviation for the command **set autocommit on.**

Enabling Users to Use Autotrace

Some administration is required with Oracle8 before users can use
autotrace successfully. The SQL statements shown in the next listing are in
the PLUS80\PLUSTRCE.SQL file underneath the Oracle home directory on
a Windows NT Server. Note the ORA-01919 error after the first command;
this is because the role did not exist when the **drop role** was issued.

```
SQL> drop role plustrace;
drop role plustrace
              *
ERROR at line 1:
ORA-01919: role 'PLUSTRACE' does not exist
SQL> create role plustrace;
Role created.
SQL> grant select on v_$sesstat to plustrace;
Grant succeeded.
SQL> grant select on v_$statname to plustrace;
Grant succeeded.
SQL> grant select on v_$session to plustrace;
Grant succeeded.
SQL> grant plustrace to dba with admin option;
Grant succeeded.
SQL>
```

The last statement in the previous listing empowers any user with the DBA
role to grant membership in the PLUSTRACE role to other users. Once the
PLUSTRACE role has been created, give it out to individual users, roles, or
everyone who can connect to the database, as shown in the following listing.

```
SQL> grant plustrace to public;
Grant succeeded.
SQL>
```

Autotrace Modes

By default, **autotrace** displays the query result set, reports statistics, and
shows a query execution plan for all successful **select**, **insert**, **update**, and
delete SQL statements. The help for the command in the documentation is
shown in the next listing (used with permission of Oracle Corporation).

```
AUTOT[RACE] {OFF|ON|TRACE[ONLY]} [EXP[LAIN]] [STAT[ISTICS]]
```

Command	Explain Output	Statistics	Query Results
autot on	X	X	X
autot trace	X	X	
autot on exp	X		X
autot trace exp	X		
autot on stat		X	X
autot off			

TABLE 8-13. *Options with set autotrace and Output Results*

Table 8-13 shows the commands to call for **autotrace** and the output that will be produced.

APPLICATION TUNING RULE #13

Use the **set autot trace** *command. It suppresses the display of the result set to the query and provides for the fastest way to tune your SQL since no data is returned.*

Following Rule #13 requires that a very large query complete before the report(s) is generated by autotrace, but, since no data is displayed, it will finish much sooner than it would if the result set was displayed. Sample output from the command **set autot trace** is shown in the next listing. Notice the numbers beside the steps in the Execution Plan shown in bold; they represent the parent of each step in the plan, and they match what you would expect based on the indentation convention shown.

```
SQL> select perno, name, status_desc
  2    from person, status_codes
  3    where person.status_cd = status_codes.status_cd;
14 rows selected.
Execution Plan
----------------------------------------------------------
    0       SELECT STATEMENT Optimizer=CHOOSE
    1    0   NESTED LOOPS
    2    1     TABLE ACCESS (FULL) OF 'PERSON'
    3    1     TABLE ACCESS (BY INDEX ROWID) OF 'STATUS_CODES'
```

```
   4    3         INDEX (UNIQUE SCAN) OF 'PK_SC' (UNIQUE)
Statistics
----------------------------------------------------------------
        34  recursive calls
         3  db block gets
        24  consistent gets
         2  physical reads
         0  redo size
      1121  bytes sent via SQL*Net to client
       695  bytes received via SQL*Net from client
         4  SQL*Net roundtrips to/from client
         1  sorts (memory)
         0  sorts (disk)
        14  rows processed
SQL>
```

The Hints and EXPLAIN PLAN Toolbox

While investigating the use of the cost-based optimizer, most installations will find the DBA wants to leave the initialization parameter file entry OPTIMIZER_MODE set to RULE. Hints are the way to go while tuning SQL statements for the cost-based optimizer. To do this, load a SQL statement into the PLAN_TABLE with hints in place. Run the script and inspect the output. This is an iterative process until the **cost =** value is a minimum. The following two listings gives the explain plan results using two different hints. The hints used in these examples are explained in Table 8-8.

```
QUERY_PLAN using the hint /*+ ORDERED */
----------------------------------------------------------------
  SELECT STATEMENT     Cost = 4679
    2.1 NESTED LOOPS
      3.1 MERGE JOIN
        4.1 SORT JOIN
          5.1 TABLE ACCESS FULL FND_FLEX_VALUES
        4.2 SORT JOIN
          5.1 TABLE ACCESS BY INDEX ROWID FND_FLEX_VALUE_SETS
            6.1 INDEX RANGE SCAN FND_FLEX_VALUES_SETS_1 NON-UNIQUE
      3.2 TABLE ACCESS BY INDEX ROWID FND_FLEX_VALUES
        4.1 INDEX RANGE SCAN FND_FLEX_VALUES_1 NON-UNIQUE
```

```
QUERY_PLAN using the hint /*+ FIRST_ROWS */
-----------------------------------------------------------------
 SELECT STATEMENT      Cost = 1416
  2.1 NESTED LOOPS
    3.1 NESTED LOOPS
      4.1 TABLE ACCESS BY INDEX ROWID FND_FLEX_VALUE_SETS
        5.1 INDEX RANGE SCAN FND_FLEX_VALUES_SETS_1 NON-UNIQUE
      4.2 TABLE ACCESS BY INDEX ROWID FND_FLEX_VALUES
        5.1 INDEX RANGE SCAN FND_FLEX_VALUES_2 NON-UNIQUE
    3.2 TABLE ACCESS BY INDEX ROWID FND_FLEX_VALUES
      4.1 INDEX RANGE SCAN FND_FLEX_VALUES_1 NON-UNIQUE
```

The cost figures (4679 versus 1416) are significant. They are the results from using different hints with the same SQL statement. This means that the FIRST_ROWS hint execution plan bore less than 30 percent of the cost of the plan used to execute the query using the ORDERED hint alone. Notice the drastic difference in the **cost =** value between these two examples. These amounts must be interpreted relative to one another on the same statement; they cannot be compared across statements. Note as well that step 2.1 is the same in both listings, whereas 3.1 is MERGE_JOIN in the first listing and NESTED_LOOPS in the second. There are also ten lines in the first and nine lines in the second explain plan output.

tkprof and SQL Trace

Closely related to EXPLAIN PLAN is the tkprof facility. With tkprof you can produce output that shows the three phases of SQL statement processing in hundredths of a second. To use tkprof, you (on a per-session basis) or the DBA (on an instance-wide basis) must enable tracing. To enable SQL trace by session, issue the following SQL statement:

```
alter session set sql_trace = true;
```

To disable SQL trace by session, issue the following SQL statement:

```
alter session set sql_trace = false;
```

Regardless of session or instance tracing, the entry

```
timed_statistics = true
```

must be set in the initialization parameter file. This permits the collection of statistics on the CPU and elapsed time. Instance enabling is set in the initialization parameter file with the parameter

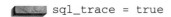 `sql_trace = true`

NOTE
Setting sql_trace=true in the initialization parameter file causes every session to produce a trace file. This can amount to a 1 percent to 5 percent performance decrease on most systems.

The trace files accumulate in the USER_DUMP_DEST directory (specified in the initialization parameter file with different default locations based on the operating system). They usually have the prefix ora_ and the extension .trc. The following listing shows part of the output from tkprof. Notice how the column headings above the parse, execute, and fetch statistics are defined at the top of the output. In addition, when tkprof is called with the EXPLAIN option, the EXPLAIN PLAN for the statement comes after the statistics for the statement.

NOTE
We call this analysis facility "tkprof" even though the executable called from the NT DOS command line is "tkprof80".

```
TKPROF: Release 8.0.3.0.0 - Production on Tue Sep 42 19:35:58 1999
(c) Copyright 1997 Oracle Corporation.  All rights reserved.
Trace file: ora00204.trc
Sort options: default
********************************************************************
count    = number of times OCI procedure was executed
cpu      = cpu time in seconds executing
elapsed  = elapsed time in seconds executing
disk     = number of physical reads of buffers from disk
query    = number of buffers gotten for consistent read
current  = number of buffers gotten in current mode (usually for update)
rows     = number of rows processed by the fetch or execute call
********************************************************************
select /*+ choose */
      substr(a.flex_value,1,4) responsibility,
      a.description            edesc,
```

```
       c.description            fdesc
  from fnd_flex_values a,
       fnd_flex_value_sets b,
       fnd_flex_values c
 where b.flex_value_set_name = 'RESP'
   and a.flex_value_set_id = b.flex_value_set_id
   and c.flex_value_set_id = b.flex_value_set_id
   and a.flex_value = c.flex_value
```

call	count	cpu	elapsed	disk	query	current	rows
Parse	1	0.00	0.00	0	0	0	0
Execute	1	0.00	0.00	0	0	0	0
Fetch	69	0.00	0.00	208	7307	0	1012
total	71	0.00	0.00	208	7307	0	1012

```
Misses in library cache during parse: 0
Optimizer goal: CHOOSE
Parsing user id: 29   (FND)
Rows    Execution Plan
-------  -------------------------------------------------------
      0  SELECT STATEMENT   GOAL: HINT: CHOOSE
      0   NESTED LOOPS
      0    NESTED LOOPS
      0     TABLE ACCESS   GOAL: ANALYZED (BY INDEX ROWID) OF
                 'FND_FLEX_VALUE_SETS'
      0      INDEX   GOAL: ANALYZED (RANGE SCAN) OF
                  'FND_FLEX_VALUES_SETS_1' (NON-UNIQUE)
      0     TABLE ACCESS   GOAL: ANALYZED (BY INDEX ROWID) OF
                 'FND_FLEX_VALUES'
      0      INDEX   GOAL: ANALYZED (RANGE SCAN) OF 'FND_FLEX_VALUES_2'
                 (NON-UNIQUE)
      0    TABLE ACCESS   GOAL: ANALYZED (BY INDEX ROWID) OF
                 'FND_FLEX_VALUES'
      0     INDEX   GOAL: ANALYZED (RANGE SCAN) OF 'FND_FLEX_VALUES_1'
                 (NON-UNIQUE)
****************************************************************************
OVERALL TOTALS FOR ALL NON-RECURSIVE STATEMENTS
```

call	count	cpu	elapsed	disk	query	current	rows
Parse	12	0.00	0.00	0	0	0	0
Execute	13	0.00	0.00	2	2	17	11
Fetch	78	0.00	0.00	208	7327	33	1049
total	103	0.00	0.00	210	7329	50	1060

```
Misses in library cache during parse: 1
OVERALL TOTALS FOR ALL RECURSIVE STATEMENTS
call       count      cpu    elapsed        disk       query     current       rows
-------   ------  --------  ----------  ----------  ----------  ----------  ----------
Parse          2     0.00       0.00           0           0           0           0
Execute       12     0.00       0.00           2           1          11           9
Fetch          3     0.00       0.00           6          15           0           3
-------   ------  --------  ----------  ----------  ----------  ----------  ----------
total         17     0.00       0.00           8          16          11          12
Misses in library cache during parse: 0
     14  user  SQL statements in session.
      1  internal SQL statements in session.
     15  SQL statements in session.
      5  statements EXPLAINed in this session.
*****************************************************************************
Trace file: ora00204.trc
Trace file compatibility: 7.03.02
Sort options: default
      1  session in tracefile.
     14  user  SQL statements in trace file.
      1  internal SQL statements in trace file.
     15  SQL statements in trace file.
     12  unique SQL statements in trace file.
      5  SQL statements EXPLAINed using schema:
          FND.prof$plan_table
            Default table was used.
            Table was created.
            Table was dropped.
    270  lines in trace file.
```

NOTE
Even though the "Trace file compatibility"
reports 7.03.02, the trace file you produce will
be against an Oracle8 database.

If the trace file contains any *recursive calls* (reads of data dictionary information from a disk that is not in the SGA), Oracle displays their statistics as well. These statistics are included in the statistics for your SQL statement processing. They should not be added in again when adding times together. For example, if your statement took 0.26 seconds of CPU time, and a recursive call initiated by your statement took 0.05 seconds, the total CPU time would be 0.26, not 0.31.

Since tkprof is an executable run from the operating system prompt, be sure that your DBA has it somewhere where you can run it. Invoke tkprof using the command

```
tkprof80 [name_of_trace_file] output=[output_file_name]
explain=[userid_password] sort=[sort_options]
```

Using the sort option with tkprof, you can get a better picture of the most troublesome statements. The following listing shows the options you may sort on.

```
prscnt   number of times parse was called
prscpu   cpu time parsing
prsela   elapsed time parsing
prsdsk   number of disk reads during parse
prsqry   number of buffers for consistent read during parse
prscu    number of buffers for current read during parse
prsmis   number of misses in library cache during parse
execnt   number of execute was called
execpu   cpu time spent executing
exeela   elapsed time executing
exedsk   number of disk reads during execute
exeqry   number of buffers for consistent read during execute
execu    number of buffers for current read during execute
exerow   number of rows processed during execute
exemis   number of library cache misses during execute
fchcnt   number of times fetch was called
fchcpu   cpu time spent fetching
fchela   elapsed time fetching
fchdsk   number of disk reads during fetch
fchqry   number of buffers for consistent read during fetch
fchcu    number of buffers for current read during fetch
fchrow   number of rows fetched
```

When examining tkprof output, we concentrate on the EXPLAIN PLAN output as well as the CPU and elapsed figures shown on all the parse, execute, and fetch sections. Inspecting these sections, we can start to zero in on problem SQL statements and get a handle on the amount of parse activity. As we pointed out earlier in this chapter, parsing an SQL statement is expensive; constant reparsing of statements may point to poor use of statements already in the shared pool.

The SQL Trace Black Hole

Finally! You can now, using yet another SYS object, initiate SQL trace against a user session already in motion. It has become increasingly difficult to trace with conventional means since, as we have discussed in this chapter, the initialization parameter entry SQL_TRACE must be TRUE or an **alter session** command must be issued by the product with which the user interacts with the database. Turning trace on is performed using the DBMS_SYSTEM package, passing it three arguments. First you need to get the SID and the SERIAL# of the desired session from V$SESSION. You query based on the OSUSER, USERNAME, or PROGRAM column as shown in the following listing.

```
SQL> select sid, serial#
  2    from v$session
  3    where osuser = 'oradba';
SID            SERIAL#
------------- ----------------
          11               17
SQL>
```

Armed with the values for these two columns, turning on trace is a matter of issuing the following statement from SQL*Plus, SQL*Worksheet, or Server Manager.

```
SQL> execute dbms_system.set_sql_trace_in_session(11, 17, true);
PL/SQL procedure successfully completed.
SQL>
```

You can turn trace off for this session by issuing the same command, passing it the text **false** rather than **true**. This package opens up opportunities to look at what a user is doing and, in situations where an enormous amount of resources are being used, zero in on problem SQL statements.

From within a PL/SQL block, you turn on trace during execution using the DBMS_SESSION package and the following command:

```
dbms_session.set_sql_trace (true);
```

Indexing Columns

Indexes are separate data segments used by Oracle for quick access to data blocks. They store values for fields in a table and pointers to the location of the actual data. You may find yourself setting up indexes during program development and going through a process of investigating their usage, dropping some, and perhaps setting up new ones. Indexes are created on one column (single-column indexes) or multiple columns (composite or concatenated indexes).

The big question is: What columns to index? Six guidelines follow to help make this difficult decision.

APPLICATION TUNING RULE #14

Know your data. Figure out the columns with good selectivity. Selectivity is the percent of rows in a table that have the same value. Columns with low selectivity are good candidates for indexing.

Our experience dictates that if a column contains few distinct values, then, even in a table with 250,000 rows, the performance using an index and doing a full table scan can be just about the same. In some instances, the performance using an indexed column that perhaps should not be indexed may even be worse than the dreaded full table scan. If you do not know what your data will look like, use EXPLAIN PLAN and constantly run a sample of your application SQL statements to see the indexes that are being used.

APPLICATION TUNING RULE #15

The best candidates for indexing are columns that are mentioned after WHERE and AND in SQL statements.

Mentioning column names in these clauses causes Oracle to use indexes when they exist. The order of the columns mentioned in the *predicate* (that part of the coding of the SQL statement following the object name(s) and preceding any **group by** or **order by** portions) may become an issue when using the cost-based optimization approach. It is possible that the order of the columns, during your experimentation, may affect the access path.

APPLICATION TUNING RULE #16
Even if a column's contents contain a wide range of values, do not index if it is always mentioned using a function (e.g., FLOOR or ABS) or string manipulation and conversion (e.g., SUBSTR or TO_CHAR).

The query

```
select substr(location,1,10) from plant_detail;
```

would be an example of this type of column usage.

APPLICATION TUNING RULE #17
When looking at and using the cost-based optimizer, ensure that your tables are analyzed to gather important column statistics that aid in the selection of indexes to create.

Gather these column statistics using the SQL*Plus **analyze** command. Most of the useful output from **analyze table** is stored in the data dictionary in USER_TABLES and USER_INDEXES, as the following listing indicates.

```
SQL> select distinct_keys, avg_leaf_blocks_per_key,
  2          avg_data_blocks_per_key, clustering_factor
  3    from user_indexes
  4    where table_name = 'GT_PERIODIC_DTL';
DISTINCT_KEYS AVG_LEAF_BLOCKS_PER_KEY AVG_DATA_BLOCKS_PER_KEY CLUSTERING_FACTOR
------------- ----------------------- ----------------------- -----------------
         2492                       1                       1              2282
SQL>
SQL> select num_rows, blocks, empty_blocks, avg_space, chain_cnt, avg_row_len
```

```
 2    from user_tables
 3  where table_name = 'GT_PERIODIC_DTL';
 NUM_ROWS    BLOCKS EMPTY_BLOCKS AVG_SPACE CHAIN_CNT AVG_ROW_LEN
--------- --------- ------------ --------- --------- -----------
    2492        59            0       364         0          36
SQL>
```

After placing an index on a table, the information stored in the USER_TABLES and USER_INDEXES views shown in the above listing can be quite helpful. Examining the output leads to the following conclusions:

- Of the over 2000 rows in the table, the columns all have distinct values, which means the column is highly selective and, therefore, this is a good index.

- Since the clustering factor of the index is closer to the number of rows than the number of blocks, it is unlikely that index entries in the same index block point to data that resides in the same block (thus I/O is performed for the index block information with a separate I/O for the data block).

APPLICATION TUNING RULE #18
When choosing candidate columns for composite indexes, look at those columns that are used in **where** *and together during your application. If they are retrieved in* **where** *and separately as well as together, two single-column indexes may be better.*

From time to time, you may find, based on your applications, that maintaining a composite index as well as multiple single-column indexes may be the way to proceed. This reinforces the need to know your data and your applications when making indexing decisions.

APPLICATION TUNING RULE #19
A composite index will only be used to satisfy a query when the leftmost column in that composite index is mentioned in **where** *or* **and**.

If there is a composite index on cola and colb on a table (and neither column has a single column index in place), the first query in the following will use that index, whereas the second will not:

```
select colc, substr(cold,1,30) from taba where cola >= 'ABC';
select colc, substr(cold,1,30) from taba where colb >= 'ABC';
```

Some syntax you may use in defining declarative integrity in tables will cause Oracle to maintain an index automatically. Notice the index called SYS_C0031346 on the ADDRESS table in the listing below. Using a **unique** or **primary key** constraint implicitly creates one of these internal indexes. If you try to manually create an index on one or more columns that Oracle has created for enforcement of integrity constraints, you will receive an error. These indexes cannot be dropped manually.

```
SQL> create table address (
  2           addr_id number primary key,
  3           city varchar2(20));
Table created.
SQL> select *
  2      from user_indexes
  3    where table_name = 'ADDRESS';
SYS_C00846                          NORMAL        FND
ADDRESS                             TABLE         UNIQUE
FND                                       2          255          10240          10240
          1          121          50                                              1
               1          10 YES

                                                                         VALID
                         1
1                                         NO  N Y DEFAULT
SQL> select *
  2      from user_ind_columns
  3    where table_name = 'ADDRESS';
SYS_C00846                          ADDRESS
ADDR_ID
               1          22
SQL>
```

Oracle provides two SQL scripts to help you assess the candidate columns for indexing. They are usually found in RDBMS80\ADMIN. Run utloidxs.sql followed by utldidxs.sql to produce output similar to that in the following listing; the ORG_COMP_TYPE column has been considered as a candidate for an index in the OCOMP table. The output produced using utloidxs.sql and utldidxs.sql is shown in the next listing.

```
SQL> @utloidxs OCOMP ORG_COMP_TYPE
TABLE_NAME        COLUMN_NAME      STAT_NAME                            STAT_VALUE
---------------   ---------------  ---------------------------------    -----------
OCOMP             ORG_COMP_TYPE    Rows - Null                                0.00
OCOMP             ORG_COMP_TYPE    Rows - Total                             205.00
OCOMP             ORG_COMP_TYPE    Rows per key - avg                        51.25
OCOMP             ORG_COMP_TYPE    Rows per key - dev                        77.94
OCOMP             ORG_COMP_TYPE    Rows per key - max                       166.00
OCOMP             ORG_COMP_TYPE    Rows per key - min                         1.00
OCOMP             ORG_COMP_TYPE    Total Distinct Keys                        4.00
OCOMP             ORG_COMP_TYPE    db_gets_per_key_hit                       70.07
OCOMP             ORG_COMP_TYPE    db_gets_per_key_miss20                   140.14
9 rows selected.
SQL> @utldidxs OCOMP ORG_CCOMP_TYPE
TABLE_NAME        COLUMN_NAME      BADNESS   KEYS_COUNT  ROW_PERCENT  KEY_PERCENT
---------------   ---------------  --------  ----------  -----------  -----------
OCOMP             ORG_COMP_TYPE       166        1          80.98        25.00
OCOMP             ORG_COMP_TYPE        34        1          16.59        25.00
OCOMP             ORG_COMP_TYPE         4        1           1.95        25.00
OCOMP             ORG_COMP_TYPE         1        1           0.49        25.00
4 rows selected.
SQL>
```

The listing displays statistics on the table and column reported. The second part can help make the indexing decision. Note that the badness factor for 80.98 percent of the rows is 166. Comparing that badness factor for that percent of rows against the badness factor for the remaining 19.02 percent of the rows shows that the ORG_COMP_TYPE column of the OCOMP table is not a good candidate for an index.

Both scripts are looking for a table name followed by a column in that table to inspect. The first script creates the tables INDEX$INDEX_STATS and INDEX$BADNESS_STATS and a view INDEX$BADNESS. You may want to drop these objects when you are done using them. Examining the output from above, the term *badness* refers to the selectivity of a column in a table. Those with high badness relative to badness counts for the same column are not good candidates for indexes.

NOTE
These scripts are intended to be an aid to the selection of columns to index. Actual experimentation with indexing and inspection of the results may clash with some of the scripts' recommendations.

In the next listing, the PIN column has been considered as a candidate for an index in the STATUS_HISTORY table. The output from the same two programs for PIN is shown after that.

```
SQL> @utloidxs STATUS_HISTORY PIN
TABLE_NAME       COLUMN_NAME      STAT_NAME                            STAT_VALUE
---------------  ---------------  -----------------------------------  --------------
STATUS_HISTORY   PIN              Rows - Null                                0.00
STATUS_HISTORY   PIN              Rows - Total                           2,288.00
STATUS_HISTORY   PIN              Rows per key - avg                         1.87
STATUS_HISTORY   PIN              Rows per key - dev                         1.21
STATUS_HISTORY   PIN              Rows per key - max                         9.00
STATUS_HISTORY   PIN              Rows per key - min                         1.00
STATUS_HISTORY   PIN              Total Distinct Keys                    1,222.00
STATUS_HISTORY   PIN              db_gets_per_key_hit                        1.59
STATUS_HISTORY   PIN              db_gets_per_key_miss                       2.65
9 rows selected.
SQL> @utldidxs STATUS_HISTORY PIN
TABLE_NAME       COLUMN_NAME       BADNESS KEYS_COUNT ROW_PERCENT KEY_PERCENT
---------------  ---------------  --------- ---------- ----------- -----------
STATUS_HISTORY   PIN                     9          2        0.79        0.16
STATUS_HISTORY   PIN                     8          1        0.35        0.08
STATUS_HISTORY   PIN                     7          9        2.75        0.74
STATUS_HISTORY   PIN                     6         10        2.62        0.82
STATUS_HISTORY   PIN                     5         30        6.56        2.46
STATUS_HISTORY   PIN                     4         68       11.89        5.57
STATUS_HISTORY   PIN                     3        125       16.39       10.23
STATUS_HISTORY   PIN                     2        365       31.91       29.87
STATUS_HISTORY   PIN                     1        612       26.75       50.08
9 rows selected.
```

By examining the output, you can see that the highest badness is 9 and the lowest is 1. This column is a good candidate for an index, as 31.91 percent of the PIN column values in the table have two rows for that PIN. The first part of this output shows less than two percent (1.87 percent) average rows per key. Thus, of the 2,288 rows in the table, there is an average of less than two rows per PIN value.

Locking

Oracle establishes different forms of locking to ensure consistency, concurrence, and integrity of its data. *Data consistency* ensures that users selecting data are not affected by changes to that data while the query is running. *Data concurrency* ensures that users reading data blocks do not wait for users changing those blocks and vice versa. You should allow Oracle to take care of locking resources. Oracle will acquire the least prohibitive lock necessary to accomplish a task. *Exclusive* locks do not permit sharing of the locked resource, whereas *share* locks support this sharing. Locks are released by one of the following events:

- An explicit commit by the user or program

- An implicit commit by Oracle (e.g., leaving SQL*Plus with uncommitted transactions)

- An explicit session rollback by user or program

- An implicit session rollback by Oracle (e.g., an import aborting on lack of adequate rollback segment extents)

- A rollback to a savepoint issued by the user

The PMON (process monitor) background process discussed in Chapter 2, "Memory/CPU," does user process abort cleanup and will cause locks from that process to be released. Oracle issues row and table locks to protect data where necessary. Data dictionary locks protect object definition in the data dictionary. You can expect Oracle to issue lock requests in an efficient, unrestrictive manner. Any locks issued manually during application operations should be handled likewise. The Lock Manager in the Performance Pack, shown in Figure 8-3, and a number of SQL*Plus queries can be used to monitor locking activity and detect abnormal or unnecessary locking situations and requests.

Oracle provides utllockt.sql to produce a report on lock wait situations. Prior to running this, run catblock.sql to set up objects to be used by

	Username	Session ID	Session Serial No.	Lock Type	Resource ID1	
88	Background Process	4	1	RT	1	
89	APPS	34	1597	TM	1215	
90	APPS	34	1597	TX	589925	
91	APPS	36	1321	TM	33485	
92	APPS	36	1321	TX	720991	
93	APPS_MLS	43	211	TM	4677	
94	APPS_MLS	43	211	TX	196739	
95	TAPS	79	1277	TM	102741	
96	TAPS	79	1277	TX	327816	
97	APPS	96	77	TM	8960	
98	APPS	96	77	TX	262158	
99	APPS	115	207	TM	1215	
100	APPS	115	207	TX	458752	
101	APPS	195	723	TM	6561	
102	APPS	195	723	TX	852015	

For Help, press F1

FIGURE 8-3. *The Lock Manager*

utllockt. If there are no lock wait occurrences when the report is run, it will return "no rows selected."

> **NOTE**
> *Your catblock.sql program may have an error in the SQL statement that creates the DBA_LOCK view. There may be a comment on the last line of the code that creates the view, delimited by the /* comment */ indicator. Either take the semicolon (;) off the line with the comment and put the forward slash (/) on the next line, or remove the comment.*

An alternative to using sqldba for lock monitoring is to query the V$LOCK dictionary view as shown in the following listing. The lock mode in SQL*Plus from V$LOCK is a number instead of a two-character lock code. Table 8-14 translates the numbers from the LMODE column into a lock type for the most common locks.

```
SQL> select * from v$lock;
ADDR      KADDR      SID TY  ID1  ID2 LMODE  REQUEST  CTIME  BLOCK
--------  --------   --- --  ---- ---- -----  -------- ------ ------
02202D90 02202DA0    2 MR    5    0    4       0    12481    0
02202CDC 02202CEC    2 MR    3    0    4       0    20599    0
02202CA0 02202CB0    2 MR    2    0    4       0    20599    0
02202C64 02202C74    2 MR    1    0    4       0    20599    0
02202BEC 02202BFC    2 MR    4    0    4       0    20599    0
02202BB0 02202BC0    3 RT    1    0    6       0    20606    0
6 rows selected.
SQL>
```

Note that the TYPE column values when using SQL*Plus will also include listings of Oracle internal locks. In the above listing, the *MR* refers to a lock associated with media recovery and the *RT* to a lock associated with a redo log operation. You have no control over these locks.

Value	Lock Type
1	No lock
2	Row share: Locks rows in a table with the intent to perform **update** to those rows. Others may row share lock other rows. Others may **select** all rows in table, even those with the row share lock acquired by others.
3	Row exclusive: Locks rows while applying changes to those rows. Others may row exclusive lock other rows. Others may **select** all rows in table, even those with the row exclusive lock acquired by others.
4	Share table: Locks rows in a table for **insert update** or **delete**. Others may still **select** rows in that table and acquire their own share table locks (this is the lock acquired by **lock table in share update mode** seen in older SQL*Plus programs).
5	Share row exclusive: Similar to share table, except this prevents other users from obtaining a lock that requires a share table lock while this lock is in effect.
6	Exclusive: Locks the table and permits others to only **select** data. Prevents others from successfully issuing *any type* of lock on the table.

TABLE 8-14. *Lock Mode Types in V$LOCK*

Let's Tune It

This chapter introduced techniques for monitoring access paths during the execution of SQL statements using tools delivered with Oracle. Discussion also covered the shared SQL area, what is in it, and how to make maximum use of parsed and executable statements. The use of centralized generic code, the use of hints with the cost-based optimizer, indexing considerations, and locking considerations were also discussed. In conclusion, here's some further advice:

- Develop coding conventions for the SQL statements in your installation. Decide issues such as keyword case, keyword placement, alignment of statements, and object aliasing.

- Using database triggers and procedures helps standardize code. Using generic code avoids repetition of the costly parse phase of SQL statement processing.

- Analyze database objects at night as part of backup routines. Analyzing will cause any parsed SQL statements in the shared pool to be flushed.

- When sizing for the shared pool, Oracle refers to small, medium, and large databases, which means the expected number of concurrent users and NOT the sum of the size of all the database files. Rule of thumb suggests 1 to 15 users is small, 16 to 25 users is medium, and anything above 25 is large.

- Become fluent with usage of the cost-based optimizer. Experiment with it, inspect the results, and incorporate it into your applications where they may benefit from it most. With subsequent releases, Oracle has stated that the rule-based approach may disappear. Familiarize yourself with the cost-based approach *now,* rather than rushing to learn it when you have no choice.

- Do not rule out using the cost-based optimizer. If your systems currently use rule-based optimization, be careful when turning on CBO. Prepare tests to look at the performance of the application with rule and cost and remember to analyze your objects when making the move.

- Setting SQL_TRACE=TRUE in the initialization parameter file causes every SQL session to produce a trace file. These trace files require manual cleanup and can occupy unpredictable amounts of disk space. For that very reason, do not set SQL_TRACE=TRUE in the initialization parameter file. Do tracing on a per session basis. Remember to check programs for **alter session set sql_trace=true**; before they go to production.

- Assess efficiency of indexes using EXPLAIN PLAN. See what indexes are being used for common queries and drop any that are not used. Over-indexing a table can cause added overhead. All indexes must be updated during record creation, modification, and deletion.

- When using SQL*Plus for non-**select** statement work, issue commit statements after all **update**, **delete**, and **insert** statements to release resource locks. If this is not possible according to application logic, so be it.

- When testing and coding for the cost-based optimizer, use EXPLAIN PLAN and optimizer hints to get the cost to a minimum.

- Familiarize yourself with the contents of the shared pool during program development. You may find something there that you can match rather than coding your own statement.

Oracle 7.x Specifics

Please note the following points organized by the headings for some sections throughout this chapter:

- "Oracle Enterprise Manager" Though the version of OEM is different with Oracle8, the material in this section applies to Oracle7.x.

- "The Shared SQL Area" With Oracle7.3, the Performance Pack monitorinf is available, but with 7.2.x and 7.1.x you will have to use GUI Server Manager or full-screen SQL*DBA.

- "Tuning the Shared Pool" All this information is applicable to Oracle 7.x.

- ■ "SQL Statement Processing" All this information is applicable to Oracle 7.x.

- ■ "Using Generic Code" All this information is applicable to Oracle 7.x, except the ability to define libraries and make references to external objects in PL/SQL 8.0.

- ■ "The Cost-Based Optimizer (CBO)" Some of the hints discussed in this section are new to Oracle8; many can be used in Oracle7.x.

- ■ "Where Statistics Are Stored" The definitions of the views mentioned here are different than Oracle7.x. The material on views with the "PART" text for range-based partitioning is not available with 7.x whatsoever.

- ■ "Using Hints" There are some new hints that can be used with Oracle8 and will be ignored in Oracle7.x.

- ■ "explain plan" All this information is applicable to Oracle 7.x.

- ■ "Using set autotrace" This material applies to Oracle7.3, except the portion that deals with setting up the PLUSTRACE role. Autotrace is not available with Oracle 7.2.x or 7.1.x.

- ■ "The Hints and EXPLAIN PLAN Toolbox" All this information is applicable to Oracle 7.x.

- ■ "tkprof and SQL Trace" All this information is applicable to Oracle 7.x.

- ■ "The SQL Trace Black Hole" This section does not apply to Oracle7.x.

- ■ "Indexing Columns" All this information is applicable to Oracle7.x.

- ■ "Locking" All this information is applicable to Oracle7.x.

CHAPTER
9

Performance Pack

his chapter is dedicated to a current generation management suite of tools rolled together under the banner "Performance Pack." Oracle's system management people have created a set of management tools that work alongside the server and give DBAs lights-out management capabilities. Many vendors have automated GUI-based solutions that SQL*DBA and both versions of Server Manager have not been able to deliver. The technical community has thirsted for graphs, agents, and intelligent automated suggestion-based modules for many versions of the Oracle Server.

Along comes Oracle Enterprise Manager (also known as *OEM*), which was first released with 7.2 of the Server in 1994. OEM release 1.4 is bundled with the Oracle8 OEM. This chapter is an introduction to the Performance Pack and will offer some suggestions on optimal use of the product. We will also introduce a few additional managers (e.g., Tablespace Manager and Lock Manager) that are not available with the base OEM.

OEM is a good example of Oracle moving in directions dictated by the needs and inputs from its worldwide user community coupled with the obvious direction of the industry. It is a very rich product and, with your input through vehicles such as the official enhancements process, will become even better. Oracle Corporation and some of the largest user group conglomerates around the globe cooperate to carry out this enhancements process.

NOTE

Visit the International Oracle Users Group-Americas (IOUG-A) on the Web at **www.ioug.org** *for details, or send an e-mail to* **iouga@ioug.org** *requesting information about the official enhancements process.*

We are going to call the Enterprise Manager Performance Pack EMPP from here on out. Perhaps we'll go down in history as having invented another acronym (TWANMA—the world always needs more acronyms!).

NOTE
The Performance Pack is an add-on to the base OEM product. Consult your friendly neighborhood Oracle office for details about per-seat pricing in a client server environment.

Components of Performance Pack

After a successful install of OEM with the Performance Pack add-on, you will find a folder on your desktop called Oracle Enterprise Manager, with shortcuts as illustrated in Figure 9-1.

Let's spend a bit of time looking at the major components of EMPP, through which we will inevitably begin to see the benefit of the product.

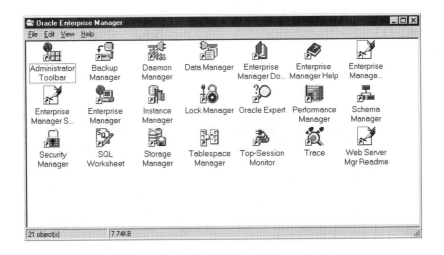

FIGURE 9-1. *OEM release 1.4 folder*

Oracle Trace

Using Oracle Trace, you can map events that occur as your systems operate and, after collecting data about those events, take action to fix problems such as processing bottlenecks. You can trace applications as they run on nodes that have been discovered through the OEM services discoverer.

PERFORMANCE PACK RULE #1
Nodes are discovered through Navigator/
Service Discovery/Discover New Services of
the OEM main console.

The discovery of nodes is reported on the Service Discovery Status screen shown in Figure 9-2. The node name is the handle used for identification of the NT node on your network.

Inspect the next few points to see how this monitoring and event mapping can assist the tuning process.

- It helps you zero in on problem areas and, after isolation of code that contributes to poor performance, address poor code segments. Response time measurement is one of the best measurements. Suppose your help desk reports over a two-week period that there have been a lot more complaints than usual about system

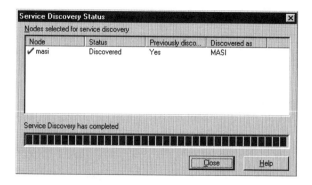

FIGURE 9-2. *Discovery of MASI node*

performance. Using Oracle Trace and the data it can collect, you can figure out where the problem lies; a feeling becomes a solution armed with information collected by Trace as per your instructions.

- By collection of data through all layers of the application, Oracle Trace permits you to find culprits—be it the network, the database itself, or the application code that may be causing bottlenecks.

- Trace provides data that can be formatted into reports that are meaningful to you; you are the database expert and, alongside your application experts, you adapt the output to meet your particular needs.

- Isolate poorly worded SQL statements and, with buy-in from the appropriate management personnel, attempt to educate your development on writing efficient SQL regardless of the programming environment in use (e.g., Oracle Forms or Visual Basic).

PERFORMANCE PACK RULE #2
Collection of data using EMPP alone will not fix your system performance. You and your developers need to invest time and energy to fix problems through planned intervention.

The Oracle Trace main console is shown in Figure 9-3.

PERFORMANCE PACK RULE #3
Collection of data by Oracle Trace depends on an Intelligent Agent running on the node upon which data is to be collected.

The Intelligent Agent on a local Oracle8 database on NT can be started through Control Panel|Services by:

- Starting the OracleAgent service manually using the Start button

- Configuring the Agent to start automatically by setting Start Type to Automatic in the service definition property sheet invoked by double-clicking OracleAgent

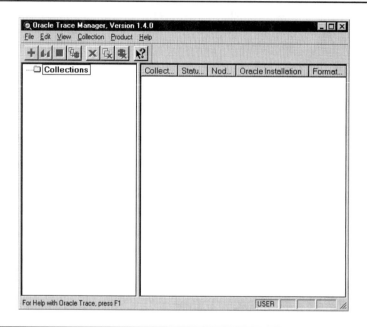

FIGURE 9-3. *Oracle Trace main console*

Oracle Expert

Oracle Expert is a knowledge-based module that assists the tuning exercise for applications and the Oracle8 instance itself. After collection of data, you use Oracle Expert to analyze the information and, based on the analysis performed, make recommendations about changes that should be considered.

Before using Oracle Expert, you can specify exactly what areas you would like to monitor and dictate guidelines you would like Expert to follow during its analysis. You choose the categories you want Oracle Expert to watch; it will produce reports in the areas of interest to you. Oracle Expert works with tuning sessions that you define through the operator interface. After creating a tuning session, you go about your business after deciding on the scope of the session and specifying control parameters.

NOTE
Oracle Expert requires a repository which will be set up when Expert is invoked if one does not already exist. The work is performed by the Oracle Repository Manager.

The Oracle Expert main console is shown in Figure 9-4.

Performance Manager

This piece will soon become the DBA's best friend. As far back as we can remember, Oracle's software bundle has included a monitoring feature that assisted us with baseline tuning. It started with the Oracle Display System (*ODS*) with version 5, then it was SQL*DBA monitor with versions 6 and 7, then GUI-based Server Manager in later releases of Oracle7, and now the Performance Pack. This section of EMPP is where we will spend most of our time in this chapter. Figure 9-5 shows the main console of the Performance Manager.

Lock Manager

The Lock Manager is where you can look at the locks held in the current database by session, broken down by username and lock mode. Figure 9-6 shows the startup screen where you are positioned after supplying login

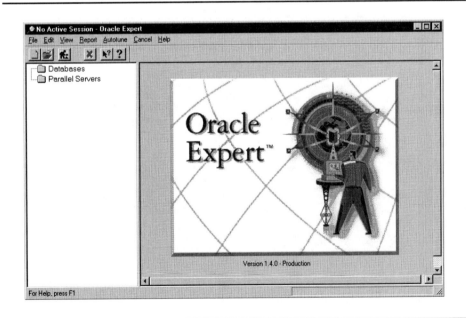

FIGURE 9-4. *Oracle Expert main console*

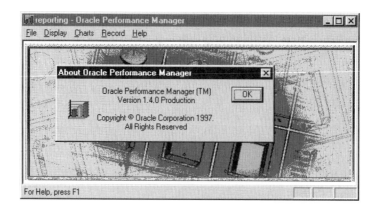

FIGURE 9-5. *Performance Manager main console*

information to the manager and it has started to collect meta data from the server. Shown in Figure 9-6 is where you can kill unwanted or problem sessions.

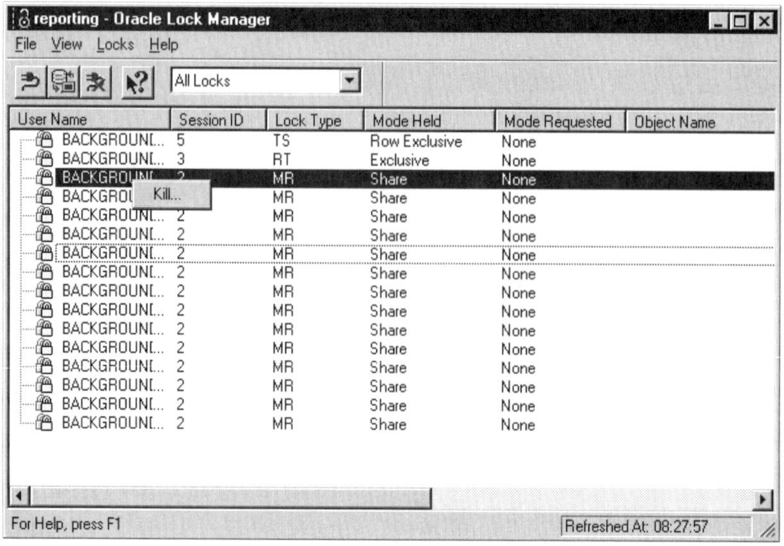

FIGURE 9-6. *Oracle Lock Manager main console*

The Lock Manager will bring up a confirmation box before killing an unwanted session. Notice the All Locks text on the button bar. You can change that lock type to Blocking/Waiting Locks by selecting it from a pick list. Monitoring this lock type may prove useful when trying to zero in after user complaints about excessive wait conditions. Resource contention, of which locks are a component, involves a user session fighting for a resource that is being tied up by someone else.

PERFORMANCE PACK RULE #4
Before panicking over some of the locks displayed in the Lock Manager, familiarize yourself with the common session lock acronyms.

To help you live by Rule #4, Table 9-1 lists the most common lock types and what they mean.

Lock Type	Notes
MR	Media recovery—Should not require any intervention since these lock requests are issued continually as Oracle8 maintains a consistent state of the instance
TX	Transaction—A lock being held on a portion of a rollback segment
UL	PL/SQL user lock—Same as TX
TM	DML—Work-a-day-world locks designed to maintain data integrity—part and parcel with Oracle8's consistency mechanisms; TM always refers to locks on a table or view
TS	Temp segment—Indicates a session has tied up portions of the user's assigned temporary segment for work requests
RW	Row wait—Session has issued a willing-to-wait lock request that has not yet been satisfied; it will be satisfied shortly since the Server knows the current holder of the row lock is in the midst of releasing the resource
TE	Table extend—A session may be temporarily prevented from working with data in a table since the table is in the midst of being extended to satisfy the need for additional space

TABLE 9-1. *Common Lock Types*

Figure 9-7 shows two locks being held by user SYSTEM and how the Lock Manager indicates one lock blocking another. The tree-fashioned display indicates the lower level lock (session ID 12) is being blocked by the one higher in the same branch (session ID 11). Also notice the familiar "-" sign beside the higher lock indicating the lock list has been expanded. If you were to close the list, a "+" sign would be placed beside the lock displayed for session 11. Note as well that the lock type pick list is expanded, where you can select Blocking/Waiting Locks rather than All Locks.

Tablespace Manager

From an organization of the database infrastructure standpoint, the Tablespace Manager is an interesting tool. Figure 9-8 shows the Tablespace Manager main console.

There are a number of interesting activities that can be accomplished from this tool. You can:

- Reorganize data and free up unused space at the end of the data segments within the chosen tablespace

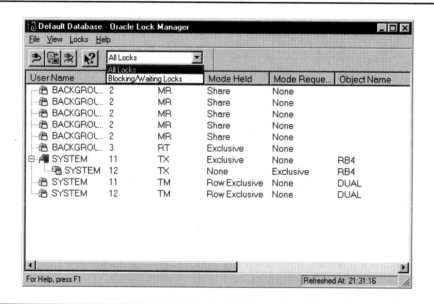

FIGURE 9-7.   *Blocking locks expansion*

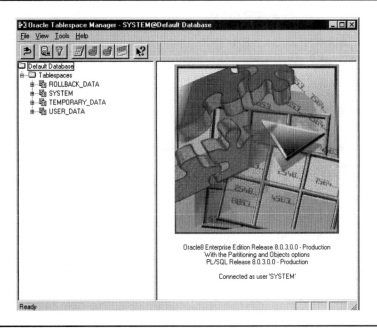

FIGURE 9-8. *Tablespace Manager main console*

- Rebuild indexes resident within the chosen tablespace

- Analyze objects within the chosen tablespace, by table, cluster, index, or partition. A wizard allows you to specify the familiar assortment of statistic collection information such as mode of analysis (i.e., compute or estimate), deletion of statistics, or reporting on chained/migrated rows.

The work done via any of the wizards submits a job to the OEM scheduling module, which must be running for the work to commence now or at some later time.

PERFORMANCE PACK RULE #5
Defragmentation activity renders the data within the affected object unavailable during the operation. Be careful when selecting a time for the job to run; it's best to communicate your intentions to affected parties before beginning a defragmentation exercise.

Oracle TopSessions

Oracle TopSessions is used to monitor database connections and isolate intensive resource consumers. The definition for resource consumption is configurable and can isolate sessions filtering by cache, SQL, operating system, or parallel server. The display of the statistics can be sorted based on the filter type selected. The TopSessions main console is shown in Figure 9-9.

As seen in Figure 9-10, the Options dialog box provides access to the highly configurable displays available in TopSessions. With the Statistic Filter selected, notice the context sensitive Sort Statistic values in the pick list—cluster key scan block gets, cluster key scans, execute count, parse time, and parse time CPU. When Parallel Server is selected, the pick list entries all start with the prefix "global lock". You can further customize the

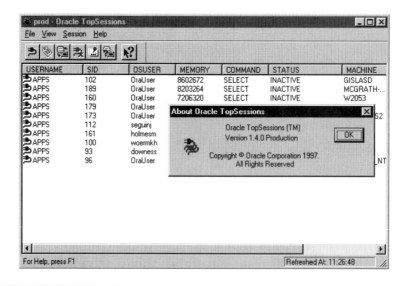

FIGURE 9-9. *Oracle TopSessions main console*

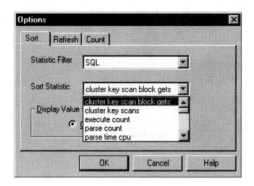

FIGURE 9-10. *Sort statistic accompanying SQL filter*

information you display by specifying manual or automatic data refresh, the rate of automatic refresh, and the number of sessions to display.

Performance Pack and the Tuning Process

Bottlenecks, ugly SQL, I/O bound, CPU bound—all terminology that conjures up visions of irate clientele coupled with the never ending hunt for reasons why these things are happening. In the next few sections, we are going to concentrate on the monitoring capabilities of EMPP and have a look at where to go to zero in on the most common performance hogs. We will look at the most common screens, charts, and graphs you will encounter during your EMPP-based mission—tune that database, tune that database, tune that database, tune that database, tune that database—that's got a familiar ring, *n'est-ce pas?*

If this is the first time you've opened up OEM while logged on to the chosen database, you will be informed that a number of repositories need to be created. Click OK on the screen shown in Figure 9-11 to accomplish this task.

We are now going to have a look at a few of our favorite charts available with the EMPP, and then we'll look at building one of our own.

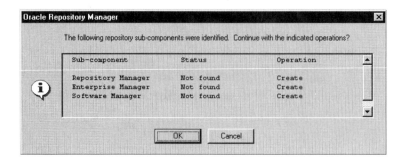

FIGURE 9-11. *OEM Create Repositories dialog box*

File I/O Rate Details

The File I/O Rate Details chart displays physical reads/blocks read and physical writes/blocks written by database file. V$FILESTAT coupled with V$DBFILE are the underlying views.

```
SQL> desc sys.v_$filestat
 Name                                Null?    Type
 ----------------------------------- -------- ----
 FILE#                                        NUMBER
 PHYRDS                                       NUMBER
 PHYWRTS                                      NUMBER
 PHYBLKRD                                     NUMBER
 PHYBLKWRT                                    NUMBER
 READTIM                                      NUMBER
 WRITETIM                                     NUMBER
SQL> desc sys.v_$dbfile
 Name                                Null?    Type
 ----------------------------------- -------- ----
 FILE#                                        NUMBER
 NAME                                         VARCHAR2(513)
SQL>
```

This chart is a logical drill-down from the File I/O Rate chart. It can be accessed from the menu on the EMPP main console or by a right-mouse click and selecting Drilldown|Object from the pop-up menu that appears on the File I/O Rate chart. By default, when the File I/O details graph appears, it uses a line type display. If your instance has a large number of

database files (i.e., more than ten, as shown in Figure 9-12), you will have
to adjust the border at the top of the file name display to see exactly what
color refers to what database file. You will probably have problems with
the color legend with many files, as it will de difficult discerning one shade
of a color from another. Better still, with a large number of files, you should
right-click on one of the four detail areas and change the display to type
Area. This enhanced output is easier to read, with the color code moved to
the I/O type (e.g., Physical Blocks Read) and a legend to the file name at
the bottom of the horizontal scrolling display.

PERFORMANCE PACK RULE #6
When monitoring activity by database file,
ensure the time slice is long enough to show
I/O rate by file is not skewed based on the
time of day during which the monitoring is
performed.

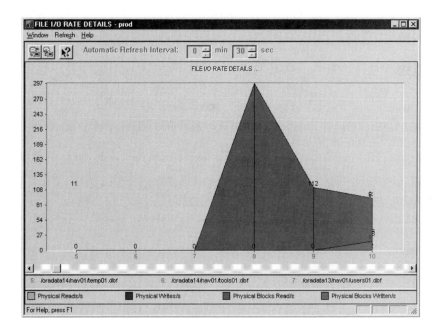

FIGURE 9-12. *File I/O Details output*

We also suggest multiple database file I/O monitoring sessions spread over a number of days. Obtaining meaningful results is a triple-edged sword:

1. Using a representative time slice—make sure the length of the monitoring activity is long enough to provide a sample long enough to be projected over a number of days. If the monitoring is done for a three-hour period, projecting three to twenty-four hours is statistically more sound than using a 30-minute period and projecting it over a full day by multiplying by 48.

2. Sample at different times during the working day—the results can easily be skewed if you don't ensure the monitoring is done at different times over the day. We recommend deliberately spacing your sessions over a three-day period and, if a 24 by 7 shop, monitoring in the quiet hours as well as the batch jobs run.

3. Ensure the data cache is primed when monitoring—the I/O activity involved in priming the data cache is representative of the load balance during the startup phase of the database. This balance could be radically different than when the cache is full and user requests for data go to disk when information is not already resident in memory.

VLDB
*Due to the sheer number of database files with repositories of this nature, we find examining the output from utlbstat/utlestat or V$FILESTAT and V$DBFILE in SQL*Plus much easier to use.*

Let's look at some sample output from a query against V$FILESTAT to see how you start to arrive at making database file placement decisions based on the output from this chart:

```
SQL> select *
  2    from v$filestat;
     FILE#     PHYRDS    PHYWRTS  PHYBLKRD PHYBLKWRT    READTIM   WRITETIM
--------- ---------- ---------- --------- --------- ---------- ----------
        1       2799       1443      2020       443          0          0
        2       1742      12787      1742     12787          0          0
        3        324       1624       324      1624          0          0
```

```
    4          0          0          0          0          0          0
    5         32       3228        162       3228          0          0
    6        483          1        881          1          0          0
    7          2          0          2          0          0          0
    8     355393       2367     469489       2367          0          0
8 rows selected.
SQL>
```

Based on this output, the total number of physical reads is 385,775 of which file #8 accounts for more than 92 percent. On the other hand, file #2 accounts for over 59 percent of the physical writes.

PERFORMANCE PACK RULE #7
Database files reporting high read/write activity compared to the average for all database files are candidates for range-based partitioning as discussed in Chapter 4.

System I/O Rate

This chart details I/O statistics for the entire instance, zeroing in on buffer gets (requests for information satisfied by memory reads), block changes, and physical reads per second. The information in this chart comes from the V$SYSSTAT view:

```
Name                             Null?    Type
-------------------------------- -------- ----
STATISTIC#                                NUMBER
NAME                                      VARCHAR2(64)
CLASS                                     NUMBER
VALUE                                     NUMBER
```

Looking at the display shown in Figure 9-13, over an 8.5 minute interval (indicated by 17 collection points with a 30-second refresh rate), the buffer gets far exceeded the other two statistics, peaking at 4,053 and bottoming out close to zero. Notice how there were close to no block changes and physical reads during that same time period.

This leads into an interesting feature in the EMPP—automatic refresh coupled with percentage resource display. Suppose you were interested in finding the relative amount of time spent on I/O for each of the three components monitored by this chart. You could change the chart type by

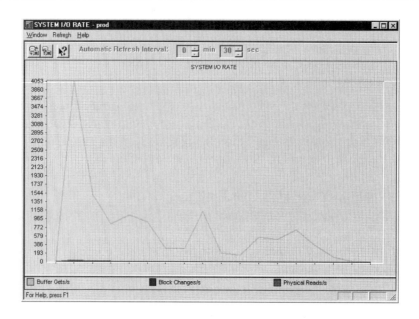

FIGURE 9-13. *System I/O output*

right-clicking and changing the Type to Pie, then setting the automatic refresh interval to five seconds. The readout would show an amount of activity performed for each of the three I/O types at a point in time and then, after the interval had elapsed, update the display.

PERFORMANCE PACK RULE #8
The buffer gets figure from the System I/O chart should far exceed those for the other indicators. This confirms the I/O work being done by the database instance is productive and conducive to optimal performance.

Memory Library Cache Details

In Chapter 6 we spoke of the library cache as part of the shared SQL area. Our travels around Oracle7/8 since the invention of the shared pool have shown us that tuning this pool is the single most effective way to optimize

	GETS	GETHITS	GETHITRATIO	PINS	PINHITS	PINHITRATIO	RELOADS	INVALIDATIONS
BODY	23951	23749	1	24042	23635	1	184	0
CLUSTER	27	12	0	15	5	0	0	0
INDEX	65	0	0	65	0	0	0	0
OBJECT	0	0	1	0	0	1	0	0
PIPE	10412	10410	1	6941	6939	1	0	0
SQL AREA	557411	528069	1	3308883	3228770	1	15386	181
TABLE/PROCEDURE	320059	314587	1	1661421	1648579	1	7132	0
TRIGGER	7687	7332	1	7170	6497	1	318	0

Window Refresh Help — LIBRARY CACHE DETAILS - prod — Automatic Refresh Interval: 0 min 5 sec — For Help, press F1

FIGURE 9-14. *Library Cache Details output*

performance of any instance. There really is no other way to look at the
status of the shared cursors in this cache. A *cursor* is a chunk of memory
allocated to process SQL statements and, after it's opened and
preprocessing is done on the statement, can be shared among multiple user
sessions. Output is shown in Figure 9-14. The quick and dirty hit and miss
ratio can be seen using a Pie type chart after selecting Display|Memory|
Library Cache Hit% from the EMPP main console. The GETHITRATIO and
PINHITRATIO should be very close to 1 in all areas except INDEX and
CLUSTER. The RELOADS should be low compared to the PINS and GETS.
As you can see in Figure 9-13, for example, most figures in the RELOADS
column are less than 1 percent of those in the GETS or PINS.

PERFORMANCE PACK RULE #9
*Six of the eight library cache hit percentages
should be no less than .90; in most cases, they
will be 1.*

The V$LIBRARYCACHE, shown in the following listing, is the
underlying object in the data dictionary view.

```
Name                            Null?    Type
------------------------------- -------- ----
NAMESPACE                                VARCHAR2(15)
GETS                                     NUMBER
```

GETHITS	NUMBER
GETHITRATIO	NUMBER
PINS	NUMBER
PINHITS	NUMBER
PINHITRATIO	NUMBER
RELOADS	NUMBER
INVALIDATIONS	NUMBER
DLM_LOCK_REQUESTS	NUMBER
DLM_PIN_REQUESTS	NUMBER
DLM_PIN_RELEASES	NUMBER
DLM_INVALIDATION_REQUESTS	NUMBER
DLM_INVALIDATIONS	NUMBER

Memory Sort Hits

As we mention many times throughout *Oracle8 Tuning*, doing as much work in memory as you can will give you the biggest bang for your buck. Sorting is a very intensive operation, initiated by activities all the way from assembling query results to creating unique indexes. A healthy instance should report a very high sort to memory percentage as shown in Figure 9-15.

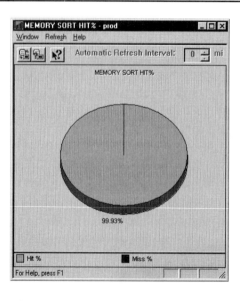

FIGURE 9-15. *Sorts to memory hit rate chart*

Requests for sort area that cannot be satisfied in memory go to secondary storage. The V$SYSSTAT, shown in the next listing, contains most of the data from which this chart is derived. The rows whose NAME column values are either "sorts (memory)" or "sorts (disk)" are the heart of this chart's output.

```
Name                            Null?    Type
------------------------------- -------- ----
STATISTIC#                               NUMBER
NAME                                     VARCHAR2(64)
CLASS                                    NUMBER
VALUE                                    NUMBER
```

PERFORMANCE PACK RULE #10
The sorts to disk should account for less than 5 percent of the sorts performed by your applications.

Rule #10 is all fine and dandy, but the question, "What should I do if the sorts on disk are greater than 5 percent?" springs to mind immediately. If more memory can be allocated to the SORT_AREA_SIZE initialization parameter file entry, that is one solution. If more memory is not available, look into acquiring some.

Rollback Nowait Hit %

This chart is accessed from the Display|Contention|NoWait Hit % menu option on the EMPP main console. Wait situations are tracked in a number of the data dictionary views; V$ROLLSTAT is dedicated to rollback segments. This view is shown in the next listing:

```
Name                            Null?    Type
------------------------------- -------- ----
USN                                      NUMBER
EXTENTS                                  NUMBER
RSSIZE                                   NUMBER
WRITES                                   NUMBER
XACTS                                    NUMBER
GETS                                     NUMBER
WAITS                                    NUMBER
OPTSIZE                                  NUMBER
```

HWMSIZE	NUMBER
SHRINKS	NUMBER
WRAPS	NUMBER
EXTENDS	NUMBER
AVESHRINK	NUMBER
AVEACTIVE	NUMBER
STATUS	VARCHAR2(15)
CUREXT	NUMBER
CURBLK	NUMBER

Rollback segment header contention can impede optimal operation of your online systems. Before a **delete**, **update**, or **insert** SQL statement can begin, the transaction needs to find itself space in a rollback segment for any undo information. The conduit to each rollback segment is its segment header that tracks extent usage and transaction activity. The Pie display shown in Figure 9-16 is the best way to view this chart.

PERFORMANCE PACK RULE #11
There should be very little or no waits for rollback segment headers, and the Rollback NoWait Hit chart should report a 99 percent to 100 percent hit rate.

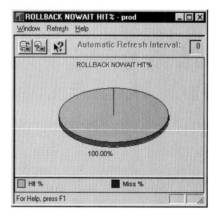

FIGURE 9-16. *Rollback Wait Hit % chart*

Overview

The last screen we are going to have a look at is the Overview chart shown in Figure 9-17.

    We have discussed many of the areas on this chart in their own sections. First, let's delve a wee bit into the three user-based areas in the middle of the output. The Users Logged On area displays information about the number of concurrent user sessions connected to the database. It uses the V$LICENSE view shown in the next listing, displaying the current value sitting in the SESSIONS_CURRENT column.

```
Name                               Null?    Type
-------------------------------- -------- ----
SESSIONS_MAX                               NUMBER
SESSIONS_WARNING                           NUMBER
SESSIONS_CURRENT                           NUMBER
SESSIONS_HIGHWATER                         NUMBER
USERS_MAX                                  NUMBER
```

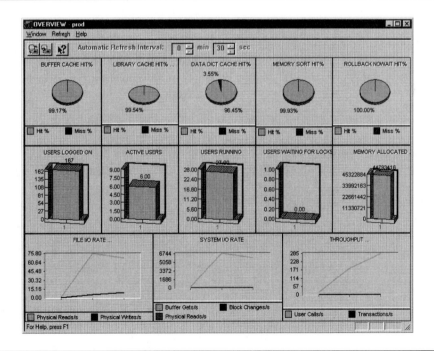

FIGURE 9-17.   *Overview chart*

The Active Users area of this display shows information from the V$SESSION view. A partial listing of this view is shown next, with the columns relative to this display bolded. The results displayed in this area are based on those rows in V$SESSION with the **status = 'ACTIVE' and type <> 'BACKGROUND'** selection criteria:

Name	Null?	Type
SADDR		RAW(4)
SID		NUMBER
SERIAL#		NUMBER
AUDSID		NUMBER
PADDR		RAW(4)
USER#		NUMBER
USERNAME		VARCHAR2(30)
COMMAND		NUMBER
OWNERID		NUMBER
TADDR		VARCHAR2(8)
LOCKWAIT		VARCHAR2(8)
STATUS		**VARCHAR2(8)**
SERVER		VARCHAR2(9)
SCHEMA#		NUMBER
SCHEMANAME		VARCHAR2(30)
OSUSER		VARCHAR2(15)
PROCESS		VARCHAR2(9)
MACHINE		VARCHAR2(64)
TERMINAL		VARCHAR2(16)
PROGRAM		VARCHAR2(64)
TYPE		**VARCHAR2(10)**

The Users Running portion of the display details the sessions currently running a transaction. The V$SESSION_WAIT, shown in the next listing, is the view sitting behind the scenes. The figure displayed counts the rows in this view with their **wait_time <> 0**.

Name	Null?	Type
SID		NUMBER
SEQ#		NUMBER
EVENT		VARCHAR2(64)
P1TEXT		VARCHAR2(64)
P1		NUMBER
P1RAW		RAW(4)
P2TEXT		VARCHAR2(64)

P2	NUMBER
P2RAW	RAW(4)
P3TEXT	VARCHAR2(64)
P3	NUMBER
P3RAW	RAW(4)
WAIT_TIME	NUMBER
SECONDS_IN_WAIT	NUMBER
STATE	VARCHAR2(19)

The Overview chart is a form of one-stop shopping. There is no need to visit other screens if this display meets your monitoring needs. If and when any problems are identified from one of the sections of the Overview chart, you can do one of the following:

■ In areas where drill-down is active, right-click in the desired area and select Drilldown then Object from the pop-up menu that appears, as shown in Figure 9-18 on the Throughput area, followed by the Oracle TopSessions target of the drill-down shown in Figure 9-19.

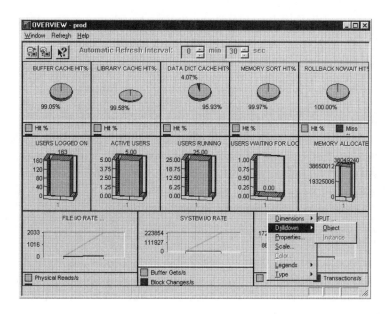

FIGURE 9-18. *Throughput area pop-up menu*

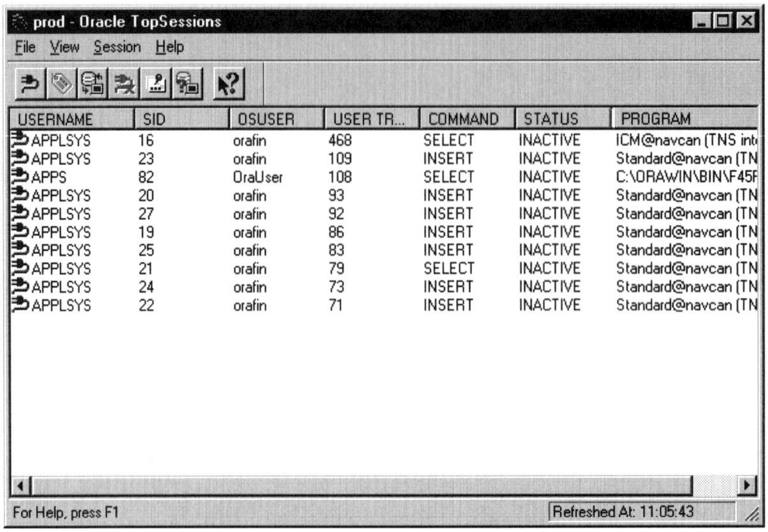

FIGURE 9-19. *TopSessions output from Throughput drill-down*

■ In areas where drill-down is not active, create your own chart to solve your desire for more detail.

To finish our discussion of EMPP, we are going to create and save our own chart to solve drill-down requirements for a detail area of the Overview chart we spoke of in the "File I/O Rate Details" section of this chapter. In that section, we pointed out that when you have an instance with more than ten database files, reading the output of the File I/O Rate Details chart becomes difficult. In the next section, we are going to look at building two user-defined charts that allow us to get the information that we are looking for by ourselves.

Custom Charts

When your needs are not met by the off-the-shelf charts, you will find yourself quickly enabling the custom charts feature of EMPP. From the EMPP main console, choose Charts|NewSQL Chart from the menu; you are presented with a dialog box where a new chart is named, drill-down defined, the SQL query entered, and display options selected.

I/O by Device

The first chart we are going to create will list the total number of physical
reads and writes by device. The query is installation-dependent; the
database we are using as an example uses the text "oradata" followed by a
sequential number to name file systems upon which the database files
reside. Figure 9-20 shows the dialog box filled in with the SQL query
shown in the next listing.

```
select substr(file_name,1,10) "Device",
       sum(phyrds) "Reads",
       sum(phywrts) "Writes"
  from sys.v_$filestat a, sys.dba_data_files b
 where a.file# = b.file_id
 group by substr(file_name,1,10)
 order by 1;
```

After closing the chart definition window, you should proceed to
File|Save Charts off the EMPP main console. The new chart is displayed by
selecting Display|User-defined, then picking the "I/O by Device" window

FIGURE 9-20. *Defining a new chart*

from the displayed pick list. The output from this chart is shown in Figure 19-21.

Let's take this a little bit further. Now that we can isolate the number of reads and writes by device, wouldn't it be nice to know what tablespaces are on each device? Armed with figures on the read and write activity by device, hot spots in the application can be isolated by knowing the tablespace(s) each device contains.

Tablespace by Device

This second user-defined chart will illustrate self-imposed drill-down. Once we have a chart that reports on I/O load by device, it would be nice to be able to drill-down to see what tablespaces are on each of those devices. Again, the exercise begins by selecting Charts|New SQL Chart from the EMPP main console. We name the new chart "Tablespace by Device" and enter the query shown in the next listing. The dialog box where the query is

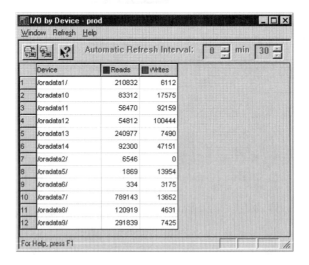

FIGURE 9-21. *I/O by Device chart output*

defined is similar to that shown in Figure 9-20. Figure 9-22 shows the
output from this chart.

```
select distinct substr(file_name,1,10) "Device",
       tablespace_name "Tablespace"
  from sys.dba_data_files order by 1;
```

To enable the drill-down between the two charts we have created, you
return to the Charts|Modify SQL Chart selection off the main console, then
select the I/O by Device chart. In the screen shown in Figure 9-20 where
the chart was initially defined, bring up the pick list beside Drilldown
Window and choose "Tablespace by Device". This establishes the hookup
between the two charts, meaning that a right-click on the I/O by Device,
then Drilldown|Object, will display the Tablespace by Device chart.

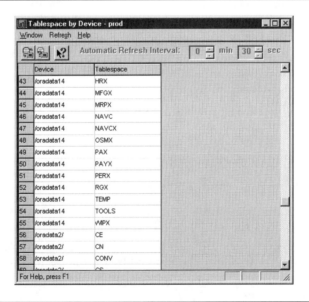

FIGURE 9-22. *Output from Tablespace by Device chart*

Usage Recommendations

Before wrapping up this chapter, let's look at a few recommendations regarding configuration, registering of nodes, and overall use of the Performance Pack.

Local versus Remote Repository

The Enterprise Manager requires a repository behind the scenes as you work with its many components, including EMPP. As we looked at EMPP and worked on this chapter, we defined a local repository in an Oracle8 Enterprise Edition database on NT 4.0. We prefer a local repository but, at the same time, with appropriate file access permissions in place, recommend placing the database files for the local instance on a drive that is backed up on a regular basis.

Some NT administrators reading this section may not be happy about you placing a local Oracle8 database on a network drive. If that's the case, you are going to have to look at either placing the repository in a database on a local drive or going the remote way. Regardless of whether you go local or remote, the EMPP is going to function the same on top of the repository you allow it to set up. Let's look at two more EMPP rules.

PERFORMANCE PACK RULE #12
When more than one client has access to OEM and EMPP, ensure that everyone knows the location of the repository and uses the correct connect information to hook up to the correct location when signing on.

PERFORMANCE PACK RULE #13
Your custom charts are saved in the EMPP repository; to enable access to these charts while connected to any database, you need to use a centralized repository across your enterprise.

The Performance Hit

Often many DBAs worry about the performance hit of monitoring a database while the user community is on the system and actively involved in day-to-day activities. We do not believe EMPP-based data collection and analysis are much of a drain on system resources, and we encourage you to use the product as much or as little as possible to meet your needs.

PERFORMANCE PACK RULE #14
Using an automatic refresh time of between five and ten minutes will suit most of your monitoring needs and ensure your session itself is not consuming too many resources.

Canned versus User-Defined Charts

As soon as we started finding our way around the Performance Manager, we found a lot of predefined charts that were never used, and we were tempted to delete them to shorten pick lists. Keep in mind though, when using a centralized repository as we suggest, that you are not the only one using EMPP. Others may find the charts you are not using quite useful.

Let's Tune It

The following points will guide you in the right direction as you decide how the Performance Pack can benefit you and your installation.

■ Oracle Trace can help you track events and activities as your Oracle systems operate and can provide useful information to Oracle Expert for a tuning exercise.

■ Oracle Expert can assist the tuning exercise and make recommendations about improvements in the database setup, memory allocations, and SQL statement activities. The rules used by Expert are configurable.

■ The Performance Manager is where you may spend a great deal of time looking around your instance and trying to zero in on problems. The off-the-shelf charts meet most of the needs of most DBAs; use the user-defined charts module when you want more information than you can glean otherwise.

■ The Lock Manager is where you go to look at lock activity on your server. Waits caused by lock requests can be a factor in performance degradation, especially when more than one session is looking for a lock on the same item of information.

■ Familiarize yourself with the Tablespace Manager; it is where you will spend time assessing the status of space consumption and the need for management activities such as defragmentation.

■ Use Oracle TopSessions to report on heavy consumers of resources. The resource types that can be monitored can be selected from many pick lists.

■ The File I/O Rate Details chart in the Performance Manager is a good starting place for looking at I/O balance.

■ The System I/O Rate chart is a good place to look when deciding if most requests for data are being satisfied in memory (a good thing) or require disk reads (a not-so-good thing—but also avoidable).

■ The Library Cache Hit % chart is where you get a handle on how well-sized your shared SQL area is; using drill-down, you can go to further details that list hit rates by components of this cache (e.g., trigger or index namespaces).

■ The Memory Sort Hits chart is a quick way to look at what proportion of sort activity is being done to memory and how much is going to disk. Well over 90 percent should be done in memory.

■ The Rollback Nowait % chart quickly shows wait situations being raised as a result of requests for rollback segment space—no transaction can begin before getting rollback.

■ Use some of your own charts to complement what Oracle delivers.

■ Use central repository so more than one user of the Performance Manager can take advantage of any custom charts others may have created.

Oracle 7.x Specifics

The Performance Pack part of the Oracle Enterprise Manager sold alongside the Oracle8 Enterprise Edition is version 1.4; OEM 1.3.5 is sold with Oracle release 7.3.x. You will find the material presented in this chapter applicable with versions 1.3.x of OEM. The way you go about doing things may be a little bit different, and the end results may not be exactly the same, but the flavor of the process and the chart will be similar.

CHAPTER
10

Putting It All Together:
A Wholistic Approach

e have discussed many issues on tuning the Oracle8 database. In this chapter, we will put it all together. To have a healthy Oracle environment, you need to tend to all the issues we have discussed, using a planned, methodical approach. We call the discussions here a *wholistic approach.* When tuning Oracle, you must look at the whole picture, not just the usual three-tiered approach of memory, I/O, and important applications. Yes, the Big Three are the most important and they give the most noticeable results. Throughout this book, though, we have looked at many issues that require your attention during the tuning process; no stone can be left unturned.

When your complete tuning exercise is done, you will have touched on most aspects of your database that require day-to-day attention. Think of your database as one of your loved ones:

- It craves your attention when you neglect it.

- It sends you messages when there is something wrong with it.

- It refuses to cooperate when you ask it to do too much.

- It confuses you when you tend to one problem when another actually needs fixing.

- It gets you up at all hours of the night.

- It tells you one thing when it means another.

- It sends you mixed messages.

- It thrives on TLC (tender loving care).

VLDB
The bigger the database, the more potential for bigger problems (just like teenage children compared to toddlers!).

But above all, you must provide it with the resources that enable it to succeed on its own! We believe that tuning Oracle is a process applied to all components of the software. Providing a stable, dependable operating environment is fundamental to a regimen that minimizes database downtime and data loss potential. This is a database administrator's most important priority. A down database is not a tuned database. We will discuss mechanisms you can put in place to care for and protect your database in the following areas:

- *Backup* The process whereby you make copies of your data from your database at fixed time intervals. Backup protects you against the assortment of hardware, software, and user-based errors that may occur.

- *Recovery* The restoration of a backup of your database from a previous time period and rolling it forward using redo log files (roll forward is discussed in the "Tuning Database Recovery" section later in this chapter).

- *Error routines* DBA-defined mechanisms that you implement to alert you when predefined error situations happen with your database.

We will also discuss the following:

- Transaction control tuning features

- Efficient overall resource management

- Clusters and their potential performance gains

In other words, miscellaneous mechanisms make you and yours more aware of Oracle8 features that enable your installation to be a better manager and developer.

Let's get started by looking at the Oracle Connection Manager which, coupled with the multithreaded server on the Server side, allows connection pooling through the Net8 transport mechanism. The Oracle Connection Manager makes a contribution to the discussions in the journey we affectionately call *Oracle8 Tuning*.

Oracle Connection Manager

The Oracle Connection Manager is a feature of Net8 that allows you to set up a pool of network connections and have them shared among client connections as they require resources on the server. The heart of Oracle Connection Manager (*OCM*) is multiplexing, where more than one session becomes a single logical connection using the same network transport. Readers familiar with the multithreaded server (*MTS*) will hear a lot of jargon and concepts similar to MTS when looking at using OCM, which intercepts requests for network services and routes them through a single channel.

WHOLISTIC RULE #1

Oracle Connection Manager communicates on the server end with a multithreaded server. If you are not running MTS on your host, connection pooling using OCM is not available.

Enabling Multiplexing

The multiplexing capability can be enabled by an OCM when a number of sessions are trying to communicate with the same multithreaded server and all the connection requests are initiated through the same OCM. The best analogy is to think of the requests as being at the top of a funnel, with the single physical connection at the bottom through which all the client requests pass. OCM maintains a logical connection to the server even when sessions are not requesting any services.

Additional Security Layer

You can introduce another layer of security using OCM since you can specify what hosts can be reached from what clients. Using OCM, you can specify a hostname or IP address of servers deemed to be reachable; an IP address is a four-part identification of servers and clients on a network. When you hear addresses such as "one three nine dot twelve dot one zero nine dot two," people are using these addresses.

WHOLISTIC RULE #2

If not already implemented, speak with your network personnel to implement a facility to use names rather than IP addresses for your servers. This especially makes sense when setting up Net8 configuration files.

In addition, destination databases can be specified to enable OCM access to some target instances and restrict access to others.

Multi Protocol Support

Using OCM, it can be easier to roll out a wide corporate network with clients communicating with servers using different protocols. OCM takes care of protocol translation, such that clients could communicate with OCM using the SPX protocol, and OCM could communicate with the server using TCP/IP.

Configuring Oracle Connection Manager

Since the dawn of SQL*Net version 2 with Oracle7, we have been working with a handful of network configuration files terminating with the file extension ".ORA". OCM is configured with its own settings, stored in CMAN.ORA. The starting point to ensuring connections are funneled through OCM is to place the following line in your SQLNET.ORA file:

```
user_cman = true
```

There are three main sections to the CMN.ORA file, details of which are available in the appropriate piece of Net8 documentation:

1. CMAN specification is where you define the listening addresses for Oracle Connection Manager.

2. CMAN_PROFILE is where you set parameters that control the environment under which OCM operates. You may control features such as the level of logging and tracing as well as the desired authentication level.

3. CMAN_RULES is where you define your network access security rules by specifying source addresses (src=), host addresses (dst=), target database identifiers (srv=), and action to follow (act=) in a rules list.

WHOLISTIC RULE #3
*When looking at access restrictions in a rules
list using CMAN_RULES, use the address
wildcard character "x" with the src= and dst=
parameters whenever possible. Totally
hard-coded IP addresses make the
maintenance of CMAN.ORA more difficult
and the contents of the configuration file
more cryptic.*

VLDB
*Oracle Connection Manager makes extra
sense with VLDBs since they usually conjure
up visions of many hundreds of users.*

A Fine Time for This

PL/SQL offers you the time to a hundredth of a second using the GET_TIME
function in the DBMS_UTILITY package. The function is designed to give
you two numbers on successive calls to GET_TIME as shown in the
following listing.

```
set echo off pages 0 feed off
var a number
var b number
begin
  :a := dbms_utility.get_time;
end;
/
   . . .
   . . .
   . . .
-- The code goes in here for the activity to be timed.
   . . .
   . . .
   . . .
begin
  :b := dbms_utility.get_time;
end;
```

```
/
print a
print b
```

The results from the two print statements at the end of the listing indicate that :a holds the value 4317050 and :b the value 4317107. By finding the difference between the two numbers, you get the elapsed time in hundredths of a second, as in the following calculation.

```
elapsed time = :b - :a
             = (4317107 - 4317050) / 100 = .57 seconds
```

Two words come to mind when we see stuff like this—way too cool!

Who Said It Can't Be Done in PL/SQL?

Oracle8 has rolled even more functionality into PL/SQL to permit transaction and session control. In this section, we bring it all together and highlight some useful procedures in a few packages created by RDBMS80\ADMIN\DBMSUTIL.SQL.

Pointing a Transaction at a Rollback Segment

The USE_ROLLBACK_SEGMENT procedure in DBMS_TRANSACTION is shown in the next listing.

```
PROCEDURE USE_ROLLBACK_SEGMENT
 Argument Name          Type          In/Out          Default?
 -------------          ----          ------          --------
 RB_NAME                VARCHAR2      IN
```

This procedure is the equivalent of **set transaction use rollback segment** we know in SQL*Plus. The name of the rollback segment is enclosed in single quotes as in

```
SQL> execute dbms_transaction.use_rollback_segment ('MONSTER');
```

The same two errors can be raised from this procedure that plague you in SQL*Plus.

1. Trying to point the transaction at a rollback segment that does not exist is shown in the first listing

```
SQL> execute dbms_transaction.use_rollback_segment ('RR');
begin dbms_transaction.use_rollback_segment ('RR'); end;
*
ERROR at line 1:
ORA-01534: rollback segment 'RR' doesn't exist
ORA-06512: at "SYS.DBMS_TRANSACTION", line 65
ORA-06512: at line 1
begin dbms_transaction.use_rollback_segment ('RR'); end;
SQL>
```

2. The call to the procedure must be the first activity in a transaction, or you will receive the following error:

```
SQL> execute dbms_transaction.use_rollback_segment ('SYSTEM');
begin dbms_transaction.use_rollback_segment ('SYSTEM'); end;
*
ERROR at line 1:
ORA-01453: SET TRANSACTION must be first statement of transaction
ORA-06512: at "SYS.DBMS_TRANSACTION", line 65
ORA-06512: at line 1
SQL>
```

WHOLISTIC RULE #4
Unlike the **set transaction use rollback segment** *statement in SQL*Plus, if the USE_ROLLBACK_SEGMENT procedure returns an error, the PL/SQL block terminates at once; it does not report the error and then go on to the next line of code.*

To illustrate this rule, the next listing shows the behavior of **set transaction use rollback segment** in SQL*Plus.

VLDB
This procedure proves especially useful when cleansing or aggregating large data sets in a data warehouse.

```
SQL> update finance
  2      set amt_owing = null
  3    where fin_id = 88771;
1 row updated.
SQL> set transaction use rollback segment fin_rb;
set transaction use rollback segment fin_rb
*
ERROR at line 1:
ORA-01453: SET TRANSACTION must be first statement of transaction
SQL> update finance
  2      set amt_owing = null
  3    where fin_id = 88771;
1 row updated.
```

VLDB
*Routines in the data warehouse that populate tables from other Oracle objects are prime candidates to be prefixed by a **set transaction use rollback segment** statement.*

Session Control

There are a few DBMS_SESSION package components we find interesting and useful. They are shown in the next listing, part of a describe on DBMS_SESSION.

```
PROCEDURE SET_NLS
 Argument Name                    Type                    In/Out Default?
 ------------------------------   ----------------------  ------ --------
 PARAM                            VARCHAR2                IN/OUT
 VALUE                            VARCHAR2                IN/OUT
PROCEDURE SET_ROLE
 Argument Name                    Type                    In/Out Default?
 ------------------------------   ----------------------  ------ --------
 ROLE_CMD                         VARCHAR2                IN/OUT
PROCEDURE SET_SQL_TRACE
 Argument Name                    Type                    In/Out Default?
 ------------------------------   ----------------------  ------ --------
 SQL_TRACE                        BOOLEAN                 IN/OUT
```

Set an NLS Parameter

NLS (National Language Support) is an issue with the proliferation of multilingual systems. The SQL*Plus **alter session** command can be used to alter some NLS parameters at the session level. The SET_NLS procedure in DBMS_SESSION allows this to be done in PL/SQL as shown in the next listing.

```
SQL> begin
  2    dbms_session.set_nls ('NLS_TERRITORY','FRANCE');
  3  end;
  4  /
PL/SQL procedure successfully completed.
```

```
SQL> select sysdate from dual;
SYSDATE
---------
06/09/97
```

```
SQL> begin
  2    dbms_session.set_nls ('NLS_TERRITORY','AMERICA');
  3  end;
  4  /
PL/SQL procedure successfully completed.
```

```
SQL> select sysdate from dual;
SYSDATE
---------
06-SEP-97
```

Note in the listing that the value for NLS_TERRITORY affects the default display for the sysdate system variable—when FRANCE it shows 06/09/97 and when AMERICA it shows the familiar 06-SEP-97.

WHOLISTIC RULE #5

The session altering statement in a PL/SQL block remains in effect for the entire session or until another such statement is encountered. The change made by SET_NLS does not disappear when its PL/SQL block terminates.

Set a Role

To accomplish this task, you invoke the SET_ROLE procedure in DBMS_SESSION somewhere within a PL/SQL block. This is illustrated in the following listing.

```
SQL> begin
  2    dbms_session.set_role ('DBTECH');
  3  end;
  4  /
PL/SQL procedure successfully completed.
```

Roles that are password-protected can not be enabled using this procedure in PL/SQL; you must use the standard **set role {role} identified by {password};** in SQL*Plus. Naturally, the role you are enabling must be in the realm of existing roles that have been granted, or you will get the following error:

```
begin dbms_session.set_role ('DBTEC'); end;
*
ERROR at line 1:
ORA-01919: role 'DBTEC' does not exist
ORA-06512: at "SYS.DBMS_SESSION", line 26
ORA-06512: at line 1
```

Set SQL_TRACE

The SET_SQL_TRACE procedure accepts the argument TRUE or FALSE and turns SQL tracing on or off as need be. You may find this quite useful when working with large packages or procedures. When they grow to a few thousand lines of code, you may need to zero in on what's going on in one spot. The procedure turns tracing on and off as shown next.

```
SQL> begin
  2    dbms_session.set_sql_trace (true);
  3  end;
  4  /
PL/SQL procedure successfully completed.
SQL> begin
  2    dbms_session.set_sql_trace (false);
  3  end;
  4  /
PL/SQL procedure successfully completed.
```

Verifying Integrity of Database Files

We recommend running a database file verify routine weekly to check the integrity of your database. The names of the files can be obtained from DBA_DATA_FILES; run the program shown in the following listing to build a batch file to scan the whole database at once.

NOTE

The verification utility expects the Oracle block size to be 2K (2,048 bytes); if your block size is different, pass the parameter **blocksize={block size in bytes}** *on the command line to avoid an error.*

```
SQL> select 'dbverf80 '||file_name
  2    from sys.dba_data_files;
dbverf c:\orant\database\sys1orcl.ora
dbverf c:\orant\database\rbs1orcl.ora
dbverf c:\orant\database\usr1orcl.ora
dbverf c:\orant\database\tmp1orcl.ora
SQL>
```

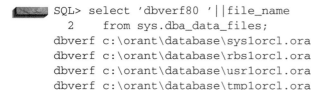

NOTE

The name of the verification utility may differ on your operating system.

When the output is passed to Oracle8 for processing, the output resembles that shown in the next listing—interesting how the system date says "Lu" for the day of the week since the client's NLS_LANG is set to display French text.

```
C:\ORANT\DATABASE> dbverf80 sys1orcl.ora
DBVERIFY: Release 8.0.3.0.0 - Production on Lu Sep 8 9:0:16 1999
(c) Copyright 1997 Oracle Corporation.  All rights reserved.
DBVERIFY - Verification starting : FILE = sys1orcl.ora
DBVERIFY - Verification complete
Total Pages Examined        : 30720
Total Pages Processed (Data) : 18315
```

```
Total Pages Failing    (Data) : 0
Total Pages Processed (Index): 6784
Total Pages Failing    (Index): 0
Total Pages Empty             : 0
Total Pages Marked Corrupt    : 0
Total Pages Influx            : 0

C:\ORANT\DATABASE> dbverf80 rbs1orcl.ora
DBVERIFY: Release 8.0.3.0.0 - Production on Lu Sep 8 9:0:46 1999
(c) Copyright 1997 Oracle Corporation.  All rights reserved.
DBVERIFY - Verification starting : FILE = rbs1orcl.ora
DBVERIFY - Verification complete
Total Pages Examined          : 10240
Total Pages Processed (Data) : 0
Total Pages Failing    (Data) : 0
Total Pages Processed (Index): 0
Total Pages Failing    (Index): 0
Total Pages Empty             : 0
Total Pages Marked Corrupt    : 0
Total Pages Influx            : 0

C:\ORANT\DATABASE> dbverf80 usr1orcl.ora
DBVERIFY: Release 8.0.3.0.0 - Production on Lu Sep 8 8:35:4 1997
(c) Copyright 1997 Oracle Corporation.  All rights reserved.
DBVERIFY - Verification starting : FILE = usr1orcl.ora
DBVERIFY - Verification complete
Total Pages Examined          : 1536
Total Pages Processed (Data) : 100
Total Pages Failing    (Data) : 0
Total Pages Processed (Index): 140
Total Pages Failing    (Index): 0
Total Pages Empty             : 0
Total Pages Marked Corrupt    : 0
Total Pages Influx            : 0
C:\ORANT\DATABASE>
```

The three readouts for Total Pages Failing (Data), Total Pages Failing (Index), and Total Pages Marked Corrupt are the ones that indicate a problem. If all is well with the database files examined, all these values should be zero. If any database files fail verification, you need to:

1. Look in the instance alert file for any ORA-00600 errors that may have been reported over the past week. If any are found, contact

WorldWide Support at Oracle for assistance armed with anywhere from one to six arguments that follow the raising of the error.

2. Either roll the database forward from the last image backup, and reverify the offending file or rebuild the offending database file and reinstantiate the data that it contained from a recent export.

3. If the offending datafile contains only indexes, drop the indexes, re-create the database file, and then re-create the indexes.

We are fond of the dbverf80 command since, in pre-release 7.3 days when it did not exist, the only way to scan the whole database, start to finish, was using export.

WHOLISTIC RULE #6
Run dbverf80 on your entire database at least once a week and e-mail the output somewhere to one or more DBAs to check for any problems with the database files.

VLDB
Due to the sheer size and number of files that hold data in a VLDB, you may consider cycling a test of database files such that all files get tested over a five-day cycle.

Resources on the World Wide Web

Let's have a whirlwind tour around some of our favorite Internet sites which we think are the most useful. There are so many places to go on the Internet to rub shoulders with professionals working with exactly the same software as you. Many organizations run discussion areas where you can ask questions and respond to requests for help from other users. Figure 10-1 is the first place to start—the newsgroups.

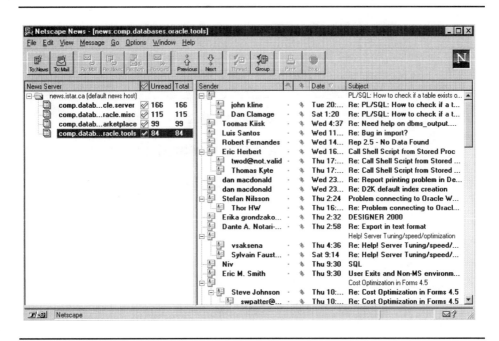

FIGURE 10-1.   *Oracle related newsgroups*

The interesting thing about these newsgroups is they are part of what we call your alternate support network. Often, questions that seem to take forever to get answered using other more conventional media are answered in real time on one of these newsgroups.

Figure 10-2 shows the Oracle User Forum and Fan Club, identified by **www.orafans.com**. The discussion groups are just off the Fan Club's home page. Notice the way the topics blend so nicely into the types of questions most users are looking for help with.

The International Oracle Users Group-Americas (IOUG-A), identified by triple-dub **ioug.org**, is a place for one-stop shopping for software, user groups, Oracle-related technical events, and membership information. Figure 10-3 shows a list of Oracle Links selected from the ORACLE RESOURCES pick list that offers choices like Oracle8 and IOUG-Alive (a yearly event sponsored by the IOUG-A on behalf of the Oracle user community).

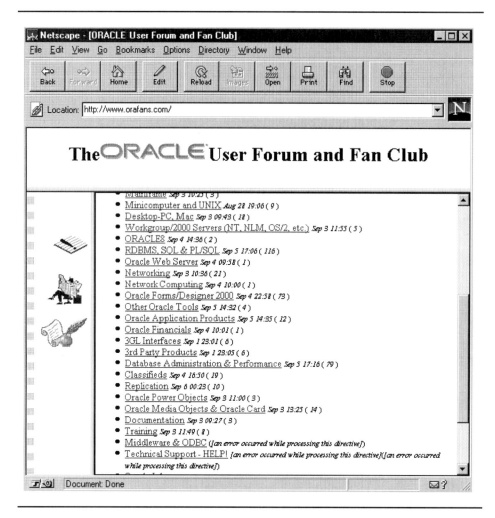

FIGURE 10-2. *www.orafans.com Discussion Groups*

Clicking the Oracle FTP Site off the IOUG-A links page takes you to the
FTP site shown in Figure 10-4. If you are interested in some of the 60-day
trial software available from Oracle, this FTP site may provide you with
what you are looking for.

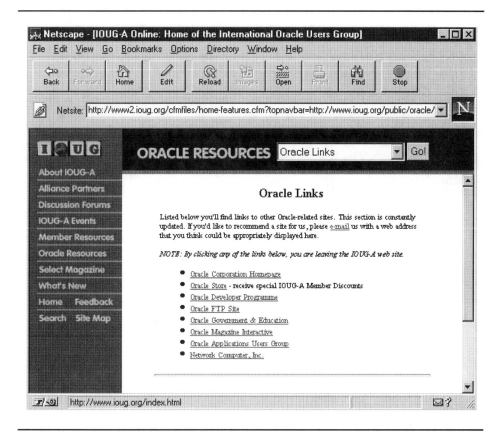

FIGURE 10-3. *www.ioug.org Oracle Links*

Oracle's corporate site (**www.oracle.com**), as well as most of their subsidiaries around the globe, maintains a support-related Web site. Some of their electronic support is carried on via these locations on the Internet. Many of you should be able to get access to the support call database from where you receive technical support; you will need a valid customer reference number to be allowed to browse this database. Speak to Oracle Corporation directly to view information in many of the Web-based support forums. The support page off the Oracle corporate Web page is shown in Figure 10-5.

FIGURE 10-4. *Oracle FTP site*

The Oracle Magazine Code Depot, shown in Figure 10-6, offers a wealth of code that you may find useful. This code depot is brought to you by Oracle Press, the people that bring you books like *Oracle8 Tuning*; it's a cooperative effort supported by people at Oracle.

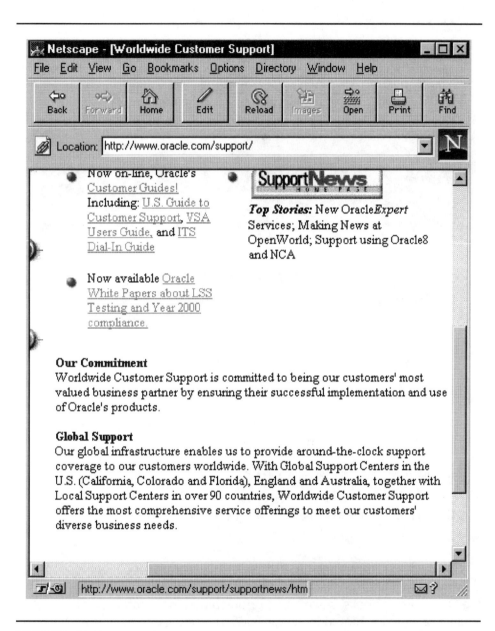

FIGURE 10-5. *Oracle corporate support page*

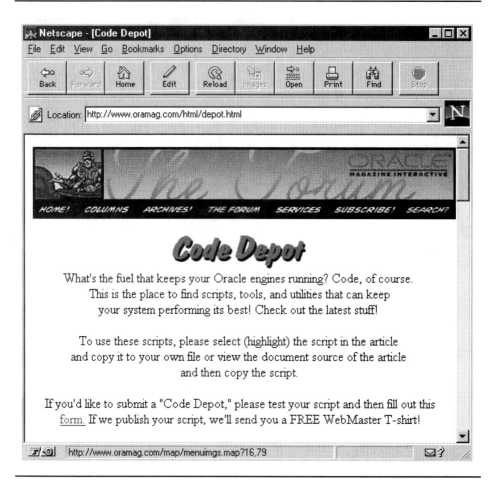

FIGURE 10-6. *Oracle Magazine Code Depot site*

Speaking of Oracle Press, many readers regularly visit the code download area at Osborne/McGraw-Hill. Code from almost all of the Oracle Press books is available for download in this area, a sample of which is shown in Figure 10-7. The best place to start is Osborne/McGraw-Hill's home page: **www.osborne.com**.

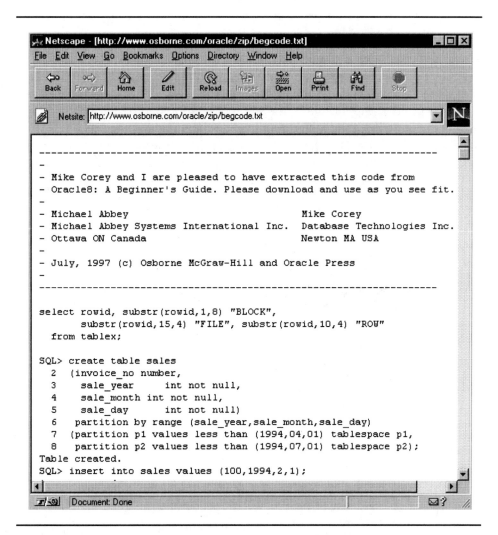

FIGURE 10-7.   Oracle8: A Beginner's Guide *code download page*

The Standby Database Facility

DBAs and other technocrats have often wondered why they couldn't have an exact replica of their production database on standby for times when something went wrong with the day-to-day environment. Using Oracle8's standby database facility, you can maintain an exact copy of your production database and have all transactions propagated to that standby site. On a moment's notice, the standby site can be switched to the primary site and business can carry on almost uninterrupted. The theory behind this facility is pretty straightforward; the implementation can be wrought with pitfalls if you do not follow the instructions in the *Oracle8 Server Backup and Recovery Guide.* Let's have a condensed look at what's involved in creating and maintaining a standby database.

Creating the Standby Database

There are two steps involved in creating the standby database. The first step is to create the control file for the alternate site using the command shown in the next listing. You must create the control file using this special syntax, which allows the standby site to be brought up in the required mode.

```
SVRMGR> alter database create standby controlfile 'prd_stby.ctl';
Statement processed.
SVRMGR>
```

The next step ensures consistency between the control file backup just created, the copy of the database files about to be written, and the current redo logs. This is shown next.

```
SVRMGR> alter system archive log current;
Statement processed.
SVRMGR>
```

Oracle suggests you can back up the production database open or closed when preparing the copy for the alternate site. The following listing shows an SQL script that can be run to create a batch file to copy the production database files and redo logs to a backup area on a Windows NT server.

```
SQL> select 'copy '||file_name||' d:\prodbkp\copy'
  2     from sys.dba_data_files
  3  union
  4  select 'copy '||member||' d:\prodbkp\copy'
  5     from v$logfile;
```

```
copy C:\ORANT\DATABASE\RBS1ORCL.ORA d:\prodbkp\copy
copy C:\ORANT\DATABASE\USR1ORCL.ORA d:\prodbkp\copy
copy C:\ORANT\DATABASE\TMP1ORCL.ORA d:\prodbkp\copy
copy C:\ORANT\DATABASE\SYS1ORCL.ORA d:\prodbkp\copy
copy C:\ORANT\DATABASE\LOG1ORCL.ORA d:\prodbkp\copy
copy C:\ORANT\DATABASE\LOG2ORCL.ORA d:\prodbkp\copy
SQL>
```

WHOLISTIC RULE #7
*When preparing a copy of the production
database for copying to the standby site, back
up the primary site while Oracle is down. The
consistency of the primary site is guaranteed if
you write an offline backup.*

Bringing Up the Standby Database

After the backup of the control file, the copy of the production database,
and any online archived redo logs are restored to their proper location, it is
time to enliven the standby database. Enlivening the standby database is
accomplished in Server Manager using the following commands.

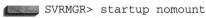

```
SVRMGR> startup nomount
ORACLE instance started.
Total System Global Area        12071016 bytes
Fixed Size                         46136 bytes
Variable Size                   11090992 bytes
Database Buffers                  409600 bytes
Redo Buffers                      524288 bytes
SVRMGR> alter database mount standby database exclusive;
Statement processed.
SVRMGR> recover standby database;
```

At this point, the standby database has been placed in total recovery
mode. It is your responsibility to manually copy archived redo logs from the
primary production site to the standby database archive destination for the
automatic recovery process on that site. You can only apply redo logs that
have been archived at the primary site against the standby database.

Name Differences Between the Two Sites

We recommend trying to keep the file names, including their directories, the same between the two sites. However, sometimes this is not possible. Name differences can be a problem, since the archived redo logs from the primary site use that site's file names for its redo logs. For example, the SYSTEM tablespace on the primary site sits in the file called H:\DATABASE\PRD\SYSTEM1.ORA, and the same name is not used on the standby site. Two parameters—DB_FILE_NAME_CONVERT and LOG_FILE_NAME_CONVERT are placed in the standby initialization parameter file to deal with name changes. Suppose these two parameters were set as shown next.

```
db_file_name_convert = "H:\DATABASE\PRD", "F:\STANDBY\DBFILE"
log_file_name_convert = "J:\REDO\PRD" , "K:\STANDBY\REDO"
```

Standby database file names are constructed by scanning file names from the primary site and, if a match is found, replacing the characters in the first string with those in the second. Thus, the SYSTEM tablespace name coming from the primary site will be converted to F:\STANDBY\DBFILE\SYSTEM1.ORA and a redo log called J:\REDO\PRD\LOG1.RDO on the primary site would become K:\STANDBY\REDO\LOG1.RDO at the standby site.

WHOLISTIC RULE #8
When planning file names for a production database that will be a primary site for a standby database, plan the file names carefully so these two initialization parameter file entries can convert database file and redo log file members on the standby site.

Activating Your Standby Database

Even though we might hope that we will never need to activate the standby database in a real life disaster, you should become familiar with this task to be prepared. Activating the standby site makes it your "new" production database at which point the "old" production database is gone. Before activating your standby database, if possible, archive any online redo logs from the soon-to-be ex-production database. After these log files are transferred to the standby database site, it is very possible that NO transactions will be lost!

The command to activate your standby database is shown next. The completion of the command dismounts the database, at which point you should back it up, then restart.

```
SVRMGR> alter database activate standby database;
Database altered.
SVRMGR>
```

NOTE
If there are any unarchived online redo logs at the old production site, they are incompatible with the new production database after the standby database is activated.

In closing, we are going to highlight a few initialization parameter file entries and database creation parameters and their relationship between the production and standby databases.

Production and Standby Parameter Synching

The following three issues come up when looking at the similarities between the two databases that play a role in this standby database magic.

- COMPATIBLE This entry must be the same in both the primary and the standby site.

- MAXDATAFILES Must be the same at both sites as well. This parameter has an effect on the size of the control file and also controls the maximum number of datafiles the instance may acquire.

- CONTROL_FILES These files must be different between the primary and standby site.

Tuning Database Backups

Tuning database backups is one of the ongoing responsibilities of the DBA. You need to create and maintain adequate system backup procedures to ensure a minimum of data loss when problems occur. Backup routines use a combination of Oracle utilities and operating system programs. Sufficient attention to detail in this area will have enormous payoffs if and when something goes wrong. Backup procedures need to include a tested recovery plan.

WHOLISTIC RULE #9
A tested recovery plan is very important; you do not have a valid backup procedure unless your well laid plans have been tested.

This means you actually run a fire drill and make sure you can restore the data. Yes, we mean you. If you're the DBA, then earn your pay. You should personally make sure the backup works. Even if it means getting up at 2:00 A.M. and watching an operator mount the tapes. Yes, we did say 2:00 A.M.—if that's the only time you can do a fire drill, then do it. Experience has taught us that a backup will never work until it has been tested.

Very Important Story, So Pay Attention!

To quote the late great Frank Zappa—"It can't happen here, Suzie Creamcheese." Guess what? It can and will! A few years ago, one of us was doing work for one of the largest banks in New England. We were working on a very large Oracle database. In fact, it was one of the largest databases in North America at the time. We know this because we were working with one of the kernel developers at Oracle on some database contention issues. Video Lad, as this kernel developer is now known, made the comment that it was one of the largest databases he had ever heard of. (Great question for a game of *Jeoracledy*: "What Oracle employee's nickname is Video Lad? Clue: It's on his business card. To get this answer, come to an Oracle user group conference and send us an e-mail or look us up at the presentation, and we will be happy to answer the question.)

To back this very large database (or *VLDB*) up in a timely manner, we were required to use a new high capacity/high speed tape drive system. As a few of the senior database consultants on duty, we wanted to develop and fire drill the new backup procedures. We also wanted to implement a secondary backup system using the Oracle export utility. Even though the database was so huge, we felt we could develop a viable nightly export. (We have taken a mature backup approach to the nth degree—we recommend that all customers develop a *triad backup scheme* consisting of cold backups [weekly or so], hot backups [daily], and export [daily].) In this case, the customer, in their infinite wisdom, decided to ignore our advice. Testing the fire drill was unnecessary. Management felt this was just a way to raise consulting fees and it was an unbudgeted item besides. We felt very strongly that not doing a fire drill was a very big mistake. We felt so strongly, we created a nightly export routine on our own time and implemented it.

A long weekend came up and I decided to take my family camping. I prefer camping as a vacation, since the computer terminal does not easily come with me. On my way out the door, I told the customer how to get hold of me if they needed me. That night, I was sitting by the fire roasting some marshmallows, when the owner of the campground came over. He had received a panic call for me. I got to the nearest phone and talked to the bank's lead DBA.

The DBA explained to me that the database was lost. When the systems group tried to restore off the new tape system, all attempts had failed. He asked if I had any pearls of wisdom. I explained that I had created a quick and dirty export of all but the biggest tables within the database. After some additional thinking, we were able to develop a plan to get back 90 percent of the database. The many months of the team's development effort were saved. The moral of this story—a backup is not valid till you take the time to fire drill it, as explained in Wholistic Rule #5.

As we stated at first, tuning database backups is one of the ongoing responsibilities of the DBA. You need to create and maintain adequate system backup procedures to ensure a minimum of data loss when problems occur. The optimal backup routines include the following two components. Tuning suggestions are included with each step.

- ■ The export and import utilities (see the following section) help protect against loss of the most granular of Oracle segments: the single table (segment types are discussed in Chapter 3).

■ Online backups (discussed in the "Tuning Online Backups" section) permit uninterrupted access and allow programs to run during the precious off-hours.

Tuning Export and Import

Export is a utility that creates an operating system file with a copy of specified data. This file is usually referred to as the *dmp* (pronounced "dump"). Import reads files created by export and brings data into the database. *Oracle8: A Beginner's Guide* (Abbey & Corey, Oracle Press, 1997), as well as many other technical works, covers the export and import utilities in detail.

NOTE
*The discussions in this section are based on the **imp80** and **exp80** utilities run from a DOS for Windows NT window. One also can run export and import from the Oracle Enterprise Manager (OEM)/Data Manager interface. The same theory applies to work done in OEM.*

You incorporate these utilities into your backup procedures to permit object recovery. It is your job to educate your developers on the use of this utility. Some of the suggested parameter values affect the speed of export and import. Some of the other suggested parameter values will assist you in ensuring that they both run their work to completion. The parameters that affect export performance are listed in Table 10-1; the parameters that affect import performance are listed in Table 10-2.

Tables 10-1 and 10-2 both list the **log** parameter. Most error situations are going to be raised during import rather than export. Nothing is more frustrating than receiving the message "Import terminated with warnings" without having a log file to inspect. The **parfile** parameter in both tables can be used when either utility is run in the foreground or background.

Parameter	Meaning	Tuning
buffer	The size of the chunk of memory in which data is assembled before it's written to the export file—asking for a few megabytes is a good place to start.	Use a large number to speed up the process—Oracle, in most cases, will grab as much memory as it can up to the number specified. Sometimes Oracle8 export errors out when it cannot find the requested amount, so watch the screen.
indexes	Controls whether the **index create** statements are written to the export file.	When you already have SQL scripts that define your indexes, do not export the index definitions because, unless you remember to place the parameter **indexes=n** in the call to import, the import will re-create the indexes.
log	Causes Oracle to write the screen I/O from the export session to a disk file.	When things go wrong, you need the screen I/O saved to a file to browse and see what went wrong.
parfile	Name of the file that contains the parameters for the export session.	Run export in the background using this keyword—it frees up your terminal to do other things at the same time.
direct	Instructs export to do a "fast write" of the data to the export file by bypassing some conventional buffering mechanisms.	Export runs between 20 percent and 40 percent faster. Your results may vary.

TABLE 10-1.   *Parameters Affecting Export Performance*

Parameter	Meaning	Tuning
analyze	Controls whether Oracle runs the **analyze** statement on objects after they have been created.	Set **analyze=n** and manually collect statistics on the objects after the import terminates.
parfile	Name of the file that contains the parameters for the import session.	Run import in the background using this keyword—it frees up your terminal to do other things at the same time.
buffer	See Table 10-1.	
commit	Controls whether Oracle issues a **commit** statement at timed intervals while inserting rows into a table.	Set **commit=y** when importing large tables or doing a full database import. Commit actually slows down the import but, since there is more likelihood that the session will run successfully, it is a way of tuning—the import will only be run once!
log	See Table 10-1.	

TABLE 10-2. *Parameters Affecting Import Performance*

As Table 10-1 suggests, setting the **indexes=n** means no index creation statements will be written to the dump file. When performing object recovery, you usually do not want to drop the object, because any grants (privileges given out to other database users) will be lost.

The optimal way to import an object is outlined in the following steps. This exercise assumes that a table called PLANT_DETAIL has been inadvertently dropped.

1. Restore a copy of the dump file from tape if it is no longer online.

2. Run import using the **indexfile** parameter to create a disk file with the **table** and **index create** statements (this will allow you to know whether enough space is free in the database to create the object).

3. Precreate the table and index(es).

4. Import the data, using **commit=y** on large objects (more than 10,000 rows), as suggested in Table 10-2.

WHOLISTIC RULE #10
Run export and import with a large buffer size.
Precreate tables before an import.

WHOLISTIC RULE #11
Use the Oracle utilities export and import to
help protect against data loss. As a DBA, you
can spend more of your time on a database
performance-tuning exercise when you have
reliable, tested backup systems in place.

Tuning Online Backups

When performing backups of the Oracle database (or any other vendors' databases), the database must be in a consistent state when the backup is written. An Oracle database is in a *consistent state* when all of the instance database files are online, accessible, and not damaged, and the time and date stamps in all of these files agree with those held in the instance control file(s). Prior to Oracle version 6, there was no mechanism in place to permit writing a consistent image of the database to tape while it was running. *Online backup* means backing up your database while it is open. Another way to think of an online backup is to call it a hot backup. In other words the database is hot with live activity. An open database can be accessed by users and, as these backups are running in the precious quiet hours, permits you to provide 24-hour access to your users.

Oracle introduced the concept of ARCHIVELOG with version 6 in 1988. When we mention running a version 6 or 7 Oracle8 database using ARCHIVELOG mode, we mean the following: ARCHIVELOG mode instructs Oracle to save a copy of each online redo log before it is reused. Think of the online redo log as a copy of every transaction that takes place in the database for a period of time. The saving of these copies and the archiving of the copies to tape (or some other secondary storage device) leads to the name given this facility: archiving. Turning on ARCHIVELOG is done using the following steps:

1. Shut down the database.

2. Edit the initialization parameter file and set LOG_ARCHIVE_START to TRUE and LOG_ARCHIVE_DEST and LOG_ARCHIVE_FORMAT to values as discussed in the *Oracle8 Server Administrator's Guide.*

3. Enter Server Manager, then log into Oracle as the SYS user (e.g., **connect internal**).

4. Start up the database with the mount option.

5. Issue the following statements:

```
SVRMGR> alter database archivelog;
Database altered.
SVRMGR> alter database open;
Statement processed.
```

When these steps are accomplished, you will have another background process supporting the database with the text "arch" embedded in its name. You will notice that the archived redo log files appear in the destination specified in your LOG_ARCHIVE_DEST. The name used for archived redo logs is a combination of the LOG_ARCHIVE_DEST and the LOG_ARCHIVE_FORMAT entries. Oracle takes these two parameters and builds a filename. For example, suppose LOG_ARCHIVE_DEST is set to

```
f:\orasys\prod\redo\arc\arch
```

and LOG_ARCHIVE_FORMAT is set to

```
_%s.prd
```

The percentages in the parameter instruct Oracle to put the log sequence number in the filename. Thus, log sequence number 1287 will end up written as the following:

```
f:\orasys\prod\redo\arc\arch_1287.prd
```

and will become an archived redo log.

You are now ready to perform online backups, which, as we mentioned before, involve making a copy of one or more of your database files while the database is open. It is a three-step process for each tablespace; the following steps use the tablespace PERSONNEL as an example:

1. Inform Oracle that the tablespace is being backed up (e.g., the tablespace is in backup mode) by issuing the following command:

```
SVRMGR> alter tablespace personnel begin backup;
Tablespace altered.
SVRMGR>
```

2. At the operating system, make a copy of the one or more datafiles that make up the PERSONNEL tablespace.

3. Inform Oracle that the tablespace backup is complete (e.g., the tablespace is out of backup mode) by issuing the following command:

```
SVRMGR> alter tablespace personnel end backup;
Tablespace altered.
SVRMGR>
```

NOTE
If you neglect to do steps 1 and 3, step 2 will still work, but the copy you made of the datafile(s) will not be usable for recovery, as discussed in the following section.

NOTE
If any tablespace is still marked as being in backup mode, you will not be able to shut down your database.

WHOLISTIC RULE #12
*Do online backups of all or part of your
database when running in ARCHIVELOG
mode. Do the backup one tablespace at a time
in order to reduce the overhead. This will
minimize the impact on your online systems.*

WHOLISTIC RULE #13
*Ensure that your control file is part of an
online backup. Copy it to the same destination
as your archived redo logs at the end of your
tablespace backup.*

The drain on system resources during an online backup is small with a
well-tuned database. However, every contributor to requests on system
resources must be taken into account using our wholistic approach.

NOTE
*Oracle needs at least two single-membered
redo log groups to run. Oracle writes
information about transactions performed on
the database to the online redo logs, and it
uses the redo log groups in a cyclical fashion:
it writes to one redo log group and, when the
redo log files in that group are full, it switches
to the other group.*

Tuning Database Recovery

There are two types of recovery when running an Oracle instance.
Every time an Oracle instance is started, automatic instance recovery
is performed. Instance recovery protects you from events that caused
the database to unexpectedly stop, for example, a power failure or an
unexpected reboot of the hardware without a shutdown of the database.
With instance recovery, nothing is broken.

When the need arises and your database is in ARCHIVELOG mode, you can also perform media recovery to rebuild a component of your database (e.g., a missing data file or rollback segment) from an image backup. To recover from instance failure and media failure is a three-step process:

1. Rolling forward applies transactions recorded in the redo logs to recover data that may not have been written to the database.

2. Rolling back undoes transactions that had been rolled back by users or by Oracle.

3. Resources are freed up that had been in use during active user sessions.

Oracle refers to the term "media failure" during discussions of recovery. *Media failure* involves an assortment of hardware problems, such as a disk failure or damage to a read/write head on a disk drive.

WHOLISTIC RULE #14
Run your database in ARCHIVELOG mode.
This allows protection against a wide range of
problems with hardware and user error. It
helps minimize instance downtime.

Tuning of the recovery process emphasizes our theme that a down database is not a tuned database. The recovery speed is a function of the speed of your disk drives coupled with the amount of transaction data in the redo logs to be applied. Recovery reads redo log files and applies their changes to the database restored from your image backup. To help speed up the process, try to keep 48 hours of archived redo log files on line, e.g., those written for the full two days prior to the current day. Also keep as much of the image backup online as possible. The most time-consuming part of the recovery exercise is reading massive amounts of data from tape.

You can perform recovery on the whole database, one or more tablespaces, or one or more datafiles that make up a tablespace. The options available and the interactive routines used to perform recovery are the subject of a chapter in the *Oracle8 Server Administrator's Guide*, and the manuals discuss what to do when parts of your database configuration are damaged.

WHOLISTIC RULE #15
Make an operating system text copy of your control file using the alter database backup controlfile to trace statement. Incorporate this into your backup routines.

WHOLISTIC RULE #16
A recovery procedure is only good if TESTED! Run a number of mock recovery situations when first putting recovery mechanisms into place. The documentation explains recovery and what-to-do-when very well, but there could be some surprises when recovering from a real-life disaster.

We admit: we have been nattering on and on about backups! At this point, you probably see the importance we give to adequate backup procedures. Let's move on to deciphering the new Oracle8 extended ROWID format.

Understanding the Extended ROWID

Just when we were so proud of ourselves by figuring out the meaning of the Oracle ROWID, it's been changed. In one of our previous works, *Oracle8: A Beginner's Guide*, we spoke of the BARF convention for the ROWID— *Block Address Row File*. Oracle8 comes with a number of stored objects that can help translate the extended ROWID into meaningful numbers along the lines of what we have become used to.

WHOLISTIC RULE #17
*Become familiar with the conversion routines
Oracle8 provides. Understanding the ROWID
components assists the tuning process by
knowing where rows are stored in
nonpartitioned tables.*

We are not suggesting you do not need to know where rows are stored
in partitioned objects, but the information is readily and easily available by
looking at the partition keys and the column values in each row placed in
the table. We discuss row placement in the "In Which Partition Do I Belong"
section of Chapter 4. SYS's DBMS_ROWID package can be used to get the
information on the extended ROWID. The ROWID_INFO procedure is
shown in the next listing.

```
PROCEDURE ROWID_INFO
  Argument Name                    Type                      In/Out Default?
  ------------------------------   ----------------------    ------ --------
  ROWID_IN                         ROWID                     IN/OUT
  ROWID_TYPE                       NUMBER                    IN/OUT
  OBJECT_NUMBER                    NUMBER                    IN/OUT
  RELATIVE_FNO                     NUMBER                    IN/OUT
  BLOCK_NUMBER                     NUMBER                    IN/OUT
  ROW_NUMBER                       NUMBER                    IN/OUT
```

Note how the procedure takes six arguments and, whether invoked from
SQL*Plus or PL/SQL, there must be placeholders passed for the last five
arguments with the ROWID passed in as the first. Let's look at some
PL/SQL that will accomplish this for us.

```
set serveroutput on size 1000000
set echo on
begin
  declare
    cursor get_data is
      select rowid
        from finance
       where rownum < 41;
    rid    rowid;
    p2     number;
```

```
        p3      number;
        p4      number;
        p5      number;
        p6      number;
    begin
      open get_data;
      fetch get_data into rid;
      while get_data%found loop
          dbms_rowid.rowid_info (rid,p2,p3,p4,p5,p6);
          dbms_output.put_line ('ROWID is '||
                                    lpad(p5,4,0)||'.'||
                                    lpad(p6,4,0)||'.'||
                                    lpad(p4,4,0));
          fetch get_data into rid;
      end loop;
    end;
end;
/
```

Now let's look at the output from the code, showing the first ten lines, then jumping to where the block number changes.

```
ROWID is AAAAASAABAAAACoAAA or 0168.0000.0001
ROWID is AAAAASAABAAAACoAAB or 0168.0001.0001
ROWID is AAAAASAABAAAACoAAC or 0168.0002.0001
ROWID is AAAAASAABAAAACoAAD or 0168.0003.0001
ROWID is AAAAASAABAAAACoAAE or 0168.0004.0001
ROWID is AAAAASAABAAAACoAAF or 0168.0005.0001
ROWID is AAAAASAABAAAACoAAG or 0168.0006.0001
ROWID is AAAAASAABAAAACoAAH or 0168.0007.0001
ROWID is AAAAASAABAAAACoAAI or 0168.0008.0001
ROWID is AAAAASAABAAAACoAAJ or 0168.0009.0001
...
...
ROWID is AAAAASAABAAAACoAAc or 0168.0028.0001
ROWID is AAAAASAABAAAACoAAd or 0168.0029.0001
ROWID is AAAAASAABAAAACpAAA or 0169.0000.0001
ROWID is AAAAASAABAAAACpAAB or 0169.0001.0001
ROWID is AAAAASAABAAAACpAAC or 0169.0002.0001
ROWID is AAAAASAABAAAACpAAD or 0169.0003.0001
ROWID is AAAAASAABAAAACpAAE or 0169.0004.0001
ROWID is AAAAASAABAAAACpAAF or 0169.0005.0001
ROWID is AAAAASAABAAAACpAAG or 0169.0006.0001
ROWID is AAAAASAABAAAACpAAH or 0169.0007.0001
ROWID is AAAAASAABAAAACpAAI or 0169.0008.0001
ROWID is AAAAASAABAAAACpAAJ or 0169.0009.0001
```

ROWID_INFO to the Max

Armed with our newfound knowledge, let's look at building on the ROWID_INFO procedure. First, we create a function that accepts a ROWID and returns it in nnnn.nnnn.nnnn format as shown in the previous listing.

```
SQL> create or replace function extoreg (rid in rowid) return varchar2 is
  2   p2 number;
  3   p3 number;
  4   p4 number;
  5   p5 number;
  6   p6 number;
  7   begin
  8     dbms_rowid.rowid_info (rid,p2,p3,p4,p5,p6);
  9     return lpad(p5,4,0)||'.'||lpad(p6,4,0)||'.'||lpad(p4,4,0);
 10   end;
 11   /
Function created.
SQL>
```

The next listing shows the function used in a query, and the results follow the query text.

```
SQL> col ct format 999999999 head 'Row count
SQL> col ba format a20 head 'Block number'
SQL> select substr(extoreg(rowid),1,4) ba,
  2          count(*) ct
  3   from finance
  4  where rownum < 211    -- Limit the length of output
  5  group by substr(extoreg(rowid),1,4);
Block number             Row count
--------------------     ----------
0168                            30
0169                            30
0170                            29
0171                            27
0848                            27
0849                            27
0850                            26
0851                            14
8 rows selected.
SQL>
```

We can now make the following deductions with the information shown in the query output.

1. Naturally, there are roughly 28 rows per block when the Row Count values are averaged over the first seven rows of the display.

2. Since the database block size is 2K or 2,048 bytes, the average row length can be estimated by the following formula. We know that Oracle reserves space in each block for overhead and there can be upwards of 10 percent of each block not used by data. Let's take that into consideration during the calculation.

```
avg_row_len = floor (9 / 10 * db_block_size /
                     avg_rows_per_block)
            = floor (9 / 10 * 2048 / 28) = 65 bytes
```

3. When running the query without the **rownum < 211** criterion, there were 107 rows returned by the query, meaning there are 107 blocks allocated to the FINANCE table. There are four series of contiguous blocks allocated to FINANCE starting with the block IDs 168, 848, 2761, and 3905. Thus, FINANCE has four extents; this can be verified by looking at the USER_EXTENTS for the table as shown in the next listing.

```
SQL> select count(*)
  2    from user_extents
  3   where segment_name = 'FINANCE';
COUNT(*)
--------
       4
SQL>
```

There is, as there always has been, a wealth of information that can be gleaned on ROWIDs. This section has opened the door perhaps on some of the mystery of the extended ROWID used by Oracle8. In the next section, we are going to discuss a habit all DBAs need to get into—inspecting trace files written by Oracle looking for errors.

DBA Error-Trapping Routines

Throughout this book, we have discussed where error situations occur and what to do about them. We will now discuss ways to contribute to the tuning process by flagging error conditions and dealing with them before they get worse.

Background Process Trace Files

Each of the Oracle support processes creates a trace file. Oracle writes to these trace files to help debug system problems if and when they occur. Use these files for their intended purpose. The location of these files is operating system dependent, but they are usually in $ORACLE_HOME/rdbms/log. On any system, you can get Oracle to tell you where these trace files are written by logging into the Server Manager, connecting to the database, and then issuing the command

```
show parameters dump_dest
```

On most systems, the output will be the directory suggested above. The trace file name is built using the four-character process name (e.g., pmon or smon), the underscore character (_), and the process identifier. Use whatever operating system commands you wish, and ensure that you look for the following situations. Table 10-3 shows some common error situations that can be alleviated using a rigid tuning methodology.

NOTE
If you initiate a session via Net8 using a database that resides on another machine, the trace file for that session will be on the host, not on the local machine.

WHOLISTIC RULE #18
Inspect your database trace files daily using an automated process. Oracle writes these files for your information—use them.

What to Do	What It Means and What May Be Wrong
Look in the instance alert file for waits during the allocation of sequence numbers for online redo log switches.	You need larger or more redo log groups—Oracle is unable to switch the redo log group because the current group is still in use.
Look in the instance alert files for ORA-04031 errors.	This error is raised when Oracle is trying to allocate more memory for an SQL statement in the shared pool, and not enough memory can be found.
Search all trace files for the series of ORA-00600 error messages.	1. Consult your own notes—there are up to size arguments after the error enclosed in []. 2. Look for the meaning of the arguments in notes you have saved from previous situations. 3. Call Oracle Support if necessary. 4. Fix the situation that caused the error.
Search all the trace files for the ORA-01547 error message.	This indicates a session needed to acquire more space in a datafile and enough space could not be found—this typically happens without any application error messages and needs your intervention.
Search all the trace files for the ORA-03113 error message.	Applications that use Net8 to read remote databases get disconnected from Oracle periodically—the trace file may contain further information that could prove helpful to Oracle support.
Inspect the file SMONORCL.TRC looking for clean-up activities on aborted processes.	The system monitor is signaled by the process monitor (PMON) when Oracle user processes abort and there has to be some post-abort cleanup work performed.

TABLE 10-3. *Common Error Conditions to Monitor*

Database Free Space

Using the two queries in the following listings, you can assess the total amount of free space in all your tablespaces and the largest chunk of free space in each tablespace. The first lists the amount of free space in each tablespace. The second displays the largest chunk of contiguous free space by tablespace. As we discussed in Chapter 3, Oracle allocates space in blocks, and adjacent chunks of blocks are referred to as *contiguous space*.

```
select tablespace_name,sum(bytes) from sys.dba_free_space
    group by tablespace_name;
select tablespace_name,max(bytes) from sys.dba_free_space
    group by tablespace_name;
```

The following listing shows the output from the first line of the code.

```
TABLESPACE_NAME                      SUM(BYTES)
------------------------------     ----------
BORIS_ABELFRANTRO                     2678784
NANCY_BESDESMITH                     18423808
FRANCIS_DEFWAYNO                     10932224
NORMAN_NADROJIAN                     40550400
ALL_INDEXES                           4861952
AUDIT_APPS                            1331200
COMMON                               13897728
DESIDERATA                            5734400
FINANCIAL                            40550400
ALL_INDEXES                           4505600
```

Let's look at this output, using the DESIDERATA tablespace as an example. Suppose there are now 10,932,224 free bytes; of that amount, the largest chunk of contiguous space is 5,734,400 bytes as shown in the previous listing. A *contiguous chunk* is defined as space that is free in adjacent Oracle blocks. Because a block identifier (e.g., 4310 or 280) is assigned to each block in each tablespace in the database, if blocks 4000 through 4020 were free, we would have 21 blocks of contiguous free space.

What is even more useful is knowing the total space allocated to each tablespace and the change in free space since the previous day. We recommend the following routine when inspecting database free space as part of the tuning exercise:

1. Create a table to hold free space information daily, as described in Table 10-4.

2. Run a script to create free space statistics for the current day.

3. Compare that amount against free space from the previous day.

4. Calculate a percentage (plus or minus) that the free space has changed since the previous day.

Using the table described in Table 10-4 (called FSPACE), the following code will populate the table with free space rows daily.

```
/* ----------------------------------------------------------- */
/*   fspace.sql                                                */
/*                                                             */
/*   Create rows in FSPACE for FREE_SPACE in the database.     */
/*                                                             */
/*   Oracle8 Tuning     Corey & Abbey & Dechichio & Abramson   */
/* ----------------------------------------------------------- */
rem *  Create rows in FSPACE for today
insert into fspace
select a.tablespace_name,
       sum(a.bytes),           /*  Allocated from DBA_DATA_FILES  */
       round(sum(b.bytes)),    /*  Free bytes from DBA_FREE_SPACE */
       '','',sysdate
  from sys.dba_data_files a,sys.dba_free_space b
 where a.tablespace_name = b.tablespace_name
 group by a.tablespace_name,'','',sysdate;
rem *  Yesterday's free space is in the rows from yesterday's
rem *  FREE_TODAY column.  The FREE_TODAY column values from
rem *  yesterday are moved into the FREE_YESTERDAY columns for
REM *  today's rows.
update fspace a
```

```
set free_yesterday =
    (select free_today
       from fspace b
     where a.tablespace_name = b.tablespace_name
         and to_char(b.system_date) = to_char(sysdate - 1))
where to_char(system_date) = to_char(sysdate);
rem *  The PERCENT_CHANGED is set to represent the following:
rem *  % change = free_today - free_yesterday / free_yesterday
rem *  expressed as a percentage.  The calculation has to use a
rem *  DECODE in case the amout of free space has not changed.
rem *  This avoids dividing by 0.
update fspace
   set percent_changed =round(decode(free_today-free_yesterday,
           0,0,  /* If no change, set PERCENT_CHANGED to zero  */
           100*(free_today-free_yesterday)/
           (free_yesterday)),2)
 where to_char(system_date) = to_char(sysdate);
rem *  Print changed free space report for today.
col tablespace_name heading 'Tablespace'
col allocated heading 'Allocated' 999,999,990
col free_today heading 'Free today' form 999,999,990
col free_yesterday heading 'Yesterday form 999,999,990
col percent_changed heading 'Pct Ch' form 90.00
select tablespace_name, allocated, free_today, free_yesterday,
       percent_changed
  from fspace
 where to_char(system_date) = to_char(sysdate);
```

Column Name	Attributes
tablespace_name	varchar2(30)
allocated	number
free_today	number
free_yesterday	number
percent_changed	number
system_date	date

TABLE 10-4. *Table to Hold Daily Free Space Output*

The output from this code looks like the report shown in the following listing. Negative numbers in the Pct Ch column indicate less free space today than yesterday. Positive numbers mean more free space today than yesterday.

```
Tablespace              Allocated        Today    Yesterday   Pct Ch
-------------------     -----------    ----------  ----------  -------
GRUNGE                  209,715,200        92,160      92,160    0.00
AUDIT_APPS               73,400,320     2,678,784   2,678,784    0.00
PAFE                    209,715,200    18,423,808  18,423,808    0.00
DESIDERATA              209,715,200    10,932,224   7,245,824   50.88
BAFF                    838,860,800    83,886,080  83,886,080    0.00
FINANCIAL               104,857,600    40,550,400  40,796,160   -6.25
ALL_INDEXES              15,728,640     4,861,952   4,861,952    0.00
DESCAP                   73,400,320    14,680,064  29,360,128   50.00
```

WHOLISTIC RULE #19
Examine database free space, using an automated process, as part of the tuning process.

User Temporary Segment

As we discussed in Chapter 3, if there is not enough memory to support a sort operation, the Oracle8 database creates sort objects in the tablespace based on the user profile. The default is the SYSTEM tablespace. As new users are created, it is your job to ensure they do not use the SYSTEM tablespace for sorting to disk. Using the code following, report on any users that are still pointed at this forbidden tablespace.

```
select username
  from sys.dba_users
 where temporary_tablespace = 'SYSTEM';
```

WHOLISTIC RULE #20
Ensure that users are not using the SYSTEM tablespace as a work area for sorts that use disk space as well as memory.

Runaway Processes

In some environments, when users disconnect abnormally, there is a chance they could leave one or more orphan processes lying around. An orphan process is most common when a user (accessing the system using Windows) does a warm boot to get out of a session that seems to be frozen. After CTRL-ALT-DEL, there is a possibility that the user's server process may not go away. In cooperation with your hardware support personnel, you must constantly look for these processes and clean up after them. Terminal emulation is an ideal candidate for this problem. Now that more and more sites are using GUI (graphical user interface) front-ends such as MS Windows and NT, this problem is even more common.

NOTE
We are not suggesting that the orphan process problem occurs frequently. We mention it to alert you of the situation and suggest you look out for it on your machine.

It is not unheard of that one of these orphan processes is consuming an unusually high amount of CPU (up to 85 percent at a time). It is your job to seek out these processes and remove them from your machine. These processes rob your machine, its CPU, and all other resources of precious processing time.

WHOLISTIC RULE #21
Monitor the processes on your machine for orphans that should be stopped. You will need the assistance of your installation's hardware superusers to remove unwanted processes that do not belong to you.

WHOLISTIC RULE #22
If you are using a multithreaded server (see Chapter 2 for details), watch out for runaway dispatcher processes. They can consume massive amounts of CPU time.

Two-Task Considerations

Most UNIX hardware runs Oracle using two-task architecture: a user process (i.e., SQL*Plus) and a database communication process called the *shadow process.* It is possible to build copies of most Oracle programs using what is referred to as single-task, which means the user process and the shadow process are one in the same. Oracle tools that are run in single-task use less overhead because the interprocess communication necessary to support two-task is not needed for single-task. A great way to test this, if you are not sure, is to remake the export executable single-task. Then time the nightly export job. You will see a substantial savings in the time the job normally takes to run.

Oracle supplies programs to rebuild your application executables such as *sqlplus* and *runform30.* In HP-UX, for example, is a program called inf_rdpms.mk in the $ORACLE_HOME/rdbms/lib directory. In the midst of tuning Oracle, you may wish to experiment with single-task and examine the results.

NOTE
*Client-server applications are not candidates
for single-task.*

The steps in a test case are as follows:

1. Using a two-task program, run a routine that accomplishes your predefined scenario.

2. Examine the statistics: elapsed time and CPU consumption.

3. Restore the data to a pre-two–task state.

4. Using a single-task program, run the same routine.

5. Compare the results.

You may find the performance of the single-task executable as high as 15 to 20 percent faster than the two-task program.

WHOLISTIC RULE #23
*If your operating system supports both
two-task and single-task architecture,
investigate using Oracle programs in
single-task.*

NOTE
*There can be a significant ripple effect when
looking at single-task. BE CAREFUL and
especially have a look at any applications in
your systems that produce disk file output
while running.*

Year 2000 Date Mask

Oracle's solution to the year 2000 has been the creation of the date mask
DD-MON-RR. This date mask is nothing new to Oracle8; we first saw it not
long after Oracle7 appeared. We all have done our best to ensure systems
ask the users for a four character year. If an application development tool
fully supports this date mask, the two character year will be properly
handled as it is written to the database. The logic behind the century that
is stored is shown in the next listing.

```
if last 2 digits of system_date >= 50
    if last 2 digits of date_entered < 50
        store century of system_date + 1
    else
        store century of system_date
    end if
elsif last 2 digits of date_entered < 50
        store century of system_date
    else
        store century of system_date - 1
    end if
end if
```

Table 10-5 summarizes the behavior of the RR portion of this date mask based on this logic.

We find, and have always found, the application of logic for the millennium storage of century digits to be confusing. One is much better off using a four character date mask YYYY and insisting that the user enter all four digits.

Problem with the RR Portion of the Mask

The biggest problem with the RR date mask happens when the system date is something like December 5, 1998, and you want to enter the date December 5, 2052 into a field with a two-character year. Following the logic shown in the previous listing, Oracle8 will store the year 1952, not 2052, since the two digits of the system date (98) are >=50 and the two digits of the year entered (52) are >= 50 as well.

System Date	Date Entered	4-digit Year Stored	Explanation
12-DEC-1999	12-DEC-99	1999	Last 2 digits of system date are >= 50 and last 2 of year entered are >=50, so the century is stored the same as system date.
12-DEC-1999	12-DEC-03	2003	Last 2 digits of system date are >=50 and last 2 of date entered < 50, so the century is stored as current system date century +1.
12-DEC-2009	12-DEC-09	2009	Last 2 digits of system date are <50 and last 2 of year entered are <50, so the century is stored the same as system date.
12-DEC-2009	12-DEC-87	1987	Last 2 digits of system date are <50 and last 2 of year entered are >=50, so the century is stored as the system date century -1.

TABLE 10-5. *How the RR Date Mask Handles Centuries*

Transaction Control Features

Oracle8 has two time-saving features, **truncate table** and **truncate cluster**. When rows are removed from a table under normal circumstances, the rollback segments are used to hold undo information; if you do not commit your transaction, Oracle restores the data to the state it was in before your transaction started. With **truncate**, no undo information is generated. Removing rows from very large tables or clusters completes in a matter of seconds. Use **truncate** rather than **delete** for wiping the contents of small or large tables when you need no undo information generated. You may not qualify a **truncate** as you may be familiar with doing with **delete**. The following two statements illustrate using **truncate**.

```
truncate table plant_detail;
truncate cluster plant_clust;
```

Be aware that, because no undo is created with **truncate** once the "Table truncated" message is returned by Oracle, the rows in the table cannot be recovered. You cannot code any qualifiers (e.g., **and** or **where**) with the **truncate** statement. A more restrictive lock is acquired when **truncate** is used instead of **delete**. You may find some Oracle lock errors returned that are similar to those you get from time to time performing an operation such as index creation. The secret with **truncate** is that because it requires fewer resources, it helps tune your applications.

WHOLISTIC RULE #24
*Use **truncate table** and **truncate cluster** where appropriate. It is faster (allows more CPU time for other database activity) and needs fewer resources (no undo is generated) to complete.*

Another transaction control feature is the following statement:

```
set transaction use rollback segment;
```

This statement appeared in Oracle version 6. The name of a rollback segment is mentioned in the statement, and that rollback segment is used until the next **commit** statement is issued explicitly (by the user) or implicitly (by Oracle when disconnecting from SQL*Plus or issuing a DDL statement, such as **create**, **grant**, or **alter**). You will aid the performance of large transactions using this feature. Because the transaction is pointed at a large rollback segment, the likelihood of encountering extent errors (when the rollback segment needs more space and cannot acquire it) in the rollback segment is reduced.

WHOLISTIC RULE #25
To tune the performance of large SQL transactions, use **set transaction use rollback segment**.

Efficient Resource Management

Of course, a finite amount of resources are available to manage the Oracle database as well as everything else your environment supports. You should incorporate a number of conventions into your applications and database management routines to minimize resource requirements and permit the sharing of these resources among more users doing more tasks. This contributes to the *wholistic* approach to tuning Oracle.

Frequency of commit Statements

During all database activity, the performance of your program is enhanced and its resource requirements are minimized by issuing frequent **commit** (i.e., saving work) statements. After all **update**, **delete**, and **insert** statements, a **commit** frees up the following resources:

- Information held in the rollback segments to undo the transaction, if necessary

- All locks acquired during statement processing

- Space in the redo log buffer cache (as described in Chapter 2)

- Overhead associated with any internal Oracle mechanisms to manage the resources in the previous three items

WHOLISTIC RULE #26
Issue frequent **commit** *statements in your*
programs to free up resources.

When using sqlloader to enter a lot of records into the database, putting
in the **commit=y** parameter will speed up performance substantially, for all
the reasons we stated. You are freeing up resources quickly.

Cursor Management Using PL/SQL

You may use PL/SQL with other SQL statements in SQL*Plus and most
other tools that work with the Oracle database. With the emergence of new
products, Oracle has adopted PL/SQL as the standard language. There are
two ways to use *cursors* (the terminology Oracle uses to refer to a segment
of memory acquired for SQL statement execution). The first way is to
explicitly define a cursor, as illustrated in the following code:

```
procedure get_items is
cursor my_cursor is
   select *
     from plant_detail
    where city_id = 12;
   temp_buffer plant_detail%rowtype;
begin
   open my_cursor;
   fetch my_cursor into temp_buffer;
   while my_cursor%found loop

     . . .

     . . .
   end loop;
   close my_cursor;
end;
```

Notice how the code manually closes the cursor at the end.
The second way is to allow Oracle to handle more of cursor management
by implicitly defining the cursor, as shown in the following listing:

```
procedure get_items is
the_cnt number;
```

```
begin
  select count(*)
    into the_cnt
    from plant_detail
  where city_id = 12;
end;
```

There is no direct coding of any text mentioning a cursor, so Oracle handles it itself. We prefer using explicit cursors: they are easier to read, and they play a part in our wholistic tuning approach, because they perform better than implicit cursors. The major performance gain with explicit cursors is that they only initiate *one* call to the database for data. In a well-tuned system, as we discussed in Chapters 2 and 3, this "database access" will actually be a request for information in one or more of the Oracle memory caches. With implicit cursors, *two* requests are issued: the first to get (or fail to get, in some cases) the desired data, and the second to check for any error conditions that the first request may have detected.

WHOLISTIC RULE #27
*Use explicit cursors in all your
PL/SQL blocks.*

Clusters

The wholistic approach to tuning the Oracle database must attend to using clusters. Clustering tables is an alternative way of storing Oracle data. A *cluster* is used to store data from one or more tables. Each cluster you build has a *cluster key*, which is one or more columns from the table(s) you are putting in the cluster that match one another in size and datatype. Oracle8 includes two kinds of clusters. *Indexed clusters* store data from one or more tables in the same data blocks of a tablespace; they provide a rapid access method, using indexes similar to the way they are used with unclustered tables. *Hash clusters* place rows from clustered tables in data blocks, after applying a hash function to the values in the cluster key columns. A hash table is maintained by Oracle for quick row retrieval from hash clusters. When we speak of *hash function,* consider the following example:

Suppose a bank wants to build account numbers so that the seventh digit of each number is the units digit of the sum of all the other account number digits. This is commonly referred to as a check-digit hash formula. Using account number 2547862 as an example, the sum of the first six digits in the account number is 32. Thus, the units digit in this sum is the digit 2, which becomes the seventh digit of the full account number. We can then say a hash function is performed on the first six digits of a new account number to arrive at the seventh digit number.

You choose whether to use indexed or hash clusters by using the keyword **hashkeys** in the **create cluster** statement. Leaving out this keyword creates an indexed cluster. The keyword **hash is**, used when creating hash clusters, cannot be coded when a cluster is created without also coding the **hashkeys** keyword at the same time. When you use clusters, you instruct Oracle to store the rows of tables in the same physical location, which can reduce the amount of I/O to retrieve the tables' data. When joins are done on clustered tables, the number of data blocks read to satisfy the query can be dramatically reduced. Candidate tables for clustering are ones that are constantly joined together and are mainly used in queries (**select** statements, as opposed to **insert**, **update**, and **delete** operations).

Clusters have been available with previous versions of Oracle, but the Oracle7 way of handling clusters further aids your efforts in tuning the performance of tables involved in joins.

Indexed Clusters

In the case of a single-table cluster, the rows sharing the same value for the cluster index column are stored in the same data blocks. In the case of multiple clusters, rows from ALL of the tables in the cluster that share column values in the cluster index are stored in the same data blocks. When creating an index cluster, it is important to pay close attention to the storage parameters even more so than when creating tables. The following steps contribute to the values you choose for some of the space parameters in a **create cluster** statement. The actual formulae used to do the calculations are not presented here. Consult the *Oracle8 Server Administrator's Guide* for the equations used for this exercise. (This summary of the steps is used with the permission of Oracle Corporation.)

1. Calculate the total block header size (the block header is a road map to the contents of each block in a cluster).

2. Calculate the available data space per block (the space for actual data in the block).

3. Calculate the combined column lengths of the average rows per cluster key.

4. Calculate the average row size of all the clustered tables (this is the minimum amount of space required by a row in a clustered table).

5. Calculate the average cluster block size (this value becomes the size parameter value when you create the cluster).

6. Calculate the total number of blocks required for the cluster (this affects the value of the **initial** parameter when you create the cluster).

If you have never worked with clusters, you will notice that the cluster index must be created before data can be inserted into the cluster. An Oracle error is raised if you try to use the cluster before making the cluster index. Oracle does not maintain index entries for indexed columns that have null values, whereas clustered tables have index entries for columns with nulls in the cluster key column(s).

WHOLISTIC RULE #28
Investigate using indexed clusters to speed up access to tables commonly joined together on a standard set of matching columns.

WHOLISTIC RULE # 29
Use documented formulae for calculating space parameters for indexed clusters based on row characteristics, volume of data, and the average number of rows per table per cluster index value.

Hash Clusters

After instructing Oracle to build a hash cluster, Oracle either performs an internal hashing routine on row cluster key values or, if you use the **hash is** keyword when the hash cluster is created, it bypasses the internal hashing mechanism. Based on the result of the hash function, Oracle places rows in the hash cluster in the same data blocks as rows whose cluster key hashes to the same value. The *Oracle8 Server Administrator's Guide* includes a discussion on working with hash clusters and necessary calculations that should be made prior to defining hash clusters. If the following three conditions have been met, consider using hash clusters instead of indexed clusters.

- You are able to allocate space for tables with preallocated amounts for future growth.

- Query performance optimization is a primary goal of your tuning exercise.

- The columns that are part of the cluster key (hashed columns) are used in equality conditions in your SQL statement WHERE clause.

WHOLISTIC RULE #30
If the appropriate conditions have been met,
use hash clusters to enhance the performance
of applications.

PL/SQL File I/O

Many readers are familiar with the first solution for file I/O (except there was no "I", just "O")—DBMS_OUTPUT. By spooling output in SQL*Plus to a file and issuing calls to the DBMS_OUTPUT.PUT_LINE procedure, you could place information in a file. For example, the code shown in the following listing would put the text "Hello world." in dbmsout.lst.

```
SQL> set serveroutput on size 1000000
SQL> set echo off trimsp on feed off pages 0
SQL> spool dbmsout
SQL> begin
  2     dbms_output.put_line ('Hello world.');
  3  end;
  4  /
PL/SQL procedure successfully completed.
SQL> spool off
```

With this handy little package called UTL_FILE, files can be written to or read directly from within a PL/SQL procedure. Let's have a look at the pieces that come together in UTL_FILE, which should become part of your DBA toolkit. The UTL_FILE package is the next generation of file I/O.

WHOLISTIC RULE #31
Become fluent on using the UTL_FILE package
to perform read, write, and append operations
to operating system files.

File Handle Declaration

A UTL_FILE file handle must be defined in the **declare** section of the procedure as **utl_file.file_type**. By inspecting the UTL_FILE package, you would notice the following lines towards the start of the package declaration.

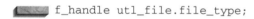
```
/*
** FILE_TYPE - File handle
*/
TYPE file_type IS RECORD (id BINARY_INTEGER);
```

As is the case with most **type** definitions in stored objects, you may then code a line in your procedure **declare** section that gives a variable. you name the type definition in UTL_FILE by coding something similar to

```
f_handle utl_file.file_type;
```

Opening the File

Within the procedure body, the file handle must be opened with the **utl_file.fopen** command followed by the path, filename, and mode. The mode **w** opens the file in write mode. The other modes include **r** for read and **a** for append. All three parameters are specified when the **fopen** is invoked.

To allow the package to work, you need to specify one or more directories in your initialization parameter file where users are able to write to and read files from. You may have multiple entries for UTL_FILE_DIR in this initialization parameter file. If you wish to allow PL/SQL file I/O to be done anywhere, instead of placing a directory name after the entry, place an asterisk (*). The next few lines enliven areas on a Windows NT server.

```
utl_file_dir = c:\orant\utl_file
utl_file_dir = c:\utl_file\users
utl_file_dir = *
```

If the platform is UNIX, be sure to include a forward slash at the end of the last directory in the path.

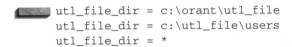

NOTE
Only ten files can be open at any one point in time. If your stored object needs to write to more than ten files, some conditional logic and UTL file commands will be required to handle the opening and closing of the files. Under these circumstances, you will open the appropriate file when it is needed and then close it after the data has been written to it. After the first time a file is opened in write mode, the second and subsequent **utl_file.fopen** *commands must be done in append mode.*

Writing to the File

Once the file has been opened, the **utl_file.put_line** command will write a new line to a file opened for output or appending. The file handle and string to be written are passed as arguments to the **put_line** command. The string must not exceed 1K (1,024 bytes); any attempt to write a longer string will raise an error and none of the string will be written to the file.

NOTE
The UTL_FILE.FFLUSH procedure can be used to dump the contents of the output buffer without waiting until it fills up.

Closing the File

The **utl_file.fclose** command is placed at the end of the file I/O code and closes the file. The file handle is passed to **fclose** as the only argument.

Putting the Pieces Together

We now present two examples of working with file I/O. The first is quick and dirty, to illustrate the pieces and how they go together. The output of the first example is a one-line file containing the text "Hey there, buddy, are you still there?" The second is commented and shows a more sophisticated scenario where an Ottawa Senators ticket flat file is being written from the STH table in an Oracle8 database.

```
SQL> begin
  2      declare
  4        f_handle utl_file.file_type;
  5      begin
  6        f_handle := utl_file.fopen ('c:\','text','w');
  7        utl_file.put (f_handle,'Hey there, buddy, are you still there?');
  8        utl_file.fclose (f_handle);
  9      end;
 10    end;
 11    /
PL/SQL procedure successfully completed.
SQL>
```

Wonderful, you say, but what good is it anyway? We have found that, once you start working with file I/O and UTL_FILE, you will wonder how you ever did without it. Let's close this section with the season tickets data file creation program (rumor has it Mark may be the Senators $38,782^{nd}$ round draft choice in 2002).

```
/* ------------------------------------------------------------ */
/*  sens_sth_select          Mark Kerzner 1997                  */
/*                             sensfan@sensfans.com             */
/*  Illustrate the use of UTL_FILE against an Oracle8           */
/*  database.                                                   */
/*                                                              */
/*  Oracle8 Tuning     Corey & Abbey & Dechichio & Abramson     */
/* ------------------------------------------------------------ */
```

```
create or replace procedure sens_sth_select (i_section_number in number,
                                             i_year in number) is
  l_sth_file_handle    utl_file.file_type;
  -- Naturally, these could be set after the BEGIN, but it is much
  -- cuter to do it here. The value assigned to "l_sth_file_path" must
  -- be mentioned in the UTL_FILE_DIR entry in INIT.ORA unless the entry
  -- says UTL_FILE_DIR = * as explained elsewhere.
  l_sth_file_path      varchar2(20) default 'c:\orant\bin';
  l_sth_file_name      varchar2(20) default 'sth_list.dat';
  l_record_buffer      varchar2(163);
  cursor sth_cur is
    select accnt_num,lst_nme,frst_nme,cmpny_nme,addr_ln1,
           addr_ln2, city, prvnc, pstl_cde, club_stts
      from sth
    where sth.sctn = i_section_number
      and sth.yr = i_year;
begin
  begin
    -- Open the file for write.
    l_sth_file_handle := utl_file.fopen (l_sth_file_path, l_sth_file_name, 'w');
    for sth_rec in sth_cur loop
      if sth_rec.club_stts = 'GOLD' then
        -- Build the output line (fixed length fields).
        l_record_buffer :=
            lpad(sth_rec.accnt_num,10,0)||
            rpad(nvl(sth_rec.lst_nme,' '),20,' ')||
            rpad(nvl(sth_rec.frst_nme,' '),10,' ')||
            rpad(nvl(sth_rec.cmpny_nme,' '),40,' ')||
            rpad(sth_rec.addr_ln1,30,' ')||
            rpad(nvl(sth_rec.addr_ln2,' '),30,' ')||
            rpad(sth_rec.city,15,' ')||
            sth_rec.prvnc||
            rpad(nvl(sth_rec.pstl_cde,' '),6,' ');
        utl_file.put_line (l_sth_file_handle, l_record_buffer);
      end if;
    end loop;
  exception
    -- Trap and deal with exceptions. We highly recommend doing this
    -- yourself to avoid aborted procedures with very little information
    -- that's useful to the end user or the help desk.
    when utl_file.internal_error then
    -- LOG_ERR is another procedure that writes error text to
```

```
      -- an error file or a table from which errors will be dumped.
          log_err ('A',SQLCODE,'Internal Error with utl_file package');
      when utl_file.invalid_filehandle then
          log_err ('A',SQLCODE,'An Invalid filehandle was declared');
      when utl_file.invalid_mode then
          log_err ('A',SQLCODE,'Invalid mode error with utl_file package');
      when utl_file.invalid_operation then
          log_err ('A',SQLCODE,'Invalid operation error with package');
      when utl_file.invalid_path then
          log_err ('A',SQLCODE,'An invalid path was specified '||
                    'for the output file');
      when utl_file.write_error THEN
          log_err ('A',SQLCODE,'An error occurred while attempting '||
                    'to write to the output file');
      when others then
          log_err ('A',SQLCODE,NULL);
  end;
  utl_file.fclose (l_sth_file_handle);
end;
/
```

SENS_STH_SELECT has the **cursor** declaration, the **put_line** command, and exceptions inside a PL/SQL block that is nested inside another PL/SQL block. This is done so that the file can be closed after the exception handling block. Even if your procedure opens and closes the file within the same PL/SQL block, you should have another **utl_file.fclose** command after the exception handling section.

NOTE
You should experiment with closing files within the exception block and perhaps also at the end of the major PL/SQL block that uses UTL_FILE. Watch out for error conditions that can creep up when you try to close a file that is no longer open!

Let's Tune It

The points we have made throughout this book contribute to a well-tuned database. As we have shown in this chapter, you need to monitor a wide spectrum of areas to cover all your bases. We can summarize the wholistic approach in the following high-level summary:

- Investigate the Oracle Connection Manager when deploying systems with Net8.

- Attend to the Big Three (I/O, memory, and CPU), but look at the bigger picture when tuning Oracle.

- Embed session and transaction control statements right in your PL/SQL using the DBMS_SESSION and DBMS_TRANSACTION packages we have featured in this chapter.

- Use the trace files written by Oracle to help pinpoint problem areas, and attend to them before they become more serious.

- Verify the integrity of your database files weekly using the dbverf80 utility.

- Tune online backups by following the recommendations we make in this chapter.

- Consult the wealth of resources on the Internet for assistance with tuning-related issues. The World Wide Web is a part of your alternate support network.

- Run your database in ARCHIVELOG mode to provide maximum protection against data loss.

- Use **truncate table** to wipe out the contents of tables—it creates no undo information and is much faster than **delete**.

- Use the UTL_FILE package for file I/O from PL/SQL.

- Consider using indexed and/or hash clusters when storing static data—the retrieval times for columns in clustered tables can enhance performance of some applications.

■ Know your data, know your users, and know your applications.

■ Use explicit cursors in PL/SQL blocks—they require less I/O than implicit cursors.

■ Look at using clustering with Oracle8 tables accessed frequently together.

■ Whenever possible, issue frequent **commit** statements in all your programs; locks, latches, and other resources are freed up when a transaction does a commit or rollback.

■ Use export and import as part of your ongoing backup and recovery mechanisms.

■ Use a large buffer size (upwards of 10MB, or 10,240,000 bytes) for export and import.

■ Always use the **log** parameter with export and import; partial imports especially are a nuisance when trying to figure what did not get imported if you have no import session log file to inspect.

■ When working with extended characters, ensure they are not lost during data movement activities.

■ Set the **commit** parameter to **y** when importing large tables (greater than 100,000 rows).

■ Inspect and test your applications for year 2000 compliance and look at the DD-MON-RR date mask.

■ Make copies of your control file in Server Manager during system backups, using both of the following statements:

```
alter database backup controlfile to 'location' reuse;
alter database backup controlfile to trace;
```

■ Write a recovery plan and test it out on a nonproduction database to ensure the bugs are out before you have to do the real thing.

■ Run export and import in the background using the parameter file keyword (parfile=).

Oracle7.x Specifics

Please note the following points organized by the headings for some of the sections of this chapter:

- ■ "Oracle Connection Manager"   Does not apply to any version of Oracle7 whatsoever.

- ■ "A Fine Time for This"   The GET_TIME function appeared with Oracle 7.2 and is not available for 7.1.x.

- ■ "Who Said It Can't Be Done in PL/SQL?"   This material applies to Oracle7.3.x and 7.2.x, but had not yet arrived with 7.1.x.

- ■ "Verifying Integrity of Database Files"   Only applies to Oracle 7.3.x and no lower versions.

- ■ "The Standby Database Facility"   Can be used with Oracle 7.3.x but not 7.2.x or 7.1.x.

- ■ "Tuning Database Backups"   Applies to Oracle 7.x except the discussion of the **direct** parameter to export which did not appear until 7.3.2.

- ■ "Tuning Database Recovery"   Applies to all versions of Oracle7.x.

- ■ "Understanding the Extended ROWID"   Is only applicable to Oracle8.

- ■ "DBA Error-Trapping Routines"   Applies to all Oracle7.x.

- ■ "Year 2000 Date Mask"   Applies to all Oracle 7.x.

- ■ "Transaction Control Features"   Applies to all Oracle 7.x.

- ■ "Clusters"   Applies to Oracle7.x.

- ■ "PL/SQL File I/O"   First appeared with Oracle 7.2 and was not available with release 7.1.

CHAPTER
11

Scripts and Tips

his chapter will present various scripts and tips that we have used or created from our years of working with the Oracle database. Because of our travels around the Oracle software over the past decade, we find ourselves armed with an assortment of tips and tricks. We have gained this knowledge from the trials and tribulations of our real-life Oracle experiences. A large number of our Oracle scripts help tune the database and contribute to efficient resource management. A great deal of experimentation with this and that has helped us to keep current with the advancing technology and to take advantage of new and better functionality as soon as it is released by Oracle.

We find the server technology that Oracle has implemented needs more information and tips disseminated than Oracle alone is capable of producing. This chapter highlights some areas we feel are high-level examples of what to look for to help you manage your Oracle databases and keep them running and running and running and running...

We will cover database backups, space management issues, accessing and using the important information in the SYS V$ and DBA_ views, renaming a column in a table (preserving the well thought out space considerations you have painstakingly put in place), and the ever-popular trick of using SQL to write SQL.

Tips on Backing Up Your Database

When deciding on a backup strategy, one of the first questions you need to ask is, "If we experience hardware failure, how up to date does our database need to be after recovering from a backup?" Hardware failure is not common, but preparing a strategy to deal with problems if and when they happen is a wise decision.

ARCHIVELOG Mode

The following may convince you that there is no need to run your database in NOARCHIVELOG mode. After we present the almost bulletproof protection ARCHIVELOG offers, we know you will start using it at once.

SCRIPTS AND TIPS RULE #1
*Use ARCHIVELOG mode as part of the
backup strategy in your production database.*

We now present four common "excuses" we hear for not using
ARCHIVELOG mode, and we'll lead you through a discussion of why these
(and all other reasons) should not keep you from using ARCHIVELOG.

1. Our database is not used during the quiet hours, and there is no
need to leave it up 24 hours a day—backing it up while it is not
running is sufficient.

■ Using the regimen described in Chapter 2, where we
recommend you move reporting jobs into the quiet hours, the
need to leave the database up all the time becomes obvious.

■ As we discussed in Chapter 2 and elsewhere in this book, when
the database is closed and restarted, you lose all the
information held in the numerous caches that Oracle maintains
as your instance operates. These caches must be filled all over
again each time the database is started. The filling of these
caches leads to unnecessary disk I/O.

■ We discussed continuous monitoring that you should perform
on your database (especially the utlbstat.sql and utlestat.sql
performance diagnostic programs) in Chapter 6. The secret to
monitoring is to provide the program you use with the best time
slice to perform the statistics gathering. Closing your database
daily for backups limits this time slice to a period always less
than 24 hours.

2. Export offers us all the protection we need (refer to Chapter 10 for
details on the role export can play in tuning your database), and
nobody uses the instance during the night anyway.

■ You have no idea when users access your database. The only
time you truly know they are not logged on is when the
instance is not running. For this reason, using export alone is
questionable. There is a possibility that someone may be on
the machine when you least expect it.

■ Using export alone means a single point of failure. If, for example, the export does not work (the message "Import terminated with warnings" is displayed at the end) or the disk you are exporting to fills up, the file written by export may be unusable or incomplete.

3. The disk space used to store archived redo logs is just not available on our computer (refer to Chapter 10, where we discuss how this works).

■ While keeping in mind concepts such as disk striping and table/index splitting (as discussed in Chapter 3), you should consider moving database files around your disks to free up space on a dedicated drive to hold these archived redo log files.

■ When there is no disk space to be found, purchase more. Seems easier said than done; however, an $8,000 disk drive is far cheaper than running the risk of losing a full day's transactions when not running in ARCHIVELOG mode.

4. We run huge reporting jobs, which produce so many archived redo logs that the disk holding archived redo logs would be filled to capacity.

■ Look at running those jobs on the same machine using another database that is not in ARCHIVELOG mode. Then, when using the application that accesses that data, read it from the other database using Net8.

■ Move the large amount of archived redo logs to tape during the reporting job itself.

■ In UNIX, for example, compress your archived redo logs periodically during the day. They are compressed anyway as they are written to tape.

SCRIPTS AND TIPS RULE #2
Use a combination of online backups
(refer to Chapter 10 for details) and export
for system backups.

SCRIPTS AND TIPS RULE #3
Test your recovery routines before you need to use them in a real emergency. Do so on a separate instance of Oracle, and go through the steps involved. Consult the *Oracle8 Server Backup and Recovery Guide for details.*

The next section discusses writing hot backups as your database runs in ARCHIVELOG mode and, mainly due to the size of your database, the backup has to be written in cycles.

Hot Backup Cycles

When running your Oracle8 database in ARCHIVELOG mode, we recommend running your hot backups to disk, then copying the information from that holding area to your preferred backup medium. Often the size of the database dictates designing a plan that backs up portions of the database each day in a cyclical fashion.

Let's look at one of many approaches to setting up a series of three cycles to back up a 15 gigabyte database. When backing up using a cycle-based approach, the following points explain how to perform the backups (with our sample configuration plugged in to formulas):

1. Figure out how many cycles based on the size of the database and the space available on disk for hot backups.

   ```
   number of cycles = floor (size of database / space on disk + 1)
                    = floor (15 gigabytes / 7 gigabytes + 1) = 3
   ```

2. Each cycle is dependent on the successful completion of the previous. Thus 2 cannot run until 1 succeeds, 3 until 2 succeeds, and 1 until 3 succeeds. If for some reason cycle 2 does not complete on a Wednesday morning, the Thursday morning job reruns cycle 2.

3. The successful completion of each cycle triggers writing that cycle number to a file. Each time the backup routine runs, it brings the contents of the file into the job and then decides what cycle is to be run that day.

4. You must decide whether to:

- Run the backup from UNIX—this entails figuring out how to take the tablespaces in and out of backup mode

- Run the backup from within SQL*Plus—this entails shelling out to UNIX to do the copy command

NOTE
We prefer the first approach that involves echoing the appropriate text and piping the display into line-mode Server Manager.

Let's get started. The next listing shows two objects used to create the hot backup script. The first holds database file information and the second ends up being used to create the lines for the backup script.

```
SQL> desc hot_data
 Name                              Null?     Type
 -------------------------------   --------  ----
 CYCLE                                       NUMBER(1)
 TABLESPACE_NAME                             VARCHAR2(30)
 FILE_NAME                                   VARCHAR2(100)
 BYTES                                       NUMBER
SQL> desc hot_write
 Name                              Null?     Type
 -------------------------------   --------  ----
 CTR                                         NUMBER
 TEXT                                        VARCHAR2(100)
```

The next listing we present accomplishes two things. In the first scripts, after arbitrarily deciding that the threshold for each of the three cycles is five gigabytes, we create rows in HOT_DATA. In the second program, using the information placed in HOT_DATA, we write a program to do the hot backup. The code is commented to explain what is being done.

NOTE
The machine we use as an example is HP-UX 10 running Oracle Financials. Thus, the code is a UNIX shell script in an environment running the posix shell.

```
/* ----------------------------------------------------------- */
/*  hot_data.sql                                               */
/*                                                             */
/*  Create rows in HOT_DATA with tablespace and data file     */
/*  information.                                               */
/*                                                             */
/*  Oracle8 Tuning    Corey & Abbey & Dechichio & Abramson    */
/* ----------------------------------------------------------- */
set echo on term off pages 0 feed off
set serveroutput on size 1000000
begin
  declare
    high_end        number := 5368709120;
    accum           number;
    cycle           number := 1;
    file_row        sys.dba_data_files%rowtype;
    -- Get all the information about tablespaces and datafiles
    cursor get_data is
      select *
        from sys.dba_data_files
        order by tablespace_name,file_name;
  begin
    delete hot_data;
    commit;
    accum := 0;
    -- Loop through the information in DBA_DATA_FILES, inserting rows
    -- into HOT_DATA. When the ACCUM variable is larger than HIGH_END, the
    -- cycle is incremented and we carry on into the next cycle.
    for file_row in get_data loop
      accum := accum+file_row.bytes;
      if accum > high_end then
        cycle := cycle+1;
        accum := 0;
      end if;
      -- Put the cycle number, tablespace name, file name, and file size in
      -- HOT_DATA.
      insert into hot_data values
            (cycle,file_row.tablespace_name,
             file_row.file_name,file_row.bytes);
    end loop;
  end;
end;
/
```

When this completes, HOT_DATA contains information as illustrated in the next listing for backup cycle #3.

```
CYCLE       TABLESPACE FILE_NAME                                            BYTES
---------- ---------- ------------------------------------------ ----------
        3 POX         /oradata10/masii/pox01.dbf                       419430400
        3 QA          /oradata2/masii/qa01.dbf                          10485760
        3 QAX         /oradata13/masii/qax01.dbf                        10485760
        3 RBS         /oradata5/masii/rbs01.dbf                       1677721600
        3 RBS1        /oradata6/masii/rbs101.dbf                      1677721600
        3 RG          /oradata13/masii/rg01.dbf                         10485760
        3 RG          /oradata13/masii/rg02.dbf                         20971520
        3 RGX         /oradata14/masii/rgx01.dbf                        10485760
        3 SYSTEM      /oradata1/masii/system01.dbf                     524288000
        3 SYSTEM      /oradata1/masii/system02.dbf                     262144000
```

Now shown is the script we use to create the UNIX hot backup routine. It is commented as well, highlighting what we are doing and why.

```
/* ---------------------------------------------------------- */
/*  hot_write.sql                                             */
/*                                                            */
/*  Create rows in HOT_WRITE using the information in         */
/*  HOT_DATA. We use the HOT_WRITE table simply to format     */
/*  and dump rows as the backup script is created.            */
/*                                                            */
/*  Oracle8 Tuning    Corey & Abbey & Dechichio & Abramson    */
/* ---------------------------------------------------------- */

truncate table hot_write;
begin
  declare
    t_bytes           number := 0;    -- Keeps track of tablespace bytes
    f_bytes           number := 0;    -- Keeps track of datafile bytes
    ctr               number := 0;
    ts_name           varchar2(30);
    f_name            varchar2(100);
    l_cycle           number := 1;
    cursor get_files is
      select file_name,bytes
        from hot_data
       where tablespace_name = ts_name;
    cursor get_ts is
      select distinct tablespace_name
        from hot_data
```

```
      where cycle = l_cycle;
begin
  -- The next few lines place the UNIX RCS header information in the
  -- backup script. Each time we write to HOT_WRITE we increment a counter
  -- so we can get the rows back in order.
  ctr := ctr+1;
  insert into hot_write values (ctr,'#');
  ctr := ctr+1;
  insert into hot_write values (ctr,'# $Header$');
  ctr := ctr+1;
  insert into hot_write values (ctr,'#');
  ctr := ctr+1;
  insert into hot_write values (ctr,null);
  ctr := ctr+1;
  insert into hot_write values (ctr,'cd $HOME/backups');
  ctr := ctr+1;
  -- Write the line to place us in the correct directory.
  insert into hot_write values (ctr,'export ORACLE_HOME=/home/oracle');
  ctr := ctr+1;
  -- Set the ORACLE_SID properly.
  insert into hot_write values (ctr,'export ORACLE_SID=masii');
  ctr := ctr+1;
  insert into hot_write values (ctr,null);
  ctr := ctr+1;
  -- This line gets the last completed cycle number from the disk file
  -- mentioned in numbered point 3 at the top of this "Hot Backup Cycles"
  -- section.
  into hot_write values (ctr,'cycle=`cat hot_cycle`');
  ctr := ctr+1;
  insert into hot_write values (ctr,null);
  for i in 1..3 loop
    ctr := ctr+1;
    -- Build the start of the IF statement.
    insert into hot_write values (ctr,'if [ "$cycle" = '||
                                  l_cycle||' ]; then');
    ctr := ctr+1;
    insert into hot_write values (ctr,null);
    ctr := ctr+1;
    insert into hot_write values (ctr,'   #');
    ctr := ctr+1;
    insert into hot_write values (ctr,'   # Cycle '||l_cycle);
    ctr := ctr+1;
    insert into hot_write values (ctr,'   #');
    open get_ts;
    fetch get_ts into ts_name;
```

```
while get_ts%found loop
  -- Outer loop gets the name of all the tablespaces.
  ctr := ctr+1;
  insert into hot_write values (ctr,null);
  ctr := ctr+1;
  -- The next line will place the desired tablespace in backup mode.
  insert into hot_write
         values (ctr,'   echo "alter tablespace '||ts_name||
                     ' begin backup;" | $ORACLE_HOME/bin/sqlplus /');
  open get_files;
  fetch get_files into f_name,f_bytes;
  while get_files%found loop
    -- Inner loop gets all the file names and sizes for the tablespace
    -- selected in the outer loop.
    ctr := ctr+1;
    -- Create the line that copies the datafile to the disk backup
    -- location.
    insert into hot_write values (ctr,'   cp '||f_name||' /backups/hot');
    fetch get_files into f_name,f_bytes;
    t_bytes := t_bytes+f_bytes;
  end loop;
  ctr := ctr+1;
  -- The next line takes the desired tablespace out of backup mode.
  insert into hot_write
         values (ctr,'   echo "alter tablespace '||ts_name||
                     ' end backup;" | $ORACLE_HOME/bin/sqlplus /');
  close get_files;
  fetch get_ts into ts_name;
end loop;
ctr := ctr+1;
insert into hot_write values (ctr,null);
ctr := ctr+1;
insert into hot_write values (ctr,'   #');
ctr := ctr+1;
-- This line simply writes out the size of the cycle just completed.
insert into hot_write values (ctr,'   # Cycle size --- '||
                                  to_char(t_bytes,'99,999,999,990'));
t_bytes := 0;
ctr := ctr+1;
insert into hot_write values (ctr,'   #');
ctr := ctr+1;
-- Write the end of if statement for UNIX.
insert into hot_write values (ctr,'fi');
ctr := ctr+1;
insert into hot_write values (ctr,null);
```

```
        -- Having just completed a cycle, go on to the next.
        l_cycle := l_cycle+1;
        close get_ts;
      end loop;
    end;
end;
/
spool off
set echo off
spool hot_backup.sh
select text
  from hot_write
 order by ctr;
prompt if [ "$cycle" = 1 ]; then
select '   echo 2 > $HOME/backups/hot_cycle' from dual;
prompt elsif [ "$cycle" = 2 ]; then
select '   echo 3 > $HOME/backups/hot_cycle' from dual;
prompt else
select '   echo 1 > $HOME/backups/hot_cycle' from dual;
prompt fi
spool off
```

The information is dragged out of HOT_WRITE using the statement
select * from hot_write order by 1;. Part of the backup script is shown in
the next listing. The ellipses (...) indicate where code is not displayed.

```
#
# $Header$
#
cd $HOME/backups
export ORACLE_HOME=/home/oracle
export ORACLE_SID=masii
cycle=`cat hot_cycle`
if [ "$cycle" = 1 ]; then
    #
    # Cycle 1
    #
    echo "alter tablespace AP begin backup;" | $ORACLE_HOME/bin/sqlplus /
    cp /oradata9/masii/ap01.dbf /backups/hot
    echo "alter tablespace AP end backup;" | $ORACLE_HOME/bin/sqlplus /
    echo "alter tablespace APX begin backup;" | $ORACLE_HOME/bin/sqlplus /
    cp /oradata10/masii/apx01.dbf /backups/hot
    echo "alter tablespace APX end backup;" | $ORACLE_HOME/bin/sqlplus /
...
...
```

```
    echo "alter tablespace GL begin backup;" | $ORACLE_HOME/bin/sqlplus /
    cp /oradata7/masii/gl01.dbf /backups/hot
    cp /oradata7/masii/gl02.dbf /backups/hot
    echo "alter tablespace GL end backup;" | $ORACLE_HOME/bin/sqlplus /
    #
    # Cycle size ---   4,206,886,912
    #
fi

if [ "$cycle" = 2 ]; then
    #
    # Cycle 2
    #
...
...
```

Space Management Tips

Implementing routines and automated procedures to help track space allocation events in your database will help the tuning exercise. In Chapter 7, we discuss extent issues and the maximum number of extents a table may acquire. In this section, we will present a way to monitor the number of extents allocated to tables.

Part of space management for the database as a whole involves monitoring the free space by tablespace. Let's look at one of many ways to monitor free space and present you with results that list the percentage of space free by tablespace. Because Oracle tracks and allocates space to tables by blocks, we will discuss the concept of how Oracle8 tracks contiguous space in tablespaces. *Contiguous space* is space in adjacent blocks. In a 4K (4,096-byte) block size, if 300 blocks of free space are adjacent to one another in a tablespace, then 1,228,800 bytes of contiguous space are available.

Extent Monitoring

You need to continually inform yourself of tables in your database that are overextended or are reaching their **maxextents** limit. Bringing this information to your attention now before extent problems occur helps keep your database tuned.

Overextended Tables and Indexes
(More Than Five Extents Allocated)

The following listing will inform you of the tables and indexes that are overextended. We use the term *overextended* when a table or index has more than five extents.

```
SQL> select owner "Owner", segment_name "Segment Name",
  2         segment_type "Type", tablespace_name "Tablespace",
  3         extents "#Ext", max_extents "Max"
  4    from sys.dba_segments
  5    where extents > 5
  6      and owner not in ('SYS','SYSTEM')
  7    order by owner,segment_name;
```

Owner	Segment Name	Type	Tablespace	#Ext	Max
USER1	ACC_TABLE	TABLE	TBSP_TESTONE	7	99
USER1	TBL_SECONDS	TABLE	TBSP_TESTONE	7	99
USER1	ACTORS	TABLE	TBSP_TESTONE	16	120
USER1	XFERS	TABLE	TBSP_TESTONE	6	120
USER2	HISTORY_FILE	TABLE	TBSP_TESTTWO	8	120
USER2	HISTORY_INDEX	INDEX	TBSP_TESTTWO	9	120
USER2	TEMP2	INDEX	TBSP_TESTTWO	8	120
USER3	FORM	TABLE	TBSP_TEST3	13	120
USER3	MENU	TABLE	TBSP_TEST3	21	120
USER3	REPORT	TABLE	TBSP_TEST3	8	120

```
10 rows selected.
SQL>
```

The consolidation of extents into one chunk of contiguous space can be accomplished by following these steps:

1. Export the table (the grants and indexes will automatically be written to the export file with Oracle8).

2. Drop the table.

3. Import the table.

Consider the following query and its results before these three steps are performed.

```
SQL> select segment_name, extents
  2    from sys.dba_segments
```

```
  3  where table_name = 'MY_TABLE' and owner = 'USER1';
SEGMENT_NAME        EXTENTS
----------------- -------
MY_TABLE               101
SQL>
```

After exporting, dropping, and importing the table, the same query results would be

```
SEGMENT_NAME        EXTENTS
----------------- -------
MY_TABLE                 1
SQL>
```

This method works if the data in the extents can fit into the originally sized initial extent of the table; however, if this is not the case or you want to allow for some extra expansion, we recommend you follow our next rule.

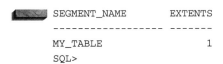

SCRIPTS AND TIPS RULE #4
*When defragmenting overextended tables, set the **initial** parameter for the table to the size of the data that is currently in the table, and if extra expansion space is desired add that on also.*

Using the export file created for the defragmentation of the table MY_TABLE, perform the following steps to create the table with a properly sized **initial** space allocation.

1. Run import table using the following command:

   ```
   imp userid=user1/password indexfile=my_table.sql
   ```

   By using the INDEXFILE parameter with import, you have instructed Oracle to write table and index creation information to the file specified, rather than to bring the data back into the table. The file will contain **create** statements for the table and any indexes. Any triggers and declarative integrity (refer to Chapter 8 for a brief discussion of declarative integrity) defined for the table will be brought back in step #4.

2. Edit the file my_table.sql:

- Remove all "REM" text at the start of lines.

- Look for and delete any rows that contain the word "Connect."

- Look for and delete any rows that start with the word "Rows."

- Look for the **initial** and replace it with the new space desired.

3. Run my_table.sql in SQL*Plus.

4. Import the table data using the command

```
imp userid=user1/password ignore=y tables=my_tabledata
```

This command must mention the keyword **ignore=y** to force Oracle to bring in the table data even though the table already exists after step #3 has completed. If **ignore** is not coded on the call to import, it defaults to N, and the import will not bring rows in, because the table already exists.

SCRIPTS AND TIPS RULE #5
When defragmenting a table using export and import, always use **ignore=y** *to bring the table data in after the table has been re-created.*

Throughout this exercise, we have assumed that there is enough space in the tablespace where the table resides to accommodate the additional requests needed for the table. If this were not the case, you would have to either add another datafile to the tablespace or rebuild the entire tablespace with a larger datafile.

Tables and Indexes Reaching Maxextents

It's all fine and dandy to look at objects with more than a specified number of extents, but the proactive technician will dig for extent information beforehand. One of our favorite tricks is to search through the data dictionary looking for objects that have consumed a number of extents approaching the maximum number they are allowed. This will answer a question such as, "What tables are within 2 of reaching their maximum allowable extent allocation?" or, in more technical terms, what tables are 2 away from their MAXEXTENTS?

We use a NUM_EXT function as shown in the next listing to tell us the number of extents allocated to an object. The function accepts an object name and returns the number of extents currently in use. Inspect the code for some pertinent comments.

```
create or replace function num_ext (object_name in varchar2)
   return number is
  m_extid    number;
  begin
    --
    -- Each table's initial allocation is tracked in USER_EXTENTS as extent
    -- with EXTENT_ID = 0. Thus, we add 1 to the largest extent ID to get
    -- the number of extents in use. If a table had 4 extents, the EXTENT_IDs
    -- would be 0 1 2 and 3. This function also assumes that every object
    -- name (regardless of object type) is unique within schema. Hence, if
    -- a schema has a table called STADIUM, it will not have a SEQUENCE with
    -- the same name.
    --
    select max(extent_id)+1
      into m_extid
      from user_extents
     where segment_name = upper(object_name);
    return m_extid;
  end;
/
```

Once this function is built, we use it in the following SQL script to compare extents in use against maximum available. Our user-defined functions (e.g, function NUM_EXT) can be used in SQL*Plus just as the ones embedded in the Oracle SQL*Plus engine can (e.g., TO_CHAR or MAX). The next listing shows the script and some sample output for the MAYTAG schema.

```
SQL> /* ----------------------------------------------------- */
SQL> /*  exinuse.sql                                          */
SQL> /*                                                       */
SQL> /*  Report on tables and indexes whose extent allocation is */
SQL> /*  within the specified maximum number allowed for the   */
SQL> /*  object.                                               */
SQL> /*                                                       */
SQL> /*  Oracle8 Tuning    Corey & Abbey & Dechichio & Abramson */
SQL> /* ----------------------------------------------------- */
SQL> set pages 20 echo off ver off trimsp on
SQL> col eiu          form 999 head 'In Use'
```

```
SQL> col table_name   form a30 head 'Table name'
SQL> col index_name   form a30 head 'Index name'
SQL> col max_extents form 999 head 'MExtents'
SQL> repheader 'Tables within 2 extents of max allowed ...' skip 2
SQL> select table_name,max_extents, num_ext(table_name) eiu
  2     from user_tables
  3   where max_extents - num_ext(table_name) < 3;
Table name                        MExtents In Use
------------------------- -------------- ------
NEPTUNE                                12     10
FIXEMUP                                99     98
SQL> repheader 'Indexes within 2 extents of max allowed ...' skip 2
SQL> select index_name,max_extents, num_ext(index_name) eiu
  2     from user_indexes
  3   where max_extents - num_ext(index_name) < 3;
Index name                        MExtents In Use
------------------------- -------------- ------
NEPTUNE_PK                             48     46
SQL>
```

SCRIPTS AND TIPS RULE #6
Become fluent in writing and using your own functions, remembering they return one and only one value of your specified datatype. We have found functions especially helpful when working with multilingual data (e.g., French and English, when Y is for Yes in English and O is for the French equivalent).

Contiguous Space Monitoring

The DBA_FREE_SPACE is the place to look to see the status of the free space in your database. The next listing reports on the free space in the USERS7 tablespace in an Oracle8 database.

```
SQL> select *
  2     from sys.dba_free_space
  2   where tablespace_name = 'USERS7'
  3   order by block_id;
TABLESPACE_NAME      FILE_ID    BLOCK_ID      BYTES     BLOCKS
---------------- ---------- ---------- ---------- ----------
USERS7                    16         817      49152         12
```

```
USERS7                     16       829     356352         87
USERS7                     16      5359    1024000        250
USERS7                     16      5609     409600        100
USERS7                     16      5709     565248        138
USERS7                     16      8463   13897728       3393

6 rows selected.
```

By examining Table 11-1, you can assess the true amount of contiguous free space. For each row, you take the starting block ID and add the number of blocks that are free. If that equals the block ID of the next row, then the two rows in DBA_FREE_SPACE are contiguous even though Oracle does not present the output that way.

Periodically, the system monitor (SMON) background process (Chapter 2 discusses the Oracle background processes) coalesces adjacent chunks of free space to make larger contiguous chunks. After SMON does its work, the same query on the USERS7 tablespace is quite a bit different. Notice how the contiguous chunks of free space are now clumped together.

```
TABLESPACE_NAME      FILE_ID   BLOCK_ID      BYTES     BLOCKS
----------------  ----------  ----------  ----------  ----------
USERS7                    16        817      405504          99
USERS7                    16       5359     1998848         488
USERS7                    16       8463    13897728        3393

3 rows selected.
```

There is also the SQL command **alter tablespace … coalesce**; which will collapse all contiguous free extents into larger contiguous extents for each

Begin Block ID	Blocks of Free Space	Actual Contiguous Space (Blocks)
817	12	99
829	87	(part of the 99 above)
5359	250	488
5609	100	(part of the 488 above)
5709	138	(part of the 488 above)
8463	3393	3393

TABLE 11-1. *Actual Contiguous Free Space*

datafile in the tablespace. You can use the DBA_TABLESPACES view and the following code to periodically coalesce free space in your tablespaces.

NOTE
This query assumes the names of the temporary and rollback tablespaces are TEMP and ROLLBACK; they may need to be changed for your purposes.

```
SQL> set echo off pages 0 trimsp off feed off
SQL> spool coalesce
SQL> select 'alter tablespace '||tablespace_name||' coalesce;'
  2    from sys.dba_tablespaces
  3    where tablespace_name not in ('TEMP','ROLLBACK');
alter tablespace SYSTEM coalesce;
alter tablespace REP_DATA1 coalesce;
alter tablespace REP_INDEX1 coalesce;
alter tablespace CENTRAL coalesce;
SQL> spool off
SQL> set echo on feed on
SQL> @coalesce.lst
SQL> alter tablespace SYSTEM coalesce;
Tablespace altered.
SQL> alter tablespace REP_DATA1 coalesce;
Tablespace altered.
SQL> alter tablespace REP_INDEX1 coalesce;
Tablespace altered.
SQL> alter tablespace CENTRAL coalesce;
Tablespace altered.
SQL>
```

NOTE
There will be no entry in DBA_FREE_SPACE for any tablespace that has NO free blocks. This is a Trojan horse to be watched for!

NOTE
Oracle8 does not coalesce free space in any tablespace that has the default storage parameter PCTINCREASE set to 0. Watch out for this.

SCRIPTS AND TIPS RULE #7
On reports that display the free space totals by tablespace, ensure the number of rows returned is the same as the number of tablespaces in the database. This will alert you if a situation occurs where a tablespace has no free space whatsoever.

Free Space by Tablespace Monitoring

Along with monitoring the number of extents that segments have, the monitoring of the free space in a database should be done on a regular basis. This monitoring can be used to determine if too much space is allocated to a tablespace or if additional space needs to be allocated.

The following SQL script reports on the allocated space in each tablespace, the amount of free space for each tablespace, and percentage of allocated space that remains free.

```
SQL> select b.file_id "File #",
  2           b.tablespace_name "Tablespace name",
  3           b.bytes "# bytes",
  4           (b.bytes - sum(nvl(a.bytes,0))) "# used",
  5           sum(nvl(a.bytes,0)) "# free",
  6           (sum(nvl(a.bytes,0))/(b.bytes))*100 "%free"
  7    from sys.dba_free_space a, sys.dba_data_files b
  8    where a.file_id(+) = b.file_id
  9    group by b.tablespace_name, b.file_id, b.bytes
 10    order by b.tablespace_name;
```

File#	Tablespace Name	# Bytes	# Used	# Free	%Free
1	SYSTEM	104857600	26503168	78354432	74.7
3	TBSP_INDEX001	83886080	78610432	5275648	6.3
9	TBSP_INDEX001	10485760	6907904	3577856	34.1
5	TBSP_PROD001	3145728	2048	3143680	99.9
6	TBSP_PROD002	5242880	3381248	1861632	35.5
7	TBSP_PROD003	52428800	50563792	1835008	3.5
8	TBSP_PROD004	5242880	2021376	3221504	61.4
2	TBSP_ROLLBACK	157286400	47310848	109975552	69.9
4	TBSP_USER_TEMP	31457280	2048	31455232	100.0
10	TBSP_WORK	31457280	11300864	20156416	64.1

This listing shows that in tablespace TBSP_INDEX001, a mere 6.3 percent of space allocated is not being used, and in tablespace TBSP_PROD003, only 3.5 percent of space allocated is not in use. The SYSTEM tablespace is only using 25.3 percent of the space allocated to it. The following recommendations from this report may help you make the sizing decisions that help tune your database.

1. The INDEX001 and PROD003 tablespaces have too low a percent of space not in use.

2. If the database is in a production mode (persons use the database daily to undertake the business of your installation), the SYSTEM tablespace is using too little of its space to be sized at 102.4 megabytes.

3. Tablespace PROD001 may have too much space allocated, unless it has been preallocated for a large load of data.

SCRIPTS AND TIPS RULE #8
If the free space in a tablespace containing tables that experience high insert and update activity falls below 15 percent, add more space to the tablespace.

SCRIPTS AND TIPS RULE #9
If a tablespace holds static table data, reduce the amount of file space allocated to it if there is more than 20 percent free space.

SCRIPTS AND TIPS RULE #10
Increasing the amount of free space in a tablespace may not always involve adding an additional datafile. Tablespace reorganization using export and import may free up large quantities of space, alleviating the need to add another datafile.

SCRIPTS AND TIPS RULE #11
*The only way to decrease the amount of space
allocated to the SYSTEM tablespace is to
re-create the database.*

User Information

There will be times when, either for auditing purposes or user requests, user
information will need to be gathered. We have used Oracle Reports to
create a report that gives the username, the date it was created, roles that
have been granted to the user, the user's default, and temporary tablespaces.

```
select username "Username", created "Created",
       substr(granted_role,1,15) "Roles",
       default_tablespace "Default TS",
       temporary_tablespace "Temporary TS"
  from sys.dba_users, sys.dba_role_privs
 where username = grantee (+)
 order by username;
```

An example of the output that is produced from this report follows.

```
                              USER LIST
PAGE: 1                                              DATE: 09-SEP-99


Username         Created   Roles           Default TS       Temporary TS
--------------   --------  --------------  --------------   --------------
ADAMS            03/18/99  CONNECT         TBSP_WORKDEV     TBSP_TEMPORARY
FORMS30          03/18/99  CONNECT         TBSP_WORKDEV     TBSP_TEMPORARY
FORMS30          03/18/99  RESOURCE        TBSP_WORKDEV     TBSP_TEMPORARY
OPS$USER1        03/18/99  CONNECT         SYSTEM           SYSTEM
OPS$USER1        03/18/98  DBA             SYSTEM           SYSTEM
OPS$USER1        03/18/97  RESOURCE        SYSTEM           SYSTEM
OPS$USER002      03/18/98  CONNECT         TBSP_WORKDEV     TBSP_TEMPORARY
OPS$APPLIC1      03/18/98  CONNECT         TBSP_DATA001     TBSP_TEMPORARY
OPS$APPLIC1      03/18/99  RESOURCE        TBSP_DATA001     TBSP_TEMPORARY
SYS              03/17/98  CONNECT         SYSTEM           SYSTEM
SYS              03/17/98  DBA             SYSTEM           SYSTEM
SYS              03/17/98  EXP_FULL_DATABA SYSTEM           SYSTEM
SYS              03/17/98  IMP_FULL_DATABA SYSTEM           SYSTEM
SYS              03/17/98  RESOURCE        SYSTEM           SYSTEM
```

As can be seen, the users are listed alphabetically by their username and appear multiple times if they have been assigned multiple Oracle roles.

SCRIPTS AND TIPS RULE #12
Gather user information as part of your daily backups—it will assist you when trying to set up new users or groups of users.

Accessing All V$ and DBA_ Dictionary Views

Throughout this book, we make continual reference to the assortment of V$ views owned by Oracle user SYS. The assortment of views prefixed by the characters DBA_ prove useful to the DBA and application developers as well. Regardless of what is done at installation time, our experience dictates that you should manually give access to these views. A script that will grant select access to PUBLIC on all V$ and DBA_ views is shown next. It must be run connected to the database as Oracle user SYS.

```
set echo off feed off pages 0
spool veedollar_dba.sql
select 'grant select on '||view_name||' to public;'
  from sys.dba_views
 where view_name like 'V_$%'
    or view_name like 'DBA_%;
set echo on feed on
@veedollar_dba
```

After this script completes, all database users will be able to access the desired dictionary views. Public synonyms are in place for the V$ tables. None are in place (unless you put them there) for the DBA_ views. When using these DBA_ views, simply qualify the view name with the SYS account qualifier.

SCRIPTS AND TIPS RULE #13
Do not create public synonyms for the DBA_ views. Developers who need to use them can use the account qualifier syntax (e.g., the DBA_FREE_SPACE view is referenced using the name SYS.DBA_FREE_SPACE).

Sizing the Shared Pool

Finding the optimal size for the shared pool can be an elusive exercise. As DBAs and application programmers, we are all too familiar with Oracle error ORA-04031:

```
ORA-04031: unable to allocate num bytes of shared memory num, num, num

Cause: More shared memory is needed than was allocated in the operating system
process. SGA private memory has been exhausted.

Action: Either use the DBMS_SHARED_POOL package to pin large packages,
reduce your use of shared memory, or increase the amount of available
shared memory by increasing the value set for the SHARED_POOL_SIZE
initialization parameter.
```

Using the code that follows, that figure can be calculated. There are a few points worth noting in the listing. They are embedded in the code as remarks.

```
SQL> /* ---------------------------------------------------------- */
SQL> /*  spsizing.sql                                              */
SQL> /*                                                            */
SQL> /*  Report on shared pool sizing for entered number of        */
SQL> /*  concurrent users using a user logged on as a sample of    */
SQL> /*  the amount of memory that will be used per session.       */
SQL> /*                                                            */
SQL> /*  Oracle8 Tuning    Corey & Abbey & Dechichio & Abramson    */
SQL> /* ---------------------------------------------------------- */
set echo off ver off feed off pages 0

rem * You are prompted for the Oracle ID of someone currently
rem * logged on. That person's memory consumption will be used
rem * as a sample amount. You are also asked for the # of
rem * concurrent users to base this calculation on.

accept username prompt 'User to use?? '
accept numusers prompt '# of users ?? '

rem * Get that user's session identifier by joining v$process
rem * and v$session matching the ADDR column from v$process
rem * against the PADDR column from v$session, and matching
rem * the USERNAME column from v$session against the username
rem * entered before
```

```
set term off
col a new_value snum
select sid a
  from v$process p, v$session s
 where p.addr = s.paddr
   and s.username = upper('&username');

rem * Now that we have the sample user's session
rem * ID, we can go to v$sesstat for the amount of memory
rem * that user is consuming.  We use STATISTIC# = 16 which is
rem * the MAX SESSION MEMORY per user maintained in
rem * v$sesstat for each user connected to the database.

col b new_value pumem
select value b
  from v$sesstat
 where statistic# = 16
   and sid = &snum;

rem * Get the amount of memory in the shared pool that is
rem * currently in use (i.e., the size of the SQL sitting in the
rem * shared pool).
col c new_value spl
select sum(sharable_mem) c
  from v$sqlarea;
rem * Using the following formula, make the optimal shared
rem * pool size calculation.
rem * optimal size = 1.3 * (per_user_memory * number _users +
rem *                       size_of_sql_in_pool)
col d new_value size1
col e new_value size2
select (&pumem*&numusers+&spl) d,
       (&pumem*&numusers+&spl)+3/10*(&pumem*&numusers+&spl) e
  from dual;

col pmem form 99,999,990
col nu   like pmem
col sss  like pmem
col tmu  like pmem
col s1   like pmem
col s2   like pmem
set term on
prompt
prompt
prompt
```

```
prompt =====================================================
select 'Per user memory requirement:  ', &pumem pmem
   from dual;
select 'Number of users              :  ', &numusers nu
   from dual;
prompt =====================================================
select 'Total memory for users      :  ', &numusers*&pumem tmu
   from dual;
select 'Size of stuff in shared SQL:  ', &spl sss
   from dual;
prompt =====================================================
select 'Base shared pool size        :  ', &size1 s1
   from dual;
select 'Pool size with 30% free      :  ', &size2 s2
   from dual;
prompt =====================================================
```

You will receive output similar to the following when you run this code.

```
SQL> @pool
User to use?? ops$jonespg
# of users ?? 30
=================================================
Per user memory requirement:      198,116
Number of users           :            30
=================================================
Total memory for users    :     5,943,480
Size of stuff in shared SQL:    10,360,432
=================================================
Base shared pool size     :    16,303,912
Pool size with 30% free   :    21,195,086
=================================================
```

SCRIPTS AND TIPS RULE #14
Run this script to estimate optimal shared pool size at regular intervals during the business day and NEVER within 24 hours of instance startup.

Notice the figure "30%" as free space in the shared pool. We believe that shared pool sizing is the single activity you are responsible for that has the biggest payback in the tuning exercise. Fine-tuning the SHARED_POOL_SIZE entry in the initialization parameter file can be

assisted using this script. Watch
provides more and more tools with each new release of the software.

SCRIPTS AND TIPS RULE #15
*When sizing the shared pool, allow an extra
30 percent free space. If and when the
concurrent user load increases, revisit shared
pool sizing programs.*

Use of Database Block Buffers in the SGA

It is handy to know whether all the buffers specified in the initialization
parameter file entry DB_BLOCK_BUFFERS are being used during
day-to-day operations. The next script must be run as the Oracle user SYS.

```
select decode(state,0,'FREE',
                     1,'Read and Modified',
                     2,'Read and Non-Modified',
                     4,'Current Block Read','Other'),count(*)
  from x$bh
 group by decode(state,0,'FREE',
                     1,'Read and Modified',
                     2,'Read and Non-Modified',
                     4,'Current Block Read','Other');


DECODE(STATE,0,'FREE'  COUNT(*)
---------------------  ---------
FREE                         62
Other                        20
Read and Modified           118
```

The figure to pay the most attention to is the FREE buffers. This is the
number of database block buffers in the cache that are not in use. They can
be unused for one of two reasons. It can be due to a very small concurrent
use of the database (as in quiet off-hours). It could also be that the entry for
DB_BLOCK_BUFFERS in the initialization parameter file is set too high. The
former reason requires no intervention. For the latter, you may want to
decrease the value of this parameter.

SCRIPTS AND TIPS RULE #16

*If the FREE buffer count is nonzero over an
extended sampling period (e.g., after running
script once an hour between 9:00 and 5:00
and inspecting the results), consider lowering
the value of DB_BLOCK_BUFFERS and
restarting the instance.*

Creating an Instance Control File

When backing up the database, we recommend creating a text copy of
the code required to re-create a control file. This is done in SQL*Plus using
the command

```
alter database backup controlfile to trace;
```

Oracle will respond with "Database altered" when the command
successfully completes. The SQL script written by the command is placed
in the directory specified by the USER_DUMP_DEST entry in the
initialization parameter file. Windows NT, by default, will put the output
trace file from this command in the RDBMS80\TRACE directory. Through
our experience, this copy of the control file can be a lifesaver. The output is
shown in the next listing. As you can see, part of it is a bona fide SQL script
that could be used to create a control file. The code would be run in Server
Manager or the SQL*Worksheet tool of the Enterprise Manager—hence the
character is used as the comment indicator.

```
Dump file C:\ORANT\RDBMS80\trace\ORA00220.TRC
Tue Sep 09 14:26:03 1999
ORACLE V8.0.3.0.0 - Production vsnsta=0
vsnsql=c vsnxtr=3
Windows NT V4.0, OS V5.101, CPU type 586
Oracle8 Enterprise Edition Release 8.0.3.0.0 - Production
With the Partitioning and Objects options
PL/SQL Release 8.0.3.0.0 - Production
Windows NT V4.0, OS V5.101, CPU type 586
Instance name: orcl
Redo thread mounted by this instance: 1
Oracle process number: 10
pid: dc
```

```
Tue Sep 09 14:26:03 1999
Tue Sep 09 14:26:03 1999
*** SESSION ID:(10.700) 1999.09.09.14.26.03.993
# The following commands will create a new control file and use it
# to open the database.
# Data used by the recovery manager will be lost. Additional logs may
# be required for media recovery of offline data files. Use this
# only if the current version of all online logs are available.
STARTUP NOMOUNT
CREATE CONTROLFILE REUSE DATABASE "ORACLE" NORESETLOGS NOARCHIVELOG
     MAXLOGFILES 32
     MAXLOGMEMBERS 2
     MAXDATAFILES 32
     MAXINSTANCES 16
     MAXLOGHISTORY 1630
LOGFILE
   GROUP 1 'C:\ORANT\DATABASE\LOG2ORCL.ORA'   SIZE 200K,
   GROUP 2 'C:\ORANT\DATABASE\LOG1ORCL.ORA'   SIZE 200K
DATAFILE
   'C:\ORANT\DATABASE\SYS1ORCL.ORA',
   'C:\ORANT\DATABASE\USR1ORCL.ORA',
   'C:\ORANT\DATABASE\RBS1ORCL.ORA',
   'C:\ORANT\DATABASE\TMP1ORCL.ORA',
   'FND.DBF'
;
# Recovery is required if any of the datafiles are restored backups,
# or if the last shutdown was not normal or immediate.
RECOVER DATABASE
# Database can now be opened normally.
ALTER DATABASE OPEN;
```

This script can be used to change some of the database creation parameters that previously could only be given a new value by re-creating the database. For example, the **maxlogmembers** entry in the **create database** indicates the maximum number of redo log group members. As we have discussed throughout this book, redo log files are written by Oracle and contain transaction and rollback information about activities against the database. Redo log files are used for database recovery. With Oracle8 you can instruct Oracle to write simultaneously to a number of redo logs. This facility is called using *multiplexed redo logs*. The redo log files that are written to at the same time are referred to as a *redo log group*. Each group of redo logs can have up to the value specified in **maxlogmembers** members written to at the same time.

SCRIPTS AND TIPS RULE #17
Incorporate **alter database backup controlfile to trace** *into your system backup routines. Use the output to change database parameters that cannot be altered using the SQL command* **alter database**.

Renaming a Column in a Table

There is no SQL statement to accomplish this. Time and time again, it has been suggested to Oracle that there be an **alter table modify** where the name of a column can be changed. Oracle, like other database vendors, has no plans to implement this functionality. There are strict rules set out by ANSI (American National Standards Institute) that do not allow this operation for databases that conform to the SQL standards ANSI controls. The best way to do it is by using the SQL statement

```
create table as select
```

with a column list. For example, consider the following table definition for the JOBS table.

```
Name                 Null?    Type
-----------------    -------- ----
FY_CODE              NOT NULL VARCHAR2(5)
JOB_NUM              NOT NULL VARCHAR2(6)
PROJ_NUM             NOT NULL NUMBER(2)
SDESC_E                       VARCHAR2(30)
SDESC_F                       VARCHAR2(30)
LDESC_E                       VARCHAR2(60)
LDESC_F                       VARCHAR2(60)
BUDGET_HOURS                  NUMBER(7,2)
STATUS                        VARCHAR2(2)
```

Suppose you wanted to change the name of the BUDGET_HOURS column to BUD_HOURS. The first suggestion would be to issue the SQL statements that follow.

```
rem * Create a temp table with the new column name.
create table jobs_temp (fy_code, job_num, proj_num, sdesc_e, sdesc_f,
                        ldesc_e, ldesc_f, bud_hours, status)
as select * from jobs;
```

```
rem * swap names of tables.
rename jobs to jobs_old;
rename jobs_temp to jobs;
```

This exercise seems to complete the task. However, the following problems may have been introduced.

1. Any indexes that existed on the old jobs table are not present in the new table.

2. Any grants on the jobs object have been lost.

3. Any views built on the old column names in the jobs table are invalid if the view definition included the old column name.

4. The storage parameters of the new jobs table may not match those of the old table.

5. Any constraints on the jobs object have been lost or marked invalid.

The following steps will ensure that indexes, grants, and storage parameters will be preserved.

1. Export the existing table definition using the following command. This will create a file called jobs.dmp, which will be input to the next step.

   ```
   exp userid=user/password tables=jobs rows=n compress=n file=jobs
   ```

2. Using import with the INDEXFILE option, create an SQL script using the following command. This will create a file called jobs.sql with the existing table and index definitions with all their existing storage parameters.

   ```
   imp userid=/ indexfile=jobs.sql file=jobs
   ```

3. Run the following script in SQL*Plus to preserve the grants on the old jobs table. The script will produce a file called regrant_jobs.sql that can be run in SQL*Plus against the new jobs table. Notice the **decode** that is done on the values in the GRANTABLE column in USER_TAB_PRIVS_MADE. This is necessary to preserve the **with grant option** grants given out on the existing jobs table.

```
set echo off feed off pages 0
spool regrant_jobs.sql
select 'grant ' || privilege || ' on ' || table_name || ' to ' ||
grantee || decode (grantable,'YES',' with grant option;',';')
   from user_tab_privs_made
  where table_name = 'JOBS';
spool off
```

4. Create a SQL script to drop any indexes on the old jobs table. Using the following, a script called jobs_idrop.sql will be created.

```
set pages 0 feed off echo off
   spool jobs_idrop.sql
   select 'drop index ' || index_name || ';'
     from user_indexes
    where table_name = 'JOBS';
   spool off
```

5. Issue the following statement to rename the jobs table to jobs_old.

```
rename jobs to jobs_old;
```

6. Run jobs_idrop.sql to drop indexes on the jobs_old table. With version Oracle8 you may only have one object, regardless of object type, by the same name. If you left the indexes in place on the jobs_old table, the index creation in the next step would fail, because like-named indexes still exist on jobs_old.

7. Precreate the new jobs table by running the jobs.sql script that was created in step 2 of this exercise. Before running the script, edit jobs.sql and change the old column name in the table create script BUDGET_HOURS to BUD_HOURS. Also, remove all the REM text from the start of any lines, remove any lines that start with the text CONNECT, and remove any lines that contain a number followed by the word "rows".

```
CREATE TABLE "STEVANOVIC"."JOBS" ("FY_CODE" VARCHAR2(5) NOT NULL,
"JOB_NUM" VARCHAR2(6) NOT NULL, "PROJ_NUM" NUMBER(2, 0) NOT NULL,
"SDESC_E" VARCHAR2(30), "SDESC_F" VARCHAR2(30), "LDESC_E"
VARCHAR2(60), "LDESC_F" VARCHAR2(60), "BUD_HOURS" NUMBER(7, 2),
"STATUS" VARCHAR2(2)) PCTFREE 40 PCTUSED 60 INITRANS 1 MAXTRANS 255
STORAGE(INITIAL 5242880 NEXT 1064960 MINEXTENTS 1 MAXEXTENTS 240
PCTINCREASE 20 FREELISTS 1 FREELIST GROUPS 1) TABLESPACE "USERS" ;
```

```
CREATE INDEX "STEVANOVIC"."JOBS_1" ON "JOBS" ("FY_CODE" , "JOB_NUM",
"PROJ_NUM" ) PCTFREE 10 INITRANS 2 MAXTRANS 255 STORAGE (INITIAL 835584
NEXT 81920 MINEXTENTS 1 MAXEXTENTS 240 PCTINCREASE 20 FREELISTS 1)
TABLESPACE "INDEXES" ;
CREATE INDEX "STEVANOVIC"."JOBS_3" ON "JOBS" ("PROJ_NUM" ) PCTFREE
10 INITRANS 2 MAXTRANS 255 STORAGE (INITIAL 565248 NEXT 40960 MINEXTENTS 1
MAXEXTENTS 240 PCTINCREASE 20 FREELISTS 1) TABLESPACE "INDEXES" ;
CREATE INDEX "STEVANOVIC"."JOBS_2" ON "JOBS" ("JOB_NUM" ) PCTFREE
10 INITRANS 2 MAXTRANS 255 STORAGE (INITIAL 589824 NEXT 61440 MINEXTENTS 1
MAXEXTENTS 240 PCTINCREASE 20 FREELISTS 1) TABLESPACE "INDEXES" ;
```

8. Move data from jobs_old to jobs by issuing the statement

```
insert into jobs select * from jobs_old;
```

9. Run regrant_jobs.sql to put back the grants as they existed on the old table.

10. Drop all foreign key constraints on the original table (jobs_old).

11. Drop the jobs_old table.

12. Re-create all foreign key constraints on the new table (jobs).

You will now have a properly indexed and properly sized jobs table that has the BUDGET_HOURS column renamed to BUD_HOURS. The last task is looking in the data dictionary for any view built using the old BUDGET_HOURS column. These views, if any, are now flagged as invalid and must be re-created. The following query will list the names and owners of any views mentioning the BUDGET_HOURS column.

```
select owner, table_name, column_name
  from sys.dba_tab_columns
 where column_name = 'BUDGET_HOURS';
```

There is no way to automatically re-create any views that use the old BUDGET_HOURS column name. You must manually intervene and rebuild these views.

NOTE
The exercise we just led you through will not work as expected if there are constraints on the table (e.g., primary key or check constraints). The migration of the constraints to the new table will be problematic, thereby requiring manual intervention.

Using SQL to Write SQL

If you are not familiar with this technique, now is the time to learn! With the spooling capabilities of SQL*Plus and the correct wording of SQL statements, it is possible to create a spool file from a SQL command that is SQL itself. Suppose you wanted to drop all objects belonging to a user (OPS$FRANCISL in this example) but did not have enough privileges to issue the SQL command

```
drop user charroel;
```

The following code will accomplish this for you. When you are done, there will be a script called nukeuser.sql with the drop statements.

```
set echo off pages 0 feed off trimsp on
spool nukeuser.sql
select 'drop '||object_type||' '||owner||'.'||object_name||';'
  from sys.dba_objects
 where object_type in ('VIEW','SEQUENCE','SYNONYM')
   and owner = 'CHARROEL';
select 'drop ' ||object_type||' '||owner||'.'||object_name||
       'cascade constraints;'
  from sys.dba_objects
 where object_type =  'TABLE'
   and owner = 'CHARROEL';
spool off
```

Taking this one step further, let's rebuild the tablespace quotas given out to your users using this technique. The following will do this for you and create a SQL script as output called ts_quotas.sql.

```
spool ts_quotas.sql
select 'alter user quota ' || max_bytes || ' on ' || tablespace_name || ';'
  from sys.dba_ts_quotas
 where nvl(max_bytes,0) > 0;
spool off
```

Why not use SQL to dynamically build a parameter file for use with export? Let's create a parameter file to export all the data for any user that has objects in the tablespace YR_TRANS. This script, unlike the previous two, uses a combination of SQL and SQL*Plus statements.

```
set pages 0 feed off echo off
spool yr_trans.parfile
prompt userid=system/manager
prompt file=yr_trans
prompt buffer=10240000
prompt indexes=y
prompt grants=y
prompt owner=(
select unique owner || ','
  from sys.dba_tables
 where tablespace_name = 'YR_TRANS'
   and  owner <>
   (select max(owner)
     from sys.dba_tables
   where tablespace_name = 'YR_TRANS');
select max(owner) || ')'
  from sys.dba_tables
where tablespace_name = 'YR_TRANS';
spool off
```

The sky's the limit. Once you get started with this technique, you will end up finding a host of situations where you can use it. Why not use the information stored in the data dictionary to assist your backup procedures by creating a SQL script to rebuild your rollback segments?

```
select 'create rollback segment '||segment_name||chr(10),
       '           tablespace '||tablespace_name||chr(10),
       '           storage (initial    '||initial_extent||chr(10),
       '                    next       '||next_extent||chr(10),
       '                    minextents '||min_extents||chr(10),
       '                    maxextents '||max_extents||');'
    from sys.dba_rollback_segs a,v$rollstat b,v$rollname c
   where segment_name <> 'SYSTEM'
     and b.usn = c.usn
     and a.segment_name = c.name;
```

Re-creating Stored Objects

The code for all your procedures, packages, and functions is stored in the USER_SOURCE and DBA_SOURCE data dictionary views. In most installations we have experience with, the DBA has granted **select** on the DBA_ series of dictionary views. We will use the DBA_SOURCE view in the following code so anyone can reconstruct the SQL to create stored objects. Let's look at a few programs that can be used to drag the code out of the dictionary.

Code to Re-create Packages

Even though the package (TYPE='PACKAGE') definition or package body ((TYPE='PACKAGE BODY') can be compiled separately, the code shown next does both parts together. The **create or replace** text is not stored in DBA_SOURCE, and is put in the output by decoding the LINE column and placing it there when the column value is 1.

```
/* ---------------------------------------------------------- */
/*  mpkg.sql                                                  */
/*                                                            */
/*  Receive the package name and the owner on the command    */
/*  on the command line.                                      */
/*                                                            */
/*  Oracle8 Tuning    Corey & Abbey & Dechichio & Abramson    */
/* ---------------------------------------------------------- */
set space 0 ver off pages 0 feed off echo off trimsp on lines 999
def package_name = "&1"
def owner = "&2"
spool package.sql
prompt /*
prompt
prompt SQL to recreate &&owner.'s PACKAGE &&package_name
prompt
prompt */
prompt
prompt set echo on feed on
prompt spool package
prompt
select decode(line,1,'create or replace '||text,text)
  from sys.dba_source a
 where type = 'PACKAGE'
   and name = upper('&&package_name')
```

```
   and owner = upper ('&&owner')
 order by line;
prompt /
prompt
select decode(line,1,'create or replace '||text,text)
  from sys.dba_source
 where type = 'PACKAGE BODY'
   and name = upper('&&package_name')
   and owner = upper ('&&owner')
 order by line;
prompt /
prompt spool off
spool off
```

Code to Re-create Procedures and Functions

Procedures and function can be handled together since they only contain one part. This can be done for a whole schema at once by placing a call to this program in a separate SQL script, with a line to re-create each procedure or function in the schema.

```
/* ----------------------------------------------------------- */
/*  mpfn.sql                                                    */
/*                                                              */
/*  Receive the object name and the owner on the command       */
/*  on the command line.                                        */
/*                                                              */
/*  Oracle8 Tuning    Corey & Abbey & Dechichio & Abramson      */
/* ----------------------------------------------------------- */
def prfn_name = "&1"
def owner = "&2"
spool prfn
prompt
prompt /*
prompt SQL to recreate &&owner.'s PROCEDURE or FUNCTION &&prfn_name
prompt
prompt */
prompt
prompt set echo on feed on
prompt spool prfn
prompt
select rtrim(decode(line, 1,'create or replace '||text, text)) col1
  from sys.dba_source
```

```
  where owner = upper('&&owner')
    and name = upper('&&prfn_name')
  order by line;
prompt /
prompt spool off
spool off
```

Compiling a Whole Schema

This can be accomplished in SQL*Plus using the following code. The most important keyword in the SQL statement used to build the output is **distinct**. Each line in the USER_SOURCE view contains the name of the stored object.

```
/* ------------------------------------------------------- */
/*  recomp.sql                                             */
/*                                                         */
/*  Write an SQL*Plus script to recreate the stored        */
/*  objects for an entire schema.                          */
/*                                                         */
/*  Oracle8 Tuning    Corey & Abbey & Dechichio & Abramson */
/* ------------------------------------------------------- */
set echo off feed off pages 0
spool recomp.do
select distinct 'alter '||type||' '||name||' compile;'
  from user_source
 where type <> 'PACKAGE BODY';
spool off
set echo on feed on
spool recomp
@recomp.do
spool off
```

The result of this code will be the "recomp.do" file with a line to compile each object; a few lines are shown in the next listing.

```
alter package WEMBLEY compile;
alter function YORN compile;
alter procedure DISNEY compile;
```

Let's Tune It

We have provided you with some food for thought in this chapter, drawing your attention to some issues (and their resolutions) that you will wrestle with tomorrow (if not today) or have already visited. In this book, we repeatedly state that the tuning process is ongoing—and you need to attend to every facet of managing the resources to get the best return from your tuning investment.

- Run your database in ARCHIVELOG mode—you provide yourself with almost bulletproof protection against data loss due to a variety of emergencies (e.g., disk drive headcrash or mistaken erasure of a database file).

- Develop a plan of attack when doing hot backups of a large database by splitting the tablespaces into a number of cycles and doing each cycle when and only when the previous cycle runs to completion. If a cycle does not complete on its first attempt, keep trying it again until it succeeds.

- Monitor and report on extent allocations to tables and indexes to help you manage space effectively.

- Keep up-to-date user information at your fingertips to assist you if you need to prepare reports for auditors or reset privileges for users or a class of users.

- Grant access to the assortment of V$ and DBA_ data dictionary tables to allow your developers and co-DBAs to access a wide assortment of performance information they need to make tuning decisions.

- Compute the optimal setting for the SHARED_POOL_SIZE entry in your initialization parameter file that will turn on the light at the end of the shared-SQL-area-sizing tunnel.

- Monitor the activity of the buffers in the database buffer cache—if some buffers are not being used steadily, consider adjusting the DB_BLOCK_BUFFERS entry in your initialization parameter file.

- When renaming a column in a table, use our method—it preserves grants, indexes, and storage parameters.

- Incorporate the scripts we presented that take **create** statements out of the USER_SOURCE or DBA_SOURCE views for all packages, procedures, and functions in a schema or the whole database.

Oracle 7.x Specifics

All sections in the chapter apply to Oracle 7.x.

Shutdown

This ends the saga we have grown to love called Oracle8 Tuning. The tuning business is littered with pitfalls and time consuming tasks. Fortunately, there has been a proliferation of assistants (i.e., books such as this) to aid you during this never-ending process. The leaders in the field are keeping current with the latest and greatest trends in the tuning bag of tricks. Two words continually come to mind when we think of tuning: education and experience. There is no substitute for education and there never will be. Experience helps you master the seemingly insurmountable tasks involved in tuning Oracle8.

Rub shoulders with your counterparts at Oracle user group and other software conventions around the globe—you will always see the likes of Corey, Abbey, Dechichio, and Abramson there. We live and breathe Oracle—it tastes good—give it a shot! Thanks, merci, gracias, danke schoen, todah rabah.

APPENDIX

A

Describes of Tables Referenced Throughout this Book

he following data dictionary tables and miscellaneous Oracle objects are referenced throughout *Oracle8 Tuning*. These commands are extracted from the Oracle 8.0.3 data dictionary. Column names may change in subsequent releases of the Oracle Server. These views are owned by Oracle user SYS. You may have to connect to the SYS account and grant **select** on these objects to allow others to use them. We have included them here for reference and to keep the reader from having to balance *Oracle8 Tuning* on one hand and the *Oracle8 Server Reference* on the other.

NOTE
You will have to use the **desc sys.v_$** *convention when trying to look at the structure of the SYS v$ data dictionary views. If you use the syntax you may now be familiar with,* **desc v$**, *you will get error ORA-24332: invalid object type.*

Describes of Miscellaneous Tables

DBA_AUDIT_OBJECT

```
Name                             Null?    Type
-------------------------------- -------- ----
OS_USERNAME                               VARCHAR2(255)
USERNAME                                  VARCHAR2(30)
USERHOST                                  VARCHAR2(128)
TERMINAL                                  VARCHAR2(255)
TIMESTAMP                        NOT NULL DATE
OWNER                                     VARCHAR2(30)
OBJ_NAME                                  VARCHAR2(128)
ACTION_NAME                               VARCHAR2(27)
NEW_OWNER                                 VARCHAR2(30)
NEW_NAME                                  VARCHAR2(128)
SES_ACTIONS                               VARCHAR2(19)
COMMENT_TEXT                              VARCHAR2(4000)
SESSIONID                        NOT NULL NUMBER
ENTRYID                          NOT NULL NUMBER
STATEMENTID                      NOT NULL NUMBER
```

```
RETURNCODE                          NOT NULL NUMBER
PRIV_USED                                    VARCHAR2(40)
OBJECT_LABEL                                 RAW MLSLABEL
SESSION_LABEL                                RAW MLSLABEL
```

DBA_EXTENTS

```
Name                             Null?    Type
------------------------------   -------- ----
OWNER                                     VARCHAR2(30)
SEGMENT_NAME                              VARCHAR2(81)
PARTITION_NAME                            VARCHAR2(30)
SEGMENT_TYPE                              VARCHAR2(17)
TABLESPACE_NAME                           VARCHAR2(30)
EXTENT_ID                        NOT NULL NUMBER
FILE_ID                          NOT NULL NUMBER
BLOCK_ID                         NOT NULL NUMBER
BYTES                                     NUMBER
BLOCKS                           NOT NULL NUMBER
RELATIVE_FNO                     NOT NULL NUMBER
```

DBA_FREE_SPACE

```
Name                             Null?    Type
------------------------------   -------- ----
TABLESPACE_NAME                  NOT NULL VARCHAR2(30)
FILE_ID                          NOT NULL NUMBER
BLOCK_ID                         NOT NULL NUMBER
BYTES                                     NUMBER
BLOCKS                           NOT NULL NUMBER
RELATIVE_FNO                     NOT NULL NUMBER
```

DBA_SOURCE

```
Name                             Null?    Type
------------------------------   -------- ----
OWNER                            NOT NULL VARCHAR2(30)
NAME                             NOT NULL VARCHAR2(30)
TYPE                                      VARCHAR2(12)
LINE                             NOT NULL NUMBER
TEXT                                      VARCHAR2(4000)
```

DBA_SYNONYMS

Name	Null?	Type
OWNER	NOT NULL	VARCHAR2(30)
SYNONYM_NAME	NOT NULL	VARCHAR2(30)
TABLE_OWNER		VARCHAR2(30)
TABLE_NAME	NOT NULL	VARCHAR2(30)
DB_LINK		VARCHAR2(128)

DBA_TABLES

Name	Null?	Type
OWNER	NOT NULL	VARCHAR2(30)
TABLE_NAME	NOT NULL	VARCHAR2(30)
TABLESPACE_NAME		VARCHAR2(30)
CLUSTER_NAME		VARCHAR2(30)
IOT_NAME		VARCHAR2(30)
PCT_FREE		NUMBER
PCT_USED		NUMBER
INI_TRANS		NUMBER
MAX_TRANS		NUMBER
INITIAL_EXTENT		NUMBER
NEXT_EXTENT		NUMBER
MIN_EXTENTS		NUMBER
MAX_EXTENTS		NUMBER
PCT_INCREASE		NUMBER
FREELISTS		NUMBER
FREELIST_GROUPS		NUMBER
LOGGING		VARCHAR2(3)
BACKED_UP		VARCHAR2(1)
NUM_ROWS		NUMBER
BLOCKS		NUMBER
EMPTY_BLOCKS		NUMBER
AVG_SPACE		NUMBER
CHAIN_CNT		NUMBER
AVG_ROW_LEN		NUMBER
AVG_SPACE_FREELIST_BLOCKS		NUMBER
NUM_FREELIST_BLOCKS		NUMBER
DEGREE		VARCHAR2(10)
INSTANCES		VARCHAR2(10)

```
CACHE                              VARCHAR2(5)
TABLE_LOCK                         VARCHAR2(8)
SAMPLE_SIZE                        NUMBER
LAST_ANALYZED                      DATE
PARTITIONED                        VARCHAR2(3)
IOT_TYPE                           VARCHAR2(12)
TEMPORARY                          VARCHAR2(1)
NESTED                             VARCHAR2(3)
BUFFER_POOL                        VARCHAR2(7)
```

INDEX_STATS

```
Name                            Null?    Type
------------------------------- -------- ----
HEIGHT                                   NUMBER
BLOCKS                                   NUMBER
NAME                                     VARCHAR2(30)
PARTITION_NAME                           VARCHAR2(30)
LF_ROWS                                  NUMBER
LF_BLKS                                  NUMBER
LF_ROWS_LEN                              NUMBER
LF_BLK_LEN                               NUMBER
BR_ROWS                                  NUMBER
BR_BLKS                                  NUMBER
BR_ROWS_LEN                              NUMBER
BR_BLK_LEN                               NUMBER
DEL_LF_ROWS                              NUMBER
DEL_LF_ROWS_LEN                          NUMBER
DISTINCT_KEYS                            NUMBER
MOST_REPEATED_KEY                        NUMBER
BTREE_SPACE                              NUMBER
USED_SPACE                               NUMBER
PCT_USED                                 NUMBER
ROWS_PER_KEY                             NUMBER
BLKS_GETS_PER_ACCESS                     NUMBER
```

INDEX_HISTOGRAM

```
Name                            Null?    Type
------------------------------- -------- ----
REPEAT_COUNT                             NUMBER
KEYS_WITH_REPEAT_COUNT                   NUMBER
```

OBJ$

Name	Null?	Type
OBJ#	NOT NULL	NUMBER
DATAOBJ#		NUMBER
OWNER#	NOT NULL	NUMBER
NAME	NOT NULL	VARCHAR2(30)
NAMESPACE	NOT NULL	NUMBER
SUBNAME		VARCHAR2(30)
TYPE#	NOT NULL	NUMBER
CTIME	NOT NULL	DATE
MTIME	NOT NULL	DATE
STIME	NOT NULL	DATE
STATUS	NOT NULL	NUMBER
REMOTEOWNER		VARCHAR2(30)
LINKNAME		VARCHAR2(128)
FLAGS		NUMBER
OID$		RAW(16)
SPARE1		NUMBER
SPARE2		NUMBER
SPARE3		NUMBER
SPARE4		VARCHAR2(1000)
SPARE5		VARCHAR2(1000)
SPARE6		DATE

USER_EXTENTS

Name	Null?	Type
SEGMENT_NAME		VARCHAR2(81)
PARTITION_NAME		VARCHAR2(30)
SEGMENT_TYPE		VARCHAR2(17)
TABLESPACE_NAME		VARCHAR2(30)
EXTENT_ID	NOT NULL	NUMBER
BYTES		NUMBER
BLOCKS	NOT NULL	NUMBER

USER_PART_KEY_COLUMNS

Name	Null?	Type
NAME		VARCHAR2(30)
COLUMN_NAME		VARCHAR2(30)
COLUMN_POSITION		NUMBER

USER_SOURCE

```
Name                                  Null?    Type
------------------------------------- -------- ----
NAME                                  NOT NULL VARCHAR2(30)
TYPE                                           VARCHAR2(12)
LINE                                  NOT NULL NUMBER
TEXT                                           VARCHAR2(4000)
```

USER_IND_PARTITIONS

```
Name                                  Null?    Type
------------------------------------- -------- ----
INDEX_NAME                            NOT NULL VARCHAR2(30)
PARTITION_NAME                                 VARCHAR2(30)
HIGH_VALUE                                     LONG
HIGH_VALUE_LENGTH                     NOT NULL NUMBER
PARTITION_POSITION                    NOT NULL NUMBER
STATUS                                         VARCHAR2(8)
TABLESPACE_NAME                       NOT NULL VARCHAR2(30)
PCT_FREE                              NOT NULL NUMBER
INI_TRANS                             NOT NULL NUMBER
MAX_TRANS                             NOT NULL NUMBER
INITIAL_EXTENT                                 NUMBER
NEXT_EXTENT                                    NUMBER
MIN_EXTENT                            NOT NULL NUMBER
MAX_EXTENT                            NOT NULL NUMBER
PCT_INCREASE                          NOT NULL NUMBER
FREELISTS                                      NUMBER
LOGGING                                        VARCHAR2(3)
BLEVEL                                         NUMBER
LEAF_BLOCKS                                    NUMBER
DISTINCT_KEYS                                  NUMBER
AVG_LEAF_BLOCKS_PER_KEY                         NUMBER
AVG_DATA_BLOCKS_PER_KEY                         NUMBER
CLUSTERING_FACTOR                              NUMBER
NUM_ROWS                                       NUMBER
SAMPLE_SIZE                                    NUMBER
LAST_ANALYZED                                  DATE
BUFFER_POOL                                    VARCHAR2(7)
```

USER_PART_COL_STATISTICS

```
Name                              Null?     Type
--------------------------------  --------  ----
TABLE_NAME                        NOT NULL  VARCHAR2(30)
PARTITION_NAME                              VARCHAR2(30)
COLUMN_NAME                                 VARCHAR2(30)
NUM_DISTINCT                                NUMBER
LOW_VALUE                                   RAW(32)
HIGH_VALUE                                  RAW(32)
DENSITY                                     NUMBER
NUM_NULLS                                   NUMBER
NUM_BUCKETS                                 NUMBER
SAMPLE_SIZE                                 NUMBER
LAST_ANALYZED                               DATE
```

USER_TAB_COL_STATISTICS

```
Name                              Null?     Type
--------------------------------  --------  ----
TABLE_NAME                        NOT NULL  VARCHAR2(30)
COLUMN_NAME                       NOT NULL  VARCHAR2(30)
NUM_DISTINCT                                NUMBER
LOW_VALUE                                   RAW(32)
HIGH_VALUE                                  RAW(32)
DENSITY                                     NUMBER
NUM_NULLS                                   NUMBER
NUM_BUCKETS                                 NUMBER
LAST_ANALYZED                               DATE
SAMPLE_SIZE                                 NUMBER
```

USER_TAB_PARTITIONS

```
Name                              Null?     Type
--------------------------------  --------  ----
TABLE_NAME                        NOT NULL  VARCHAR2(30)
PARTITION_NAME                              VARCHAR2(30)
HIGH_VALUE                                  LONG
HIGH_VALUE_LENGTH                 NOT NULL  NUMBER
PARTITION_POSITION                NOT NULL  NUMBER
TABLESPACE_NAME                   NOT NULL  VARCHAR2(30)
```

PCT_FREE	NOT NULL	NUMBER
PCT_USED	NOT NULL	NUMBER
INI_TRANS	NOT NULL	NUMBER
MAX_TRANS	NOT NULL	NUMBER
INITIAL_EXTENT		NUMBER
NEXT_EXTENT		NUMBER
MIN_EXTENT	NOT NULL	NUMBER
MAX_EXTENT	NOT NULL	NUMBER
PCT_INCREASE	NOT NULL	NUMBER
FREELISTS		NUMBER
FREELIST_GROUPS		NUMBER
LOGGING		VARCHAR2(3)
NUM_ROWS		NUMBER
BLOCKS		NUMBER
EMPTY_BLOCKS		NUMBER
AVG_SPACE		NUMBER
CHAIN_CNT		NUMBER
AVG_ROW_LEN		NUMBER
SAMPLE_SIZE		NUMBER
LAST_ANALYZED		DATE
BUFFER_POOL		VARCHAR2(7)

V_$ARCHIVED_LOG

Name	Null?	Type
RECID		NUMBER
STAMP		NUMBER
NAME		VARCHAR2(513)
THREAD#		NUMBER
SEQUENCE#		NUMBER
RESETLOGS_CHANGE#		NUMBER
RESETLOGS_TIME		DATE
FIRST_CHANGE#		NUMBER
FIRST_TIME		DATE
NEXT_CHANGE#		NUMBER
NEXT_TIME		DATE
BLOCKS		NUMBER
BLOCK_SIZE		NUMBER
ARCHIVED		VARCHAR2(3)
DELETED		VARCHAR2(3)
COMPLETION_TIME		DATE

V_$DATAFILE

Name	Null?	Type
FILE#		NUMBER
CREATION_CHANGE#		NUMBER
CREATION_TIME		DATE
TS#		NUMBER
RFILE#		NUMBER
STATUS		VARCHAR2(7)
ENABLED		VARCHAR2(10)
CHECKPOINT_CHANGE#		NUMBER
CHECKPOINT_TIME		DATE
UNRECOVERABLE_CHANGE#		NUMBER
UNRECOVERABLE_TIME		DATE
LAST_CHANGE#		NUMBER
LAST_TIME		DATE
OFFLINE_CHANGE#		NUMBER
ONLINE_CHANGE#		NUMBER
ONLINE_TIME		DATE
BYTES		NUMBER
BLOCKS		NUMBER
CREATE_BYTES		NUMBER
BLOCK_SIZE		NUMBER
NAME		VARCHAR2(513)

V_$FILESTAT

Name	Null?	Type
FILE#		NUMBER
PHYRDS		NUMBER
PHYWRTS		NUMBER
PHYBLKRD		NUMBER
PHYBLKWRT		NUMBER
READTIM		NUMBER
WRITETIM		NUMBER

V_$LATCH

```
Name                             Null?     Type
-------------------------------- --------  ----
ADDR                                       RAW(4)
LATCH#                                     NUMBER
LEVEL#                                     NUMBER
NAME                                       VARCHAR2(64)
GETS                                       NUMBER
MISSES                                     NUMBER
SLEEPS                                     NUMBER
IMMEDIATE_GETS                             NUMBER
IMMEDIATE_MISSES                           NUMBER
WAITERS_WOKEN                              NUMBER
WAITS_HOLDING_LATCH                        NUMBER
SPIN_GETS                                  NUMBER
SLEEP1                                     NUMBER
SLEEP2                                     NUMBER
SLEEP3                                     NUMBER
SLEEP4                                     NUMBER
SLEEP5                                     NUMBER
SLEEP6                                     NUMBER
SLEEP7                                     NUMBER
SLEEP8                                     NUMBER
SLEEP9                                     NUMBER
SLEEP10                                    NUMBER
SLEEP11                                    NUMBER
```

V_$LIBRARYCACHE

```
Name                             Null?     Type
-------------------------------- --------  ----
NAMESPACE                                  VARCHAR2(15)
GETS                                       NUMBER
GETHITS                                    NUMBER
GETHITRATIO                                NUMBER
PINS                                       NUMBER
```

```
PINHITS                          NUMBER
PINHITRATIO                      NUMBER
RELOADS                          NUMBER
INVALIDATIONS                    NUMBER
DLM_LOCK_REQUESTS                NUMBER
DLM_PIN_REQUESTS                 NUMBER
DLM_PIN_RELEASES                 NUMBER
DLM_INVALIDATION_REQUESTS        NUMBER
DLM_INVALIDATIONS                NUMBER
```

V_$LOG

```
Name                          Null?    Type
----------------------------- -------- ----
GROUP#                                 NUMBER
THREAD#                                NUMBER
SEQUENCE#                              NUMBER
BYTES                                  NUMBER
MEMBERS                                NUMBER
ARCHIVED                               VARCHAR2(3)
STATUS                                 VARCHAR2(16)
FIRST_CHANGE#                          NUMBER
FIRST_TIME                             DATE
```

V_$LOG_HISTORY

```
Name                          Null?    Type
----------------------------- -------- ----
RECID                                  NUMBER
STAMP                                  NUMBER
THREAD#                                NUMBER
SEQUENCE#                              NUMBER
FIRST_CHANGE#                          NUMBER
FIRST_TIME                             DATE
NEXT_CHANGE#                           NUMBER
```

V_$LOGFILE

```
Name                          Null?    Type
----------------------------- -------- ----
GROUP#                                 NUMBER
STATUS                                 VARCHAR2(7)
MEMBER                                 VARCHAR2(513)
```

V_$PQ_SESSTAT

Name	Null?	Type
STATISTIC		VARCHAR2(30)
LAST_QUERY		NUMBER
SESSION_TOTAL		NUMBER

V_$PQ_SYSSTAT

Name	Null?	Type
STATISTIC		VARCHAR2(30)
VALUE		NUMBER

V_$PQ_TQSTAT

Name	Null?	Type
DFO_NUMBER		NUMBER
TQ_ID		NUMBER
SERVER_TYPE		VARCHAR2(10)
NUM_ROWS		NUMBER
BYTES		NUMBER
OPEN_TIME		NUMBER
AVG_LATENCY		NUMBER
WAITS		NUMBER
TIMEOUTS		NUMBER
PROCESS		VARCHAR2(10)
INSTANCE		NUMBER

V_$ROWCACHE

Name	Null?	Type
CACHE#		NUMBER
TYPE		VARCHAR2(11)
SUBORDINATE#		NUMBER
PARAMETER		VARCHAR2(32)
COUNT		NUMBER
USAGE		NUMBER
FIXED		NUMBER

```
GETS                             NUMBER
GETMISSES                        NUMBER
SCANS                            NUMBER
SCANMISSES                       NUMBER
SCANCOMPLETES                    NUMBER
MODIFICATIONS                    NUMBER
FLUSHES                          NUMBER
DLM_REQUESTS                     NUMBER
DLM_CONFLICTS                    NUMBER
DLM_RELEASES                     NUMBER
```

V_$SESSTAT

```
Name                             Null?      Type
-------------------------------  --------   ----
SID                                         NUMBER
STATISTIC#                                  NUMBER
VALUE                                       NUMBER
```

V_$SGASTAT

```
Name                             Null?      Type
-------------------------------  --------   ----
POOL                                        VARCHAR2(11)
NAME                                        VARCHAR2(26)
BYTES                                       NUMBER
```

V_$SQLAREA

```
Name                             Null?      Type
-------------------------------  --------   ----
SQL_TEXT                                    VARCHAR2(1000)
SHARABLE_MEM                                NUMBER
PERSISTENT_MEM                              NUMBER
RUNTIME_MEM                                 NUMBER
SORTS                                       NUMBER
VERSION_COUNT                               NUMBER
LOADED_VERSIONS                             NUMBER
OPEN_VERSIONS                               NUMBER
```

```
USERS_OPENING                        NUMBER
EXECUTIONS                           NUMBER
USERS_EXECUTING                      NUMBER
LOADS                                NUMBER
FIRST_LOAD_TIME                      VARCHAR2(19)
INVALIDATIONS                        NUMBER
PARSE_CALLS                          NUMBER
DISK_READS                           NUMBER
BUFFER_GETS                          NUMBER
ROWS_PROCESSED                       NUMBER
COMMAND_TYPE                         NUMBER
OPTIMIZER_MODE                       VARCHAR2(25)
PARSING_USER_ID                      NUMBER
PARSING_SCHEMA_ID                    NUMBER
KEPT_VERSIONS                        NUMBER
ADDRESS                              RAW(4)
HASH_VALUE                           NUMBER
MODULE                               VARCHAR2(64)
MODULE_HASH                          NUMBER
ACTION                               VARCHAR2(64)
ACTION_HASH                          NUMBER
SERIALIZABLE_ABORTS                  NUMBER
```

V_$SQLTEXT

```
Name                         Null?    Type
--------------------------- -------- ----
ADDRESS                               RAW(4)
HASH_VALUE                            NUMBER
COMMAND_TYPE                          NUMBER
PIECE                                 NUMBER
SQL_TEXT                              VARCHAR2(64)
```

V_$STATNAME

```
Name                         Null?    Type
--------------------------- -------- ----
STATISTIC#                            NUMBER
NAME                                  VARCHAR2(64)
CLASS                                 NUMBER
```

V_$SYSSTAT

```
 Name                             Null?    Type
 -------------------------------- -------- ----
 STATISTIC#                                NUMBER
 NAME                                      VARCHAR2(64)
 CLASS                                     NUMBER
 VALUE                                     NUMBER
```

V_$TYPE_SIZE

```
 Name                             Null?    Type
 -------------------------------- -------- ----
 COMPONENT                                 VARCHAR2(8)
 TYPE                                      VARCHAR2(8)
 DESCRIPTION                               VARCHAR2(32)
 TYPE_SIZE                                 NUMBER
```

V_$WAITSTAT

```
 Name                             Null?    Type
 -------------------------------- -------- ----
 CLASS                                     VARCHAR2(18)
 COUNT                                     NUMBER
 TIME                                      NUMBER
```

APPENDIX
B

Object Management

ppendix B is dedicated to an object management tool, serving as an example of the contribution that can be made to the tuning process when the DBA and the developer are able to:

- Easily view, create, and modify any object type on any server in an enterprise network of Oracle databases

- Ensure stored objects (i.e., procedures, functions, and packages) are identical on all nodes involved in a corporate Oracle network

- Easily assess the impact of making schema changes

One of many themes we have discussed time and time again in *Oracle8 Tuning* is using generic code and utilizing the shared SQL area to improve performance. By looking at Sylvain Faust International's SQL-Programmer, we will give you a flavor of the robust object management capabilities that assist the DBA's tuning efforts.

Before we move on to looking at SQL-Programmer, we will take a quick look at defining a service in the Net8 Assistant, which must be done to enable hookup to an Oracle8 database (local or remote).

Accessing an Oracle8 Database

This section will show you how to set up a service name in the Oracle Net8 Assistant to point at a local Oracle8 database for Windows NT.

NOTE
If you want to access a database on a remote server, the information entered in the assistant's dialog boxes may be different.

Begin by double-clicking on the Net8 Assistant shortcut in the Oracle for Windows NT folder. When the Assistant's main console appears, highlight Service Names, then click on the Create button (the "+" sign on the foremost left of the button bar) to display the screen shown in Figure B-1. Enter your desired service name where we have entered **local8** as an example, then click Next to carry on.

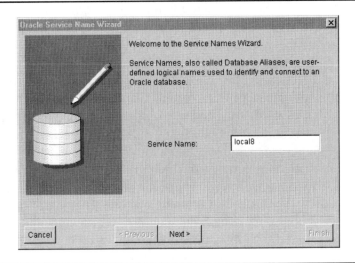

FIGURE B-1.   *Service creation dialog box*

When the next screen appears, as shown in Figure B-2, highlight the Bequeath (Local Database) selection, then click Next to continue.

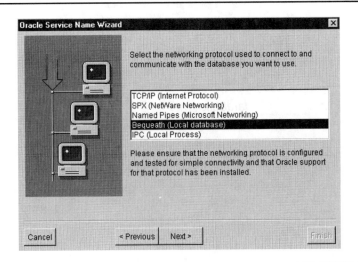

FIGURE B-2.   *Choosing a protocol for the new service*

The Net8 Assistant then informs you that there is no extra information to be entered since this is a local connection, so click Next to go to the screen where you specify the system identifier (SID) of the local database. The Assistant may suggest the text ORCL as a SID; accept it if this is correct or enter the correct SID, then click Next. The test service screen then appears from where the new service can be tested. Click the test button, then enter a username and password. If the test of the service completes successfully, the text "The connection test was successful" is displayed, as shown in Figure B-3.

Save the network configuration through the File|Save menu option. The service specified in the first screen where the name was selected is now available for use with your local Oracle8 database. The definition of the local8 service is shown in Figure B-4.

Prior to Net8 and the Net8 Assistant, many of us used the SQL*Net Easy Configuration front end for defining services. The Net8 Assistant will update the local tnsnames.ora as did its predecessor, the Easy Configuration.

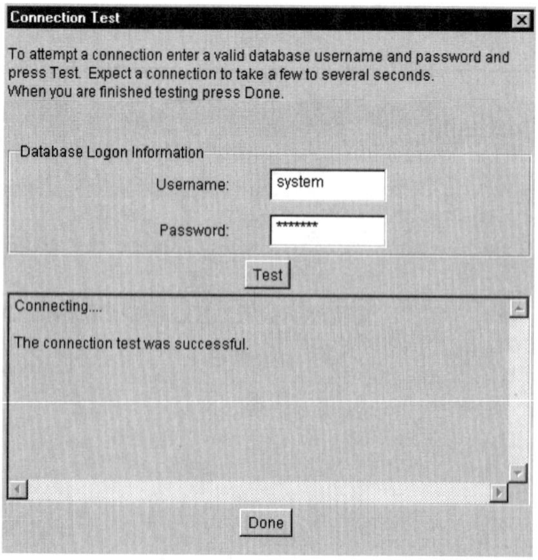

FIGURE B-3. *Successful test confirmation message*

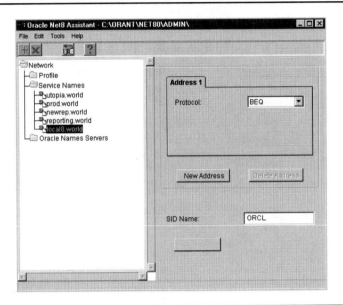

FIGURE B-4.   *local8 service properties*

SQL-Programmer

In this section we will have a look at some of the features of
SQL-Programmer release 2.1 for a 32-bit environment. We have found in
our travels that a robust and flexible object management assists the overall
tuning exercise. We assume that the product has been successfully installed
on your Windows NT client. Figure B-5 shows version information on the
copy of SQL-Programmer we used for this section.

The first time you open SQL-Programmer, connect to the desired
database as the SYS in order to create a repository that sits behind the
scenes as you interact with the Oracle8 database. At creation time, the
repository occupies roughly 20K (20,480 bytes); after working with some of
the source code control features of the product, the repository can grow to
a number of megabytes. Regardless of the size of the repository, we
recommend placing it in a non-SYSTEM tablespace and monitoring its size
regularly. Click OK on the screen shown in Figure B-6 to bring up the
SQL-Programmer Login dialog box. Notice that you can specify a
tablespace for the SQL-Programmer repository in the Create Repository
dialog shown in Figure B-6.

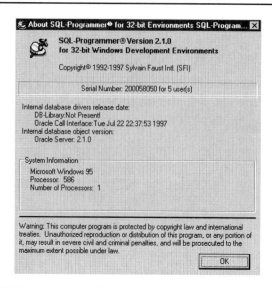

FIGURE B-5. *SQL-Programmer splash screen*

The Login screen is looking for the familiar Server, Type, Login ID, and Password. Enter the information as shown in Figure B-7, then click Connect. When the connection is established, notice the Connected To information filled in as well. Click Done to dismiss the login screen and position yourself at the main console.

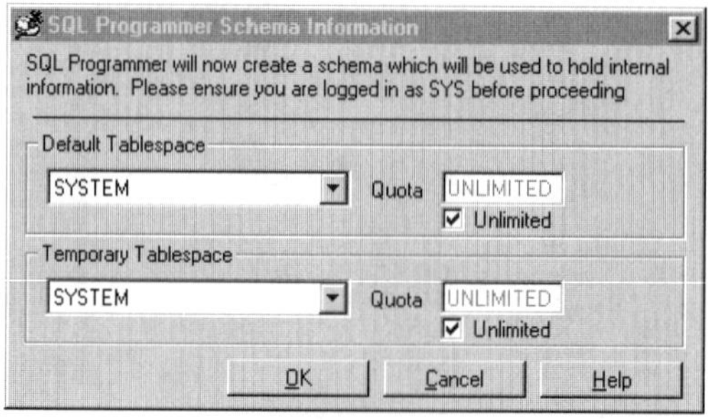

FIGURE B-6. *Create Repository dialog*

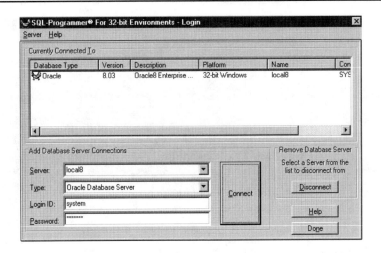

FIGURE B-7. *Login dialog displaying database connection information*

There are two tools accessible from the main console we are going to have a look at.

■ The Database Explorer is accessible from the main console by clicking the globe icon, using the shortcut key CTRL-B, or selecting the Database Explorer option from the view menu shown in Figure B-8. The principal purpose of the SQL-Programmer Explorer is to provide access to and information on objects of the connected servers. Virtually any object contained within a connected server can be accessed through the Explorer. A context-sensitive toolbar and menu expose functionality which can be applied to these objects.

NOTE
Becoming familiar with the objects on your server(s) is part of the tuning process. Some applications have so many objects (tables, views, synonyms, stored procedures, etc.) that their management becomes unwieldy without a graphical user interface.

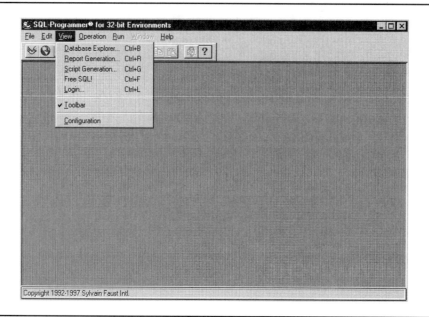

FIGURE B-8. *View pull-down menu to access the Database Explorer*

■ The Script Generator is accessible from the main console by clicking the script icon (two over from the globe icon), using the shortcut key CTRL-G, or selecting the Script Generator option from the menu shown in Figure B-8. This interface provides the means to select one or more objects to be submitted for script generation.

NOTE
We have always found it time consuming and a nuisance having to dig object creation scripts out of the Oracle data dictionary manually. Again, this type of graphical user interface assists the process and makes it easier to stay on top of exactly what is in your database instance.

Using the Explorer, you can inspect and work with the assortment of objects in the Oracle8 database. We are going to have a closer look at doing some work with this tool and show you how it can assist the overall tuning process.

The Database Explorer

When the Database Explorer startup screen appears, there are the familiar Windows NT interface items with the "+"sign for expansion and, when lists are expanded, the "–" sign to collapse a list. Figure B-9 shows the Host: local8 (Oracle) expanded to display objects that can be further expanded.

Using the Database Explorer, let's go through two activities we found quite intriguing. First we will create a stored procedure, then we will propagate that procedure to another schema. In our travels around Oracle systems for the past few hundred years (so it seems!), we have found many tuning exercises that didn't succeed when schemas that were supposed to be identical were out of synch.

NOTE
The code used in the procedure is artificially simple to illustrate the concept rather than the code itself.

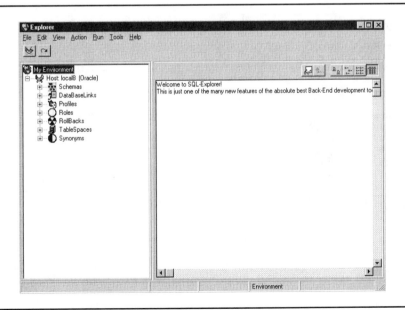

FIGURE B-9.   *Default database (local8) object expansion*

Creating a Stored Procedure

We start by expanding the Schemas list, then further expanding the schema owned by DEMO. After highlighting the Procedures item in the list underneath DEMO's schema, we right-click on Procedures to display the pull-down menu shown in Figure B-10.

We then select the Create option from that menu and are presented with a screen where the procedure can be named, the code for the procedure body created and compiled, and the code can be stored in the database to which we are connected. Figure B-11 shows the screen with the code entered but not compiled.

Let's highlight a few areas and features of the screen shown in Figure B-11. The button two over from Save that looks like a tent is used to compile the code. After compilation, if all goes well, the status of the procedure will change from INVALID to VALID. For those familiar with coding procedures in SQL*Plus, the **create or replace tester** line as well as the slash ("/") that terminates the PL/SQL block are not entered into the Database Explorer create procedure dialog. The right arrow beside the compile button is used to execute the procedure after a successful compile. After the compilation, we

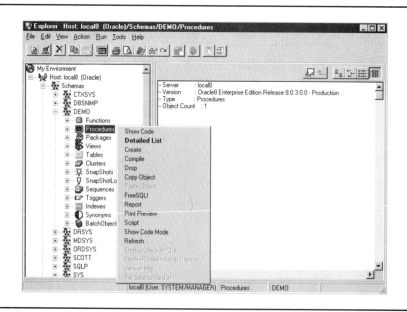

FIGURE B-10. *Pull-down menu for Procedures*

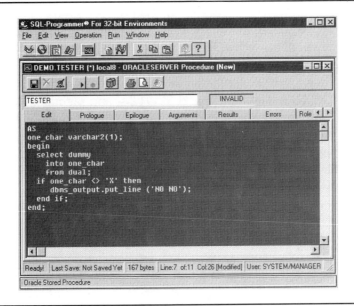

FIGURE B-11. *Creating procedure dialog*

store the code in the database by clicking the Save button on the button bar. Now that the stored object is in the database and marked as ready to execute, let's synch another schema with the same procedure.

NOTE
For the sake of this exercise, we are propagating the procedure to another schema in the same database; in real life we would be copying the code to one or more other databases whose connections have been established in the same session.

Propagating the Procedure Elsewhere

NOTE
This activity can be accomplished via the familiar Windows drag-and-drop functionality. The method we use in this section is an alternative approach preferred by some, scorned by others.

First, the TESTER procedure is placed in a buffer, then it's copied to the desired schema. Highlight the TESTER procedure, then right-click to bring up the drop-down menu shown in Figure B-12.

Select Copy Object in that menu and, shortly thereafter, the object is in the copy buffer. Let's drop a copy of the object into SCOTT's schema. We first collapse DEMO's schema, expand SCOTT's, and highlight Procedures, then right-click to bring up a drop-down menu. Click on Paste Object to bring up the screen shown in Figure B-13.

When the activity completes successfully, you are informed "Procedure: DEMO.TESTER on server: local8 copied to SCOTT.TESTER on server: local8". Notice the options on Figure B-13, especially the Privileges check box. Any privileges are copied with the code when the TESTER procedure

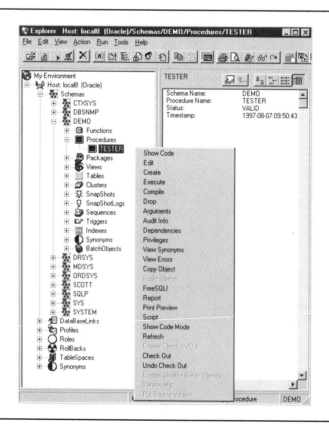

FIGURE B-12. *Procedure context sensitive drop-down menu*

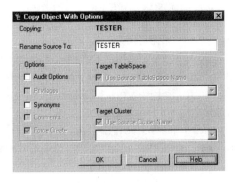

FIGURE B-13. *Paste object dialog*

is placed in the copy buffer. When pasting the object, clicking Privileges causes the grants to be placed in the target schema alongside the procedure.

Before moving on, let's look at copying multiple objects from one schema to the other. First, you highlight Procedures and do a right-click to bring up a drop-down menu. Select the Detailed List from that menu to bring up the list shown in Figure B-14. With the detail list on the right pane

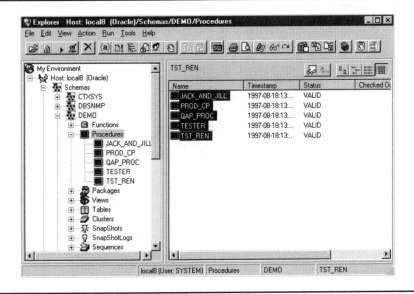

FIGURE B-14. *Detailed object list on right window pane*

of the screen, the CTRL left mouse convention can be used to select multiple items in the list. The objects can then be copied to another schema by dragging them on top of the name of another schema.

When presented with the Copy Object With Options dialog box, simply click OK to accept all names, thereby using the same names in the target schema. As the copy activity is initiated, SQL-Programmer displays a Copy Status window with progress information, as shown in Figure B-15. When finished, SQL-Programmer informs you of how many objects were copied and where. Click OK to dismiss this information box, then click Done to return to the Explorer.

We now move on to illustrate the script generation capabilities of SQL-Programmer. DBAs that manage wide corporate database networks with a mixture of local and remote repositories will find the script module helpful; easy creation of object definition text files assists a robust backup routine in any Oracle environment, especially one with many nodes in a corporate environment.

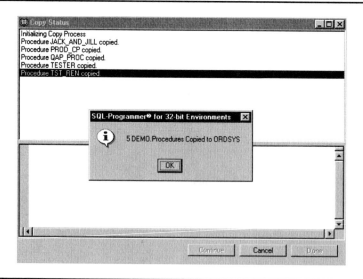

FIGURE B-15. *Status and results display for copy objects*

The Script Generator

From the Database Explorer main console, the Script Generator is invoked. As shown in Figure B-8, the generator can be called via the menu, the CTRL-G shortcut key, or the Scripts icon (fourth from the left). Before using the generator, you may need to visit the SQL-Programmer configuration box off the main console. Click on the hammer/pliers icon to bring up the Configuration dialog, then click Results. Change the Oracle End-of-Batch signal to the forward slash ("/") if necessary. Let's look at generating a script for a schema as a whole, and then we'll look at a few stored objects.

Total Schema

In this section we will look at generating a script for a whole schema. We have found in our travels around Oracle databases all over the galaxy that quick and easy access to object creation scripts enhances our ability to:

■ Clone an object from one schema to the other

■ Build a more well-rounded disaster recovery methodology

■ Ensure objects that are intended to be clones of one another actually are

We have successfully connected to the local8 database shown in Figure B-7—let's get started. Once the main console is open, you need to select the View by Connection option to display the screen shown in Figure B-16.

Expand the Schema list, then proceed to the desired schema. Right-click to display a context sensitive pop-up menu, and choose Select All from that menu when it appears. Once that has been done, the object type list is expanded for the selected user, and the work begins. The generator marches one by one through the object types and updates its status lines with the number of objects selected. When done, SQL-Programmer opens up object type icons when it has found a certain object type in the selected schema.

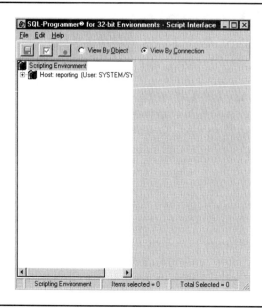

FIGURE B-16. *Script generator expanded by connection*

Click the diskette icon on the menu bar to bring up the Save dialog box, and enter a file name within which the source code will be saved. The top of output from the exercise resembles that shown in the next listing.

```
/*
   Script for Server local8 (Oracle8 Enterprise Edition Release 8.0.3.0.0 -
   Production) on 32-bit Windows
*/
/*
   Table(s)
*/
CREATE TABLE CTXSYS.CTX_PROPER_NAME
(PRP_KEY VARCHAR2(80) NOT NULL
,PRP_PHRASE VARCHAR2(80) NOT NULL
,PRP_PHRLEN NUMBER NOT NULL
,PRP_COUNT NUMBER
,PRP_VALID VARCHAR2(1) DEFAULT 'T'
)
PCTFREE 10
PCTUSED 40
INITRANS 1
MAXTRANS 255
```

```
TABLESPACE USER_DATA
    STORAGE (  INITIAL  10K
    NEXT  5M
    MINEXTENTS 1
    MAXEXTENTS 121
    PCTINCREASE 50
            )
/
```

Let's look at how a professional object management environment such as SQL-Programmer can assist productivity which, in the long and the short run, allows your IT organization to enjoy the fruits of your labor in a shorter time-to-market.

Assisting the Tuning Process

During this brief look at SQL-Programmer, we have given you a taste of a comprehensive object management and developer programming assistant. Object management is an increasingly important requirement as more and more applications come on board. With centralized storage of corporate information, a complete object management solution ensures that developers and DBAs can get quick and easy access to current object definitions.

With many client/server implementations, we are strong believers in doing as much processing as possible on the server. When this approach is followed, you end up with a sophisticated network of stored objects. SQL-Programmer is an example of a product that delivers modules that enhance the productivity of your development organization by:

- Providing production quality reports that serve as documentation and aid the developers by zeroing in on current object names

- Providing a debugging environment where the developer can test and code on an ongoing basis

- Providing a facility to do "what-if" testing for modification of objects without affecting existing code

- Providing a means to analyze references made from one object to another to assist impact analysis exercises

■ Providing a check-in/check-out facility that ensures nobody clobbers another's efforts by registering object names and tracking who has done what with what object and when

More Information

Sylvain Faust International can be seen at most Oracle conferences around North America and points beyond. Visit them on the World Wide Web at **http://www.sfi-software.com** or send requests for information by email to **info@sfi-software.com**.

APPENDIX
C

Creating a Second Database on NT

s the NT Server becomes a more powerful and efficient computer, many will find themselves developing applications that run against an Oracle8 instance on one of these servers. Many readers of this and the previous *Tuning Oracle* work have created a second database instance. This appendix will guide you through using the Database Assistant on Oracle8 for Windows NT. The Oracle Database Assistant is invoked using a shortcut in the Oracle for Windows NT folder. The assistant can be used to create or delete a database from the server. After starting the assistant, you will be presented with the screen shown in Figure C-1.

NOTE
On Windows NT, you need to be logged onto the server as a user with administrator privileges or, better still, the administrator account itself.

The next screen shown in Figure C-2 is where you tell the assistant if you wish to create a new, or delete an existing database.

You then are asked to specify the choice between a custom or typical database. If you choose the former, you are cautioned that this option is only for those experienced with advanced database creation procedures. Don't worry, the ensuing dialog is straightforward, and you can always back up to this screen using the Previous button seen on most windows. Click Custom and then Next to continue. See Figure C-3.

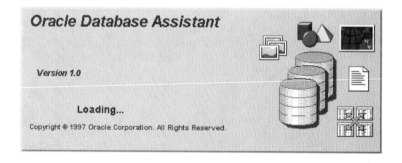

FIGURE C-1. *Database Assistant splash screen*

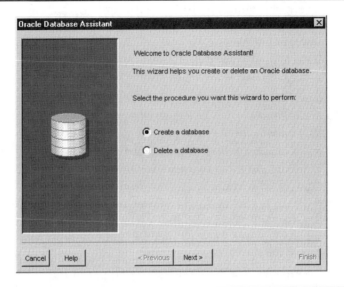

FIGURE C-2. *Choice of creating or deleting a database on NT*

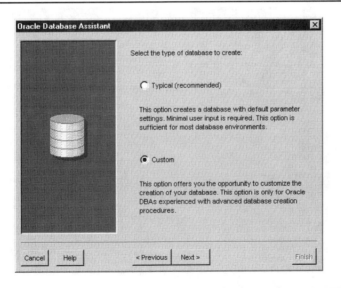

FIGURE C-3. *Selecting creation type—Typical or Custom*

The next screen, shown in Figure C-4, is where you specify the data cartridges you wish to include in the database being created. Notice how the Spatial, ConText, and Image choices are inactive, and the Advanced Replication option is available. Simply click Next here without doing anything else.

The next screen is where you start to specify characteristics of the database you are creating. The choice among Small, Medium, or Large you make here simply causes the Assistant to use different default values for suggested file sizes and some memory structures later in the creation process. You can override most of these defaults as the appropriate dialog box is presented. Click on Large, as shown in Figure C-5.

The Change Character Set button is where you can change the character sets for your database. The Assistant brings up two pick lists where the value for these sets can be changed. The first pick list is shown in Figure C-6.

The next screen, shown in Figure C-7, is where you start to specify some identification information for the database. Though not required, we suggest using the same name for the database as for the SID, and keep the name three to five characters long. Once you have entered values for the

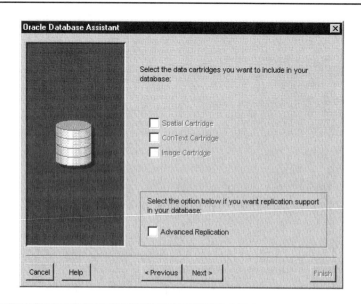

FIGURE C-4. *Choosing cartridges for new database*

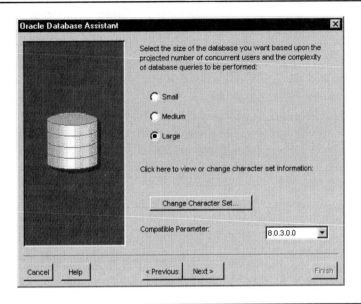

FIGURE C-5. *Specifying a size for the new database*

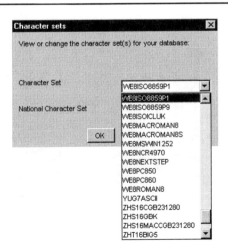

FIGURE C-6. *Character set pick list*

first two fields and move to the Initialization Filename, the Assistant will build the default name based on the value you entered for SID. Choose a secure database password that can be easily remembered. Most DBAs choose the password "oracle", which is fine but provides little security. Click Next to continue.

The next screen, shown in Figure C-8, is used to specify control file information all the way from the names of the first two control files to a number of instance-specific parameters. Notice the Re-use Control Files box that is usually checked in case the files already exist in the specified location. The names the Assistant suggests are built using the SID that was selected in Figure C-7. Keep in mind that the values entered for Maximum Datafiles, Maximum Log Files, and Maximum Log Members affect the size of the control files. Here's another neat trick—if you select Re-use Control Files and like-named files exist with a different file size than the one that will be generated with these values, the **create database** statement will fail. Click Next after filling in the desired information.

Next, you are presented with a screen, shown in Figure C-9, that contains five folders—one for each of the five default tablespaces. All six

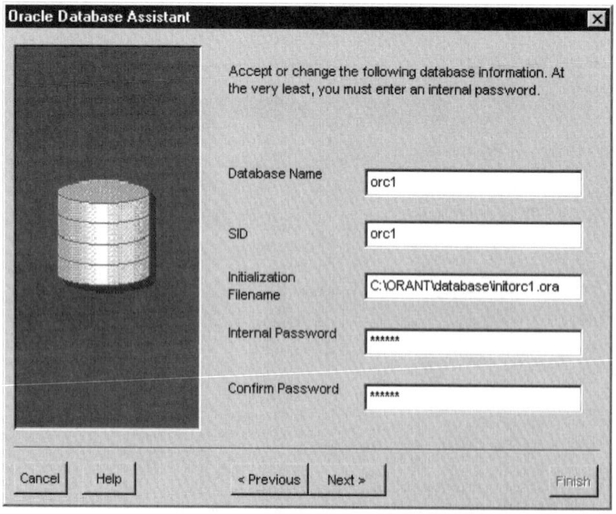

FIGURE C-7. *Entering database identification information*

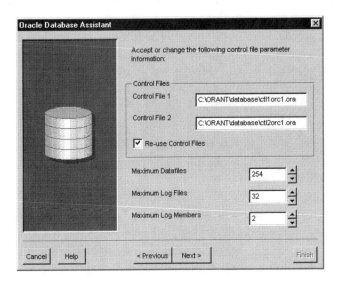

FIGURE C-8.   *Control file specification*

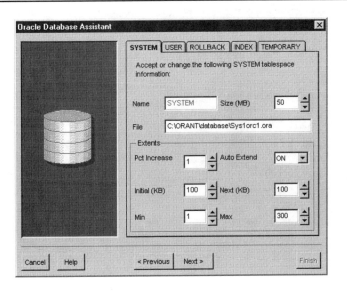

FIGURE C-9.   *Specifications for the system tablespace*

fields in the Extents area must be filled in. Note that the values specified here end up being passed to the Oracle8 database engine as part of the **create database** statement for the SYSTEM tablespace, or the **create tablespace** statement for all others. Using the values shown in Figure C-9, the storage component would be worded as in the following:

```
autoextend on default storage (initial 100k next 100k pctincrease 1
                               minextents 1 maxextents 300)
```

Inspect Figures C-10 through C-13 to see the values and what needs to be entered for the other four default tablespaces—USER, ROLLBACK, INDEX, and TEMPORARY.

The next screen is where the names and sizes of the first redo log groups are specified. Again, the value chosen for SID is embedded in the log file member names. Since we are creating a large database, the displayed values for log file size (200K) are probably inadequate and they should be changed to something around 4096 (which will end up making each log file 4MB). This screen is shown in Figure C-14.

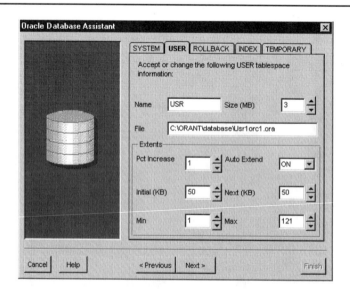

FIGURE C-10. *USER tablespace folder*

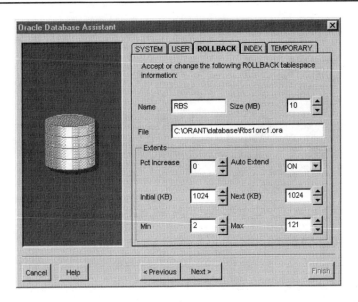

FIGURE C-11. *ROLLBACK tablespace folder*

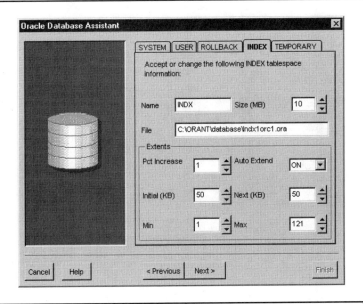

FIGURE C-12. *INDEX tablespace folder*

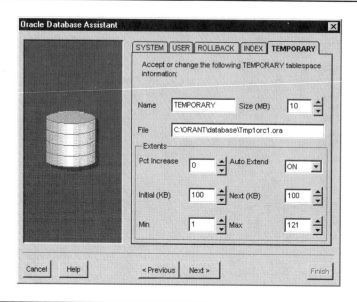

FIGURE C-13. *TEMPORARY tablespace folder*

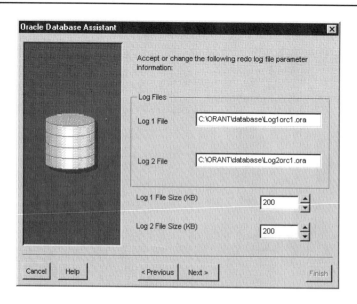

FIGURE C-14. *Log file member specifications*

Clicking Next will position you at the screen shown in Figure C-15, where you describe the logging environment for the database. We have accepted the default values specified. We have discussed the concept of checkpointing in a few spots throughout this book. Click Next to move on.

The next screen, shown in Figure C-16, presents some SGA information where a number of parameters are tweaked that affect the size of the database's system global area. Using the values entered, the shared pool size will be just under 12 megabytes, the database will support 200 concurrent processes, and the Oracle data block size will be 2K. Click Next to continue.

Figure C-17 shows the next screen where the directories are specified for the trace files written by user and support processes as the database operates.

The journey is just about over. The screen shown in Figure C-18 asks if the database should be created now or the information written to a script to be run at a later time. We select to do it now. Since we are sure of what we are doing, we click Yes in the information box shown in Figure C-19, and Oracle8 gets a hold of the information and begins to create the database.

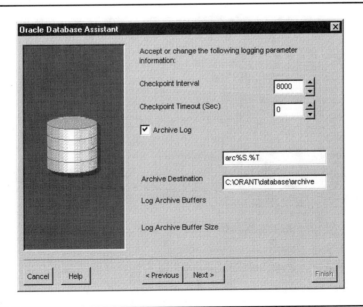

FIGURE C-15.   *Logging specifications*

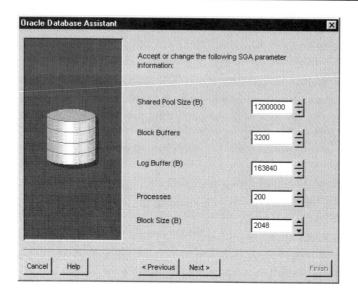

FIGURE C-16. *SGA sizing parameters*

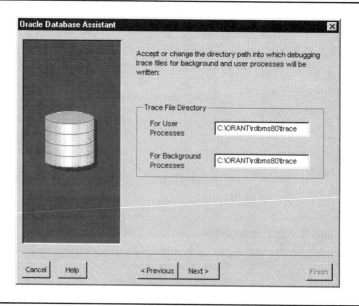

FIGURE C-17. *Trace file location specifications*

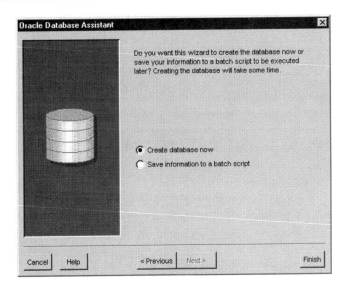

FIGURE C-18.   *Confirmation of create database activity*

The alert shown in Figure C-20 informs you of the name of the database and the Oracle system identifier. Click OK to continue.

As the database is created, a Progress indicator screen is displayed, where a hand moves from one activity to the other. This is shown in Figure C-21.

Before the invention of the Database Assistant, we were surprised at the number of Oracle DBAs who had never created a database. We trust that these people may have developed a disaster recovery routine for their installations, but wonder if they ever experimented with a mock disaster.

FIGURE C-19.   *Making sure of what we want done by the Assistant*

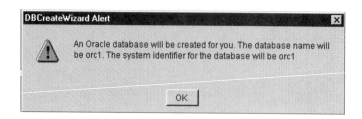

FIGURE C-20. *Name of database and SID alert*

After all, in some situations the complete re-instantiation of an Oracle database must start with running a **create database** activity using some form of interface—line-mode Server Manager, the SQL*Worksheet, or our newest best friend, the Database Assistant as featured in this appendix.

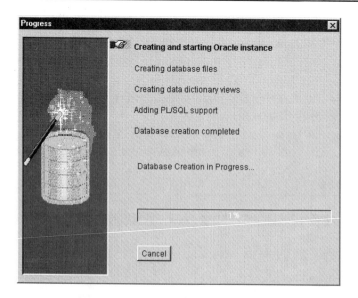

FIGURE C-21. *Progress of database creation*

INDEX

G

H

F

P

V

W

Y

Get Your **FREE** Subscription to Oracle Magazine

Stay informed and increase your productivity with every issue of *Oracle Magazine*. Inside each FREE, bimonthly issue, you'll get:

- Up-to-date information on the Oracle RDBMS and software tools

- Third-party software and hardware products

- Technical articles on Oracle platforms and operating environments

- Software tuning tips

- Oracle client application stories

Three easy ways to subscribe:

1 **MAIL:** Cut out this page, complete the questionnaire on the back, and mail to: *Oracle Magazine*, 500 Oracle Parkway, Box 659952, Redwood Shores, CA 94065.

2 **FAX:** Cut out this page, complete the questionnaire on the back, and and fax the questionnaire to **+ 415.633.2424.**

3 **WEB:** Visit our Web site at **www.oramag.com.** You'll find a subscription form there, plus much more!

If there are other Oracle users at your location who would like to receive their own copy of *Oracle Magazine,* please photocopy the form on the back, and pass it along.

☐ YES! Please send me a FREE subscription to <u>Oracle Magazine</u>. ☐ NO, I am not interested at this time.

If you wish to receive your free bimonthly subscription to *Oracle Magazine,* you must fill out the entire form, sign it, and date it (incomplete forms cannot be processed or acknowledged). You can also subscribe at our Web Site at **http://www.oramag.com/html/subform.html** or fax your application to *Oracle Magazine* at **+415.633.2424.**

SIGNATURE (REQUIRED) ✓   **DATE**

NAME _____ TITLE _____

COMPANY _____

STREET/P.O. BOX _____

CITY/STATE/ZIP _____

COUNTRY _____ TELEPHONE _____

You must answer all eight of the questions below.

1 What is the primary business activity of your firm at this location?
(circle only one)
01. Agriculture, Mining, Natural Resources
02. Communications Services, Utilities
03. Computer Consulting, Training
04. Computer, Data Processing Service
05. Computer Hardware, Software, Systems
06. Education—Primary, Secondary, College, University
07. Engineering, Architecture, Construction
08. Financial, Banking, Real Estate, Insurance
09. Government—Federal/Military
10. Government—Federal/Nonmilitary
11. Government—Local, State, Other
12. Health Services, Health Institutions
13. Manufacturing—Aerospace, Defense
14. Manufacturing—Noncomputer Products, Goods
15. Public Utilities (Electric, Gas, Sanitation)
16. Pure and Applied Research & Development
17. Retailing, Wholesaling, Distribution
18. Systems Integrator, VAR, VAD, OEM
19. Transportation
20. Other Business and Services ____

2 Which of the following best describes your job function? *(circle only one)*
CORPORATE MANAGEMENT/STAFF
01. Executive Management (President, Chair, CEO, CFO, Owner, Partner, Principal, Managing Director)
02. Finance/Administrative Management (VP/Director/Manager/Controller of Finance, Purchasing, Administration)
03. Other Finance/Administration Staff
04. Sales/Marketing Management (VP/Director/Manager of Sales/Marketing)
05. Other Sales/Marketing Staff ____
TECHNICAL MANAGEMENT/STAFF
06. Computer/Communications Systems Development/Programming Management

07. Computer/Communications Systems Development/Programming Staff
08. Computer Systems/Operations Management (CIO/VP/Director/Manager MIS, Operations, etc.)
09. Consulting
10. DBA/Systems Administrator
11. Education/Training
12. Engineering/R&D/Science Management
13. Engineering/R&D/Science Staff
14. Technical Support Director/Manager
15. Other Technical Management/Staff
_____

3 What is your current primary operating system environment?
(circle all that apply)
01. AIX	12. Solaris/Sun OS
02. HP-UX	13. SVR4
03. Macintosh OS	14. Ultrix
04. MPE-ix	15. UnixWare
05. MS-DOS	16. Other UNIX
06. MVS	17. VAX VMS
07. NetWare	18. VM
08. OpenVMS	19. Windows
09. OS/2	20. Windows NT
10. OS/400	21. Other ____
11. SCO	

4 What is your current primary hardware environment? *(circle all that apply)*
01. Macintosh
02. Mainframe
03. Massively Parallel Processing
04. Minicomputer
05. PC (IBM-Compatible)
06. Supercomputer
07. Symmetric Multiprocessing
08. Workstation
09. Other ____

5 In your job, do you use or plan to purchase any of the following products or services
(check all that apply)

SOFTWARE
	Use	Plan to buy
01. Accounting/Finance	☐	☐
02. Business Graphics	☐	☐
03. CAD/CAE/CAM	☐	☐
04. CASE	☐	☐
05. CIM	☐	☐
06. Communications/Networking	☐	☐
07. Database Management	☐	☐
08. Education	☐	☐
09. File Management	☐	☐
10. GIS	☐	☐
11. Image Processing	☐	☐
12. Laboratory Control	☐	☐
13. Materials Resource Planning (MRP, MRP II)	☐	☐
14. Multimedia Authoring Tools	☐	☐
15. Office Automation	☐	☐
16. Order Entry/Inventory Control	☐	☐
17. Programming/Systems Development	☐	☐
18. Project Management	☐	☐
19. Scientific and Engineering	☐	☐
20. Spreadsheets/Financial Planning	☐	☐
21. Systems Management Products	☐	☐
22. Workflow	☐	☐

HARDWARE
	Use	Plan to buy
23. Macintosh	☐	☐
24. Mainframe	☐	☐
25. Massively Parallel Processing	☐	☐
26. Minicomputer	☐	☐
27. PC (IBM-Compatible)	☐	☐
28. Supercomputer	☐	☐
29. Symmetric Multiprocessing	☐	☐
30. Workstation	☐	☐

PERIPHERALS
	Use	Plan to buy
31. Bridges/Routers/Hubs/Gateways	☐	☐
32. CD-ROM Drives	☐	☐
33. Disk Drives/Subsystems	☐	☐
34. Tape Drives/Subsystems	☐	☐
35. Video Boards/Other Multimedia Peripherals	☐	☐

NETWORK/COMMUNICATIONS
	Use	Plan to buy
36. Communications Controllers	☐	☐
37. Local Area Networks	☐	☐
38. Modems	☐	☐
39. Wide Area Networks	☐	☐

SERVICES
	Use	Plan to buy
40. Computer-Based Training)	☐	☐
41. Education/Training	☐	☐
42. Maintenance	☐	☐
43. Online DatabaseServices	☐	☐
44. Support	☐	☐
45. **None of the above**	☐	☐

6 What Oracle products are in use at your site? *(circle all that apply)*
SERVERS
01. Oracle7
02. Oracle Media Server
03. Oracle7 Workgroup Server
04. Personal Oracle7
05. Oracle Rdb
TOOLS
06. Designer/2000 (CASE)
07. Developer/2000 (CDE, Forms, Reports, Graphics)
08. Oracle Media Objects
09. Oracle Power Objects
APPLICATIONS
10. Oracle Financials
11. Oracle Human Resources
12. Oracle Manufacturing
13. Other ____
14. **None of the above**

7 What other database products are in use at your site? *(circle all that apply)*
01. CA-Ingres	11. Progress
02. DB2	12. Sybase System 1
03. DB2/2	13. Sybase System 1
04. DB2/6000	14. Sybase SQL Serve
05. dbase	15. VSAM
06. Gupta	16. Other ____
07. IMS	17. SAP
08. Informix	18. Peoplesoft
09. Microsoft Access	19. BAAN
	20. **None of the abov**
10. Microsoft SQL Server	

8 During the next 12 months, how much do you anticipate your organization will spend on computer hardware, software, peripherals, and services for your location? *(circle only one)*
01. Less than $10,000
02. $10,000 to $49,999
03. $50,000 to $99,999
04. $100,000 to $499,999
05. $500,000 to $999,999
06. $1,000,000 and over

OM